BUDDHISM

PATH TO NIRVANA

BUDDHISM

Path to Nirvana

A Perspective

K. N. Upadhyaya

Radha Soami Satsang Beas

I pay homage to the Buddha,
whose majesty is inconceivable,
whose mind is unattached, and who has taught
the inexpressible Dharma out of compassion.

Nāgārjuna[1]

Published by:
J. C. Sethi, Secretary
Radha Soami Satsang Beas
Dera Baba Jaimal Singh
Punjab 143 204, India

First edition 2010

17 16 15 14 13 12 11 10 8 7 6 5 4 3 2 1

ISBN 978-81-8256-920-1

Printed in India by: Replika Press Pvt. Ltd.

Contents

Pronunciation Key xi
Foreword xiii
Author's Note xv

ONE
An Introduction 1

TWO
The Life of the Buddha: A Teaching Story 11

THREE
The Buddha and the Doctrine of the Triple Body 60
Three Dimensions of the Buddha 61
The Importance of the Historical Buddha 68
Down to Earth 71

FOUR
Human Life 74
Human Life Is Difficult to Obtain 74
All Is Within the Human Body 77
Human Life Is Impermanent and Perishable 81

Human Life Fulfilled 84
Human Life Wasted 89

FIVE
A World of Impermanence 93
Three Marks of the Phenomenal World 93
Impermanence 94
Suffering 96
Non-Self 100

SIX
A Perspective on Buddhist Views on Soul and God 108
The Buddhist Perspective on Soul 108
The Five Constituents of Personality 110
Differentiating the Soul (*ātmā* or *ātman*) from the Personal Self (*attā*) 111
Soul as Jīva 116
Soul and Nirvāṇa 118
The Buddhist Perspective on God 121
Buddhism and the Contemporaneous Literature on God 122
The Law of Cause and Effect 128
Ultimate Reality and Brahman 131
Is There a Personal God? 139

SEVEN
The Enlightened One 145
The Buddhist Perspective 145
Taking Refuge in the Buddha 152
The Indispensability of a Teacher 154
The Necessity of a Living Teacher 160

Masters Are Always Present in the World 164
The Unbroken Chain of Living Teachers 166
The Teacher's Responsibility 171
The Disciple's Attitude 174
The Disciple's Duty 179
Discrimination in Finding a Fully Enlightened Master 188
Faith and Devotion 196

EIGHT
THE ETERNAL PATH: PERSPECTIVES AND PRACTICES 208
The Three Jewels 209
Bodhichitta 214
The Essential Practice of the Eightfold Path 215
The Five Essential Precepts or Abstentions 218
Reverence for Life and Vegetarianism 222
Control of the Mind 229
Detachment 232
The Meditation Practice – Dying While Living 234

NINE
INNER EXPERIENCES OF SOUND AND LIGHT 243
All Is Sound and Light 244
The Buddha's Enlightenment: An Experience of Light and Sound 246
The Transcendent Voice of the Buddha 249
Experiencing the Transcendent Form of the Buddha 252
Experiencing Light and Sound in Meditation Practice 254

TEN
THE FUTILITY OF AUSTERITIES,
RITUALS AND THE CASTE SYSTEM 265
Futility of Rituals 265
Futility of Caste Distinctions 274

CONCLUSION 279

Appendix: Texts Included
in the Pali Canon (*Tipiṭaka*) 283
Endnotes 285
Key to Abbreviations of Texts Quoted 285
Glossary 299
Bibliography 341
Index 365
Addresses for Information and Books 381
Books on This Science 387

PRONUNCIATION KEY

Symbol	*Pronunciation*
ā	as 'a' in car
ḍ	as 'd' in drum
ḥ	short form of 'ah!'
ī	as 'ee' in week
ṁ	as 'an' in kangaroo
ṇ	as 'n' in Karṇa (Arjuna's brother)
ṅ	as 'n' in hunger
ñ	as 'nj' in inject
ṭ	as 't' in ant
ū	as 'u' in rude

Note that the sound generally represented by *ṣ* or *ś* in many diacritical systems is represented by *sh* in this book, and the sound generally represented by *c* is represented by *ch* for ease of pronunciation for readers not familiar with these symbols.

FOREWORD

Buddhism: Path to Nirvana explores the teachings of Buddhism from the perspective of a perennial philosophy that links all yearning for truth through a common foundation. The author, Professor K. N. Upadhyaya, has studied the ancient languages of Sanskrit and Pali, and his field of specialization has been the philosophies of India. He has also been associated for many years with a lineage of adept teachers of *surat shabd yoga* (the yoga of uniting the soul with the sound current). For this book, he has brought his scholarship and personal understanding of the philosophy of the eternal way to his exploration of Buddhism and the earliest Buddhist texts in their original.

If we look to the heart of any of the world's great religions, we see how much they have in common. They all say that there is a beginningless beginning, a reality beyond time and matter. Thus, Truth remains eternal – the same for all groups and for all time. This supreme reality is also presented by every scripture and by every account of the personal quest for understanding as ineffable and beyond the reach of words and mind.

The common message of Buddha and other spiritual giants is that enlightened teachers keep coming through the ages and their teachings are for everyone without distinction. All indicate one Truth for the whole world; all speak of life's source as compassion, non-violence and love; and all say that this love is accessible and available to all. Buddhism, in common with other spiritual traditions, emphasizes the paramount need for regular spiritual practice, for making one's best effort to gain insight into the reality beyond intellect and words and to experience this reality. It is the hope of the publishers that this book will contribute towards this understanding.

J. C. Sethi
Secretary
Radha Soami Satsang Beas

Author's Note

Among all living beings only human beings are endowed with the faculty of reasoning and discrimination. Therefore, we have a natural inclination, whether mild or strong, to know about ourselves, unravel the mystery of the world and realize the objective of human life. To do so, it is very helpful to know what the great sages, saints and Enlightened Ones, whether of the East or West, have said regarding these matters, especially regarding the ultimate Truth and the way to realize it.

Gautama, the Buddha, is certainly one of the greatest masters to ever appear in this world. He is widely known for his sincere quest for the truth, persistent endeavours, moral earnestness, spiritual insight and finally his compassionate resolve, after his enlightenment, to preach and propagate his teachings for the good and happiness of many.

The Buddha established his Dharma (teachings) more than two thousand five hundred years ago, but his thoughts and deeds are still alive and vibrant today in the minds and hearts of a multitude of his devoted followers. Many kingdoms and empires established by mighty kings and emperors on the strength of brutal force, arms and ammunition proved short-lived when compared to the long life of the Dharma established by the Buddha on the foundation of his love and compassion and his heart-felt desire to do ultimate good to people. Kings and emperors live to increase the power, wealth and importance of their own selves, whereas sages and the Enlightened Ones efface their self and live for others. The former appear and, after glittering for a while, disappear into oblivion, whereas the latter appear to show the way to immortality to a multitude of people lost in ignorance and misery.

The Buddha is not to be looked upon as an ordinary individual who quietly fades out from this world. All Buddhas are wise and compassionate luminaries who have been coming to this world in succession since time immemorial and will continue to do so for all times to come. Gautama, the Buddha, himself refers to the previous Buddhas[2] and speaks of himself as one who has known and seen the Truth and the way to it, as others had known and seen in the past.[3] The teaching of one who has attained enlightenment or Buddhahood, a universal or immortal state, is called Buddhism. Thus, it signifies a universal teaching having a universal appeal.

In the long course of its history, Buddhism developed many schools and sub-schools. Its literature – canonical, exegetical and systematic – is vast and varied. It is written in various languages such as Pali, Sanskrit, Chinese, Tibetan and several others, besides having numerous translations and independent works in English and other Western languages.

It may be a commendable venture to undertake the study of the huge growth of Buddhism in all its phases and with all its glory and grandeur. But, for the purpose of this short book, we shall try to bring out the essence and spirit of Buddhism from the vast literature of many of its schools and make a clear presentation of its central moral and spiritual teachings. Buddhism points out that to attain enlightenment or the deepest insight is the ultimate goal of human beings. For this it lays emphasis on leading a good moral life, on being steadfast in one's meditation under the guidance of a competent living master and on making one's best effort to gain insight into the realm beyond intellect and speech. This indeed is the core of the common human heritage of wisdom emphasized by many renowned sages and saints all over the world.

We know that the Buddha had an intensely practical outlook. He avoided answering metaphysical questions. He felt that any answer given would be intellectually incomprehensible and of little practical use to the questioner with only limited understanding. He therefore drew attention to the universal problem of ignorance and suffering, and showed the way to enlightenment and freedom from all suffering. In preparing this book, this practical approach of the Buddha has been duly borne in mind.

The presentation of this book is based mainly on original texts of Buddhism. Materials from the vast literature of Buddhism which are directly linked to or implied by the early Buddhist texts, particularly the early stratum of the Pali Canon, have been duly utilized. The base of early Buddhism has been supported and supplemented by later Buddhist texts and treatises. Quotations from the original Pali and Sanskrit texts generally follow the standard English translations listed in the bibliography. At times the translations have been modified for clarity or to make the translations closer to the author's understanding of the original language. This book has made use of a few diacritical marks, as listed in the beginning of the book, mainly for Pali and Sanskrit words. A glossary has been provided, which includes entries for the authors and books most quoted.

In our modern hi-tech society, the living tradition of spiritual knowledge and practice is being increasingly marginalized. Yet there may still be some people willing to lend their ears to the time-tested teachings of the Buddha and tread the path prescribed by him.

It is precisely with this thought that the Buddha resolved to preach:

Among beings there are some
   with just a little dust in their eyes.
Not hearing the truth, they are languishing;
   if taught, they will see the truth.[4]

K. N. Upadhyaya
Former Professor and Chair
Department of Philosophy
University of Hawaii, USA

1

An Introduction

Buddhism, as it is known today, is a multi-faceted tradition followed in different variations by millions of people all over the world. The diverse schools and practices of Buddhism are derived from the oral teachings of the Buddha, who was originally named Siddhārtha Gautama (Gotama in Pali). After attaining enlightenment, Nirvāṇa, he came to be known as 'the Buddha' – the Enlightened One or Awakened One. Thus, 'Buddha' is a title or an epithet evoking reverence. Since his father, King Shuddhodana, belonged to the Shākya clan, the Buddha is also called Shākyamuni, the sage from the family of the Shākyas. In many texts he is also called the Tathāgata, one who has 'thus gone', that is, one who has transcended the comings and goings of transmigration.

Arising in India in the sixth century BCE, Buddhism gradually evolved into various schools. It flourished in India for nearly fifteen hundred years and spread from there to many other countries. The teachings of the Buddha were transmitted orally from generation to generation until the first century CE, when the different schools wrote down their scriptures. The three principal scriptures are called *Tipiṭaka* in Pali (*Tripiṭaka* in Sanskrit), meaning 'three baskets'. Pali is one of the major languages in which these teachings are preserved (the others are Chinese and Tibetan), and is based upon a dialect, Old Māgadhi, spoken by the Buddha. The baskets consisting of *Sutta Piṭaka* (Skt: *Sūtra Piṭaka*), the Buddha's discourses and dialogues; *Vinaya Piṭaka*, codes of conduct for the religious community; and *Abhidhamma Piṭaka* (Skt: *Abhidharma Piṭaka*), philosophical theories, are said to be the earliest scriptures.* But these are not identical in all the versions.

Within the first five centuries after the Buddha's death, at least eighteen 'schools' or interpretations of Buddhism are said to have emerged. Subsequently, many more schools and sub-schools developed, giving rise to a great mass of literature. In China we find a vast Chinese *Tripiṭaka*, consisting primarily of translations of Indian texts. In Tibet we find a similar *Tripiṭaka* in the Tibetan language. From China the *Tripiṭaka* was taken to Japan (via Korea) where, in each subsequent edition of the *Tripiṭaka*, new volumes were added. Thus a definitive *Tripiṭaka* published in Tokyo in 1929, edited by J. Takakusu, K. Watanabe and G. Ono, had expanded to one hundred volumes of about a thousand pages each.

There are today three main traditions of Buddhism: 1) Theravāda, 'The Teaching of the Elders', which flourishes in Sri Lanka and Southeast Asia; 2) Mahāyāna, the 'Great Vehicle',† which is generally followed in Tibet and East Asia; and 3) Vajrayāna or Mantrayāna, the 'Diamond' or 'Mantra Vehicle', a form of Mahāyāna practised mainly in Tibet and Japan. Each tradition saw many distinguished exponents and writers, and varied philosophical schools and sub-schools developed within the traditions. Most of these schools had fully developed and thrived in India

* The *Tipiṭaka* consists of numerous texts. For an outline of the different scriptures contained in the *Tipiṭaka*, many of which are quoted in this book, see the Appendix.

† The description of different forms of Buddhism as 'vehicles' (literally, carts) comes from a parable in the Mahāyāna *Lotus Sūtra* in which the Buddha tells the story of a kind father who promises to reward his children with toy carts (*yana*) of different kinds according to their preferences, but then gives all of them a cart which exceeds anything they could have imagined. The underlying concept of the Great Vehicle is that it encouraged more lay people to practise than in the early days of Buddhism, when monastic practices were foremost.

before Buddhism declined there in the eleventh century CE, when some of its literature was lost. But long before that time, these schools had already taken root beyond the subcontinent.

A concerted effort to take Buddhism abroad was begun by King Ashoka in the third century BCE. He sent his son and daughter to Ceylon (Sri Lanka) to accomplish this goal. Buddhism was first taken to the countries south of India, and later to the countries north of India. Theravāda took deep root in southern countries such as present-day Sri Lanka, Burma, Thailand, and Cambodia, while Mahāyāna flourished in northern countries such as Tibet, Mongolia, Korea, China and Japan. Vajrayāna prospered in Tibet and neighbouring Himalayan countries.

Theravāda scriptures were written in Pali, while Mahāyāna doctrines were written in Sanskrit. Most of this vast literature was translated into the languages of the countries where Buddhism spread. Many such translations have been utilized to restore important Sanskrit works lost in India during foreign invasions between the ninth and tenth centuries CE.

It is not possible to compress such a wealth of material into a single short volume. If we try to identify the original teachings of the Buddha, we see no objective and incontrovertible criteria by which to isolate the original words of the Buddha from later developments. Although "there is an overall harmony to the Canon, suggesting 'authorship' of its system of thought by one mind",[5] often Gautama Buddha's own teachings seem to be masked by sectarian divisions. Therefore, all attempts to trace the direct utterances of the Buddha back to a so-called authentic source lead to dispute, which is the reason why any "project of reconstructing an 'original Buddhism' is seen to be misguided".[6]

There are several factors that contribute to this complexity:

- The Buddha's teachings were not committed to writing until probably at least four hundred years after his death.

Indeed, the Buddha wrote nothing himself; what we have are accounts by his followers.

- The Buddha, according to all schools, frequently declared that the truth, the Dharma*[7] realized by him, was "profound, difficult to see and comprehend, serene, excellent, beyond reason, subtle, and comprehensible only by the wise".[8]
- The Buddha and his principal disciples remained silent, rejected, or disregarded[9] some of the major metaphysical questions, such as whether the world is eternal or non-eternal, finite or infinite; whether the soul is identical with or different from the body; and whether the Liberated One exists, does not exist, both exists and does not exist, or neither exists nor does not exist after his death.
- A distinction was made between what the Buddha taught and discussed in open general meetings and what he esoterically conveyed or transmitted in seclusion to a select few. On one occasion, the Buddha is reported to have said: "The Dhamma [Dharma]† has been taught by me, Ānanda, without making any distinction between exoteric and esoteric. The Tathāgata does not have the closed fist of a teacher (*āchariya muṭṭhi*) who holds back something relating to the Dhamma."[10] On another occasion he is said to have taken a handful of siṁsapa‡ leaves and asked the monks whether the leaves he held in his hands or those in the forest were greater in number. The monks naturally answered that the leaves in the forest were obviously much greater in number,

* The Sanskrit 'Dharma' (Pali: Dhamma) is a term with a range of meanings. Originally meaning 'that which holds or supports', it is the underlying law, the truth, the teachings of the Buddha and the way to follow the teachings

† In this book, the Sanskrit forms of words like 'dharma' and 'karma' are generally used in the text, while the Pali variants ('dhamma' and 'kamma') are used when quoting from or discussing quotations from the Pali Canon.

‡ It is not sure which tree this was; it might be a rosewood tree common to India and Southeast Asia.

whereupon the Buddha remarked: "Similarly, O monks, what I know but have not taught is greater, and what I have taught is very little."[11]

- The Buddha himself is said to have discouraged the habit of taking his words as sacrosanct and of chanting or reciting them in the Vedic manner.[12]
- Finally, the Buddha also suggested that one should care more for meanings than for mere words.[13]

Thus, by interpreting his utterances in diverse ways and by emphasizing one aspect of his teachings rather than another, different schools represented what they understood to be Buddha's teachings in varied ways. Since Buddhism naturally came to be expressed differently in the diverse social, cultural, and religious backgrounds of the countries to which it spread, the core teachings will certainly have been overlaid to some extent by further cultural interpretation. Also, a simple truth or concept that arose from practical experience, when subsequently analyzed by a philosopher or logician, may become subtler or even unintelligible to the less intellectual. Being extensions of the original teachings, these later developments may well have been implied in the original lessons of the Buddha and may not be altogether untrue. The Buddha's simple statement about the impermanence (*anitya*) of worldly things and beings, for instance, which he frequently emphasized, is a case in point. This original concept of impermanence turned into the complex doctrine of momentariness (*kshaṇikavāda*), and finally into that of emptiness (*shūnyavāda*) in some later schools.

In view of all this, it would not be appropriate to consider any one school of Buddhism as the sole representative of the original teachings of the Buddha. Yet it is not impossible to trace the core of his teachings with sufficient plausibility if we examine the texts of various schools in an objective way. This is possible because almost all schools of Buddhism, despite some divergences, contain certain common elements that suggest a common origin. In addition, it is universally recognized that Buddhism is based upon the enlightenment experience and subsequent teachings of the Buddha, and thus some basic elements from these teachings are apparent in all schools.

Looking for some 'core' teachings, therefore, is perhaps the best way to understand this ancient tradition. His Holiness, the XIV Dalai Lama (1935–), also makes a similar suggestion for approaching old religious traditions such as Buddhism. In his book, *The Power of Compassion*, he says:

> I think it is quite important to be able to make a distinction between what I call the 'core' and 'essence' of religious teachings and the cultural aspects of the particular tradition.[14]

In response to a question asking whether religion is still an appropriate path in the modern world, the His Holiness adds:

> Many years have passed since various religious traditions started, so certain aspects are, I think, perhaps out of date.... Therefore, it is important to look at the essence of different religions, including Buddhism.[15]

Speaking of the essence of Buddhism in a nutshell, we must note that the Buddha had a rigorously practical outlook. Putting aside metaphysical questions, he exhorted people to strive to attain enlightenment (Skt: Nirvāṇa, Pali: Nibbāna), which, he asserted, should be the primary goal in human life. To reach this goal he lays stress on meditation (*samādhi*), which is central to his path. Noble conduct (Skt: *shīla*, Pali: *sīla*) serves as the foundation for meditation and, through meditation, wisdom or insight (Skt: *prajñā*, Pali: *paññā*) endowed with compassionate loving-kindness (*karunā*) is gained. Thus, *shīla*, *samādhi* and *prajñā* endowed with *karunā* are the chief ingredients of the Buddhist path.

Highlighting the centrality of meditation in Buddhism, Edward Conze, the well-known translator of many Buddhist texts, aptly remarks: "In Buddhism the meditational practices are the well from which springs all that is alive in it."[16] When one dives deep into the well of meditation, one obtains the gem of wisdom whereby ignorance, the root cause of worldly bondage, is removed and Nirvāṇa attained.

The path taught by the Buddha is not something new. He claims simply to have rediscovered "an ancient path, an ancient way travelled by Enlightened Ones of former times."[17] In the early stratum of the Pali Canon, he makes reference to past and future Buddhas,[18] and even mentions some names of past Buddhas such as Vipashyī, Sikhī, Vishvabhū, Krakuchchhanda and Konāgamana.[19] The number of past Buddhas is simply innumerable according to Mahāyāna Buddhism.[20]

Since all the Buddhas who come to this world are emanations from the Dharmakāya, the real spiritual body or truth body that is eternally one and the same, it is only the physical forms of the Buddhas that are subject to birth and death, while, in essence, they are undying and immortal. The Buddha therefore declares himself to be Dharmakāya,[21] and asserts:

> He who sees the Dhamma [ultimate reality] sees me.[22]

The following passage amplifies this point:

> From the Dharma should one see the Buddhas;
> from the Dharma body comes their guidance.[23]

Thus, both the Buddhas and the truth they teach (the Dharma) come from the eternal Dharmakāya. The truth they embody is one and eternal, and their teachings are eternal, and for all.

It must also be noted here that the truly Enlightened Ones and their true spiritual teachings are always present for men and women who earnestly seek them. In other words, the chain of the master and the disciple ever continues, whether people uninterested in spirituality are aware of it or not. It is no wonder, therefore, that the Tibetan master Patrul Rinpoche (1808–1887) is said to have "held a continuous line of transmission coming down from the Buddha himself."[24] Numerous other masters and teachers in the Buddhist tradition are said to belong to a continuous line of transmission.

In *Tibetan Yoga and Secret Doctrines* W. Y. Evans-Wentz points out:

> The gurus themselves tell us that their actual method of transmitting the secret teachings is as ancient as man.[25]

Further, in the Tibetan text *The Supreme Path, the Rosary of Precious Gems*, Gampopa Rinpoche (1079–1153) says:

> It is a great joy to realize that the Path to Freedom which all the Buddhas have trodden is ever-existent, ever unchanged, and ever open to those who are ready to enter upon it.[26]

It is only out of mercy and compassion that true masters emanate from the Dharmakāya and work for the good and happiness of many.[27] Since wisdom is inseparably intertwined with compassion, the wise and enlightened cannot but be kind and compassionate to all. Indeed, there can be no spirituality without kindness and compassion. Therefore, those who are wise, compassionate and truly spiritual always serve all, treat everyone everywhere alike and make no distinctions of caste, creed, colour, country, race or religion. The Buddha, unquestionably, was a unique example of such a wise and compassionate teacher.

As long as we are on the worldly plane and have not had the inner experience of reality or have not reached the transcendent goal, we deal merely with names and concepts when we talk about the Buddha, the guru, God, or this or that higher realm. On the worldly plane we may argue and even quarrel about them, but these names and concepts cannot be taken for the reality, for they are liable to be limited by our own interpretations. We may use the same name or concept, yet understand it differently than another does, or we may use different names or concepts and yet mean the same thing. Unlike people who are guided by mere names and concepts, the Buddha, the Enlightened One, is guided by and speaks from his own inner experience. As the Buddha points out:

> The Tathāgata teaches only after having himself known and realized the truth.[28]

Unlike many people who claim the superiority of their own masters, teachers, or religious founders, and, for that reason, quarrel and fight with others, true spiritual teachers never look down upon others or speak ill of other traditions. In fact, they themselves refer to other mystics to reveal the universality of their doctrines or principles. The Buddha, for example, refers to other masters in support of his view that spiritual truth or the path (Dharma) is not subject to change. He points to the authority of the saints and other enlightened masters while stating that Dharma remains unchanging amidst all changing things of the world. As he says:

> The splendid chariots of kings become worn out;
> The body also comes to old age.

> But the Dhamma of the Noble Ones never grows old;
> Thus do the saints proclaim about the Noble Ones.[29]

There is a clear difference between scholars and mystics. The former deal with names and concepts, and debate about their meaning; the latter deal with direct and personal experience of the Sublime and may prefer to remain silent, though even in their silence there is great eloquence.

When Buddhas or true mystics teach, they speak from their direct and personal experience. This explains why we find an essential unity in their teachings, notwithstanding the use of different terminology.

What follows is an account of the Buddha's life, philosophy and thought, based particularly on the original texts of Buddhism, with supporting quotations from the wealth of teachings of various Buddhist schools. Buddha's wise, pragmatic, and compassionate approach is reminiscent of all great spiritual teachers, whose sole purpose of coming to this creation is to be a living example of spirituality and to help us attain enlightenment.

2

The Life of the Buddha

A Teaching Story

It is generally accepted that Gautama Buddha was a historical figure, but since most of the historical facts of his life are mixed with legendary material and supernatural stories, it is not possible to present an accurate historical account of the Buddha's life. It appears that Indians of ancient times had little interest in preserving historical accounts of individual sages or thinkers, however illustrious they might have been. It is the thought and not the thinker which was of abiding interest to them and which they tried to preserve with utmost care.

The whole of Vedic and Upanishadic literature contains no historical account of any sage or seer. In them we come across only the names of certain sages or teachers and their prominent disciples, or those who listened to them expounding doctrines or theories. It is no wonder, therefore, that a biography of the Buddha has not come down to us from ancient times. Whatever biographical works on the Buddha appeared at later times are found to contain elements of supernatural and legendary material from which it is impossible to separate the bare historical facts of his life.

The earliest biographical work is the *Buddhacharita*, which was composed about six hundred years after the Buddha's death. It is a poetic composition in Sanskrit by the Indian philosopher-poet Ashvaghosha, who lived in the first and second centuries CE. Another biographical work is the *Lalitavistara*, whose author is unknown. This also is a Sanskrit work, partly in prose and partly in poetry, the poetic versions being mostly a versified presentation of the prose passages. It has twenty-seven chapters, and it seems to have been composed between the second and third century CE. *Mahāvastu* is still another biographical work, mainly in Sanskrit, which seems to be of somewhat later origin and is not the composition of a single author. Its arrangement of the subject matter is unsystematic and its treatment of the subject is mostly mythological.

Apart from these books, some autobiographical materials that relate mostly to the Buddha's post-enlightenment period are found scattered in the Buddhist Canonical literature. Therein the Buddha is found explaining and discussing his doctrines to various learned brahmins, prominent lay people and rulers of different states. All this sheds light on the social, political and religious conditions of those parts of India that were visited by the Buddha in the sixth century BCE.

What we receive, a few thousand years later, is an account of a life that encapsulates the whole of Buddhist understanding. While what is fact and what is legend in the story of the Buddha's life will never be known, the Buddhist path does not depend on the historical accuracy of the story. The truths found in the story may not be historical, but they serve as metaphors, and through the account of the Buddha's life and experiences, fundamental truths are illustrated.

The Buddha preached and proclaimed the Dharma, the spiritual path, which he said is eternal. He was therefore not an inventor of a new Dharma, but a torchbearer, a discoverer and propagator of the ancient and eternal Dharma. The path, the Dharma, is central, but the Buddha did not create it. Therefore the path does not depend upon the Buddha for its existence, and the Buddha himself said that he only spoke of what he had rediscovered, the 'path of the Enlightened Ones':

> I have, monks, seen an ancient path, an ancient way travelled by Enlightened Ones of former times.[30]

> It is by following this path that men crossed the ocean of existence in the past, cross it now and will cross it in the future.[31]

In other words, the Dharma did not originate from or depend on the Buddha, the person, but knowledge of the Dharma certainly depended on him. He was a channel through which the Dharma was made known and expressed to people who were drawn to him.

Although the focus of Buddhism is on the Buddha's teachings, it is good to begin with an account of the Buddha's life. His life illustrates the spiritual journey of Buddhism, a journey to realize the state of perfect wisdom – the state of complete enlightenment from which the Buddha taught.

It is generally accepted that Gautama Buddha was born in the sixth century BCE and lived for some eighty years, but there is some controversy about the exact years of his birth and death. After a careful examination of the various opinions in this regard, some are led to the conclusion that the most probable year of his birth is 563 BCE and that he passed away in 483.[32] Recent scholars have argued for later dates: 480–400 BCE[33] or even 470–350 BCE.[34]

His father was the ruler Shuddhodana of Kapilavastu and his mother was Mahāmāyā. Kapilavastu, situated in the foothills of the Himalayas, was the capital of the Shākya people. Because he was born among the Shākya people, Gautama became known in the Mahāyāna tradition as Shākyamuni, the Shākyan sage. Shākya was at that time a prosperous state under the larger kingdom of Kosala, ruled by King Prasenjit. The small state was ruled by a council of householders, one of whom was the father of Gautama. Later traditions, however, see Gautama as the son of a king.[35]

From Heaven to the Earthly Plane

The Buddha went through the process of birth and rebirth, perfecting himself in many lives before being born as Siddhārtha Gautama. Many aeons ago, in one of his past lives, he was an ascetic named Sumedha. After meeting a previous Buddha, Dīpaṅkara, Sumedha aspired to Buddhahood. In his previous incarnation, Gautama Buddha was a bodhisattva, a being aspiring to future Buddhahood, dwelling in the Tushita heaven, when he saw that the time was right and conditions were conducive to his taking birth in Kapilavastu. As Peter Harvey writes in his *Introduction to Buddhism*:

> The traditional biography does not begin with Gautama's birth, but with what went before it.... In his penultimate life he was born in the Tushita heaven, the realm of the 'delighted' gods. This is said to be the realm where the Bodhisatta Metteyya* now lives, ready for a future period in human history when Buddhism will have become extinct, and he can become the next Buddha.[36]

The sūtras, the discourses of the Buddha, recount that Buddha was 'mindful and fully aware' when he passed from the Tushita

* According to the traditional Buddhist belief, Bodhisatta Metteyya (Skt: Bodhisattva Maitreya) will be the successor of Gautama Buddha. He is a being of great compassion who, like all bodhisattvas, dwells in the Tushita heaven, awaiting the time when he can take birth, become enlightened and assist others on the path to enlightenment.

heaven and was conceived in his mother's womb. One night King Shuddhodana's chief queen, Mahāmāyā, had a dream that a majestic white elephant had entered her womb without causing her any pain or discomfort. The next morning, the queen related her dream to the king, who sought its interpretation from knowledgeable brahmins. They explained to the king that the queen had conceived and that she would be the mother of a glorious son. If this son were to remain a householder, he would be a universal monarch, but if he were to renounce the household life, he would become a fully enlightened master. According to Buddhist tradition, the elephant symbolizes the descending of the potential Buddha, an embodiment of purity and splendour, from the Tushita heaven to this earth.

The queen passed her time in good health, without any ailment or fatigue. In the tenth month of her pregnancy, she desired to visit the pleasure garden of Lumbinī, well known for its clusters of *sāla* groves* and other beautiful trees and flowers. Accompanied by the king and her female attendants, she went to the garden. While she was walking and enjoying the glorious grove with her female attendants, she sensed that the time of delivery was approaching. With beautiful shrubs and flowers serving as a curtain, she grasped a branch of a *sāla* tree, which is how, it is said, she gave birth almost painlessly to an unusual child who was later proclaimed as the Buddha. When the group returned home, there was great festivity in the palace and throughout the kingdom over the birth of the king's first son, who was naturally taken to be heir to the kingdom.

The sage Asita had a vision of the birth of this glorious child, and he came to the king's palace. He expressed his desire to the king to see the royal baby, and the king took the sage to

---

*The *sāla* or cannonball tree has flowers of heavenly fragrance. The Buddha is said to have been born and died in a *sāla* grove.

the chamber where the baby was kept. Taking the baby in her arms, Queen Mahāmāyā tried to make the baby bow his head in reverence to the feet of Asita. But Asita himself reverently bowed at the feet of the child. He gazed intently at the glowing face of the baby, and tears trickled down from his eyes. The king and the queen were amazed but also dismayed to see this unusual behaviour of the sage, and they asked if he foresaw any trouble or danger for the prince. The sage explained that he was not thinking of any impending danger or trouble to the prince; rather, he was disappointed that he himself would not live long enough to hear the teachings of this glorious baby, who was to become an Enlightened One and who would impart the teachings that lead to the termination of the cycle of birth and death. The sage was sad that he still fell short of attaining that final goal, which he could reach if only he were to live long enough.

The sage told the king that there was no reason for him to grieve. He said that they alone should grieve who would never have the good fortune of listening to a Buddha, either because they were too deluded or intoxicated with the world or because they could not meet a living teacher.

King Shuddhodana later asked the learned brahmins to foretell the future of the young prince. All except one offered two versions of the future: if the prince were to lead a householder's life, he would be a universal monarch; but if he were to renounce the household life, he would become fully enlightened. One brahmin, however, insisted that there was no possibility of the prince remaining a householder, and that he would definitely become fully enlightened and unravel the truth to the world. He was given the name Siddhārtha – *siddha* means 'accomplished' or 'fulfilled' and *artha* means 'objective' or 'aim'. Thus, this name signifies one who will have the objective of his life accomplished or fulfilled. His family name being Gautama, he came to be known as Siddhārtha Gautama.

Just a week after giving birth, Queen Mahāmāyā left her mortal frame and took abode in heaven. Her younger sister Mahāprajāvatī, the king's second queen, lovingly took over the responsibility of rearing the prince. The prince had a happy childhood. He acquired the necessary knowledge and skills suited to a royal prince in much less time than others would normally require. Since the king was aware of the possibility of Siddhārtha renouncing household life, he made special arrangements to keep Siddhārtha in the most pleasant and luxurious surroundings. He was lodged in a mansion which had rooms suited to each season. According to one story, the king had three special palaces built for him, one for the winter, another for the summer and the third for the rainy season. The best dancers and musicians continually entertained him. Every precaution was taken to ensure that he would never see anything that could disturb his mind.

It is said that once, while some Shākyan princes were enjoying the beauty of the pleasure garden, Siddhārtha's cousin Devadatta saw a goose flying overhead, and he at once shot it with his arrow. The goose fell wounded near Siddhārtha. Siddhārtha held it tenderly, extracted the arrow and bandaged its wound. Devadatta claimed the bird, but Siddhārtha would not give it to him, saying that it belonged not to him who had attempted to take away its life, but to him who saved its life. This was the first experience of suffering in Siddhārtha's life. The king accepted Siddhārtha's plea, and Siddhārtha cared for the goose until it was able to fly away.

One day the king assembled all the Shākyan princes and sons of ministers and, followed by a large retinue, took them to witness the festival of ploughing. While most of them were enjoying the festivities, Siddhārtha went to his father's orchard with his attendants. Looking for a convenient place to rest, he saw a secluded spot under a *jambu* (rose apple) tree. He bade his attendants disperse, as he desired to be left alone. When they left, Siddhārtha sat cross-legged under the shade of the tree in a meditative posture and entered into his first trance.* After a while, someone saw him in that state and at once informed the king, who rushed to the spot and was amazed to see Siddhārtha sitting in contemplation. The king inwardly offered salutations to his son, but at the same time he felt alarmed at the prince's indifference to amusements and festivities.

The Buddha's Marriage

The king consulted with his counsellors, who advised the king to get the youthful prince married at once. This, they suggested, would tie him to the pleasures of youthful life and prevent him from renouncing his home. Siddhārtha was an exceptionally handsome youth, and it was not easy to find a suitable match for him. But the king's emissaries succeeded in finding an exquisitely beautiful and exceptionally noble princess named Yashodharā (also called Gopā). However, as we read in the *Lalitavistara*,[37] the father of the girl, Shākya Daṇḍapāni, did not want to give away his daughter to Gautama. He said to the king, "Sir, the prince has grown up in prosperity, but it is the custom of our family to give a daughter only to one who is proficient in the arts. The prince is not proficient in the arts, nor in the martial arts such as the sword or archery." So Gautama offered to display his skills against anyone who volunteered. Five hundred Shākyan nobles came to the occasion and competed against him, but Gautama was victorious in every field, whether in writing, printing, mathematics, philosophy, athletics, dancing, singing, playing musical instruments, shooting darts while riding an elephant, arm-exercise or archery. So Shākya Daṇḍapāni, realizing Gautama's worth, gave

---

*The Buddha referred to this incident later in the course of explaining the meditative practice to Mahā Sachchaka in the Mahā Sachchaka Sutta of *Majjhima Nikāya*, where he said: "I recollected how I entered the first trance in the bliss of solitude, detached from worldly enjoyments and defilement, sitting under the cooling shade of a rose-apple tree in the orchard of my father." (*MN.i*, p.246)

permission for his daughter Gopā to be married, and the ceremony took place with regal pomp and grandeur.

The couple was provided with immense luxury and comfort, and their time was spent in heavenly surroundings. One day, the prince was told by the entourage of women who entertained him about an enchanting pleasure garden near the city. Feeling like an elephant confined inside a house, the prince set his heart on an excursion outside the city and asked the charioteer to prepare his chariot. The king heard of his plans and ordered his men to arrange the prince's pleasure excursion, clearing the royal road of unpleasant sights so that nothing would agitate the prince's mind.

The Revelation of Death and Suffering

It happened, however, that while the prince was travelling in his chariot, he saw an old man whose body was bent and shaking with weakness. He was walking slowly with the help of a stick. The prince was astonished to see such a man and he enquired of his charioteer why the man's body, hair, teeth and entire appearance looked so unseemly. The charioteer explained to the prince what happens when one grows old and pointed out that all are subject to old age; no one is exempt from it. Fixing his eyes on the old man, it is recounted that Siddhārtha sighed deeply, shook his head and said:

> So that is how old age destroys indiscriminately the memory, beauty and strength of all! And yet with such a plight before people, they go on quite unperturbed! Since such is our condition, enough of this journey to the pleasure grove. Turn round the horses, charioteer. Go quickly back home.[38]

When the prince returned to his palace, he was so lost in anxiety that this same palace now seemed empty. According to the *Buddhacharita*, the gods of the five heavens of the Pure Abode (Shuddhadhivāsa) had conjured up the illusion of the old man to induce the prince to leave his home.

On another day, as the prince proceeded on his second pleasure excursion, he came upon a diseased man. In the words of the *Buddhacharita*, "The same gods conjured up a man with a body afflicted with disease."[39] The prince looked at the man with great compassion, and hearing from his charioteer that disease and sickness are common to all, he uttered in a low voice:

> This then is the calamity of disease that afflicts people. The world sees it, and yet does not lose its confident ways! Deep, indeed, is the ignorance of people who make merriment under the constant threat of disease. Enough of this pleasure excursion; turn back the chariot, charioteer, and go straight to the palace. Having heard about the danger of disease, my mind is repelled from pleasures and seems to sink into itself.[40]

On the third excursion, the prince saw a dead body, and so the charioteer explained the meaning of death, pointing out that death spares no one. The prince was dismayed and said in a distressed voice:

> This is the end fixed for all, yet the world throws off fear and takes no heed! Hardened, indeed, are men's hearts, for they feel quite at ease even while going along the road to destruction. Turn back the chariot, charioteer. This is not the time and place for a pleasure excursion. How could an intelligent man be heedless in the hour of disaster, when he knows of his impending destruction?[41]

Each time the prince returned to the palace, having gone only about halfway to the pleasure grove, the disturbing incident was reported to the king who, becoming increasingly apprehensive, provided the prince with more entertainments and increased the number of his guards. But the prince now seemed to be pensive, indifferent to the young women's dancing and music. Encouraged by the king, a young man named Udāyin came to cheer up the prince and to fan his desire to enjoy all the pleasures of life for which the world craves and which were so easily and abundantly available to him. Udāyin therefore urged the prince not to let that wonderful opportunity for enjoyment pass him by, because the prince's vigour, beauty and youth would be like a garden without flowers if he were to deprive himself of the sense pleasures and refrain from enjoying them to the full. The prince replied:

> It is not that I despise sense objects, and I know that the world runs after them. But when I find them to be transitory, I can take no delight in them. If the triad of old age, disease and death did not exist, then I too might have taken pleasure in the loveliness of sensory objects. If the beauty of women were imperishable, my mind would have taken pleasure in the passions, even though they are full of evils.... If people who are doomed to face old age, disease and death are unperturbed in their enjoyments with others who are likewise subject to old age, disease and death, they are indeed like birds and beasts....
>
> Such being the case, you [Udāyin] should not lead me astray to the ignoble passions, for I am afflicted with suffering, and it is my lot to become old and to die. How strange it is that your mind is firm and unflinching, and you find substance in the fleeting pleasures of the senses. You cling to sense objects in the midst of the most frightful dangers, even while you see the whole creation on the way to death. I, on the other hand, am frightened and exceedingly distressed reflecting on the horrors of old age, disease and death. I find neither peace nor contentment, much less any pleasure here, for the world appears to me as if ablaze with all-consuming fire.[42]

RENUNCIATION

By now it was clear that an estrangement from worldly pleasures was taking deep root in the prince's heart. Hoping that the solitude of the forest might induce peace, with the king's permission he left for the nearby forest accompanied by the ministers' sons, chosen for their reliability and skilfulness in telling entertaining stories. This time, the prince came upon a recluse, and the prince asked him who he was. In answer, the recluse said:

> Since the world is doomed to destruction, I seek salvation, the most blessed state, which is free from destruction. Kinsmen and strangers I treat alike, and there is no attraction or hatred in me for objects of the senses. I dwell wherever I happen to be, at the foot of a tree or in a deserted sanctuary, on a hill or in the forest. Possessions I have none; no expectations either. Intent on the supreme goal I wander about, accepting any alms I may receive.[43]

This provided a clue to the prince that he should seek abiding happiness and peace, and his mind was set on leaving his palace for the wandering life. Absorbed in the thought of renunciation, he returned from the forest.

Before long, King Shuddhodana was informed that the prince's wife, Princess Yashodharā, had given birth to a son. The king joyfully asked the messenger to run to the prince to bring him this delightful news. On hearing the news, the prince is said to have exclaimed, "*Rāhula*!" (an eclipse), by which he may have meant a fetter or bondage binding him to the family and home. When the king heard that the prince had uttered the word *rāhula*, he said that his grandson would be named Prince Rāhula. Great celebrations and festivities began in the palace. But Siddhārtha became increasingly impatient to leave.

It occurred to him that he must not leave the palace without seeking his father's permission. Accordingly, he went to his father and respectfully requested permission to leave the palace for the purpose of seeking salvation. Hearing these words, the king was dismayed, and in a voice choked with emotion, he said:

> Refrain, dear one, from this talk. For it is not yet the time for you to give yourself up to Dharma [the spiritual discipline]. For they say the practice of Dharma in the first bloom of youth, when the mind is still unbalanced, is full of dangers.... Now it is indeed, O lover of Dharma, my time to seek Dharma, after I have handed over the sovereignty to you, on whom all eyes are endearingly fixed.... Therefore, give up this resolve of yours. Devote yourself for the present to the duty of a householder. For entry to the forest is agreeable to a man after he has enjoyed the delights of youth.[44]

In great distress, the king asked the prince to have pity on the royal family, himself and the kingdom. He said the prince could ask for any boons he wished, and he would grant them all. Then the sweet-tongued future Buddha said:

> O lord, I wish for four boons. Kindly grant them to me, if you can. Then I shall stay here, I shall not renounce this home, and you will always see me here. I wish that old age should never assail me and that my youth, beauty and attractive complexion should endure forever; that I should enjoy good health and never fall victim to any disease; that I should have a never-ending life; and that no disaster should ever befall me.

Hearing these words, the king was greatly afflicted and distressed. He said:

> You are asking for things which no one can grant. These are beyond my powers.

The prince replied:

> If you cannot grant me, lord, the four boons of making me free from old age, disease, death and disaster, then kindly listen to still another boon that I wish for. I should have no rebirth after giving up this body here.[45]

The king urged the prince once again to give up this idea, which was going too far beyond reason. The prince then politely but firmly said to his father:

> It is not right to hold back a man who wishes to escape from a house that is being consumed by fire. Seeing that separation [from dear ones] is the fixed rule of the world, is it not better that I myself make the separation for the sake of Dharma? Will not death sever me helplessly from all, while I still remain unsatisfied and I leave without attaining my goal?[46]

The king did not prolong this discussion, and the prince returned to his palace, having conveyed his resolve to his father. But now the king alerted his guards and further increased their number, and Queen Mahāprajāvatī instructed the female dancers and musicians to make the finest display of their skills in order to keep the prince always cheerful and amused.

Flight from the Palace

The prince was now intent on escaping from the palace. He had no more interest in anything or anyone around him. At night, when the female attendants noticed that the prince was lying down with his eyes closed, indifferent to them, they fell asleep scattered around him. The prince, who was actually quite awake, opened his eyes, and the sight of the women lying in careless abandon now seemed loathsome. He quietly descended from the palace and went straight to the stables. He roused Chhandaka, the groom, and ordered him to saddle his swift-footed horse, Kaṇṭhaka.

The prince wanted to see his son before he left, so while Chhandaka saddled Kaṇṭhaka, he walked up to the chamber where Rāhula was sleeping with his mother. The prince opened the door of the chamber, within which a lamp of incense oil was lit. He saw Rāhula's mother sleeping with her hand covering the baby's face. The prince thought that if he were to move his wife's hand to see his son's face, his wife would awaken, and that would present a great obstacle to his renunciation. He then decided to leave and to come back to see his son after attaining enlightenment. According to the *Jātaka* commentary, Prince Rāhula was then only seven days old.[47]

The prince immediately turned away and walked to the place where Chhandaka was ready with his horse. Taking Chhandaka with him, the prince left the palace. The gods saw to it that everyone remained fast asleep, that the rumbling sound of the horses' hooves was muffled and that all the gates were wide open. When the prince was safely out of the city, he looked back. The city was shining in the light of the full moon of the month of July (Āshāḍha). The prince was in the prime of his youth; he was only twenty-nine years of age. Yet his resolve to attain enlightenment was firm and unshakeable. As the *Lalitavistara* puts it:

> Looking at his palace, he, a person of discerning intellect, spoke in a sweet voice: "I will not enter the city of Kapilavastu without attaining enlightenment, which brings an end to the cycle of birth and death."[48]

Prince Siddhārtha renounced his palace precisely to seek spiritual illumination. It is a general belief in the Buddhist tradition that all the potential Buddhas (bodhisattvas) of the past also left their homes in their youth in search of the right path. Indeed, the Buddha said in the Sangarava Sutta [Skt: Sangarava Sūtra] from the *Majjhima Nikāya*:

> Household life is crowded and dusty; life gone forth [the way of one who renounces household life] is wide open. It is not easy while living in a home to lead the holy life, utterly perfect and pure as a polished shell.[49]

However, it is not necessary for all who seek the true way to leave their homes. In the Subha Sutta, also from the *Majjhima Nikāya*, the Buddha said:

> I do not speak one-sidedly.... I praise the right way of practice on the part either of a householder or one gone forth; for whether it be a householder or one gone forth, one who has entered on the right way of practice, by reason of his right way of practice, is accomplishing the true way, the Dhamma that is wholesome.[50]

The main purpose is not to renounce one's home and family, but to become detached from all worldly entanglements and to attain enlightenment. By right guidance and earnestly following the right path, one is automatically detached from all worldly things and is led to enlightenment, even as a householder. Vimalakīrti, the famous householder of Vaishālī, is a good example. After taking instructions from the Buddha, he practised the disciplines earnestly and attained perfection. The *Vimalakīrti Nirdesha Sūtra* says:

> While dwelling in the Buddha's awe-inspiring majesty, his mind was extensive like the great ocean. He was praised by all Buddhas and revered by the gods Indra and Brahmā.*[51]

---

*Indra is the king of the gods. Brahmā is the creator-god, the first deity of the sacred Hindu trinity.

In later Buddhism we find many more such examples of spiritually accomplished Buddhist householders, also referred to as 'married monks' and 'married nuns'. It must be noted that Prince Siddhārtha left his palace while he was still seeking a path. During his time, renouncing household life was considered the first step towards leading a holy life. This way of life was evident in the Buddha's reference to hundreds and thousands of renunciates practising austerities and other disciplines under imperfect teachers, or simply wandering about without any teacher. After Siddhārtha found the path and attained enlightenment, he returned to his kingdom, Kapilavastu, where he met his father and kinspeople, visited his wife and son and offered them the benefit of his hard work and real achievement, as we shall shortly see.

Parting from Chhandaka

To return to the story, Prince Siddhārtha and Chhandaka rode far away on the swift-footed horse till dawn, when a hermitage came into view. They dismounted, and the prince then took off his jewels and ornaments, handing them to Chhandaka and asking him to go back with the horse to the palace. He asked Chhandaka to tell his father and all the people of his kingdom that they should not feel sorry for him, since he was not leaving his home out of moody resentment or because of lack of affection, but with the objective of putting an end to old age, disease and death. In the words of the *Buddhacharita*, he sent the following message to his father:

> I have entered the forest to put an end to birth and death, and certainly not because I yearn for paradise or feel no affection for you, or because I am in a state of anger. Therefore, you should not grieve for me. All unions must come to an end someday, however long they may have lasted.... There is no reason for you to grieve for me, because I have gone forth to get rid of all

> grief. Rather, grieve for those who are slaves of passion and who greedily cling to sensuous objects, which are the very roots of grief.… In case you feel that I have gone forth to the forest at the wrong time, I can only submit that there is no such thing as a wrong time for Dharma, our hold on life being so uncertain. Therefore, my resolve is to begin to strive for the supreme goal this very day. Because when death confronts me constantly, what reliance can be placed on life?[52]

Chhandaka, however, was in tears, and he appealed to the prince not to leave and to take into consideration his loving and aged father, who yearned so much for his son; his foster mother, who had exhausted herself in bringing him up; the inhabitants of Kapilavastu, who looked upon him as the successor to the kingdom; and poor Chhandaka himself, for whom the prince was his only refuge. The prince remained self-possessed, speaking with great firmness:

> Chhandaka, stop this grief over parting from me. Separation is a fixed law for all beings who are embodied, and that is how they keep on moving from birth to birth. Should affection lead me not to quit my kinsfolk of my own accord, still death would one day tear us all apart against our wills. Think of my mother, who bore me in her womb with pains and great longing. Fruitless proves her labour now. What am I now to her; what she to me? As birds collect on the roosting tree and then go their separate ways again, so is the union of all beings, which inevitably ends in their parting.…
>
> Since this world is in a state of continuous parting, it is unwise and improper to have the feeling that 'this is mine'. Coming together in this world is transitory, as in a dream.… This being so, go back now, my good friend, and be not aggrieved. Further, you should say to the people of Kapilavastu, who love me so

> dearly: "Cease to be so dearly attached to him, and hear his firm resolve. Either he will put an end to the chain of birth and death, and then will quickly come back to you, or he will perish, lacking in right effort and failing to reach the goal."[53]

The prince then took the sharp sword from Chhandaka's hand, cut off his well-groomed and beautiful hair, and threw it into the air, thinking it unfit for the life of a recluse. He exchanged his embroidered silk garments for the coarse, saffron-coloured robe of a hunter who happened to appear, and they both were happy at the exchange. Thus, assuming the garb of the recluse, he disregarded Chhandaka's weeping and walked resolutely away in search of the way to enlightenment.

Chhandaka, stricken with grief, returned to Kapilavastu with a very heavy heart, bringing the shocking news of the prince's renunciation. Sobbing, he described the prince's firm resolution, and a cloud of gloom descended on the entire kingdom. The distress of King Shuddhodana, Queen Mahāprajāvatī and Princess Yashodharā in particular knew no bounds. They felt completely devastated, like a stand of trees wantonly ravaged by a mighty elephant. Men were ready to be sent in all directions to search for the prince, but according to *Lalitavistara*, the wise ones stopped them when Chhandaka made it quite clear that the prince's resolve not to return to Kapilavastu before attaining enlightenment was so unshakeable that it would be impossible to bring him back.[54]

According to the *Buddhacharita*, however, the king decided to send his trusted counsellor and family priest, accompanied by a suitable retinue, to find the prince and make every effort to fetch him. They went to the hermitage where Chhandaka had left the prince and were told by the ascetics living there that he had already left for the hermitage of Ārāḍa Kālāma, a Sāṅkhyan (one of the six schools of classical Indian philosophy) teacher who lived near Rājagriha, the capital of Magadha kingdom.[55] Starting off in the direction of the hermitage, they found the prince sitting on the roadside at the foot of a tree. The prince listened calmly to their appeals, but he pointed out that the men were more emotional than rational. Accordingly, he conveyed his unshakeable resolve:

> The sun may fall to the earth, the Himalayan mountains may lose their firmness, but I will not return to my family as a worldly man with my senses turned only to the worldly objects and with no realization of the ultimate Truth. I would rather enter a blazing fire than enter my home with my goal unattained.[56]

Disappointed, the counsellor and priest left for Kapilavastu, leaving trustworthy men to covertly watch where the prince went and how he fared.

Meditation

The prince arrived at the hermitage of Ārāḍa Kālāma, where he was welcomed and accepted as a disciple, and was trained in spiritual practices. With purity and sincerity, the prince practised the discipline in a solitary dwelling, and before long mastered that system of meditation. Ārāḍa was greatly pleased with the success of this new disciple and asked him to lead the assembly of three hundred disciples as Ārāḍa's own equal. But the prince felt that this system fell short of full enlightenment. He respectfully took his leave and travelled to the hermitage of another teacher, Udraka Rāmaputra. Here also he received a warm welcome and was instructed in a spiritual discipline that would lead to a higher stage of enlightenment. Siddhārtha soon mastered this system. Here also he was asked by his teacher to be a co-equal and to jointly lead a large assembly of seven hundred disciples. But again, not fully satisfied with the method, Siddhārtha left that place and travelled onwards, intent on full enlightenment.

Passing through the kingdom of Magadha and meeting several ascetics along the way, he came to Gayā. There, near the village of Senānī in the area of Uruvelā (Uruvilva), he looked for a quiet place where he might spend time. Five disciples of Udraka Rāmaputra who had been practising the latter's spiritual discipline for a considerable time were greatly impressed by Siddhārtha's fast progress. Hoping that he would attain enlightenment, they followed him to Uruvelā. There they found lovely, peaceful places with pleasant trees and groves near the beautiful Nirañjanā River with its clear water and shady fords. The surrounding villages would provide them with alms. Siddhārtha decided to remain there to make his utmost effort to attain enlightenment.

He had seen ascetics engaged in various kinds of penances and fasting. Reasoning that self-mortification was a means of self-purification that would lead onward to inner illumination, he embarked upon rigorous austerities, penances and prolonged fasting. His body became so emaciated that he turned into a skeleton and looked like a dead man. After six years of these austerities, it dawned upon him that this kind of physical denial was merely wearing his body out. This could not be the way to achieve insight. There must be another path. He had thought that Ārāḍa Kālāma and Udraka Rāmaputra's meditative practices were not sufficiently fulfilling, but at least they had been uplifting and had provided him with some inner experiences. He recollected how, when he had gone to the ploughing festival while still living with his father, he had experienced the bliss of his first inner experience sitting cross-legged in solitude under the shade of the *jambu* tree. So Siddhārtha decided to return to this same practice of meditation.

But he needed more physical strength to carry on meditation in an effective way, because unless the body is reasonably nourished and free from undue strain, it is difficult to concentrate. So he started to take juices, rice gruel and finally some solid food.

Seeing this, the five disciples of Udraka Rāmaputra who had followed Siddhārtha to Uruvelā were disappointed. They had been attending to him during his austerities, hoping that after attaining enlightenment he would share his knowledge and help them realize their goal. But now they deserted him, thinking that he had failed and had taken to ease and comfort. They left for the Deer Park of Rishipatana (now Sāranātha) near Vārāṇasī.

The Quest for Enlightenment

Siddhārtha gradually regained his strength and natural physical beauty. On the full moon of the month of Vaishākha, he got up in the morning after his usual meditation. After attending to his bodily needs, he went to a peepal tree and sat quietly awaiting the time to go begging for alms. He did not know that the tree was sacred to the local people. Sujātā, the daughter of the chief of Senānī village, had begged the tree's god for the blessing of a son as her first child. She had been blessed with that son, and on that day she went to make her promised offering of milk-rice that she had piously prepared. Seeing a serene figure with a glowing face quietly sitting at the foot of the sacred tree, she thought that the tree-god had manifested in order to receive her offering into his own hands. Elated, she placed the vase of milk-rice before Siddhārtha, who accepted the offering, content to have a special meal without even having to move from his seat.

This was the last meal that Siddhārtha took before he sat down that evening for his most fulfilling meditation, the meditation that brought him full enlightenment. Some biographers say that it was the first meal Siddhārtha received after his prolonged austerity and fasting. In any case, Sujātā is said to have acquired great merit for offering such a good meal to the future Buddha on this crucial occasion. Siddhārtha prepared himself for his momentous meditation: he collected fresh grass from a grass-cutter, went to the auspicious peepal tree, and spreading the grass to serve as his cushion, he sat down cross-legged with the following resolution:

> My body may dry up, my skin, bones and flesh may be destroyed; yet my body shall not move from this posture without attaining enlightenment, so hard to attain even in many aeons.[57]

Siddhārtha's resolve struck fear into Māra, the tempter, who feared that his realm would become empty if Siddhārtha were to attain enlightenment and proclaim his way to the world. He first offered friendly advice to Siddhārtha, urging him not to engage in such a vain endeavour, saying, "It is impossible for you to find enlightenment."[58] In addition, continued Māra, if Siddhārtha were to return home, being fabulously rich, he could perform many religious sacrifices and charitable acts; thus, while enjoying royal happiness in the world, he would also secure heavenly bliss in the future. When Siddhārtha sternly told Māra to stop, Māra assembled his army of demons and attacked. But it was impossible for Māra and his army to vanquish Siddhārtha, who was equipped with the weapons of purity and wisdom and fully protected by his armour of unshakeable resolve. Māra was defeated and his forces of darkness ran helter-skelter.

Attaining Enlightenment or Nirvāṇa

Freed from disturbances, Siddhārtha became absorbed in deep meditation. The Buddha later described in his dialogues how one gradually ascends in meditation from the first to the fourth state of awareness, in which the mind becomes placid, pure and well concentrated. Then one begins to gain higher knowledge, as he points out:

> When the mind is concentrated, pure, cleansed, free from blemishes, purged of defilements, supple, pliant, steady and

> unperturbed, then one turns and directs his mind towards knowledge and insight.[59]

At this point it is possible to see that one's consciousness is different from the body, as the Buddha explains:

> One knows thus: 'This is my corporeal body, and this is my consciousness, which is enveloped and bound by it [the body]'... just as, if a man were to pull out the reed from the sheath of the *muñja* grass, he would know, 'This is the reed, and this is the sheath. The reed is one thing and the sheath is another.'[60]

Then he gradually acquired the following six-fold higher powers: the capacity to assume multiple forms; the divine ear to hear and the divine eye to see; the knowledge of others' minds; the knowledge of past lives; and the knowledge of the destruction of impurities. The divine ear and the divine eye are of special value, as they prove immensely helpful in ascending within to higher regions. Describing the emergence of the bright light and sonorous sound that one hears within, Ashvaghosha says:

> When the Buddha realized the truth ...the quarters shone bright with crowds of *siddhas*, and mighty drums resounded in the sky.[61]

When he finally gained the knowledge of the destruction of all impurities, he attained freedom and enlightenment. Describing his experience, the Buddha said:

> On becoming enlightened, I gained knowledge, and freedom was achieved. Exhausted is rebirth; the holy life has been lived; whatever was to be done is done, and nothing further remains after this.... Ignorance is destroyed; wisdom is arisen; darkness is dispelled and light is arisen.[62]

With this inner experience, Siddhārtha attained enlightenment. It was dawn in the full moon of the month of Vaishākha (May). The Buddha remained seated in the same posture for a week, enjoying the bliss of Nirvāṇa, the final liberation. Then he got up, walked to the Nirañjanā River and, refreshed, sat down under a banyan tree. Two passing merchants, Trapusha and Bhallika, saw him and were the first to pay homage to the Enlightened One and give him alms. The Buddha then reflected:

> This Dhamma won by me is deep, difficult to see and comprehend, tranquil, excellent, beyond reason, subtle and comprehensible only by the wise. But this is a world delighting and rejoicing in sensual pleasure. For people of such nature, this would be difficult to see.... If I were to teach Dhamma and others were not to understand me, my efforts would result only in my weariness and fatigue.... For people immersed in the darkness of ignorance, attachment and hatred, this Dhamma is subtle, profound and hard to comprehend. It would be like going against the current.[63]

Brahmā Sahampati* saw the mind of the Buddha and realized that if the Buddha were not encouraged to preach the Dhamma, the world would be ruined. Therefore Brahmā said:

> Let the Blessed One teach the Dhamma, let the Sublime One teach the Dhamma. Among beings there are some with just a little dust in their eyes. Not hearing the Dhamma, they are languishing; if taught, they will see the truth.[64]

> Sound the sublime trumpet of Dhamma. Blow the conch of true Dhamma; establish the great pillar of Dhamma, and kindle the luminous lamp of Dhamma.[65]

* A particular Brahmā or god who lives in the Pure Abodes and is a protector of Buddhism.

Brahmā Sahampati continued:*

In the past there appeared among the Magadhans†
An impure Dhamma [teaching]‡
Devised by those still stained.
Throw open this door to the Deathless!
Let them hear the Dhamma
That the Immaculate One discovered.

Just as one standing on a mountain peak
Might see below the people all around,
So, O wise one, universal eye,
Ascend the palace made of the Dhamma.
Being yourself free from sorrow, behold the people
Submerged in sorrow, oppressed by birth and decay.

Rise up, O hero, victor in battle!
O caravan leader, O debt-free one, wander in the world!
Teach the Dhamma, O Blessed One:
There will be those who will understand.[66]

Sound the sublime trumpet of Dhamma;
Blow the conch of true Dhamma.
Establish the great pillar of Dhamma
And kindle the luminous lamp of Dhamma.[67]

Approving in silence, in his great compassion the Buddha surveyed the world with his Buddha eye, and saw some people under the sway of passion and others suffering in poverty. Addressing Brahmā Sahampati, he declared:

---

* In the Nikāyas, text is sometimes in prose followed by poetry, as is shown here.
† Magadha was one of the principal kingdoms of northern India at the time of the Buddha.
‡ The Sanskrit word is 'Dharma', meaning 'that which holds'.

Opened are the doors to Deathlessness;
Those who have ears to hear may hear with faith.
Foreseeing trouble, O Brahmā, I did not speak
The refined, sublime Dhamma among human beings.[68]

Brahmā Sahampati then thought, "The Blessed One has given his consent regarding the teaching of the Dhamma," and paying homage to the Blessed One, disappeared.

Pondering to whom he should impart his teachings and who would be able to understand, the Buddha immediately thought of his two teachers, Ārāḍa Kālāma and Udraka Rāmaputra. They were wise, intelligent and had remained free from corruption. At that moment a voice sounded within him, saying that Ārāḍa Kālāma had died a week before and Udraka Rāmaputra had died only the previous night. With his new inner vision, the Buddha saw this to be true. Then he thought of the five disciples who had waited on him during the period of his austerities. He inwardly saw that they were at the Deer Park at Rishipatana (Sāranātha) in Vārāṇasī (Kāshī). After spending some time near Uruvelā, he set off on foot for Vārāṇasī.

Along the road between Bodhagayā, where the Buddha had attained *bodhi* (enlightenment), and the city of Gayā, he met a naked ascetic named Upaka. On seeing the pure, calm and majestic figure of the Buddha, Upaka enquired who he was, under which guru he was being trained and why he looked so bright and attractive. Seeing the Buddha's youthful body – he was only thirty-six years old at the time – Upaka took him for a spiritual student who, he felt, was practising holy discipline under a teacher. To remove that misunderstanding and to communicate that he was already a Buddha who had overcome all passions, the Buddha said:

Those who look like me are to be known as
  Jinas [conquerors] who have destroyed all defilements.

I have conquered the sinful tendencies;
therefore, I am indeed a Jina, O Upaka....
I shall go to Vārāṇasī, and having gone there –
to the city of Kāshī – I shall kindle
the incomparable light for people lost in blindness.
And I shall beat the drum of Deathlessness
for people devoid of *shabd* [inner sound].[69]

When the Buddha described himself as a Jina, Upaka was puzzled and said, "May it be so, friend." Shaking his head, he took a bypath and departed, in sheer disbelief.[70]

Some people, even those of a spiritual leaning, do not take interest in a spiritual teacher, even though they may see the purity and sublimity of the teacher and are convinced that his teachings are beyond reproach.* They simply remain indifferent.

One should not think that the Buddha had no guru. The Buddha himself made mention of his two gurus by name. In the celebrated text the *Lotus Sūtra* (*Saddharmapuṇḍarīka*) the Buddha states that he had previously been trained by many teachers:

> Formerly, in the company of many Buddhas, I have followed the course which is profound, subtle, difficult to know and difficult to see.[71]

Then referring to the endless succession of Buddhas who shall "follow one another in regular succession", the Buddha declares:

> Moved by benevolence and compassion, they shall in succession foretell each other's destiny, saying: "This one is to be my immediate successor, and he is to command the world as I do at present."[72]

---

* According to the *Majjhima Nikāya Atthakatha*, Upaka, after a difficult marriage, returned to the Buddha, entered the order, and was reborn in the Aviha heaven, where he attained arahantship. (*Middle Length Discourses of the Buddha*, tr. B. Ñāṇamoli, p.1218n)

The First Disciples

It is then recounted that the Buddha arrived at the Deer Park of Rishipatana (Sāranātha) in Vārāṇasī, where his five former disciples saw him coming and conferred among themselves:

> "This recluse Gautama is coming. He took to a life of ease and comfort, and deviated from his striving. He has reverted to a life of abundance. He should not be greeted. Nor should we get up to receive him, nor should we receive his bowl and robe. However, we may put out a seat for him, and he can sit if he so wishes." But as the Buddha was approaching closer and closer towards the five recluses, they were not able to adhere to their own decision, and they went ahead to receive him. Some received his bowl and robe, some prepared a seat for him and some brought water to wash his feet.[73]

The Buddha revealed that he had become fully enlightened and that he would be pleased to share his attainments. Although they felt respectful towards the Buddha, they were hesitant to accept him as a teacher, asking him how, by leading a life of relative comfort and wavering from his penances and fasts, he could attain the enlightenment that he had failed to reach even after massive austerities. The Buddha explained that he had not wavered and that he had not taken to comfort or luxury. In fact, he had found the right path, striven very hard and had succeeded in attaining the goal. He finally said:

> "Did I speak to you, recluses, like this before?"
> "No, revered sir," they answered.[74]

The Buddha persuaded them that he had attained what he had been striving for. They now listened in earnest to his teachings, and he then explained the Middle Path. He pointed out that there are two extreme approaches: one is to indulge in sensual pleasures, and the other is to subject oneself to austerities and self-mortification. Avoiding these two extremes and following the Middle Path under proper guidance leads to inner tranquillity and full enlightenment.

The Four Noble Truths and the Eightfold Path

The Buddha then taught them the Four Noble Truths, which explain the fundamentals of the Buddhist path. Because they are so central to Buddhism, these four principles are presented below in their essential form:

1. Life in the world is full of suffering (*dukkha*).
2. There is a cause of this suffering (*dukkha-samudaya*).
3. It is possible to bring an end to suffering (*dukkha-nirodha*).
4. There is a path that leads to the cessation of suffering (*dukkha-nirodha-gāminini-paṭipadā*), which is the Noble Eightfold Path (*ariya-aṭṭhaṅgika-magga*).

The usual translation of the Pali word *dukkha* as suffering is actually too severe. 'Suffering' gives the impression that life is nothing but pain, but the Buddha does not deny happiness in life; he simply teaches that suffering occurs because of the impermanent nature of happiness. *Dukkha* therefore embraces the usual meaning of 'suffering' but it also encompasses deeper concepts.

The Buddha taught that the Noble Eightfold Path, which he called the Middle Path or Middle Way (*majjhimā paṭipadā*), brings an end to suffering when one follows eight disciplines:

1. Right View (*sammā-diṭṭhi*)
2. Right Thought (*sammā-saṅkappa*)

3. Right Speech (*sammā-vācā*)
4. Right Action (*sammā-kammanta*)
5. Right Livelihood (*sammā-ājīva*)
6. Right Effort (*sammā-vāyāma*)
7. Right Mindfulness (*sammā-sati*)
8. Right Concentration (*sammā-samādhi*)*

These eight steps can be subsumed under three broad headings: Wisdom (Pali: *paññā*), the preliminary stage on the path, which includes the disciplines of right view and right thought; Morality (Pali: *sīla*), the preparation for *samādhi*, which includes right speech, right action and right livelihood; and Concentration (*samādhi*), the realization of the Dhamma, which includes right effort, right mindfulness and right concentration.

The Saṅgha Grows

There, in the Deer Park of Rishipatana in Vārāṇasī, the Buddha set in motion the wheel of the Dharma – he started giving out his teachings. He continued to reinforce his teachings in the minds of the five monks, and they practised assiduously. In the course of time they all attained enlightenment. Gradually many more people from Vārāṇasī and adjoining areas came to the Buddha and were ordained by him. When the number of enlightened monks (*arahants*) grew to sixty, the Buddha, out of compassion for the whole world, instructed them to go in different directions and preach the noble Dharma for the good and happiness of many. He enjoined them to go on their mission separately, no two monks taking the same route.

The Buddha then came back to Uruvelā in Gayā. He found an ascetic known as Uruvelā Kashyapa living there with his

---

* *Sammā* (Pali) means 'right' in the sense of correct, straight and beneficial.

five hundred disciples. The Buddha began to dwell in a grove close to the hermitage of Kashyapa. After a few days with the Buddha, Uruvelā Kashyapa was so impressed by the greatness of his teaching and the purity of his conduct that he and his five hundred followers became disciples of the Buddha, and then the other ascetics living in that area also joined the Buddha's saṅgha (community).

From Gayā, the Buddha left for Rājagriha (the capital of the Magadha Kingdom) with a large retinue of monks. There he was visited by King Bimbisāra of Magadha, who was deeply influenced by the Buddha's teachings and requested that the Buddha accept him as a lay disciple. The king invited the Buddha and all his monks to his palace for a meal. The Buddha accepted his invitation, and the king personally served food to the Buddha and all the monks. The king, after reflecting on the most suitable residence for the Buddha and his monks, donated his bamboo grove.

At the bamboo grove of Rājagriha, the Buddha found his three chief disciples, Shāriputra, Mahā Maudgalyāyana and Mahā Kāshyapa. Shāriputra and Maudgalyāyana would die before the Buddha, but Mahā Kāshyapa would take charge of the order upon the Buddha's death. The first two were wealthy brahmins of neighbouring villages who had become ascetics, leading a religious life under the guidance of a wandering ascetic, Sañjaya. The third was the only son of a brahmin, Kapila of Magadha. This son, Kāshyapa, had no desire to marry, but under pressure from his father, was compelled to marry a beautiful girl. But soon after the marriage, he and his wife renounced their home and went in search of a spiritual teacher. Seeing Shāriputra and Maudgalyāyana at a distance, the Buddha is said to have remarked in a soft voice, "Here come the two friends, my two great disciples." Kāshyapa was automatically drawn to the Buddha, and hearing his teachings, he at once begged for ordination. The Buddha took him along to the bamboo grove and granted ordination to him.

Return to Kapilavastu

The Buddha in due course proceeded to Kapilavastu, gathering new disciples as he travelled. There he received a warm welcome. King Shuddhodana, the Buddha's father, was the first to offer obeisance to the Buddha and the monks accompanying him. The former Prince Siddhārtha, who had ridden in the royal chariot in regal glory, was now walking through the same city with his head shaven, wearing a yellow robe and holding a begging bowl. King Shuddhodana was overcome with emotion, but containing his feelings, he told the Buddha that he had been right to leave his luxurious palace, right to make strenuous efforts to win Nirvāṇa, and now right to be so compassionate to his father and the relatives who loved him so dearly.

After everyone had taken their meal at the palace, all the residents of the palace except the Buddha's wife, Yashodharā, came and bowed deeply to the Buddha and the other monks. It is recounted that when Yashodharā was urged to come and make her obeisance to the Buddha, she softly replied that since she had been a loyal and virtuous wife, the one who had deserted her would himself come to her. The Buddha went to her chamber and sat on the seat offered. She fell at his feet and washed them with her unceasing tears. The Buddha consoled her. As he rose to leave, she said that he had come to her door as a beggar, and that he had left her nothing which she could offer him as a gift except their son, Prince Rāhula. She offered Prince Rāhula as a gift, and so the Buddha took Rāhula and went on his way.

According to another account, when the Buddha came to Yashodharā's chamber, she told her son, "That is your father. Go and ask him for your inheritance." Young Rāhula went to the Buddha, stood before him and said, "O Venerable One, your very shade is very pleasing to me." The Buddha rose from his seat and left, but young Rāhula followed him, pleading, "Give me,

Venerable One, my inheritance." Then the Buddha asked Venerable Shāriputra, who was then accompanying him, to take the young prince along and ordain him.

The following day the Buddha went for alms to the house of Nanda, his half-brother, the son of Mahāprajāvatī. This was the day of Nanda's installation as heir apparent, as well as his marriage to the most beautiful young woman in the kingdom. The Buddha gave Nanda his bowl to hold and, wishing him good luck, left without taking back the bowl. Out of respect for the Buddha, Nanda did not ask the Buddha to take back the bowl, but followed him, hoping that he would soon take it. As Nanda began to leave, his betrothed impatiently asked him to turn back. Her words pierced Nanda's heart. But the Buddha continued on until they reached the monastery, where he asked Nanda if he would like to enter the order. Out of respect for the Buddha, Nanda could not say no. The Buddha ordered him ordained right away, although in Nanda's ears the sweet voice of his betrothed still rang.[*75] What the Buddha did may appear drastic to many – removing a young man from his betrothed. But the perspective of the true Enlightened One is different from that of the average person; the former can clearly see one's potential and destiny, while the latter cannot.

First Ordination of Women

After the death of King Shuddhodana, Queen Mahāprajāvatī, the sister of prince Siddhārtha's mother who had raised him so lovingly after his mother died, came to the Buddha along with five hundred wives of princes who had entered the order. She

*It is said that Nanda continued to be troubled by this event and did not seem to make much progress in his meditation. He thought of quitting the order, but the Buddha called him one day and asked him to sit in meditation. The Buddha, through his power, let Nanda see heavenly nymphs far superior in beauty to Nanda's beautiful betrothed. Nanda finally decided to remain in the order. (*Udāna* 3:2, p.21)

asked the Buddha to kindly grant ordination to her and the other women, but he declined her request. The Buddha eventually departed Kapilavastu for Vaishālī. Mahāprajāvatī left the palace, shaved her hair, donned the saffron robe and, followed by the five hundred women, went to Vaishālī, where the Buddha was staying. Ānanda, the Buddha's favourite attendant, saw her at the gate, covered with dust, with swollen feet and tearful eyes. On being asked why she had travelled such a long distance and arrived in such an exhausted state, she explained that the Buddha had refused to grant ordination to women, and she had come to ask again. Ānanda again took her request for ordination, and the Buddha again refused it.

Thereupon, Ānanda asked the Buddha if it were possible for a woman to renounce the world and thus advance in the holy practice to enlightenment. The Buddha answered yes, and so Ānanda argued on the queen's behalf, reminding him that Mahāprajāvatī, the sister of his mother, had served him faithfully during his childhood. She had breastfed him when his mother died and had brought him up lovingly. Ānanda requested that she be allowed to enter the order. The Buddha decreed that women could be ordained if they agreed to follow the stringent rules of the order. Mahāprajāvatī and the five hundred ladies gladly agreed, and all were granted ordination. Thus, the first order of nuns came to be established. Soon after the establishment of the order of nuns, Yashodharā, the mother of Rāhula, joined the order. And the woman whom Nanda had left to follow the Buddha entered the order along with Yashodharā.

Another beautiful young woman named Nandā, the daughter of Mahāprajāvatī, entered the order when she found that her mother and Yashodharā had become nuns. But she used to hear the Buddha's teachings only from other nuns, trying to avoid facing the Buddha directly because she believed that he disapproved of beauty and youth. But when some nuns told her that without appearing before the Buddha and listening to his instructions directly, one couldn't properly become his disciple, she reluctantly appeared before him. She was astonished to see a young lady much more beautiful than she fanning him. All her pride in beauty and youth, all her shyness and hesitancy, disappeared.

The Grove of Jeta

After receiving offerings from the gentry as well as the humble and ordaining many of them, the Buddha returned to Magadha. One day at the bamboo grove, a wealthy merchant from Rājagriha invited the Buddha along with all his monks to his estate. Another merchant from Shrāvastī named Anāthapiṇḍaka (giver of food to the helpless), who was married to the sister of the wealthy merchant, was visiting on business and was astonished to see his brother-in-law deeply involved in organizing his servants and cooks. Usually the brother-in-law would stop and engage in conversation. Perhaps, he thought, the king and his courtiers had been invited, or there was to be a marriage. But when he enquired, it was explained that the Buddha had granted the merchant a special privilege – that of providing meals the following day to the Buddha and the other monks of the bamboo grove.

Anāthapiṇḍaka could not believe his ears. A true Buddha, he thought, is rarely found in the world. If a Buddha really dwelled here, Anāthapiṇḍaka thought, he should seize the first opportunity to see him. The Rājagriha merchant told him that it was too late in the day to visit the Buddha, but that the next morning before the Buddha's mealtime he should visit. So Anāthapiṇḍaka went to the Buddha's monastery early the next morning. After the Buddha had explained his doctrines, Anāthapiṇḍaka at once requested that the Buddha accept him as his lay disciple from that day on, and his request was accepted. After the Buddha and the other monks had finished eating, the Buddha gave a discourse. Thereupon Anāthapiṇḍaka reverently invited him to visit Shrāvastī along with his monks and to stay there as long as he wished. The Buddha accepted.

On returning to Shrāvastī, Anāthapiṇḍaka looked for a quiet place and found a park owned by Prince Jeta. But the prince was unwilling to sell, saying he would not part with it even if it were covered with *crores* (tens of millions) of gold pieces. Although this was merely a figure of speech, Anāthapiṇḍaka offered to buy the park on those terms. But Jeta still said that no deal had been struck. When this issue was referred to the king's ministers of justice, however, they decided in favour of Anāthapiṇḍaka, who brought cartloads of gold pieces and covered the park with them. Only a small section was left uncovered, so Anāthapiṇḍaka ordered his men to bring more gold to cover it. Prince Jeta felt that the cause for which Anāthapiṇḍaka was sacrificing so much of his gold must be very good, and with this thought, he told Anāthapiṇḍaka not to bring any more gold but to accept the uncovered part of the park as a gift from him. After spending some time in Magadha, the Buddha proceeded towards Shrāvastī, ordaining people along the way. He finally reached Shrāvastī, and by that time Anāthapiṇḍaka had already donated the grove to the Buddha. It came to be known as the Grove of Jeta (Jetavana) and it remained a favourite retreat of the Buddha during his stay at Shrāvastī.

Attack by Devadatta

After staying at Shrāvastī for a long time, the Buddha returned to Rājagriha. By this time his fame had spread far and wide. He had won over most of the leading brahmins and even brought early opponents to his path. But his own cousin, Devadatta, who had joined the order early, had developed certain inner powers (*siddhis*) and, although encouraged and praised by the Buddha, he now became envious. While the Buddha was preaching to a large gathering, Devadatta, impelled by eagerness for honour and fame, suddenly stood up and requested that the Buddha, now old and weary, should rest and allow Devadatta to lead the monks and lay community. The Buddha's rejection of this suggestion angered and humiliated Devadatta. Even in his childhood Devadatta bore a degree of malice against the Buddha, but he now became so desperate that he even planned to kill the Buddha. With this end in mind, he would try to win the favour of King Bimbisāra's son, Prince Ajātashatru, hoping to overawe him with his miraculous powers. He then planned to conspire with the prince to kill the king and take over Magadha.

Devadatta assumed the form of a child dressed in a girdle of snakes and appeared on Prince Ajātashatru's lap. The prince was startled and stood up in panic. Then appearing in his own form, Devadatta smiled and asked the prince why he was so scared by a monk. Ajātashatru, marvelling at his psychic power, became his supporter. Devadatta advised the prince that if he did not get rid of his father, who would still have many years remaining as king, Ajātashatru would have little chance of becoming king. Ajātashatru was later caught in an attempt to kill his father, but out of love for his son, the king abdicated in his favour. But because Devadatta had performed yet more miracles to win over Ajātashatru, he then lost the powers developed after long years of arduous spiritual practice.

Devadatta then tried to have the Buddha killed at the hands of Prince Ajātashatru's men. But when they failed, Devadatta himself decided to murder the Buddha. While the Buddha was walking along Griddhakūṭa Hill, Devadatta hurled a large rock down at him. Two protrusions prevented the rock from falling on him, and only a splinter struck the Buddha's foot, which caused some bleeding. The Buddha looked up. Seeing Devadatta, the Buddha observed that he had been foolish and created great demerit.

The news caused a great commotion among the monks, but the Buddha pacified them and told them to keep quiet. In response to their idea to provide protection for him, he told them that he needed no protection, for none could kill him unless he so willed.

Devadatta then conspired with Prince Ajātashatru's elephant keepers. He directed them to let loose the fierce elephant Nālāgiri on the Buddha while he was walking along a street. The monks who were following the Buddha raised the alarm, asking the Buddha to turn back and escape from the killer elephant. They ran away to safety, but the Buddha calmly proceeded, once again saying that none could kill him. Nālāgiri rushed towards the Buddha, but the Buddha extended the power of universal compassion towards the elephant, which became quiet and subdued and stood before him, lowering its trunk. The Buddha stroked its trunk and walked away. News spread, and Devadatta was challenged. Claiming innocence, he even managed to gain the confidence of some newly-ordained monks, creating a schism within the order.

Illness in the Mango Grove

After some time the Buddha set out northward with a large group of monks. He stopped at Nālandā and then continued on to Pātaligrāma, where the Magadha ministers were building a fortress. The ministers invited him and his monks for a meal, and after everyone had partaken of food, the Buddha gave a discourse, during which he prophesied the future greatness of the place. This indeed came to be true, and Pātaligrāma became the capital of the Magadha kingdom, known as Pātaliputra (modern Patna). Then, crossing the river Ganges, he and his monks reached Vaishālī and stayed in the mango grove of a well-known courtesan, Ambapālī. Hearing that the Buddha had come to Vaishālī and was at her mango grove, Ambapālī at once went out to see him. She made her obeisance to the Buddha, and after listening to his discourse, invited him and the monks to share her hospitality. The Buddha kindly accepted her invitation. While returning to her place with joy and pride, she saw the Lichchhavi princes coming. She knew that they also were going to see the Buddha and drove up to their chariots, whereupon they had this conversation:

> "Why do you, Ambapālī, drive like this, axle-to-axle, wheel-to-wheel, and yoke-to-yoke against the young Lichchhavis?"
>
> "This is because, my lords, I have just invited the Blessed One with his community of monks for their meals tomorrow at my residence," said she.
>
> "Ambapālī, please give this chance to us for a hundred thousand gold coins," they said.
>
> "No, my lords, even if you were to offer me the entire Vaishālī with all of its colonies, I would not give up such an honourable opportunity," said Ambapālī.
>
> Then the Lichchhavis snapped their fingers and said, "We have been outdone by this woman of the mango grove."[76]

Even so, they proceeded on to see the Buddha, and after listening to his instructions invited him and the monks to their house. But the Buddha told them that he had already accepted an invitation from Ambapālī, and they returned home frustrated. The next day, when the Buddha and his monks arrived at her mango grove, she personally served the most delicious food to them, and at the end of the meal donated her grove to the Buddha and his order. The Buddha accepted. After staying at the grove for some time and asking the monks to utilize it as a retreat, he moved on to Veṇugrāma. Spending the rainy season there, the Buddha became seriously ill and was in great pain, but he hid his illness, for it would not be fitting for him to die without having first addressed the community of monks.

Ānanda's Question on Refuge

When the Buddha felt a bit better, Ānanda, his close attendant and companion, approached him and said:

> On account of the illness of the Exalted One, my body became weak, I could not see in any direction, nor could I take interest in the Dhamma.[77]

At this the Buddha replied:

> "What, Ānanda, does the order of monks expect of me? The Dhamma has been taught by me, Ānanda, without making any distinction between exoteric and esoteric. The Tathāgata [the Buddha] does not have the closed fist of a teacher who holds back something relating to the Dhamma. Surely, Ānanda, if there were anyone who were to harbour the thought that he should lead the order or that the order were dependent on him, he would indeed give guidance on anything concerning the order. But the Tathāgata thinks that he is not that one.... I am now, Ānanda, old, full of years; I have lived my span and am at the close of my days. I am turning eighty years of age. And just as a worn-out cart, Ānanda, can be kept going only with the help of thongs, so the body of the Tathāgata can be kept going only by bandaging it up.... Therefore, Ānanda, live with the lamp kindled unto yourself, take refuge unto yourself and seek no other refuge. Hold fast to the Dhamma as a lamp, the Dhamma as a refuge and no other refuge."[78]

Thus the Buddha indicated that those who were ordained by him should not worry. There was no need for them to seek and take refuge in any other teaching or teacher. That is why the Buddha clarifies that the Dharma, the holy discipline or spiritual path taught by him, is the sole refuge of his disciples, and that they should practise this Dharma to the best of their ability and kindle the light within themselves. As we shall see, the Buddha told his disciples explicitly that after his death his teachings alone should suffice for them, and that his followers should respectfully adhere to them. They should seek guidance only from his teaching and none else.

Three Months to Live

The demon Māra appeared before the Buddha and noted that the Dharma was well established. His monks, nuns and lay disciples had become mature enough to carry on the order, and the time was nigh for him to pass away. The Buddha told Māra that he would leave his mortal frame three months from that day. When he conveyed his decision to Ānanda, the latter was greatly distressed and entreated the Buddha to remain alive longer. The Buddha answered:

> Have I not already explained to you, Ānanda, that we have to be separated from all things near and dear, we have to leave or part company with all things… and all are subject to dissolution? So, how can you have anything forever? It is not possible for anything that is born, created or brought into existence to remain indestructible.[79]

The Buddha then asked Ānanda to assemble the Vaishālī monks. When all were assembled in the big hall, the Buddha delivered a powerful discourse, urging his monks and all other disciples to practise his teachings strenuously and to obtain mastery over them. He asked them to be steadfast in their meditation, keep the Dharma pure and propagate it for the good and happiness of many. He then added:

> I exhort you, O monks: all compounded things are subject to decay. Work for your salvation with earnestness. Before long the Tathāgata will pass away. The Tathāgata will attain Parinibbāna [final Nirvāṇa] three months from now.[80]

The next day, the Buddha went to Vaishālī for alms, and after taking his meal, he looked back at Vaishālī and told Ānanda that it would be his last sight of Vaishālī. The Buddha always had great admiration for this prosperous city, where people led a disciplined and democratic way of life.

The Last Meal

After spending time in several places, the Buddha arrived at the city of Pāvā and stayed in the mango grove of Chunda, the blacksmith. Chunda invited him and his accompanying monks for a meal. He had a wide variety of excellent food prepared, along with a large quantity of delicious milk-rice (*sūkara maddava*).* The Buddha asked Chunda to serve him only the *sūkara maddava*, while serving all the dishes to the other monks. After speaking with Chunda, the Buddha left the grove. Some time after this meal, the Buddha was afflicted with dysentery and severe pain, but with steadfast mind he bore the agony, remained composed and proceeded to Kusinārā. Along the way he paused, asking Ānanda to spread a robe for him to sit and rest under the shade of a tree. He asked Ānanda to bring water, as he was thirsty, but Ānanda hesitated to go to the nearby stream since five hundred carts had just passed through it, making its water muddy and turbid. He suggested that not far away

*The phrase *sūkara maddava* means 'tasty rice and milk'. This word is not to be mistaken for *sūkara maṁsa*, 'pig's meat' (pork). There are repeated references to holy people, Buddhist and non-Buddhist, being served milk-rice, but nowhere is meat served to holy men in that part of India where the Buddha took his last meal. Deliberately serving meat to monks is clearly forbidden by the Buddha. (*MN.i*, p.368–371, *LAN*, p.212–221)

was the river Kakudhā, with cool and clear water. This would be better for the Exalted One. But when the Buddha asked Ānanda for the third time, he went to the stream and was wonder-struck to find the stream clear and pure. The Buddha's thirst was quenched.

Last Hours

A man named Pukkasa of the Malla clan, a disciple of Ārāḍa Kālāma, the first guru of the Buddha, came to him. In the course of the interview, the Buddha told him about a deeper state of meditation than his master's, so he at once begged the Buddha to accept him as his disciple and offered him a pair of gold shawls. The Buddha accepted the gift but asked Pukkasa to give one to him and the other to Ānanda. When Pukkasa left, Ānanda covered the Buddha's body with both shawls and observed that their gold seemed faint compared to the radiance of the Buddha's body. The Buddha told Ānanda that the Enlightened One gains a special radiance on two occasions: when he attains Nirvāṇa, and when he attains Parinirvāṇa. So the time came, in the last watch of that night at Kusinārā, to attain Parinirvāṇa.

The Buddha walked with Ānanda, Chunda and several other monks to the River Kakudhā, where he bathed in the river and drank. Walking to a mango grove, he lay down. He instructed Ānanda that Chunda might feel remorseful, thinking that the Buddha had passed away because of his food. He said that it should be pointed out to Chunda that two meals offered to the Buddha are of special merit: the one offered to him before he attains Nirvāṇa (served to Siddhārtha by Sujātā), and the other offered to him before attaining Parinirvāṇa; and that Chunda should therefore be happy for the great fortune of serving the Buddha's last meal. Then the Buddha, accompanied by his monks, came finally to the *sāla* grove of Kusinārā, the last destination of his earthly journey. There he spoke to Ānanda:

> Prepare me a bed with its head to the north between the twin *sāla* trees. I am tired, and I wish to lie down.[81]

Ānanda did so, and the Buddha lay down, completely self-possessed. The twin *sāla* trees were in full bloom out of season, and flowers gently fell in reverence on the Buddha's body. Divine flowers and sandalwood powder dropped from the sky and the atmosphere resounded with divine music. Then the Exalted One addressed Ānanda:

> Although, Ānanda, all these offerings are made in honour of the Tathāgata, it is not thus that the Tathāgata is rightly honoured, venerated, revered and worshipped. If monks, nuns, and lay disciples were to live in accordance with my teachings and strictly follow my teachings, they would be honouring me and venerating me rightly, and paying me true respect and true reverence. Therefore, Ānanda, you should act according to my teaching, following all the instructions, and it should be so taught to others. This would be the highest worship, which would please me most.[82]

Ānanda asked how matters should be handled when the Buddha would not be there for guidance. Ānanda then went to a nearby cottage, a place for communal ceremonies, his mind filled with the dreadful thought of the impending event. Here he stood leaning against the door lintel, weeping and feeling deserted by his master, even before the event had occurred. The Buddha called Ānanda to console him, pointing out that all things must change and that meeting and parting are inevitable in this world. He said that Ānanda had no reason to grieve, as he had wholeheartedly served the Buddha for a long time in thought, word and deed, with unbounded love. He exhorted Ānanda to continue to strive for enlightenment, and assured him that he would soon be free from all impurities. He explained Ānanda's wonderful qualities to the other monks. Ānanda then tried to point out to the Buddha that Kusinārā was an insignificant place for a Blessed One to pass away, and that he should instead think of an important city as the place of his passage. The Buddha said that Kusinārā once had been a renowned city and the capital of the great King Mahāsudarshana.

Ānanda did, however, obtain the Buddha's consent to inform the people of Kusinārā about his impending Parinirvāṇa so that they might not later repent for being denied a last glimpse. Ānanda went to Kusinārā and found the Malla princes and other gentry assembled. They rushed to the *sāla* grove in great grief, and were fortunate enough to obtain their last sight of the Buddha during the first watch of that night.

The Last Disciple

Just then an ascetic named Subhadra came to see the Buddha. He had heard that a Buddha is rarely found in this world and now, finding that one had come to Kusinārā and was to pass away during the last watch of that night, Subhadra was desperate to see the Buddha. Ānanda did not want to disturb the Buddha, who was tired and ill. Subhadra insisted three times that he must see the Buddha. The Buddha overheard their conversation and asked Ānanda to let Subhadra come in. Subhadra mentioned the names of other ascetics and asked the Buddha if any one of them was enlightened, so that he could be advised by one recommended by the Buddha. The Buddha refrained from expressing any opinion, but asked Subhadra what he needed to have clarified. Subhadra was so impressed by the Buddha's answers that he begged the Buddha to grant him ordination at that hour. The Buddha asked Ānanda to make preparations at once for Subhadra's ordination; then the Buddha fulfilled Subhadra's wish, ordaining his last disciple.

Last Words

The Buddha's final words are given below in the words of the *Dīgha Nikāya*, an early text from the Pali Canon:

> Then the Buddha called Ānanda and said to him, "It may be, Ānanda, that after my passing away you might think: 'Gone is the utterance of our master; we have no master anymore.' But you should not think so, Ānanda, for the doctrine [*dhamma*] and discipline [*vinaya*] which I have taught to you and prescribed to you will be your master [guide] after my death."[83]

Thus, before his passing away, the Buddha made it clear to his disciples through Ānanda that they had no need for another teacher, and that his instructions to them were sufficient for the guidance of his followers. The Buddha directly instructed them to regard him as their sole guide and master.

> Then the Buddha said to the assembled monks: "If any of you has any doubt or uncertainty whatsoever concerning the Buddha, the teaching, the community of monks and nuns, the path or the practice, you may seek clarification now. Do not say later that you had no opportunity to ask questions when the Buddha was face-to-face before you."[84]

The Buddha repeated this three times, but no one asked a question, and he felt satisfied that his disciples were free of any doubt concerning his teachings. He addressed the monks for the last time:

> Now, O monks, I exhort you: All compounded things are subject to decay. Work for your salvation with earnestness.[85]

These were the Buddha's last words. He retired, gradually raised his consciousness, and in the fourth watch of the night entered into the state of deathlessness. A profound silence descended upon him, and Ānanda pronounced, "The Lord has attained Parinirvāṇa."

Lighting the Pyre

There followed lamentations from the less advanced monks, but those who were more elevated remained composed, consoling their brethren and reminding them of the teaching of the Exalted One that change and separation are inevitable in this world. The news spread like wildfire. People from distant places and from all directions began pouring into the city, and elaborate arrangements were made for the cremation of the body. The body was kept for six days, and on the seventh was taken for cremation. Four chiefs of the Mallas tried to light the pyre, but they could not. Anuruddha saw with his inner vision that Mahā Kāshyapa was on his way to Kusinārā with five hundred monks, and he asked the Mallas to wait. It is said that when they arrived, Mahā Kāshyapa reverentially adjusted his robe, placing it on one shoulder, and with folded hands went round the pyre three times. Thus he offered his reverence to the Buddha and bowed to him with great devotion. The five hundred monks also paid their respects to the Buddha, after which the pyre was lit with no difficulty at all.

After the cremation a dispute arose over the ashes. The chiefs of eight different states each demanded a share of the ashes, but the Mallas maintained that as the Buddha had passed away in their state, his ashes belonged entirely to them. A brahmin named Droṇa, however, intervened and appealed to all, saying that it was inappropriate to quarrel over the ashes of such a distinguished and honourable teacher, whose whole life had been spent spreading the message of love and peace. Finally, acknowledging that the

Buddha and his teachings were not the monopoly of anyone, they agreed to divide the ashes into eight equal parts, one for each of the eight claimants, and the dispute was peacefully resolved.

Thus was the physical passing of a great guide, a torchbearer who showed the way to immortality to a multitude of people. He shunned the pomp and grandeur of the world to seek solitude and peace, and abandoned earthly fortune to discover spiritual treasure. Though born the son of a prosperous king and brought up amidst luxuries and comforts, he took birth in the natural surroundings of a grove and also left his body in a grove. A lover of the pure and simple life, kind and forgiving, with a mind possessed of wisdom and a heart full of love, he chose not to occupy a royal throne. But kings, princes and royalty bowed to him in reverence, and he won the hearts of people regardless of their rank and position. As an embodiment of Dharma, a fountainhead of spiritual powers and a repository of compassion, he worked for the good and happiness of humanity. His grace and bounty uplifted and fulfilled all who turned to him, and he left a legacy that still serves as a beacon for the world.

3

The Buddha and the Doctrine of the Triple Body

In the preceding chapter we recounted the traditional Buddhist story of the life of Gautama Buddha. How much of this story is legend and how much historical fact can never be ascertained. What is important is the message that it conveys to us. The Buddha came into a human body to bring a timeless truth, the Dharma. Depending on its context, 'Dharma' has many meanings, such as ultimate reality, perfect wisdom, ultimate truth, true path. When the sūtras tell us that the Buddha came to this world to explain the Dharma, they refer to both the ultimate truth as well as the path by which it may be realized.

So how does Buddhism portray Lord Buddha? Does the fact that the Buddha took birth and died at a certain place and time mean that he also, like any other thing or being, was bound by space and time? In other words, was he also, like other worldly objects or persons, finite and impermanent? If so, then is there any way he can be considered different from other worldly beings? Moreover, can anything finite and impermanent be considered real? Can ultimate reality be finite? And can it ever cease to be?

THREE DIMENSIONS OF THE BUDDHA

In the early Pali Canon, the Buddha himself seems to have provided suggestions as to how we should understand the idea of the Buddha. Later, the Mahāyāna school extended the implications of these suggestions and developed the doctrine of the triple body (*trikāya*). This doctrine, to put it briefly, explains that the Buddha can be seen in his three dimensions, namely, earthly, heavenly, and the absolute. Accordingly, he is said to have three forms or bodies: Nirmāṇakāya, the physical body; Sambhogakāya, the blissful or glorious body that exists in heavenly realms; and Dharmakāya, the Dharma-body or truth body that is one with absolute reality.

In the Vakkali Sutta from the *Saṁyutta Nikāya* of the Pali Canon, the Buddha distinguishes his Dharma-body from his physical body. This sutta tells of a monk, Vakkali, who, when seriously ill, sent a message to the Buddha requesting that he kindly visit him. When the Buddha went to see Vakkali, the latter was troubled by remorse and regret at not having seen the Gautama Buddha for a long time and said:

> "For a long time, Lord, I have been longing to have the sight of the Exalted One, but I had not strength enough in this body to come to see the Exalted One." Thereupon the Buddha said, "What is there, Vakkali, in seeing this corruptible body [*pūti kāya*]? He who sees Dhamma sees me; he who sees me sees Dhamma. Seeing Dhamma, Vakkali, he sees me; seeing me, he sees Dhamma."[86]

Elsewhere in the Pali Canon, in the course of his dialogue with a brahmin named Dona, the Buddha indicates that his value is not in his human form:

Then Dona, following the Lord's footprints, saw that he was sitting under a tree, calmly, faith-inspiring, his sense faculties and his mind peaceful, having attained the calm of uttermost control, restrained, tamed and guarding his sense faculties. Seeing the 'elephant' (a great being), Dona approached the Lord and said:

"Is your reverence a deva [a god]?"
"No indeed, Brahmin, I am not a deva."
"Then a *gandharva* [a heavenly being]?"
"No indeed, Brahmin."
"A *yakkha* [a non-human spirit] then?"
"No indeed, Brahmin, I am not a *yakkha*."
"Then is your reverence a human being?"
"No indeed, Brahmin, I am not a human being."
"You answer 'no' to all my questions.
Who then is your reverence?"

The Buddha then said:

"Take it that I am Buddha, Brahmin."[87]

As the well-known Japanese Buddhist scholar Junjirō Takakusu (1866–1945) has noted, the Buddha further added:

If you keep to my teachings and practise them, is it not the same as if my Dharma-body remained here forever?[88]

Explaining this, Takakusu says, "The Dharmakāya here means that his body remains as Dharma ... after the death of his physical body."[89]

The Pali Canon also illuminates the meaning of the Sambhogakāya (the blissful or glorious body) when the Buddha is described as visiting various gods and their abodes in his heavenly, non-physical embodiment. For example, the Buddha once visited Baka Brahmā, one of the gods of Buddhism, and Māra, the tempter in Buddhism, while the Brahmā was holding court with his assembly of gods. There, the Buddha urged Baka Brahmā to give up his misconception that his world was eternal.[90]

This story reveals that the roots of the doctrine of the triple body (*trikāya*) were already established in early Buddhism. The doctrine was developed and systematized by the Mahāyāna masters; in the Mahāyāna, the physical manifestation of the Buddha is clearly distinguished from the Truth that was manifested through him. In other words, the historical Buddha was regarded as an embodiment of the Dharma, but the Dharma surpasses his psycho-physical body. A few quotations from Mahāyāna texts will clearly bring this out. In the *Perfection of Wisdom Sūtra in Eight Thousand Lines* (*Ashṭasāhasrikā Prajñāpāramitā*), for example, the Buddha is quoted by the king of gods, Shakra:

> The Dharma-body is the Buddha, the Lord. But, monks, you should not think that this individual body is my body. Monks, you should see me from the accomplishment of the Dharma-body.[91]

In the same work, it is again said:

> Tathāgatas certainly do not come from anywhere, nor do they go anywhere. Because Suchness [*Tathatā*] does not move, and the Tathāgata is Suchness.... Foolish are all those who imagine the coming or going of a Tathāgata. For a Tathāgata cannot be seen from his form-body [*rūpkāya*].* The Dharma-body is the Tathāgata.[92]

---

*Tathāgata is an epithet for the Buddha that denotes his oneness with ultimate reality or the Absolute; *rūpkāya* is a synonym for the *nirmāṇakāya*, the physical body of the Buddha.

As the ninth-century Ch'an master Huang-Po, also known as Hsi Yun, explains:

> All the Buddhas and all sentient beings are nothing but the One Mind,* beside which nothing exists. This Mind, which is without beginning, is unborn and indestructible. It is neither green nor yellow, and has neither form nor appearance. It does not belong to the category of things which exist or do not exist, nor can it be thought of in terms of new or old. It is neither long nor short, big nor small, for it transcends all limits, measures, names, traces and comparisons. It is that which you see before you – begin to reason about it and you at once fall into error. It is like the boundless void which cannot be fathomed or measured.
>
> The One Mind alone is the Buddha, and there is no distinction between the Buddha and sentient things, but that sentient beings are attached to forms and so seek externally for Buddhahood. By their very seeking they lose it, for that is using the Buddha to seek for the Buddha and using mind to grasp Mind. Even though they do their utmost for a full aeon, they will not be able to attain it. They do not know that, if they put a stop to conceptual thought and forget their anxiety, the Buddha will appear before them, for this Mind is the Buddha and the Buddha is all living beings. It is not the less for being manifested in ordinary beings, nor is it greater for being manifested in the Buddhas.[93]

The same is reiterated by the Buddha in the *Diamond Sūtra* (*Vajrachchhedikā Prajñāpāramitā*):

---

*Huang-Po was not entirely satisfied with the choice of the word 'Mind' to symbolize the inexpressible reality beyond reach of conceptual thought, for he explained that the One Mind is not really mind at all. But he had to use some term and 'Mind' – *hsin* in Chinese – had often been used by his predecessors.

Tathāgata, Subhūti [a senior monk], is synonymous with true Suchness [Tathatā].[94]

It further adds:

Whosoever says that the Tathāgata goes or comes... does not understand the meaning of my teaching. And why? 'Tathāgata' is called [refers to] one who has not gone anywhere, nor come from anywhere. Therefore, he is called 'the Tathāgata, the Arhat, the fully Enlightened One'.[95]

The Mahāyāna *Lotus Sūtra* (*Saddharmapuṇḍarīka*) explains why the everlasting Tathāgata makes a show of taking birth and dying in this illusory world. Whatever he does is a magical show, as is everything we experience in this world. The *Lotus Sūtra* points out that by coming to the level of worldly beings, the compassionate Tathāgata simply utilizes the best and most skilful means (*upāya-kaushalya*) to educate and awaken those beings who otherwise would neglect their primary duty of attaining salvation. As the *Lotus Sūtra* explains:

The Tathāgata has an endless span of life, he lasts forever. Although the Tathāgata has not entered Nirvāṇa, he makes a show of entering Nirvāṇa, for the sake of those who have to be educated.... Because it might be that if I stayed here too long and could be seen too often, beings who have performed no meritorious actions, who are without merit, a poorly lot, eager for sensuous pleasures, blind, and wrapped in the net of false views, would, in the knowledge that the Tathāgata stays, get the notion that life is a mere sport, and would not conceive the notion that the Tathāgata is hard to obtain. In the conviction that the Tathāgata is always at hand, they would not exert their

> vigour for the purpose of escaping from the triple world, and they would not conceive of the Tathāgata as hard to obtain.
>
> Hence the Tathāgata, in his best or most skilful means, has uttered to those beings the saying, "Rarely, O monks, do Tathāgatas appear in the world."... When they do not see the Tathāgata, they will long for the sight of him.... Considering this, the Tathāgata, although he does not actually enter Nirvāṇa, announces his entering into Nirvāṇa, for the sake of those to be educated. And that is a discourse on Dharma by the Tathāgata himself. When he utters it, there is in it no false speech on the part of the Tathāgata.[96]

Sambhogakāya is the glorious or blissful body in which the Buddha appears in the pure heavenly worlds, where he shares the bliss of Dharma with bodhisattvas, pure and compassionate beings. The following few quotations indicate the glory of the Sambhogakāya and the bliss of the realm where he dwells:

> Then the Blessed One, beholding again his great assembly with his wisdom-eye, which is not the human eye, laughed loudly and most vigorously like the lion-king, emitting rays of light from the tuft of hair [point: *ūrṇā*] between the eyebrows... like a luminous rainbow, like the rising sun, blazing brilliantly, gloriously, which were observed from the sky by Shakra, Brahmā, and the guardians of the world.[97]

A similar description of the Buddha is found in the *Lotus Sūtra*:

> At that time a ray of light was emitted from the point between the two eyebrows of the Blessed One. It covered the eighteen thousand Buddha-fields in the east. All these Buddha-fields were illuminated by the light of this ray, which extended right from the dreadful hell, Avīchi, to the highest heaven.[98]

Indicating the bliss and beauty of Sukhāvatī, the highest heaven where one dwells before obtaining the highest wisdom or enlightenment,* the *Pure Land Sūtra* (*Sukhāvatī-Vyūha*) says:

> And, O Ānanda, the world called Sukhāvatī [Pure Land or Blissful Abode], belonging to the Bhagavat Amitābha, the Buddha of that realm, is prosperous, rich, good to live in.... There are gem trees there of golden colour and made of gold ... of silver colour and made of silver ... of diamond colour and made of diamond....
>
> There are lotus flowers there, half a yojana [ten kilometres] in circumference ... one yojana ... two, three, four or five yojanas in circumference; nay, there are some as much as ten yojanas in circumference....
>
> In that world Sukhāvatī, O Ānanda, there flow different kinds of rivers ... resounding with sweet ... sound which is deep, unknown, incomprehensible, clear, pleasant to the ear....
>
> O Ānanda, in that world Sukhāvatī, beings do not take food consisting of gross materials of gravy or molasses; but whatever food they desire, such food they perceive, as if it were taken, and become delighted in body and mind. Yet they need not put it into their mouth.[99]

These quotations regarding the triple body indicate that the Dharmakāya or Truth Body is the real Buddha. 'Kāya' (body or form) is used here in a special sense: it signifies only a centre of power or energy; it does not imply any limitations. Dharmakāya, for example, being pure consciousness, has no physical or material element which could limit it in any way. It is recognised as the

---

* As the Buddha points out: "O, Ānanda, those bodhisattvas who have been born, are being born, or will be born there [in Sukhāvatī], are all bound to one birth only [i.e. the birth they presently have in Sukhāvatī], and will thence indeed obtain the highest perfect knowledge; barring ... those bodhisattvas who are devoted to the work of helping all people to attain Parinirvāṇa." (*The Larger Sukhāvatī-Vyūha*, in *Buddhist Mahāyāna Texts*, tr. F. M. Müller, p.51–52)

ultimate reality, the ultimate ground of all, in Buddhism. It is the absolute, wholly transcending space and time, utterly beyond and at the same time coterminous with the phenomena of our world. The other two bodies emanate from it and are supported by it, although the Absolute itself is not thereby divided. It ever remains one and the same.

This Absolute or the real Buddha or Tathāgata appears in 'glorious' or 'blissful' non-physical forms known as Sambhogakāya for the sake of teaching bodhisattvas in the pure Buddha-fields, the paradises or Lands of Pure Bliss. In different Buddha-fields different glorious forms of the Tathāgata are seen and heard. Likewise, on the physical plane, a Buddha appears in a physical form. This form is known as Nirmāṇakāya, which carries on the work of saving the miserable beings of this physical world.

Some Buddhists have also referred to four Buddha-bodies.[100] We have seen that the Buddha is understood to assume different forms and visit different heavens to help, educate or dispel the doubts of the gods, Brahmās and others. Hence, there is no rigidity in speaking of three, four or many forms (bodies) of the Buddha. It all depends on whether we make a broad or a more detailed division of the various planes of existence.

The Importance of the Historical Buddha

If the real Buddha is the Dharmakāya, what then is the importance of the historical Buddha? What role does he play? Realizing that ultimate reality is non-dual and the real Buddha is not divided even though he appears in different manifestations, one will find the clue to resolve these questions.

The real Buddha is perfect wisdom, which is inseparably intertwined with infinite compassion (*mahākaruṇā*). This truly wise and compassionate one alone can devise the best or most skilful means by which to save the ignorant and miserable people of the world. This best or most skilful means is known as *upāya-kaushalya* (skill in means) in Mahāyāna Buddhism. Using the most skilful means, the real Buddha descends to the world in a physical form for the good and happiness of many out of compassion for the people of the world.[101] It is only through the physical form that he can awaken people in the physical world and guide them to their ultimate destination. There is no other way to achieve this purpose. As the *Perfection of Wisdom Sūtra in Eight Thousand Lines* (*Ashṭasāhasrikā Prajñāpāramitā*) says:

> The physical personality of the Tathāgata is the result of skill in means of the perfection in wisdom. And that becomes a sure foundation for (the acquisition of) the cognition of the all-knowing (by others). Supported by this foundation the revelation of the cognition of the all-knowing takes place.[102]

The physical garb of the Buddha only conceals his real identity from worldly people. But in essence he always remains the same. In the *Lotus Sūtra*, the Buddha in the physical form declares:

> I am the Tathāgata, the Blessed One, the Unconquered One. I have taken birth in this world for the sake of saving others.[103]

In the *Avataṁsaka Sūtra* (*Flower Ornament Scripture*) we read:

> The Buddha freely appears in the world
> To teach all living beings,
> Showing the ways to truth,
> having them understand and enter,
> Putting them in a position to realize highest wisdom.[104]

The Dharmakāya or the real Buddha is inaccessible at the level of the physical world. Unless the Buddha, in his compassion for the people of the physical world, descends to their level to be accessible to them, they will never be able to see him, communicate with him or derive any benefit from him. Therefore, despite the physical form being a veiled presentation, and not ultimately real, this form is of supreme value to the people of this world who cannot otherwise be awakened and saved. The Japanese Buddhist D. T. Suzuki explains this Buddhist view in terms of the Christian concept of the Trinity (the Father, the Son and the Holy Spirit). He says:

> We may regard the Dharmakāya as corresponding to the Christian idea of Godhead. The Dharmakāya is also known as Svabhāvakāya, meaning "self-nature-body" [*tzû-hsing-shên*], for it abides in itself, it remains as such retaining its self-nature. It is in this sense the absolute aspect of the Buddha, in whom perfect tranquillity prevails.[105]

Suzuki further clarifies:

> The essence of the Buddhahood is the Dharmakāya, but as long as the Buddha remains such, there is no hope for the salvation of a world of particulars. The Buddha has to abandon his original abode, and must take upon himself such forms as are conceivable and acceptable to the inhabitants of this earth. The Holy Spirit emanates, as it were, from Absolute Buddhahood and is seen by those who are prepared by their previous karma to see him.[106]

Therefore, anyone who is desirous of attaining perfect wisdom and salvation must find a Buddha and follow his instructions most reverently. As the eighth-century writer Anaṅgavajra enjoins us:

> So a wise man must resort to a good master, for without him the Truth cannot be found even in millions of ages. And if Truth is

> not found, the final goal can never be reached.... So when in the course of life one comes upon masters with this Truth... wondrous as a wish-granting gem... one should honour them to the best of one's ability if final perfection of the self is really one's aim. It is by means of their splendour that the bliss of infinite enlightenment is gained.... So good men who desire their own perfection always pay with their whole being full honour to their master, who is the bestower of infinite rewards.[107]

It is worth noting that the Buddha, even in his physical form, remains glorified by the Dharmakāya, the ultimate and unconditioned reality. This helps a discerning person to distinguish him from others. He is thus recognized in the world, and people pay heed to his teachings. Presenting this idea in a succinct form, the *Diamond Sūtra* says:

> [The] Absolute exalts the holy persons.[108]

Commenting on this very sūtra, Edward Conze says:

> This is a difficult idea, and a difficult word is chosen to express it. 'Exalts' – the word *prabhāvitā* – contains a great wealth of meanings, and 'exalts' is the best I can do. One could also say, 'are glorified by', 'draw their strength from', 'owe their distinction to', or 'derive their dignity from'. The idea is that the holy persons have 'arisen' from the Unconditioned, have been 'produced' from it, and are 'brought forth' by it.[109]

Down to Earth

Having considered the high and immutable form of the Buddha, it is important to note that the Pali sūtras teach that in his physical form Gautama Buddha was a pragmatic spiritual guide. He was down to earth and did not give answers to questions that were unconnected with the practice of the questioner.

In the sutta from the *Dīgha Nikāya* known as The Delightful Discourse, the Buddha was asked by the novice Chunda what wanderers of other sects should be told when they question why the Buddha refused to respond to metaphysical assertions. The Buddha answered:

> They should be told: "Friend, this [responding to metaphysical assertions] is not conducive to one's welfare, or to the Dhamma, or to the higher holy life, or to disenchantment, dispassion, cessation, tranquillity, realization, enlightenment, Nibbāna [Nirvāṇa]. That is why the Lord has not revealed it."…
>
> Then they may say "Why has this been declared by the ascetic Gotama?"
>
> They should be told: "Friend, this is conducive to one's welfare, to the Dhamma, to the higher holy life, to disenchantment, to dispassion, to cessation, to tranquillity, to realisation, to enlightenment, to Nibbāna. That is why the Lord has revealed it."[110]

This perfectly expresses the practical approach of the Buddha. The fourteenth-century Zen master Bassui Tokushō (1327–1387) underlines this, explaining that though "there is no Buddha or Dharma outside of the One Mind inherent in all people",[111] the teacher will always instruct in accordance with the student's capacity:

> If you say there are two Dharmas, you slander the Tathāgata. But even though according to this there aren't two Dharmas, there are, depending on the karma of ordinary people, the sharp and the dull, and thus sudden and gradual realizations of the Way, and shallow and deep journeys from delusion to enlightenment.

> And depending on the depth of the journey, there are lofty and feeble degrees of attainment.[112]

Buddha taught the Dharma to sentient beings in accordance with their own capacities and in a way they could understand from their own experience. Indeed, one of the characteristics of Buddhism is that though there is one Dharma, there are many different ways of teaching it.

4

Human Life

Human Life Is Difficult to Obtain

Buddhism teaches that the cosmos contains many worlds and creatures, all of which are trapped in a cycle of birth and death (saṁsāra)* due to their past actions. Deliverance from this cycle of creation is only possible by following the path taught by one of the Buddhas who appear from time to time in the creation. Without this physical contact there may be a happy rebirth for a long time in one of the temporary heaven-worlds, but no permanent deliverance from the perils of the cycle of birth and death.

Among the various life forms in the Buddhist cosmos, the human life is a rare and invaluable gift. It is granted to us so that we may work for our release from the cycle of birth and death. No other form of life provides the same privilege of striving for and attaining liberation. It is only during the limited span of the human life that we can make or mar our future. As the account of Lord Buddha illustrates, we cannot afford to fritter away this priceless opportunity. The Buddha speaks of the rarity of human life through the following simile:

---

*Saṁsāra' literally means 'flowing on' or 'wandering together'.

> Suppose, monks, a man were to throw a yoke with only one hole into the vast ocean. An easterly wind might take it westwards, a westerly wind might take it eastwards, a northerly wind might take it southwards, a southerly wind might take it northwards. Suppose a blind turtle were to come to the surface of the ocean once in a hundred years. What do you think about this, monks? Could that blind turtle put its neck through that one hole in the yoke?
>
> Not so, revered sir; and if it could do so at all, it would possibly be only once after a very long time.
>
> So I say, monks, more difficult than the blind turtle putting its neck through the one hole in the yoke would it be for a fool who had brought upon himself his own downfall to gain once again a human birth.[113]

This simile is repeatedly referred to in Buddhist literature to emphasize the rarity of the human birth. In the *Bodhicharyāvatāra*, for example, Shāntideva, the famous eighth-century exponent of Mahāyāna Buddhism, says:

> Therefore, the Blessed One has said:
> "It is extremely difficult to obtain a human birth.
> It is like a turtle putting its head by chance
> through a hole in the yoke tossed about
> in the vast ocean."[114]

Explaining the import of this analogy, Pabongka Rinpoche (1878–1941), renowned master of the Tibetan Buddhist Gelugpa school, says:

> The elements of this analogy are taken to mean the following. The ocean is the samsaric state [endless cycle of existence]; the turtle is ourselves; his blindness, ignorance; the yoke, a Buddha's teachings; and so on.[115]

Patrul Rinpoche takes this analogy further still:

The ocean symbolizes the depth and vastness of the three lower realms of rebirth and their infinite sufferings. The blind turtle symbolizes the beings of these three worlds who are without the two eyes of adopting what is beneficial and abandoning what is harmful. The fact that the turtle only rises to the surface once every hundred years symbolizes the difficulty of escaping from those states. The one hole in the yoke symbolizes the rarity of human and celestial existences. The wind which propels it this way and that represents dependence on favourable circumstances.[116]

Acknowledging these difficulties, the Buddha himself says:

Difficult it is to obtain a human birth;
Difficult is human life.
Difficult it is to be able to hear the true teachings;
And rare is the appearance of the Enlightened Ones.[117]

Shāntideva exhorts us, therefore, to be mindful of our real task in this difficult-to-obtain human life:

Having obtained the boat of the human life,
cross the dreadful river of suffering.
This is not the time to sleep, O fool;
this boat is hard to obtain again.[118]

The human life represents a critical juncture at which we can go up within ourselves and attain the highest goal, or go down to a lower form of species and remain revolving thereafter in various lower forms of species. As Patrul Rinpoche says:

Now that we have this free and well-endowed human birth, now that we know what we should and should not do, our decision at

> this juncture, when we have the freedom to choose, marks the turning point which will determine our fate, for better or worse, far into the future. It is crucial that we choose between saṁsāra and Nirvāṇa once and for all and put the instructions of our teacher into practice.... As a human being, your positive actions are more powerful than those of other kinds of beings.... But your negative actions are more powerful too.[119]

This rare and invaluable human life is obtained only for a short while, and hence it is important to make the best use of it. Pabongka Rinpoche tells us:

> This opportune physical form
> Is worth more than a wish-granting gem.
> You only gain its like the once.
> So hard to get, so easily destroyed,
> It's like a lightning bolt in the sky.[120]

And Zen master Ryokan (1758–1831) warned complacent Buddhist clergy of his time:

> The three worlds are but a temporary abode and human life as fleeting as morning dew. A good opportunity is easily lost, the true teaching hard to encounter. You've got to make a fresh start! Don't wait for me to tell you again and extend a helping hand. I'm pleading with you earnestly now, but for me it's a cheerless task. From here on, I want you to reflect carefully and change your ways. Strive hard, you successors of the Buddha, that you may have no regrets![121]

All Is Within the Human Body

The teachings of the Buddha can be likened to a river that gives rise to rivulets and takes on colour as it travels through the soil of space and time. By the time the teachings reached modern times, the Buddhist path had gained many different streams and colourations. However much these streams may appear to be different from each other, the core teachings contain the same essential elements. Meditation, for example, a technique of diving deep within oneself, is central to Buddhism and appears in all its streams. In Buddhism the reason for practising meditation is to understand reality through direct experience. Ultimate reality, the Buddha taught, cannot be understood except by personal practice. The purpose is to understand ourselves and, finally, as Zen master Shunryū Suzuki (1904–1971) says, to "forget ourselves".[122] All spiritual knowledge and power are obtained by going within – by practising meditation. All that is worth obtaining is contained within oneself. The inner path is therefore greatly emphasized in Buddhism.

It is well known that the Buddha attained enlightenment through intense meditation, and he declared that the profound truth he discovered "can be realized only personally by the wise".[123] To make this point all the more explicit, the Buddha says:

> I do declare to you that within this very body, mortal as it is and only six feet in length, are the world, the origin of the world, the ceasing of the world, and likewise the path that leads to this cessation.[124]

Indicating that the inmost region of consciousness lies beyond the reach of the mind, intellect and empirical consciousness, the famous Mahāyāna text *Laṅkāvatāra Sūtra* says:

> All things are to be comprehended by transcending the *chitta* [intellect], *manas* [mind] and *vijñāna* [empirical consciousness] as is done by thee. Thou shouldst look inwardly and not become attached to the letter and a superficial view of things.[125]

The more contemporary Japanese poet-recluse Ryokan also refers to inner consciousness in this verse:

> Even if you consume as many books
> As the sands of the Ganges
> It is not as good as really catching
> One verse of Zen.
> If you want the secret of Buddhism,
> Here it is: Everything is in the Heart![126]

And Zen master Musō Kokushi (1275–1351) explains:

> There is a vast potential, latent within human beings, that remains undiscovered, because of the limitations placed on consciousness by habitual preoccupations. The recommendation that all cravings be relinquished does not mean that detachment itself is a goal; it is a means of breaking through self-imposed restrictions and opening up this inexhaustible treasury of potential.[127]

Because this "inexhaustible treasury of potential" is contained within the human body, it is considered invaluable. Saraha, one of the earliest and most eminent among the masters of the Vajrayāna tradition of Buddhism, emphasizes that all spiritual knowledge is contained within this body and can be discovered only from within. It is futile, therefore, to search for Truth in outward rituals or written scriptures, when the bodiless reality or ultimate Truth is hidden in this body itself. As he says:

> Here [within the body] is the sacred River Yamunā,
> And here is the River Ganges;
> Here are [the holy places of] Prayāga and Benares,
> Here are Sun and Moon.

I have visited in my wanderings
Shrines and other places of pilgrimage,
But I have not seen another shrine
Blissful like my own body.
All these pandits [scholars] expound the treatises,
But the Buddha who resides within the body
  is not known.
The bodiless form is concealed in the body.
He who knows this is therein released.[128]

Similarly, the *Hevajra Tantra* says:

All beings are Buddhas,
But this is concealed by adventitious stains.
When their stains are purified,
  their Buddhahood is revealed.[129]

This purification is accomplished by meditation. In his *Encouragement to Practice*, Sŏn (Korean Zen) master Chinul (1158–1210) quotes Kuei-feng Tsung-mi:

> We know that a frozen pond is entirely water, but the sun's heat is necessary to melt it. Although we awaken to the fact that an ordinary man is Buddha, the power of Dharma is necessary to develop cultivation. When that pond has melted and its water flows freely, it can be used for irrigation and cleaning. When falsity is extinguished, the mind will be numinous and dynamic; then the effulgence of spiritual powers will manifest. There is no other approach to practise but cultivation of the mind.[130]

In *The Platform Sūtra*, the Sixth Patriarch of Ch'an, Hui-neng (638–713), says that our true nature can be realized within our own body, and that through the realization of our true nature, we realize the Buddha:

> Everyone's physical body is a city. Your eyes, ears, nose, tongue, and skin are the city gates. These five gates are on the outside, and on the inside is the gate of the intellect. Your mind is the kingdom, and your nature is the king. When your nature is there, so is the king. When your nature is gone, the king is gone too. When your nature is present, your body and mind are present. When your nature is absent, your mind and body cease to exist. The Buddha is a creation of your nature. Don't look outside your body. When you're blind to your own nature, the Buddha is an ordinary being. When you're aware of your own nature, an ordinary being is the Buddha.[131]

Human Life Is Impermanent and Perishable

Buddha and Buddhist teachers refer frequently to the impermanent and perishable nature of the world and life. They try to awaken us to seek the state of deathlessness. It is recounted that it was the sight of old age, suffering, disease and death that turned Prince Siddhārtha away from the pleasures of the world towards the path of enlightenment. Witnessing each of these common phenomena only once was enough for the highly pure and perceptive prince to be estranged from life's transitory and perishable nature, and he at once made a firm determination to search for the state beyond change, decay and destruction – the state of deathlessness.

Although our human life is rare, invaluable, and endowed with immense potential, it is short and fragile. We therefore do ourselves a disservice to spend our limited time in frivolous pursuits. Life being so uncertain, it is a grave mistake to think that old age and death are yet distant from us, to allow the few moments of our life to pass in procrastination and idleness. The Buddha presents the stark reality of life and cautions us to be mindful of our real task in this transitory world:

Before long, alas, this body
Will lie on the earth,
Despised, without consciousness
And useless like a burnt log....

Even while gathering life's flowers,
One's mind is distracted,
And while yet unsatiated by pleasures,
Death overpowers him....

Knowing that this body is like foam,
Considering it to be of the nature of a mirage,
One should go beyond the sight of the king of death,
Breaking the flowery snare of Māra [the tempter].[132]

Again, he says:

This body is worn out;
It is a nest of diseases and very frail.
This vile body breaks apart;
Life indeed ends in death....

All created things are impermanent.
When one realizes this by wisdom,
He rises above suffering;
This is the path to purity.[133]

Calling attention to our habit of procrastination and our undue attachment to worldly relatives, Shāntideva in the *Bodhicharyāvatāra* says:

It is not proper to sit comfortably,
thinking that death is not coming today itself.

That time will certainly come
    when I shall not remain here....

Discarding this world of people,
    family members and acquaintances,
Leaving aside all friends and foes,
    I shall be going somewhere alone.
What then have I to do with anyone?...

Many have been wealthy
    and many have been famous;
Yet, despite their wealth and fame,
    it is not known where they have gone.[134]

Using the metaphor of people meeting in an inn for the night and then going their separate ways in the morning, Shāntideva points out that no one really belongs to anyone else, and thus exposes the futility of our worldly relationships:

How can one impermanent being be affectionately
    attached to another, similarly impermanent,
When that dear one, even in thousands of births,
    is never to be seen again?...

Just as travellers meet in an inn for the night,
    so also we,
In the course of our worldly journey,
    meet for just a while with others.[135]

Pointing out that all who are born are sure to die, Patrul Rinpoche exhorts us to engage now in the spiritual practice that leads to liberation from death and rebirth. He warns us:

> Once born, every human in the world is sure to die. But how, why, when and where we are going to die cannot be predicted.[136]

He thus urges us:

> From this very moment onwards never slip into laziness and procrastination. Meditate sincerely on impermanence and how important it is to practise the true Dharma, which is the only thing that can really help at the moment of death.[137]

Gampopa says:

> For a religious devotee to make far-reaching plans as though he were going to establish permanent residence [in this world] instead of living as though each day were the last he had to live, is a grievous mistake.[138]

Human Life Fulfilled

The Buddha teaches that human life has immense potential. We have the choice to uncover, develop and utilize this potential and thereby attain immortality, the very goal of this life; or to disregard, degrade and misuse it and thereby remain caught in the cycle of birth and death, wasting this life. Thus, we can go up or down, rise or fall, by using or misusing this life. Buddhism therefore emphasizes the need to be vigilant and to make sincere efforts to attain immortality and liberation, thereby fulfilling the highest possibilities of this human life.

Indicating the importance of vigilance and right effort in pursuing the path of the pure Dharma that leads to immortality, the Buddha says:

> Vigilance takes one to immortality;
> Negligence takes one to death.

Those who are vigilant do not die;
Those who are negligent are as if dead already....

The life of a single day of a person
Who exerts himself to see the immortal state
Is better than the life of a hundred years of him
Who does not exert himself to see the immortal state.

Better than the life of a hundred years
Spent without perceiving the excellent Truth
Is a single day spent
Perceiving the sublime Dhamma....

One should hasten towards attaining merit,
And should restrain his thoughts from sin.[139]

We have a choice either to run after worldly gain or to work for the bliss of Nirvāṇa; therefore the Buddha explains how a disciple should conduct himself in this world. The extent to which we use or misuse this human life will determine the nature of our future birth or whether we can achieve absolute freedom from the cycle of birth and rebirth. As the Buddha says:

One is the path that leads to worldly gain
And another leads to Nibbāna.
Having learnt this, let the holy aspirant,
The disciple of an Enlightened One,
Not seek other people's respect,
But strive to develop wisdom....

Some enter the womb,
Evil-doers go to hell,
The good go to heaven,

And those free from worldly
desires attain Nibbāna.[140]

It is worth noting an important point here in relation to linking effort with the guiding grace received by the disciples of a Buddha or true teacher. Not realizing that both effort and grace are necessary and relying exclusively on only one of these elements leads to frustration and disappointment. Those who think that by their efforts alone they can undergo the tortuous and rugged path of the inner journey without the grace and guidance of a spiritual adept expose themselves to a double-edged sword.

One edge of the sword is the impossibility of such a journey with the limited power of an individual body and mind and no guidance or support from an experienced guide. Seekers will inevitably face challenges and irresistible temptations that make it impossible for them to find a way through the labyrinth of the mind.

The other edge of the sword consists of the danger of an inflated ego – the subtle but extremely strong conceit awakened when one relies exclusively on one's own efforts. The conceit of 'I' and 'mine' is itself detrimental to spiritual success. All these challenges can be overcome by an aspirant who not only makes steadfast effort but also relies on the grace and guidance of an enlightened teacher.

In order to make proper effort, we should inculcate the state of mind known as *bodhichitta*. *Bodhichitta* means a mind (*chitta*) that has the aspiration and firm resolve to attain enlightenment (*bodhi*). Speaking of the transforming power of the *bodhichitta*, Shāntideva says:

Take with resoluteness the alchemy of *bodhichitta*,
which will transform your vile form
Into the priceless form of the Jina,
the Unconquerable One.[141]

When people experience this *bodhichitta*, they then can begin to deal with their own mind (*chitta*) in order to transform themselves. Shāntideva goes on to say that it is difficult to succeed in rooting out the evil of the world, but that people can protect themselves by filling their own mind with goodness – this is the only way to safeguard themselves. Shāntideva expresses this thought through a beautiful simile:

> Where can I find enough leather to
> cover the whole earth?
> But with just enough leather for a pair of shoes,
> I can cover the whole earth.[142]

Pabongka Rinpoche exhorts us to attain freedom from the cycle of birth and death by fully utilizing this invaluable human birth. He says:

> I have obtained the optimum human rebirth,
> So hard to achieve, which can achieve a person's aims.
> If I derive no benefit from it,
> How could I hope to inherit such a pure rebirth again?[143]

He then encourages us:

> With your present physical form you can prevent yourself from ever going to the lower realms again.... All you need do is use the opportunity.... This rebirth is worth more than one thousand billion precious jewels.[144]

Urging us to attain freedom now from the cycle of birth and death, he continues:

> In short, as long as you are not free of saṁsāra for good, you have not transcended the nature of suffering. You therefore must

> definitely become liberated from it; and you must do so while in your present rebirth.... If we cannot achieve liberation now, when shall we ever achieve it?[145]

Zen Buddhism also directs us to rise above considerations of worldly gain and loss and to realize ultimate reality, attaining freedom from the cycle of mundane existence forever. As Musō Kokushi says:

> The central benefit of Zen, in the context of the ordinary ups and downs of life, is not in preventing the minus and promoting the plus but in directing people to the fundamental reality that is not under the sway of ups and downs.[146]

In his *Secrets on Cultivating Mind* (*Susim Kyol*), written between 1203 and 1205, Sŏn master Chinul reminds us to remain conscious of our objective:

> If we consider our actions in our past wanderings in saṁsāra, we have no way of knowing for how many thousands of *kalpas** we have fallen into the darkness or entered the Interminable Hell and endured all kinds of suffering. Nor can we know how many times we have aspired to the path to Buddhahood but, because we did not meet with wise advisors, remained submerged in the sea of birth and death for long *kalpas*, dark, unenlightened, performing all sorts of evil actions. Though we may reflect on this once in a while, we can not imagine the duration of our misery. How can we relax and suffer again the same calamities as before?[147]

---

* *Kalpa* is a time unit, meaning 'world-period', an inconceivably long time. The Buddha mentioned that if a solid piece of flawless rock one mile long by one mile wide by one mile deep was rubbed with a piece of silk every hundred years, this rock would disappear quicker than a world-period, a *kalpa*. (*S.ii*, p.181)

Human Life Wasted

Human life provides our only opportunity for liberation. Given this rare chance, it is to our greatest benefit to strive to realize this goal by following the inner path revealed by an enlightened master and refraining from those actions and thoughts that divert us from the goal. To spend our time and energy in useless pursuits, disregarding our real task, is to throw away a precious diamond and pick up some worthless shells instead. This would be nothing but wasting our invaluable life and squandering our greatest potential. Patrul Rinpoche says:

> To find this precious human life
> Is more valuable than finding a precious jewel.
> Look how those who do not fear saṁsāra
> Fritter life away![148]

The Buddha says those who immerse themselves in the world instead of trying to go beyond and reach the other shore are their own worst enemy:

> Worldly enjoyments destroy the fool
> Who does not seek the other shore.
> By his craving for worldly enjoyments the fool
> Destroys himself as if he were his own enemy.[149]

Those whose actions are immoral cannot escape the consequences of their deeds, and the garb of holy ones is no protection. The Buddha says:

> One who remains undisciplined
>   and utters falsehood
> Does not become a recluse [*samaṇa*]
> Merely by shaving his head.

How can one be a recluse
When he is full of desire and greed?

There are many wearing yellow robes
Who are uncontrolled and of evil conduct.
Such evil-doers, on account of their evil deeds,
Are born in hell.[150]

In the *Bodhicharyāvatāra*, Shāntideva, instead of deploring the fate of other misguided persons, regrets his own shortcomings with utter humility. He says:

I have never cultivated
even the slightest virtue.
I have thus spent this rarely obtained
wondrous life in vain.[151]

We are encouraged by the Tibetan teacher Geshe Acharya Thubten Loden (1924–) to utilize the gift of the human form to realize ultimate happiness:

> Having taken a birth with myriad opportunities, like jewels scattered around an island, don't leave empty handed. Take something of value when you die by using this birth to accumulate the causes of happiness and the ultimate goal of enlightenment. Don't waste your opportunity and just increase your debt, because it will be difficult to obtain such a birth again in future.…
>
> If you wish to practise Dharma and meditate then the time to start is right now. Procrastinating will produce many hindrances to the development of realisations. You will follow your impulses and get caught up in countless distractions, while consoling yourself with the thought, 'I can always practise later.' Without allowing time for the mind to relax and become tranquil by meditating,

> you busily rush through life filling each moment with things that 'really must be done!' Each New Year you resolve to begin Dharma practice seriously, but end up putting it off until next month, next year, then the next year until 'next' becomes next life![152]

Addressing the challenge for those who lead a hectic life, thinking they should find time to practise Dharma but never translating the thought into action, Pabongka Rinpoche says:

> Some people are now engrossed in this life and feel, 'I should practise'; many people have already reached the time when they regret not having practised Dharma. When we see these people, we should see the damage their actions did them; we should have the courage not to attach any importance to the meaningless actions that, every day, leave us no time for Dharma practice. We must practise as much Dharma as we can before Yama, the lord of death, strikes.[153]

Not practising the Dharma brings much loss, as Gampopa points out:

> If, after having been born a human being, one gives no heed to the Holy Doctrine [Dharma], one resembleth a man who returneth empty-handed from a land rich in precious gems; and this is a grievous failure.[154]

He also states that this negligence causes us to feel remorse:

> Having obtained the difficult-to-obtain, free, and endowed human body, it would be a cause of regret to fritter life away....
>
> This human life in the Kaliyuga (or Age of Darkness) being so brief and uncertain, it would be a cause of regret to spend it in worldly aims and pursuits....

> The prime of youth being the period of development of the body, speech, and mind, it would be a cause of regret to waste it in vulgar indifference.[155]

He goes on to advise:

> During the period of youth, frequent not those who cannot direct thee spiritually, but acquire practical knowledge painstakingly at the feet of a learned and pious guru.[156]

Master Chinul says:

> You must display your ardour.... If you do not believe in your superiority and, complacently resigning yourself to being inferior, you decide that you will not practice now because it is too difficult, then even though you might have good roots from past lives, you sever them now. The difficulty will keep growing and you will move farther from the goal. Since you have now arrived at the treasure house, how can you return empty-handed? Once you lose a human body, for ten thousand kalpas it will be difficult to recover. Be careful. Knowing that there is a treasure house, how can a wise person turn back and not look for it – and yet continue to resent bitterly his destitution and poverty?[157]

Patrul Rinpoche offers this prayer:

> Although I have entered the Dharma,
> I waste time doing other things.
> Bless me and foolish beings like me that we may attain
> The very essence of the freedoms and advantages.[158]

5

A World of Impermanence

Three Marks of the Phenomenal World

According to Buddhism, a wise person cannot but be struck by the three basic marks or characteristics common to all worldly things and beings: impermanence (*anitya*); suffering (*duḥkha*); and non-self (*anattā*). Some of these aspects may be evident to any normal human being, yet the deeper significance of them may not be apparent or of much concern to an average person. But Siddhārtha Gautama, an exceedingly pure and perceptive being, was deeply moved at his very first sight of old age, disease and death. This at once showed him the impermanent and sorrowful nature of the world, making him disenchanted with its deceptively glamorous and pleasant appearance. Most of us, however, require intense meditation and deep reflection in order to have full realization of these three characteristics of the world. In other words, we need to develop higher knowledge or wisdom in order to fully understand these three marks. As the Buddha says:

> All created things are impermanent.
> When one realizes this by wisdom,

He rises above suffering;
This is the path to purity.

All created things are sorrowful.
When one realizes this by wisdom,
He rises above suffering;
This is the path to purity.

All created things are non-self.
When one realizes this by wisdom,
He rises above suffering;
This is the path to purity.[159]

Let us now see how Buddhism draws our attention to these three basic characteristics of this phenomenal world.

IMPERMANENCE

Buddhism emphasizes the impermanent and perishable nature of human life. Buddhism also expresses a keen awareness of the impermanence of the world as a whole. All that exists here is impermanent and perishable. Nothing here remains unchanged even for a moment. As is stated in the Pali Canon:

> There is not a moment, not a fraction of a moment, not an instant when a mountain river does not flow.[160]

It is again pointed out in the sutta The Shorter Exhortation to Rāhula from the *Majjhima Nikāya*:

> Whatever things come into existence, all of them are subject to destruction.[161]

People run after worldly pleasures, having little concern for the real aim of their life, but according to the Buddha, all worldly pleasures appear tempting only to those who are short-sighted. These pleasures are nothing but allurements projected by Māra, the personification of temptation and negativity, in order to blind us. They are transient and are truly the source of suffering. As the Buddha says:

> Impermanent, monks, are worldly pleasures. They are worthless, false and unreal. They are created by Māyā* to tempt and delude fools.... They are snares of Māra, baits thrown by Māra, Māra's sphere and Māra's pasturage. They give rise to evil thoughts such as covetousness, ill-will and destruction, and cause obstructions in the way of a noble disciple's holy pursuit.[162]

The Buddha therefore urges his disciples to be aware of the nature of these pleasures:

> What is impermanent is not worth delighting in, not worth approval and not worth clinging to.[163]

The four most visible signs of impermanence or ceaseless change are utterly unavoidable. Speaking of them, Pabongka Rinpoche says:

> They cannot be stopped by fleeing, by force, by wealth, by substances, mantras and medicines. What are these four? Old age, sickness, decay and death.[164]
>
> At no time, once we are born, do we deviate from the direction of our death. We have already used up so much of our life span, there is not much of it left.... When we sleep, we may be relaxed and happy, yet we are still rushing directly towards the lord of death.[165]

---

* Māyā is illusion, delusion, unreality; the phenomenal universe.

Indicating that we have no real companions in life and death, he says:

> In the beginning when you were born from your mother's womb, you were born alone. In mid-life, when you get sick, for example, only you can experience it. In the end, when you die, you go through death (utterly) alone.[166]

Death makes no distinction between rich and poor, high and low. Pabongka Rinpoche points out that death is a great equalizer:

> You may be like Brahmā, Indra or a universal emperor, but when you die you will not take a single servant with you; you will not be free to take even a single possession with you – these are no help at such a time. You may be the most powerful king ruling every country but when death comes you will not be able to take a grain of barley with you. You will be indistinguishable from a beggar.[167]

The remembrance of death can motivate the practitioner to continue making sincere efforts towards liberation. Not to think about death is to forget the aim of this human life, as Pabongka Rinpoche says:

> If you do not recollect death, you will not practise Dharma seriously, nor will you be able to practise continually.… Our not recollecting death and impermanence is to blame.[168]

Suffering

The second characteristic of the world, suffering (*duḥkha*), is thought of in a specific way in Buddhism. Being the second characteristic, it follows from the first – impermanence – and has a deeper meaning than is ordinarily understood by this word. Suffering is normally taken to mean any kind of pain, grief, trouble, distress or agony. But since it is a corollary of impermanence, whatever is impermanent or subject to change is also included in suffering.

Suppose we are deeply attached to some of our family members – parents, husband, wife, son, daughter, brother, sister, or some special friends – so much so that they are always in our thoughts. But no one is to live in this impermanent world forever, and when any one of them leaves this world, never to meet us again, we undergo heart-rending suffering. Therefore, failing to realize that no one here really belongs to anyone else and clinging to anyone or anything impermanent is nothing but suffering.

Moreover, we generally fail to remember that most people make or break relationships according to their changing interests; when a relationship changes or is broken, or a friend turns out to be an enemy, it only brings suffering.

Again, we do not clearly see that neither this world nor this body is truly ours. Both are impermanent. Any attachment to either, whether positive as attraction, or negative as repulsion, cannot but bring suffering. Yet in our deep-rooted ignorance we are seldom free from these. In the pursuit of happiness we keep running after what we like, but happiness always eludes us and we become more and more bound to this changing and sorrowful world. Edward Conze points out:

> There are some things we like and others we dislike, and as long as we stay alive we clearly assume that the first outweigh the others, and no amount of disappointment will deter us from trying again and again to build ourselves a cosy home in this world.[169]

It is a mistake to think that this impermanent world can ever be a safe refuge. Suffering is the lot of everyone everywhere. The universality of suffering is referred to in Buddhism as a 'Noble Truth' or axiom (*ārya satya*) and is realized only through spiritual wisdom or enlightenment. In the Buddhist teachings it is mentioned as the First Noble Truth, since it is by understanding that the world is full of suffering that one gains the motivation to attain liberation (Nirvāṇa) or absolute release from the world. To an Enlightened One, the whole world is seen to be ablaze with the fire of suffering. Only an Enlightened One can see through the trap of enticing worldly pleasures, which when indulged in lead people to terrible suffering.

We must therefore seek inner light to free ourselves from this suffering. As the Buddha says:

> How can there be laughter, how can there be jubilation
> While this world is always burning?
> Why do you not seek the light,
> You who are shrouded in darkness [ignorance]?[170]

Only those who have seen inner light and have experienced a higher happiness can be truly detached from the allurements of the world, realizing full well that attachment, greed, hatred and other worldly passions are all sources of suffering, and that true happiness lies only in transcending the world and attaining Nirvāṇa. As the Buddha points out:

> There is no fire like attachment,
> No defilement like hatred.
> There is no suffering like the impermanent
>   human existence
> And no happiness higher than Peace.
> Greediness is the worst disease;
> Mental propensities are the greatest sorrow.
> To him who has known this truly,
> Nibbāna is the highest bliss.[171]

The Buddha illustrates the true nature of our greed and our cravings with a few similes, pointing out that they are all sources of suffering.

> One who is greedily running after worldly objects and possessions is compared with a person moving with a blazing bundle of grass against the wind, which is sure to burn him if he does not quickly throw it away.[172]

> One engrossed in worldly enjoyment is compared with a dog who lustily gnaws a fleshless bone which, far from appeasing his hunger, only adds to his pain and discomfort.[173]

> One seeking delight in the sensual pleasures of the world is likened to a leper finding pleasure in scratching his wound, then warming it at the fire, which ultimately augments his trouble all the more.[174]

Although there are countless ways of suffering in the world, birth, old age, disease and death are particularly mentioned because they are most striking and common to all. Another common form of suffering is the loss of one's loved ones. Acknowledging this, Pabongka Rinpoche quotes the following verses from the *Great Play Sūtra*:

> Forever you are separated from dear and pleasant people.
> They will not come back, there will be no reunion.[175]

> You will be separated from your...
> relatives, friends and dear ones –
> the people from whom you cannot bear
> even an hour's separation.[176]

Indicating how much we have wept through countless lives, he quotes from *Nāgārjuna's** *Letter*:

> So many tears you have shed in saṁsāra's realms
> When separated from your dearest friends,
> The teardrops from your eyes
> Would overflow the basins of the oceans.[177]

We must remember that we go through this 'vale of tears' alone. And alone we experience this immeasurable suffering, with no one to help or give comfort.

We may wonder why Buddhism lays so much emphasis on suffering and regards it as the First Noble Truth. Is Buddhism pessimistic? Certainly not. Buddhism is realistic. It presents a true picture of the world in order to instil sufficient yearning in people for liberation, for a state of permanent bliss. As the great Tsongkhapa has said:

> If one does not think hard
> about the drawbacks of suffering,
> One has not sufficient yearning for liberation.[178]

The third characteristic of the phenomenal world is non-self (*anattā* in Pali, *anātman* in Sanskrit). The principle of non-self is much more difficult to grasp than the previous two characteristics, and there is much controversy regarding its importance.

Non-Self

According to Buddhism, what generally is considered the self is actually a conglomeration of constantly changing physical and

* Nāgārjuna is the acknowledged authority and the chief exponent of Mahāyāna Buddhism.

mental constituents (*skandhas*). All empirical life is impermanent and in a constant state of flux. All phenomena exist only in dependence on the conditions of their arising, which are non-eternal, so no true self can be found in them. Clinging to concepts and ideas of a self is therefore faulty and based on ignorance, according to Buddhism. Let us investigate this important doctrine of *anattā* (non-self).

The term *anattā* might seem at first glance to be a negative term, a term coined to deny the reality of the self or 'I'. But first it is important to know precisely what is meant by the term 'self' or 'I'. It sometimes seems to mean the body (for example, 'I am fat'), sometimes a sense organ ('I am blind'), sometimes a motor organ ('I am lame'), sometimes a mental faculty ('I am dull'), and sometimes consciousness ('I know'). Which of these should be taken to be the real meaning of the self or 'I'? Moreover, the term 'self' or 'I' usually signifies an entire person. And can the term 'self' be used as a synonym for the word 'soul'? In view of these confusions, we must try to understand what the doctrine of *anattā* precisely seeks to deny – and also not deny.

Since there are differences of opinion among interpreters regarding the exact meaning of this doctrine, we shall try to explain it in light of discussions from the Pali Canon, which is considered to be the earliest or at least one of the earliest written records of the Buddha's teachings.

Since human beings find that everything passes – and therefore leads to suffering – they develop within themselves an ardent desire for permanence or immortality and bliss. But not finding anything immortal and blissful in the world, they invent or imagine something lasting in the vague concept of I-ness, selfhood or individuality, and they cling to this notion. The Buddha calls this clinging or grasping *attavādupādāna*, (clinging to I-ness); and the erroneous belief in some permanent element in every person or individual, which leads to this clinging, is *sakkāyadiṭṭhi* (the false view of the psycho-physical body being real). He also notes that all desires, attachments, conflicts, tensions, hatreds, quarrels, stealing, robbing, violence and other wrong-minded actions have their roots in this mental construct of selfhood.

To enable us to be rid of this erroneous belief and vain clinging to I-ness, the Buddha explains that each one of the constituents of the human being is transitory and a source of suffering. The Pali Canon is full of references in which the Buddha analyses the total physical and mental being of a person, dividing it into five constituents (*skandhas*): *rūpa* (corporeality), *vedanā* (feeling), *saññā* (perception), *sañkhāra* (dispositions) and *viññāṇa* (consciousness). He explains that there is nothing permanent and eternally blissful in these aspects of our nature, and establishes the point that it is therefore erroneous to cling to any idea of a self and to have the conceit of 'I' in any of them.

The Buddha begins by asking whether corporeality (*rūpa*) is permanent or impermanent.[179] On the reply that it is impermanent (*anicca*), he further asks whether that which is impermanent is to be regarded as sorrowful or blissful. To this the natural reply is that it is sorrowful (*dukkha*). In another place he asks: "Is it proper to look upon that which is impermanent, sorrowful and changeable as, 'This is mine; I am this; this is my self?'" And the obvious reply comes, "Certainly not." By applying the same formula with regard to the rest of the constituents, the Buddha finally shows the absurdity of the conceit of 'I' and 'mine'.[180]

Elsewhere he exposes the absurdity of the notion of 'I' or the self by making it quite clear that the conceit of self can only be formed by and through the five constituents of the personality described above. He says:

> All of those ascetics and brahmins who conceive of the self in various ways regard it as either the five constituents of grasping [together] or any one of them [separately].[181]

The way in which this conceit arises in its various forms is described as follows:

> There is, O monks, an uninstructed worldling who has not seen the Noble One, who has no knowledge of the noble doctrine, no training in the noble doctrine. He regards corporeality as the self, or the self as possessing corporeality, or the corporeality as being within the self or the self as within the corporeality, [and similarly with regard to the other four constituents]. Seeing in this manner, he forms the notion, 'I am'.[182]

Thus, the self or 'I' is supposed to be identical with the five components of the personality – or to possess, or contain or be contained by them. Again, the Buddha says:

> Any kind of corporeality whatever, whether past, future or present, whether internal or external, whether gross or subtle, whether inferior or superior, whether far or near – all corporeality must with objective knowledge be regarded as 'This is not mine; this is not I; this is not myself'.[183]

And he then repeats the same thought with regard to the other components.

The Buddha's statement regarding suffering, quoted in the beginning of this chapter, is worth repeating here. He says:

> All created things are non-self.
> When one realizes this by wisdom,
> He rises above suffering;
> This is the path to purity.[184]

The concept of non-self is also founded upon the Buddha's teaching of dependent origination or interdependent co-arising, which explains that all phenomena of life are interdependent – things 'arise' from one another and depend on each other for their existence. The Buddha says:

> When this is, that is.
> From the arising of this
> comes the arising of that.
> When this isn't, that isn't.
> From the cessation of this
> comes the cessation of that.[185]

This teaching of dependent origination goes beyond the idea that cause and effect are separate entities, with causes always preceding effects. The Buddha taught that effect is related to cause as a sprout is related to the seed, and that cause is related to effect in the same way that the concept of 'short' depends on 'long'. In *The Heart of the Buddha's Teaching*, Thich Nhat Hanh says:

> According to the teaching of Interdependent Co-Arising, cause and effect co-arise [*samutpāda*] and everything is a result of multiple causes and conditions. The egg is in the chicken, and the chicken is in the egg. Chicken and egg arise in mutual dependence. Neither is independent. Interdependent Co-Arising goes beyond our concepts of space and time. "The one contains the all."[186]

Within the context of dependent origination, we can find no 'true self' in all physical and mental phenomena. According to Buddhist teaching, clinging to the idea that one has an independent self is based on ignorance, and is the very cause of being trapped in the cycle of birth and death.

The interdependent conditions of mind and body can lead one either in the direction of suffering or liberation. In the circle of dependence, for example, feeling gives rise to craving, and craving gives rise to clinging. If the mind is stilled, however, feeling is stilled, craving ceases and clinging ceases as well.

This concept of dependent origination is not easy to understand. When Ānanda claimed that it was simple, the Buddha said:

> Do not say that, Ānanda. The teaching of dependent origination is indeed deep and subtle.... It is because of not understanding and not penetrating this Dhamma that this generation ... does not go beyond transmigration.[187]

It is sufficient to say here that the concept of individual self is considered so detrimental to spiritual pursuit that in answer to the question "Which one thing is to be got rid of?" the reply is "The conceit of 'I'."[188] The Buddha says:

> I do not see, O monks, any form of clinging to I-ness that would not arouse sorrow, lamentation, suffering, agony and despair.[189]

> It is only by shaking off all conceit of 'I' in this conscious body as well as in relation to all external objects that one becomes thoroughly free from all clinging and thereby attains unfettered salvation [*anuppādā vimutti*].[190]

The strongest and subtlest form of clinging is said to be toward the 'I', and since clinging is regarded as the root cause of suffering, the greatest emphasis is naturally placed on the abandonment of this conceit. It is significant to note that, according to the Buddha, an enlightened person who is endowed with knowledge does not have any conceit of 'I' or self.

The Buddha acknowledges, however, that it is extremely difficult to disentangle oneself completely from this notion of I-ness. The attachment to 'I' is so great that even when one is confronted with the contradictions and the impossibility of identifying a 'self' as any of the five constituents of the personality, or 'groups of grasping',* one still nurtures a craving for I-ness. This is well indicated in the Khemaka Sutta from the *Saṁyutta Nikāya*, where the monk Khemaka says:

> I do not speak of anything as 'I' or 'mine' in corporeality or out of corporeality ... in or out of feeling ... in or out of perception ... in or out of dispositions ... in or out of consciousness, yet my conceit of I-ness in the five groups of grasping is present, though I do not see that this is the 'I'.[191]

The sūtra continues with an analogy to illustrate the nature of this highly persuasive obsession with 'I', ego and self. A filthy cloth, even after being thoroughly washed and made clean by the washerman, may still be left with a slight smell. Then it is explained:

> Even so, though a noble disciple has put away the five lower fetters [including the *sakkāyadiṭṭhi*, the belief in something permanent in the five aggregates], yet from among the five groups of grasping the subtle remnant of the conceit of the 'I', an attachment to the 'I', and the lurking tendency to think 'I am' is still not removed from him.[192]

The cloth is then placed in a sweet-scented coffer for the sake of removing the smell which still clings to it. Again, it is pointed out:

> Later on, he [the monk] lives contemplating the rise and fall of the five groups of grasping.... In this way, as he lives in the contemplation of the five groups of grasping, that subtle remnant of

*These five form the 'aggregates of clinging' or grasping because they are the means by which we seek to experience pleasure.

> the conceit of the 'I', the attachment to the 'I' and the lurking tendency to think, 'I am', which were not removed from him, are absolutely removed.[193]

While denying the validity of the self or 'I', however, people may still use these words without being misled by them. In using them they only conform to convention. The Buddha says:

> They are merely popular expressions, popular terms of speech, designations in common practice and usages prevalent in the world, which the Tathāgata makes use of without being misled.[194]

The Buddhist doctrine of non-self makes it clear that the notion of the 'I' or the self as a permanent ego is fictitious. Denial of the self, however, should not be taken to mean the denial of the state of non-personal reality that is Nirvāṇa. It is precisely with a view to realizing this non-personal state, so impossible to characterize, that the Buddha emphasizes the need to disentangle reality from any egoistic association.

6

A Perspective on Buddhist Views on Soul and God

Two particular aspects of Buddhism typically give rise to debate and confusion. One relates to whether Buddhism denies the reality of the soul, and the second is whether it denies the reality of God in the way that an atheist does. We shall try to present and discuss here Buddhist views on soul and God.

The Buddhist Perspective on Soul

Since the Buddha denied the reality of the 'I' or self, the doctrine of *anattā* (non-self) is universally accepted by all schools of Buddhism. The Sanskrit equivalent for the Pali word *anattā* is *anātman* (*anātmā* in Hindi), which means non-soul. This semantic confusion may have partly contributed to the controversy about whether or not the Buddha and later Buddhists sought, by denying the self, to also deny the soul (*ātman*).

Buddhism denies the notions of 'I', 'mine', self or ego, nothing more and nothing less. However, it is only the impermanent elements of the sentient being – the five *skandhas* constituting the mind and body – which are 'not the self' (*anātman*). This does not imply the denial of the essence of spiritual reality that is beyond the grasp of the senses, mind and intellect, and yet enlivens them all.

During the time of the Buddha, there may have been a popular belief in a notion of 'soul' that signified a permanent psychic entity. The Buddha may indeed have denied that popular notion of the soul. But to have a clearer understanding of whether or not the Buddha and later Buddhists sought, as a result of denying the self, to also deny the soul in the sense of true essence, it may be helpful to look at the context in which the word *ātman* or 'soul' is used.

In what follows we shall compare the way in which the Buddha used the Pali word *attā* (self) with the way in which the Sanskrit word *ātman* (*ātmā* in Hindi) was used in early Indian schools of thought, indicated below through a few selections from the *Upanishads* and the *Bhagavadgītā*.

But before doing so, we may here note one of the meanings of 'true essence' as described in the book *Dream Conversations on Buddhism and Zen*, which contains letters that the thirteenth-century Zen Buddhist Musō Kokushi wrote to a student. Among other subjects, he gives a teaching on essence. Essence can be explained in different ways, he says:

> There are many meanings to the word 'essence'. Three meanings are provisionally explained in Buddhism.
>
> One is the meaning of unvarying. The essences of pepper and sweet grass, for example, are different; pepper is not sweet, sweet grass is not pungent.
>
> Second is the meaning of distinction. This refers to the distinct natures of animate and inanimate beings.
>
> Third is the meaning of real essence. This refers to the fundamental source of all phenomena, the nondual inherent essence.[195]

This third meaning is akin to what is signified by 'soul' in the *Upanishads* and *Bhagavadgītā*, as we shall shortly see.

THE FIVE CONSTITUENTS OF PERSONALITY

The Buddha, after categorizing the psycho-physical factors that comprise the personality into five constituents and demonstrating that each one of them is impermanent and sorrowful, asks the question: "Is it proper to look upon that which is impermanent, sorrowful and changeable as, 'This is mine; I am this; this is my self'?"[196] He receives a negative answer. But this answer only reveals that according to the Buddha it is incorrect to regard the psycho-physical constituents, singly or as a group, as 'I', 'my', 'mine' or 'my self'.

This says nothing about the existence or non-existence of a spiritual reality, power or principle separate from the five psycho-physical factors, a true essence. In many Indian schools, *ātman* is considered a purely spiritual power or reality, not subject to change or suffering.

It is also clear that the Pali term *attā* (self) is conceived of only in terms of the five normally perceivable constituents of the personality. The Buddha states: "All of those ascetics and brahmins who conceive of the self in various ways regard it as either the five constituents of grasping [together] or any one of them [separately]."[197] Hence the self which the Buddha denies is what is defined as these five constituents of personality, and nothing is said affirmatively or negatively about the reality of the soul as defined as the non-dual inherent essence. Moreover, even with regards to the self, the Buddha does not state here that there is no true self, but only that it is not conceived of or apprehended.

The term *attā* is somewhat ambiguous. This term could be understood as the ego, 'I' or self – or even the transcendental spirit or the soul. Rather than engaging in prolonged discussions with a questioner about the existence and nature of an abstruse entity – the soul – the Buddha remained silent. Thus, when the wanderer Vachchhagotta pointedly asks the Buddha whether the self is or the self is not, the Buddha does not answer.[198] After Vachchhagotta's departure, when Ānanda asks the Buddha about the reason for his silence, he says that any answer, whether affirmative or negative, would have just led to more confusion because of Vachchhagotta's preconceived notions.[199] Any answer would prove detrimental to his spiritual quest.

Differentiating the Soul *(Ātmā or Ātman)* from the Personal Self *(Attā)*

Unable to realize the inmost self, many people simply mistake one or more of the ordinarily perceivable constituents of the personality, or all of them together, for the real self, the true essence, and this is what the Buddha denies. It is this rejection of the concept of self that came to be known as the Buddhist doctrine of non-self.

The Buddha laid great emphasis on this because the erroneous equation of the self with impermanent and perishable things gives rise to egotism, pride and the conceit of 'I' and 'mine' – all of which are the source of so much suffering.

There is no trace of I-ness or mine-ness in the standard non-Buddhist notion of *ātman* or *ātmā*. We provide here a few examples from the *Bhagavadgītā*, where the existence of the soul is not seen as contradicting the need to discard I-ness and mine-ness. Lord Krishṇa says:

> He who abandons all desires, who acts
> without cherishing any worldly things,
> Who is free from I-ness and mine-ness,
> he indeed attains peace.[200]

Krishṇa tells his disciple Arjuna:

He who has no ill will towards any being,
who is friendly and compassionate,
Who is free from I-ness and mine-ness,
even-minded in pain and pleasure, forgiving,
Ever content, steeped in meditation, self-controlled,
unshakeable in determination,
And who has surrendered his mind and intellect to me,
such a devotee of mine is indeed dear to me.[201]

Discarding the conceit of I-ness [*ahaṁkāra*],
one's own strength, pride, desire,
anger and possession,
Giving up the conceit of mine-ness
and being peaceful, he becomes worthy
of becoming one with Brahman.[202]

It is an established principle that whatever has a beginning in time must inevitably have an end in time. Since all the five constituents of the psychological and physical personality are subject to birth and death and are mortal, there remains nothing in this mortal being that can attain immortality. There has to be within us the presence of a non-perishable power or spiritual reality endowed with infinite potential that may, through a proper process of purification, be realized as pure consciousness, the ultimate reality – not subject to decay or death and possessed of all perfection.

Later Buddhist thinkers used some terms that are analogous to the notion of *ātman* or soul, such as Tathāgata-garbha (embryonic presence of the Tathāgata), *vijñapti-mātratā* (utterly subtle consciousness), *ālaya-vijñāna* (storehouse of consciousness), or even the true self as opposed to the false self. They may have created these terms because they were uncomfortable asserting the reality of *ātman*, since it is an exact Sanskrit equivalent of the Pali term *attā*.

We know that Dharmakāya or Tathāgata is the term for ultimate reality according to Buddhism. But unless it resides within us in potential or embryonic state, we cannot realize the state of the Tathāgata. It is this presence of the Tathāgata known as Tathāgata-garbha which is spoken of in the *Laṅkāvatāra Sūtra* as being clearly distinct from ego. This is evident from the following dialogue between Bodhisattva Mahāmati and the Blessed One, the Buddha. Mahāmati asked:

> Is not this Tathāgata-garbha taught by the Blessed One the same as the ego-substance taught by the philosophers?...
>
> The Blessed One replied: No, Mahāmati, my Tathāgata-garbha is not the same as the ego taught by the philosophers.... It is emptiness [*shūnyatā*, the ultimate reality for the Mādhyamaka Buddhists], reality-limit [ultimate reality], Nirvāṇa, being unborn, unqualified.[203]

In his *Ratnagotravibhāga*,* Sāramati, a sixth-century Indian Buddhist scholar monk, points out that the Element of the Buddha or the Tathāgata dwells within everyone. This notion is hardly any different from what is known as the embryonic presence of the Tathāgata. Thus the *Ratnagotravibhāga* says:

---

*The *Uttaratantra Shastra* (*Ultimate Doctrine*), as this work is known in Tibetan Buddhist tradition, takes as its key topic the idea of the *dhatu* (fundamental element) of the Buddha, which is present in all beings. It is an exposition of the theory that the essence of Buddhahood (*Tathāgata-garbha*), the fundamental element (*dhatu*) of the Absolute, exists in all sentient beings. This element, which had been regarded as an active force (*bija*) before, is regarded, in this text, as eternal, quiescent and unalterable, as the true essence of every living being and source of all virtuous qualities.

> If the Element of the Buddha did not exist [in everyone],
> There could be no disgust with suffering,
> Nor could there be a wish for Nirvāṇa,
> Nor striving for it, nor a resolve to win it.[204]

Not knowing our pure spiritual nature, we suffer and remain confined in this world. As Edward Conze says:

> A well-known commonplace of all spiritual tradition assures us that we are 'spirits ill at ease', and that our true immortal being has somehow got lost in this world.[205]

Indicating where this 'spirit' is hidden and how to find it, Saraha says:

> The bodiless form is concealed in the body.
> He who knows this is therein released....
> 'This is myself and this is another':
> Be free from this bond
> Which encompasses you about,
> And your own self is thereby released.[206]

Musō Kokushi says:

> What ordinary people think to be their self is not the true self... as long as they have not seen the original state before personal history. A way to see this original state is to turn the attention inward.[207]

W. Y. Evans-Wentz presents the view of celebrated Mahāyānists in these words:

> Thus – as the late Lama Kazi Dawa-Samdup and other learned Mahāyānists with whom the editor has discussed the problem

> held – an impersonal principle, this microcosmic representation of the macrocosmic, persists throughout all existences, or states of conditioned being within the Saṁsāra.... But the impersonal consciousness-principle is not to be in any way identified with the personality represented by a name, a bodily form, or a saṁsāric mind; these are but its illusory creations. It is in itself non-saṁsāric, being uncreated, unborn, unshaped, beyond human concept or definition; and, therefore, transcending time and space, which have only relative and not absolute existence, it is beginningless and endless.[208]

This principle of microcosmic representation of the macrocosmic consciousness and the concept of the presence of the Tathāgata as held in Buddhism are essentially not different from what is called soul – *ātman* or *ātmā* – in standard non-Buddhist Indian tradition. In non-Buddhist Indian literature *ātman* is called a 'particle' or 'germinal essence' (*aṁsha*) of the supreme reality (known as Purush, Ishvara, Swāmī, Rām or pure consciousness), which apparently is the same as the presence of the Tathāgata or the ultimate reality in Buddhism. The *Chhāndogya Upanishad*, for example, says:

> O Maghavan, mortal verily is this body. It is consumed by death. But it is the support of that deathless, bodiless soul.[209]

The *Maitrī Upanishad* speaks of this bodiless soul:

> Verily, a particle [*aṁsha*] of that subtle, ungraspable, invisible One, called Purush, dwells here in the body.[210]

In the *Bhagavadgītā*, Krishṇa, who is considered the manifest form of the Divinity and is the master of Arjuna, says:

> A fragment* of My own self, having become a living
> soul, eternal, in the world of life,
> Draws to itself the senses that rest in nature,
> of which the mind is the sixth.[211]

Soul as Jīva

In the Pali Canon, we find another term, *jīva*, which can be regarded as a synonym of *ātman.*† It is this term which occurs in the well-known 'ten unanswered questions' pertaining to the identity or non-identity of the soul and the body. The Buddha remained silent, since answering these questions is not "conducive to the welfare or to the Dhamma, or to the higher holy life, or to disenchantment, dispassion, cessation, tranquillity, realization, enlightenment, Nibbāna".[212]

Two of these questions concern the relationship between the soul and the body:

> Is the soul [*jīva*] identical with the body?
> Is the soul [*jīva*] different from the body?[213]

It is important to note here that these questions do not raise the issue of existence or non-existence of what can be referred to as the soul; they enquire only about the relationship between the

---

*The translator, Prof. Radhakrishnan, comments here regarding "a fragment of My own self": "This does not mean that the Supreme is capable of division or partition into fragments. The individual is a movement of the Supreme, a focus of the great one Life. The self is the nucleus which can enlarge itself and embrace the whole world, with heart and mind, in an intimate communion. The actual manifestations may be partial but the reality of the individual soul is the Divine which the human manifestation does not fully bring out." (*Bhagavadgītā*, tr. S. Radhakrishnan, p.328)

†The word itself originates from the Sanskrit *jīvas*, with the root *jīv*: 'to breathe'. It has the same Indo-European root as the Latin word *vivus*: 'alive'. In the *Bhagavadgītā* of Hinduism the *jīva* is described as immutable, eternal, and indestructible.

soul and the body. The question of identity or non-identity can arise only when the assumption is present that both the body and the soul exist at the same time. If either of the two factors were truly non-existent, there could be no question of any kind of relationship between the two.

In the Pali Canon itself, an accomplished disciple of the Buddha named Kassapa affirms the existence of the *jīva* or soul, which can be understood as the immortal essence of a sentient being.

King Pāyāsi enters into a debate with Monk Kassapa over this affirmation, and the king gives the following account to support his position:

> Take the case of a thief and criminal, O Kassapa, who is caught red-handed and brought before me. I order my men to throw him alive into a big jar, close the mouth of it and cover it over with wet leather, then add a thick cement of moist clay, put it onto a furnace and kindle a fire.... On doing so, when we know that the person must have been dead, we take down the jar, unbind it and open its mouth, and closely watch to see how his soul [immortal essence] looks while passing out. But we don't see the soul of him coming out. This, venerable Kassapa, is the evidence for my belief that there neither is another world, nor a soul, nor rebirth, nor the results of good or bad deeds.[214]

Thereupon, Monk Kassapa asks the king if he ever sleeps and dreams of enjoying himself in garden, grove, country or lakeside while being watched over by his attendants. On receiving an affirmative answer from the king, Monk Kassapa says:

> So, while you are alive, if none can see your soul leaving and entering your body, how then will you see the soul [immortal essence] of a dead person entering or leaving him? Let this be a proof to you, O King, that these things do exist.[215]

Monk Kassapa explains to the king:

> These things, O King, are not to be seen through the normal eyes of flesh, as you think. Those recluses or Brahmins who … develop the pure divine eye, they through the divine eye see both this world and the other world, as well as pure souls or beings not born of parents.[216]

SOUL AND NIRVĀṆA

Despite his reluctance to discuss transcendental subjects, the Buddha does indicate that apart from the world of mortality there is another state called Nirvāṇa – an immortal state free from impermanence, suffering and death – which is everyone's goal. Thus, in the Pali Canon the Buddha says:

> There is, O monk, the unborn, the unbecome, the uncreated, the unformed.[217]

He also explains:

> There is an unborn, unbecome, uncreated, unformed. If there were not this unborn … an escape from the born, the become, the created, the formed could not be known.[218]

> Thus the Buddha regards Nirvāṇa as a supramundane state completely incomprehensible to the mind and the intellect that can only be directly and personally realized by the wise.[219]

The same is the case with the soul (*ātman*). In the following quote, the Buddha speaks of an invisible and infinite consciousness (*viññāṇa*) as the abiding reality, distinct from the world of name and form made up of perishable elements. It is differentiated from the normal consciousness of everyday life (also called *viññāṇa*), which is under constant flux and gives rise to suffering:

> *Viññāṇaṁ anidassanaṁ anantaṁ sabbatopabhaṁ:*
> *Ettha āpo cha paṭhavī tejo vāyo na gādhati,*
> *Ettha dīghañ cha rassañ cha aṇuṁ thūlaṁ subhāsubhaṁ,*
> *Ettha nāmañ cha rūpañ cha asesaṁ uparujjhati.*
> *Viññāṇassa nirodhena etth'etaṁ uparujjhatī ti.*
>
> It is consciousness [*viññāṇa*] which is invisible, infinite
> and shining everywhere;
> Where water, earth, fire and air have no footing;
> Where long and short, fine and coarse, good and bad,
> Along with name and form, cease to be without residue.
> On account of the cessation of consciousness [*viññāṇa*],
> all this ceases to be.[220]

The word '*viññāṇa*' of the first and the last lines is clearly not used in the same sense. The first *viññāṇa*, described as "invisible, infinite and shining everywhere" is said to be a state wherein the second *viññāṇa* ceases to be.

> The second *viññāṇa* evidently refers to worldly consciousness, the fifth constituent of the personality, for all the five constituents are said to cease in the state of Nibbāna [Nirvāṇa].[221]

The final worldly consciousness (*viññāṇa*) of an *arahant* (one who achieves enlightenment) is extinguished like the flame of a lamp and passes into a state of indistinguishability. Just as fire is discerned only as long as it finds fuel to support it, and is extinguished or becomes untraceable once the fuel is exhausted, so also the worldly *viññāṇa* is to be found only in the presence of the other four constituents as its support. When one no longer clings to the other four constituents, then *viññāṇa* or consciousness of the world is also extinguished as it has nothing to support it.

Being without support (*appatiṭṭhita viññāṇa*), the worldly *viññāṇa* becomes untraceable in the state of enlightenment. The Buddha refers to the tempter Māra, who searched in vain for the *viññāṇa* of the monks Godhika and Vakkali just after their deaths.[222] Māra failed in his attempt because they had attained Parinibbāna (final Nibbāna), leaving no support for *viññāṇa*: "Their consciousness being free from its empirical basis, they attained final Nibbāna."[223]

The invisible (*anidassanaṁ*) or supportless (*appatiṭṭhitaṁ*) *viññāṇa* refers to the supramundane, incomprehensible, and indistinguishable state of pure *viññāṇa* or consciousness and may be likened to the nature of *ātman* or soul in various non-Buddhist Indian texts.

In the *Brihadāraṇyaka Upanishad*, for example, this *ātman* is considered to be the great reality and is characterized as the "infinite and limitless mass of pure consciousness".[224] The *ātman* is seen as pure consciousness because in itself it is absolutely uncontaminated by matter and mind. Again, the *Shvetāshvatara Upanishad* says, "The soul is infinite and of universal form."[225] According to the *Maitrī Upanishad*, "Infinite are the rays of that which, like a lamp, dwells in the heart."[226]

But, as the Buddha points out, this soul or self is not seen, conceived of, or apprehended, because what we normally apprehend are the five discernible constituents of the personality, which are not the essential being. In order to know and see the real self or soul, one has to dive deep within oneself and open one's inner eye. Similarly, in the *Brihadāraṇyaka Upanishad*, Yājñavalkya, a legendary sage of Vedic India, exhorts Maitreyī, his wife and fellow philosopher:

> Verily, the soul, Maitreyī, is to be [inwardly] seen, to be heard, to be reflected on, to be meditated upon.[227]

Since it is clear that the Buddha refused to answer questions concerning issues beyond our normal perception or conception, it would be inaccurate to paint a negative colour on his silence and to say that he denied the soul (*ātman*) – the immortal (*amritam*), unborn (*ajam*) and supreme (*mahāntam*) self of the *Upanishads*. Thus, questions pertaining to the origin of the creation, the nature of ultimate reality, and the relationship between soul and the body are left unanswered by the Buddha. As Yājñavalkya's exhortation to Maitreyī in the *Brihadāraṇyaka Upanishad* indicates, whatever is transmundane, such as God, soul, ultimate reality and Nirvāṇa, can only be inwardly realized or revealed, and not intellectually conceived or comprehended.

The Buddhist Perspective on God

The Buddha is acknowledged to be one of the most insightful and influential teachers ever born into this world. Some Buddhist scholars and writers characterize him as an atheist, and following their assertion, many non-Buddhists also believe that the Buddha denied the existence of God. There are, however, many religious, philosophical and mystical traditions that emphatically assert the existence of God.

Now it is most unlikely for either the Enlightened Ones or other sages and saints of penetrative insight to go wrong on the most crucial subject of the ultimate reality. It may be possible that the Buddhists and the non-Buddhists are both right in what they assert, but are construed to say much more than what they actually say. Confusion may also have arisen mainly due to different ways of expressing what is indefinable and beyond the reach of the human mind. Might there be some ambiguities in the use of the term 'God', such that Buddhists and non-Buddhists only seem to hold mutually incompatible positions? Sometimes seemingly conflicting views exist simply due to the different use of words in different languages – while these words actually indicate the same reality.

Buddhism and the Contemporaneous Literature on God

Since the notion of God is of paramount importance to many, it may be helpful to examine the Buddhist position on this in the wider context of Indian thought. The statements made in early Buddhism about God may be compared with what is stated in the contemporaneous literature such as the *Upanishads* and the *Bhagavadgītā*. This may enable us to see if the two traditions are indeed diametrically opposed to or mutually incompatible with each other in this regard.

The Pali Canon is said to represent the early records of the Buddha's teachings, and it forms the basis of much of subsequent early Buddhist thought. Therefore, probably the best way to ascertain why the Buddha is said to deny God is to turn to the early Pali Canon.

It is well known that the Buddha was averse to needless metaphysical discussion and that he brushed aside ten metaphysical questions, including those pertaining to the soul. But unlike the questions concerning the soul, the question of God is not included among the Buddha's unanswered questions. The Buddha clearly rejects what some people considered to be God during his time. Obviously, 'God' is a highly ambiguous term and is understood by people in several different senses. Fortunately, the Buddha clarifies what he really denies.

In the very first sutta of the first book of the *Sutta Piṭaka* of the Pali Canon, the Brahmajāla Sutta of the *Dīgha Nikāya*, the Buddha explains how Brahmā came to be considered as God, and he exposes the weakness of the theory that Brahmā created the world. The Buddha points out how at the beginning of each world-process, a being falls from the world of Radiance because of the exhaustion of his lifespan or merit, and is born in the empty mansion of Brahmā.[228] After living there alone for a very long period and wishing for other beings to come and join him, other beings are also reborn there due to the exhaustion of their lifespan or merit. This, according to the Buddha, gives rise to the delusion on the part of the first-born being that he is God, the Creator, since he thinks:

> I am Brahmā, the great Brahmā, the supreme one, the mighty, the all-seeing, the ruler, the lord of all, the creator, the maker [*issaro kattā nimmātā*], the chief of all, the one who assigns to each his place, the controller, the father of all that are and are to be.[229]
>
> The Buddha says that the beings who are born later also take him to be the Creator, being under the same delusion.[230]

This explanation of the Buddha exposes the absurdity of the thought, perhaps prevalent during his time, that Brahmā was the first Creator.

This so-called Creator, Controller or God, according to the Buddha, is then charged with moral responsibility for all ills of the world. As the Buddha says:

> There are recluses and brahmins who maintain and believe that whatever a person experiences, be it pleasant, unpleasant or neutral – is all caused by God's act of creation.... If that is so, then people commit murder, theft and unchaste deeds due to God's act of creation; they indulge in lying, slanderous, harsh and idle talk due to God's act of creation; they are covetous, full of hate and hold wrong views due to God's act of creation.[231]

Similar arguments are also found in the Jātakas, texts most likely of later origin included in the Pali Canon:

> If God designs the life of the entire world – the glory and the misery, the good and the evil acts, humans are only the doers of [God's] bidding, and God [alone] is tainted thereby [*issaro tena lippati*].[232]

Showing the utter incompatibility of the belief in the Creator-God with the prevailing evils of the world, the Jātakas say:

> If, indeed, Brahmā is the lord of the whole world and creator of multiple beings, then why has he not made the entire world happy, without ordaining any misfortune in the world? Why has he made the world full of injustice, deceit, falsehood and conceit? The lord of beings, then, is evil, since he has ordained unrighteousness when there could have been righteousness.[233]

Then it is repeatedly shown in the Pali Canon that the Buddha is superior to Brahmā, who is only under the delusion that he is God. In the Kevaṭṭa Sutta from the *Dīgha Nikāya*, for example, a Buddhist monk goes to Brahmā, who claims to be the all-knowing God, the Creator, to seek the answer to the question, "Where do the four great elements – earth, water, fire and wind – cease, leaving no trace behind?" Brahmā has to confess his ignorance to the monk (in private, so that his ignorance may not be revealed before his courtiers) and sends the monk to the Buddha to obtain the answer. The Buddha then satisfies the monk with the answer.[234]

In the Pāthika Sutta of the *Dīgha Nikāya*, we also find that, aside from Brahmā, some other gods even lower in status than Brahmā were considered by certain groups to be the all-knowing God. The Buddha exposes their folly also, and points out that he knows far more than all of them, yet is not proud of his knowledge.[235]

Again, in the Brahmanimantanika Sutta of the *Majjhima Nikāya*, the Buddha goes to the region where Baka Brahmā ('Crane Brahmā', one of the Brahmās) lived to help him get rid of his delusion that he and his region are eternal. Displeased with the Buddha's pronouncement that Brahmā and his region are impermanent, Baka Brahmā tries to use his maximum power to make himself invisible, but fails to do so. The Buddha then demonstrates his superiority to Brahmā by causing himself to vanish from the sight of Brahmā and his courtiers, despite Brahmā's utmost effort to prevent the Buddha from doing so, and the courtiers are wonderstruck to witness this marvel of the Buddha.[236] The Buddha does not normally make such a display of his paranormal powers, but he does so here only to make Brahmā realize his limitations and impermanence.

Apart from Baka Brahmā, the Buddha makes mention of other Brahmās, such as Sahampati Brahmā and Sanatkumāra Brahmā.[237] In fact, Brahmās are said to be many and of different grades. We find mention of Brahmās as lords of 'one thousand, two thousand, three thousand … ten thousand and one hundred thousand world-systems'.[238] But even the highest Brahmā is within the range of time and is subject to rebirth.

It is true that the idea of Brahmā as the first-born among the gods is traceable to some *Upanishads*, yet it is important to note that while considering Brahmā as the first-born among the gods and as the creator of the worlds lower than his own (not of the regions higher than his own), most of the *Upanishads* speak of a being called Brahman as higher than Brahmā, and this Brahman is usually regarded as the real cause or ground of the origin and existence of the universe.[239] Brahmā, the first-born among the gods, is called creator only because he is instrumental in executing the work ordained to him by the higher divinity, Brahman. That is why Brahmā himself tells his eldest son to attain the knowledge of Brahman. As the *Muṇḍaka Upanishad* points out:

> Brahmā arose as the first among the gods, the maker and the custodian of the universe. He spoke of the knowledge of Brahman, the foundation of all knowledge, to Atharvan, his eldest son.[240]

Brahman, however, is depicted in the *Upanishads* as an indefinable, ineffable and impersonal power, devoid of all attributes or marks.[241] Thus, while the *Upanishads* consider Brahmā to be the first-born being among the gods and the creator of the illusory world, they agree with Buddhism that Brahmā is not the ultimate Creator, and that there is a reality higher than he, whether it be called Brahman or the Buddha.

In the *Bhagavadgītā* also, Brahmā is said to have come out of the imperishable or supreme reality (Brahman).[242] Thus, the supreme reality is explicitly said to be superior to the first-creator, Brahmā.[243] In the cosmic form of Krishṇa also, Brahmā, along with Shiva and hosts of other beings, sages and heavenly *nāgas*,* has been shown to be contained in the supreme God.[244] The attainment of the region of Brahmā offers no freedom from the bond of rebirth.[245] Further, the supreme God (i.e. Brahman) is clearly spoken of as the ground, cause, father and creator of the universe.[246]

Thus, Brahmā's claim to be the supreme Lord, the real creator, God and the ultimate foundation of all is rejected not only by the Buddha, but also by the *Upanishads* and the *Bhagavadgītā*. When the identification of Brahmā with God is shown to be false, all criticisms made by the Buddha or the Buddhists against Brahmā, mistakenly considered to be God, become inapplicable to God. In relation to God, the transcendent reality that is beyond space, time, and causality, untouched by karmas and not confined to this spatio-temporal world, these criticisms are simply inapplicable.

While both Buddhism and the *Upanishads* agree that Brahmā is not the ultimate God, they address differently the issue of how an infinitely compassionate supreme reality that some call God could give rise to a world in which evil is present. The Buddha simply refuses to discuss cosmological questions, pointing out that all such discussions would be intellectually incomprehensible

---

* Entities or beings taking the form of great snakes.

and practically unprofitable. For example, regarding the beginning and end of the world, he says:

> The beginning of the world is inconceivable; its first point [*pubbākoṭi*] is not comprehended.[247]

Given his vast spiritual consciousness, the Buddha could have answered any questions pertaining to beginnings or origins. But he simply sidestepped these as being irrelevant to the more important issue of the disciple's practice of the Dharma, which brings us to the pragmatic reason for the Buddha not engaging in such questions. When a recluse asked the Buddha about the beginning, the Buddha said:

> I recollect the various forms of previous lives, for example, one life, two lives ... in all their modes, details and multiple forms, so from me a question pertaining to the beginning [*pubbantaṁ*] should be asked. I could have convinced your mind. Or I may ask someone a question pertaining to the beginning, and he may satisfy me by answering the question pertaining to the beginning, or I may satisfy him by answering the question pertaining to the beginning.... [Likewise we may satisfy each other regarding answering the question pertaining to the end.] But leave aside, O Udāyin, the questions pertaining to the beginning and end; I shall teach you the Dhamma.[248]

The Buddha's pragmatic approach can be seen as the most important reason for not giving definitive answers to transcendental questions. Through his silence he acknowledged the uselessness and irrelevance of such debate, since discussing and theorizing about esoteric subjects deflect a spiritual practitioner from his real task of walking the path. With his infinite compassion and understanding of human psychology, the Buddha saw how seekers with little spiritual experience would be confused and not helped by answers that remain conceptual. Rather than wasting the time and energy of his disciples in metaphysical discussion, he advised them to devote themselves fully to their practice in order to secure release from this impermanent and sorrowful world and attain enlightenment, the state of Nirvāṇa, beyond time and space, cause and effect.

The Law of Cause and Effect

Although the *Upanishads* present the creation as arising from the supreme reality, like Buddhism they affirm that this ultimate reality lies beyond the duality of good and evil and beyond the understanding of the human intellect. Again, like Buddhism they also consider it vitally important to resolve the question of how human beings can liberate themselves from the realm of duality, evil and suffering.

To understand how the world of duality – of cause and effect – works, we may explore the law of karma (Pali: kamma). Once we understand the law of karma, we understand how the doers of good and bad actions reap their consequences, and why human beings need to take responsibility for their actions and undertake the path of liberation to go beyond the sphere of good and evil, beyond the cycle of birth, death, and suffering.

We may recall that in both Buddhist and other Indian traditions two very different worlds are postulated, within which different conditions prevail. One world is permeated by impermanence and suffering; the other is beyond time and impermanence. The former, known as saṁsāra, the world of birth and death, is conceived in terms of space, time and causality and is regulated by the strict law of justice, the law of karma. The latter, Nirvāṇa, the region of the unborn, is beyond space, time and causality and is free from karmas.

Both traditions point out that the law of karma prevails in the entire universe of phenomena. The Buddha says:

By karma revolves the world,
by karma revolves humankind.
Like the axle holding the rolling chariot-wheels,
beings are held by karma.[249]

The *Upanishads* and the *Bhagavadgītā* explain the law of karma in a similar way. The *Brihadāraṇyaka Upanishad* says:

According to how one acts, according to how one behaves, so does he become. The doer of good becomes good; the doer of evil becomes evil. One becomes virtuous by virtuous action and evil by evil action.[250]

The *Bhagavadgītā* also points out:

The fruit of good action
is said to be good and pure in its nature,
While the fruit of passion is pain
and the fruit of dullness is ignorance.[251]

The *Chhāndogya Upanishad* says that the law of karma operates alike in both earthly and heavenly worlds:

As here on earth the worldly enjoyment earned by an act perishes, even so in the other world the heavenly enjoyment earned by meritorious religious rites perishes.[252]

The *Bhagavadgītā* explains that people deluded by the *prakritis** develop the conceit of 'I' and think that they are the doer of actions:

---

*The essential nature of mind and matter, which projects itself in various forms of emotions and actions, and which also influences the various parts of the body; prakritis are twenty-five in number and consist of five principal manifestations of the five elements in the body. Thus, 'deluded by the prakritis' means to mistake one's temporary mortal body and personality for an enduring reality.

All actions are done by the *prakritis*,
the modes of nature.
But one whose self is deluded by the conceit
of 'I' or ego thinks, "I am the doer."[253]

No one can remain even for a moment
without engaging in action.
Everyone is made to act, helplessly,
by the impulses born of the prakritis.[254]

Thus, no action performed by those who labour under the conceit of 'I', whether good, unwholesome or ignorant, can ever take them out of the cycle of birth and death.

In accordance with the law of karma that prevails in the entire universe, no one but oneself is to blame for the evil or good that we encounter in the world. We alone are responsible for our happiness and suffering, since we undergo pleasurable and painful experiences strictly in accordance with the law of karma. Putting it in simple terms, the Buddha says:

As a person does, so does he reap.... Beings are inheritors of their karmas.[255]

Buddhists point out that putting responsibility on a supernatural Creator for the events of our lives is detrimental to moral incentive and self-effort. Such people abandon their efforts to live their lives righteously and instead rely on prayer for the fulfilment of their desires. In the *Aṅguttara Nikāya* it is said:

Those who fall back on God's act of creation as the essential factor lack the impulse and effort regarding what should be done and what should not be done.[256]

However, the theistic Indian tradition also affirms that effort or endeavour is essential. Belief in God as the ultimate ground of being is not thought to undermine moral incentive and effort, as these are necessary to become receptive to the grace of God. The path to God is not a path for the lazy; it is for the brave and persevering. The *Īsha Upanishad* explains:

> Always performing one's duty for the sake of duty, one should wish to live for a hundred years. Karma does not defile a person if he lives in this way, and not in any other way.[257]

The *Bhagavadgītā* explains that work performed without desire for reward is considered worship: The *Bhagavadgītā* advises a devotee:

> By worshipping Him
> through the performance of their own actions,
> People attain perfection.[258]

Krishṇa says to his disciple, Arjuna:

> Action alone is your concern
> and never at all its fruits.[259]

Thus, according to both Buddhism and the theistic Indian tradition, none can realize the ultimate goal without following moral discipline and making strenuous efforts.

Ultimate Reality and Brahman

Recognizing that both Buddhism as well as the *Upanishads* and *Bhagavadgītā* commonly accept that Brahmā is not the ultimate reality and that we must make effort and take responsibility for our own actions, not blaming God for our weaknesses, we can now note how ultimate or transcendent reality is spoken of in similar ways in Buddhism as well as the *Upanishads* and *Bhagavadgītā*.

We find a lofty and sublime notion of Brahman in the *Upanishads* and the *Bhagavadgītā*. The realm of Brahman is immortal and beyond space, time, causality and the law of karma. The transcendent reality is totally unaffected by the criticisms levelled against Brahmā. The *Chhāndogya Upanishad*, for example, states:

> As water does not cling to a lotus leaf, so evil deeds do not cling to one who knows it [Brahman].[260]

The *Kena Upanishad* differentiates the truly sublime notion of Brahman from its popular concept:

> That which is not expressed through speech but that by which speech is expressed, know that indeed to be Brahman and not what people here worship. That which is not thought by the mind but by which, they say, the mind is thought, know that indeed to be Brahman and not what people here worship.[261]

Referring to the sublime reality, the *Shvetāshvatara Upanishad* says:

> He is the one God, hidden in all beings, all-pervading, the inner Self of all beings, watching over all works, dwelling in all beings, the witness, the knower, alone and devoid of *guṇas* [attributes].[262]

> He is subtler than the subtle, greater than the great. He is the Self dwelling in the cave [heart] of every being. One beholds him as being actionless, and when through the grace of God one sees him and his majesty, one becomes free from sorrow.[263]

The *Īsha Upanishad* also says:

> What delusion and what sorrow can there be to him who has seen the Oneness?[264]

The *Bhagavadgītā* also points to a reality that is beyond the good and evil of the world:

> The all-pervading spirit takes on
> neither the sin nor the merit of anybody.
> Knowledge is enveloped by ignorance;
> thereby creatures are deluded.[265]

Brahman is often regarded as the cause or the 'ground' of being.[266] This ground of being is depicted in the *Upanishads* as an indefinable, ineffable and impersonal reality, devoid of all attributes or marks,[267] in relation to which words are inadequate. One can only indicate Brahman by stating what it is not: "not this, not this" (*neti-neti*).[268] It is incomprehensible to the mind and inexpressible by words. As the *Taittirīya Upanishad* says:

> That from which speech along with the mind returns baffled, without attaining it – he who knows the bliss of that Brahman never fears.[269]

In the *Upanishads* the following quotations point to this reality, referred to as Brahman:

> Brahman, verily was there in the beginning.[270]

> Brahman is pure consciousness and bliss.[271]

> Verily, all this is Brahman.[272]

Krishṇa's disciple Arjuna asks Lord Krishṇa to tell him wherein lies his ultimate good.[273] Krishṇa answers:

> I shall explain to you that which is to be known
> [realized], by knowing [realizing] which,
> life eternal is gained.
> It is the supreme [*paraṁ*] Brahman,
> who is beginningless and who is said to be
> neither existent nor non-existent.[274]

Turning to the Buddhist texts, we find a similar description of a reality that is beyond the reach of the senses, mind and the intellect, as well as beyond our familiar notions of space and time. It is incomprehensible and indescribable, beyond thought and speech. While this reality cannot be said to have any name or form, the Buddha yet points to it as a transcendental realm:

> Truly, there is a realm where there is neither the earth nor water, neither fire nor air, neither ether nor consciousness ... neither sun nor moon. This I call neither being born, nor dying, nor staying; neither arising nor passing away.[275]

> There the stars shine not,
> Nor does the sun shed its light.
> Neither is there the illumination of the moon,
> Nor is there any darkness.[276]

A similar statement is made in the *Milindapañhā** concerning Nibbāna:

> The form, location, age and measure cannot be given of Nibbāna – the state that is truly real.[277]

* A Pali text included only in the Burmese edition of the *Khuddaka Nikāya*.

Buddhist texts speak of the supreme state as Brahman. One who attains Nirvāṇa is said to become Brahman – *Brahmabhūto*[*278] – and the enlightened are described as having "become one with Brahman", as we find in the following passage from the *Saṁyutta Nikāya*:

> Ah, happy indeed are *arahants* (liberated ones)! In them no craving is found, the conceit of I-ness is rooted out, confusion's net is rent asunder. Unspotted in the world, they have become Brahman (*Brahmabhūto*).[279]

The Buddha himself is described as one who has obtained Brahman (*Brahmapatta*).[280]

In the Pali Canon Brahman is clearly identified with Dharma and hence Brahmakāya and Dharmakāya are said to be synonyms. The Buddha explains to the brahmin Vāseṭṭha that one whose faith in the Tathāgata is firmly and unshakeably established – in other words, one who is truly enlightened – may say:

> I am a true son of the Exalted One, born of his mouth, born of Dhamma, formed by Dhamma, an heir to Dhamma. Why is that? Because, Vāseṭṭha, this designates the Tathāgata: 'Dhammakāya', 'Brahmakāya', 'become Dhamma', 'become Brahmā'.[†281]

The expression that the Blessed One (the Buddha) has become one with the Dhamma and one with Brahman is frequently repeated in the Pali Canon.[282] There is hardly any doubt that the words *Dhammabhūto* and *Brahmabhūto*, that is, 'becoming one with the Dhamma' and 'becoming one with Brahman', are used to indicate the highest state of Nibbāna, since along with them

---

[*] Here Brahma, a variant of Brahman, is used, and is not to be confused with Brahmā, the creator of the lower worlds.

[†] Brahmā here means 'the highest', and is used here since the Buddha is speaking to brahmins.

certain other words indicative of the supreme state of enlightenment such as *chakkhubhūto* and *ñāṇabhūto*, 'vision-personified' and 'knowledge-personified', also are frequently used.[283]

Again, the Eightfold Path leading to Nibbāna is synonymously called *Dhammayāna* or *Brahmayāna*, i.e., the path that leads to the Dhamma or Brahman.[284] It is also stated that to dwell in Brahman is to dwell in the Dhamma.[285] And the Buddha is described as turning the wheel of the Dhamma or Brahman.[286]

In addition to the terms 'Brahman' and 'Dhamma' or 'Dhammakāya', we find a number of other terms for ultimate reality in Buddhism that have impersonal connotations. Among these are: Tathāgata, Nibbāna, Buddhatva (Buddha-nature), Nishprapañcha (unimpeded), Shūnyatā (emptiness), Tathatā (Suchness), Paramārthā (ultimate reality), Bhūta-koti (ultimate limit of reality), Bhūtatā (reality), Advaitā (non-duality), and Tattva (reality).[287]

Both the Buddhist and non-Buddhist Indian traditions emphasize that no human mode of speech can adequately name, depict or characterize ultimate reality. Hence it is often called 'nameless'.

Pointing to the transcendent consciousness beyond all that is known or conceived, the *Māṇḍūkya Upanishad* says:

> It is not that which cognizes the internal objects, nor that which cognizes the external objects, nor what cognizes both of them, nor a mass of cognition. It is neither cognitive nor non-cognitive. It can neither be seen nor spoken of, nor is it graspable. It is without any distinctive marks, unthinkable and unnameable.... It is that into which the world is resolved. It is the peaceful, the benign, the non-dual.[288]

The *Māṇḍūkya Upanishad* speaks of this transcendental state as 'unnameable'. That which is truly real is undeniable, yet it is indescribable. It cannot even be said to be known or described in the familiar sense of our knowing or describing.

Buddhist texts speak of the ultimate in similar ways. Saraha, a noted Buddhist teacher of the ninth century, speaks of ultimate reality as the "Supreme Lord" and describes it in the following way:

> It is devoid of names and other qualities;
> I have said it cannot be known by discussion.
> So how may the Supreme Lord be described?
> It is like a maiden's experiencing of bliss.[289]

Indicating the insufficiency of words, Saraha says:

> The whole world is tormented by words,
> And there is no one who does without words.
> But in so far as one is free from words
> Does one really understand words.[290]

The Heroic Progress Sūtra speaks of the "subtle essence" in similar words:

> The subtle essence is complete clarity beyond all name or description.[291]

Saraha goes on to say that the only way to dissolve the confusion and conflicts created by words and names is the direct experience of the bliss of reality:

> I used to recite the text-book…
> But I drank the elixir and forgot it.
> There is but one Word that I know now.
> And of that, my friend, I know not the name.[292]

There are two commonly used terms within Mahāyāna Buddhism that are used to refer to this nameless reality. These are 'Suchness' or 'Thusness' (Tathatā), and 'Void' or 'Emptiness' (Shūnya), both pointing to the fact that ultimate reality simply 'is as it is' – beyond any name, form or feature. This is the message of Junjirō Takakusu, one of the foremost Japanese scholars of Buddhism. Regarding Suchness or Thusness, Takakusu says:

> In Mahāyāna the ultimate truth is called Suchness or Thusness.... Thusness is the ultimate foundation of Buddhist thought concerning the real state of all that exists.[293]

> Thusness, or Suchness, is the only term which can be used to express the ultimate indefinable, the unnameable reality.[294]

Regarding Shūnya he says:

> 'Shūnya' negatively means 'Void', but positively... 'devoid of specific character'.... It is nameless [*akhyātī*] and characterless [*alakshaṇa*].[295]

At this point, we are encouraged to conclude that there is great similarity in the idea of the impersonal ultimate reality of both early and later Buddhist texts and the impersonal terms of some of the principal works of the early Indian tradition. Even if one were to argue that in the above quotations taken from these systems of thought, some of the common terms or names may have slight differences in meaning, such an observation would not substantially change the basic similarity in understanding.

Given such similarities in speaking of the nameless reality, it would appear that truth cuts across the barriers of time, place, country, culture, tradition, race and religion. The enlightened of all times and places dive deeply into the core of reality and describe the same eternal path, even though their message may be expressed differently through concepts that reflect their time and place.

We might also suggest here that in their earnest quest for truth, the need for seekers to find a wise and compassionate Buddha to guide them on the right path is emphasized again and again.

Is There a Personal God?

Having explored some of the ways in which the supreme reality is understood in Buddhist and non-Buddhist Indian traditions, we may now discuss whether an impersonal ultimate reality contradicts the notion of a *personal* God.

The *Upanishads* and the *Bhagavadgītā*, as well as spiritual traditions from other parts of the world, refer to the supreme transcendent reality in both impersonal and personal terms – as both God and Godhead, to use a distinction made by the British writer Aldous Huxley. The former denotes a personal Creator or Lord, and the latter denotes the impersonal reality. It is interesting to see here how the ultimate reality can be viewed in personal as well as impersonal terms.

The well-known Buddhist scholar D. T. Suzuki has equated Dharmakāya with the Christian idea of Godhead.[296] The idea of Godhead allows us to indicate the indescribable and unknowable without personalizing it and defining it in human terms. However, if the indescribable is referred to only as impersonal reality – such as the Dharmakāya – human beings struggling with the limitations of their humanity cannot relate to it. Even though Buddhism is rigorous in not personalizing ultimate reality, it is equally pragmatic in its presentation of the Buddha, personalized and infinitely compassionate, as one with ultimate reality. Indicating this Buddhist approach, D. T. Suzuki says:

> The essence of Buddhahood is the Dharmakāya, but as long as the Buddha remains such, there is no hope for the salvation of a world of particulars. The Buddha has to abandon his original

> abode, and must take upon himself such forms as are conceivable and acceptable to the inhabitants of this earth. The Holy Spirit emanates, as it were, from Absolute Buddhahood and is seen by those who are prepared by their previous karma to see him.[297]

We have already addressed how the indescribable manifests as a human being in the form of a Buddha. Now we will look at examples of how Buddhism presents the Compassionate One.

The Tathāgata, we will note, is variously referred to as the father, the cause, the ground, the foundation of the universe, and also the Lord of all. Indicating that the Tathāgata has been coming to this world again and again on his mission of mercy and compassion, the *Lotus Sūtra* says:

> He [the Buddha] always keeps coming to the world and conducts himself according to the circumstances. He indeed is the Supreme Lord, the Lord of Dharma, and also Lord among the greatest of the world.[298]

In another verse, the Tathāgata, addressing the bodhisattvas, discloses his true nature:

> I am the father of the world [*lokapitā*], the self-born [*svayambhū*], the curer of the malady of ignorance and the protector of all beings.[299]

H. Kern, a well-known English translator of the *Lotus Sūtra* (*Saddharmapuṇḍarīka*) and one of the first in the West to study this text, says:

> There is, to my comprehension, not the slightest doubt that the *Saddharmapuṇḍarīka* intends to represent Shākya [the Buddha] as the Supreme Being, as the God of gods, almighty and all-wise.[300]

Buddhism also recognizes a primordial creative energy. As Longchenpa (1308–1364), one of the most celebrated adepts of the Tibetan Buddhist Nyingma school, states in *The Jewel Ship: A Guide to the Meaning of Pure and Total Presence, the Creative Energy of the Universe*:

> Listen, because all you beings of the three realms
> Were made by me, the creativity of the universe,
> You are my children, equal to me.
> Because you and I are not separate,
> I manifest in you.[301]

Edward Conze notes:

> Some Buddhists ... rounded off their theology with the notion of an Ādi-Buddha, a kind of omnipotent and omniscient primeval Buddha, who through his meditation originated the universe.[302]

This reference to the Ādi-Buddha has affinities, it might be said, with the notion of Ādi Deva or primeval Lord that is found in the *Bhagavadgītā*.[303] The Ādi-Buddha, the primal Buddha, is also called Samanta-Bhadra or All-Good, and is regarded as "the Foundation of all", as stated in *The Good-Wishes of the All-Good Buddha Samanta-Bhadra*:

> The Foundation of all is uncreated, uncompounded, independent, beyond mental concept and verbal definition.[304]

The *Avataṁsaka Sūtra* says:

> As in all worlds
> All the solid elements
> Have no independent existence

Yet are found everywhere,
So also does the Buddha-body
Pervade all worlds,
Its various physical forms
Without abode or origin.[305]

This reality – the Tathāgata, the Dharmakāya or the uncreated "foundation of all" spoken of above – has two major qualities: unbounded compassion and unbounded wisdom, due to which it descends to earth in a human form to impart true knowledge to the inhabitants of this earth and save them from unending suffering. These two – unbounded compassion and unbounded wisdom – are said to be the most important characteristics of the Buddha or the Tathāgata who appears in the world. Thus, we see the interconnectedness of the personal and impersonal aspects of ultimate reality.

In later Buddhism these two characteristics are ascribed to two distinct divinities named Avalokiteshvara and Mañjushrī. Edward Conze explains that Avalokiteshvara means 'a being who looks down with compassion' on those suffering in this world. He says that while Avalokiteshvara personifies compassion, Mañjushrī – Avalokiteshvara's equal in popularity – personifies wisdom.[306]

Both the *Upanishads* and Buddhism also use the word 'consciousness' for absolute reality. For example, the *Brihadāraṇyaka Upanishad* says:

Brahman is pure consciousness and bliss.[307]

The *Taittirīya Upanishad* also speaks of Brahman in these terms:

Brahman is the reality, consciousness and infinite.[308]

Again it is said:

> Brahman alone, who is of the nature of reality, consciousness and bliss, is all this.[309]

Similarly, Lama Thubten Yeshe (1935–1984) explains the oneness of Reality and consciousness, as recounted in the book *Reincarnation*. He says:

> The Tibetan explanation is this: Reality and consciousness embrace each other. They are completely one.
>
> Now Christians describe God in terms of being omnipresent, don't they? God is omnipresent, He completely embraces reality, totally. It is said like this.
>
> And in Buddhism it says that consciousness is omnipresent, it completely embraces all existence, externally and internally, under the earth and in the sky, whatever there is. So there is no existence which cannot be comprehended by consciousness.[310]

In Buddhism, the impersonal reality – the Tathāgata or Dharmakāya – appears in the world in human form again and again. We have already quoted a few verses from the *Lotus Sūtra* in this section to establish this point. In the same text, the Buddha, the Blessed One, speaks of many future Buddhas who will appear in the world.[311]

Similarly, in D. T. Suzuki's work on the *Laṅkāvatāra Sūtra*, we read:

> The Buddha [as the Dharmakāya] ... must take upon himself such forms as are conceivable and acceptable to the inhabitants of this earth.[312]

If a person really wants to understand supreme reality, there is nothing in the world with which it can be compared. Direct experience is the only way to know or understand it. The Buddha therefore placed strong emphasis on direct personal experiment and the inner verification of what is truly real:

> It is a come-and-see kind of thing, accessible and realized only personally by the wise.[313]

7

The Enlightened One

The Buddhist Perspective

To enquire into the Buddhist perspective on the spiritual teacher, it may be helpful first to review the meaning of the term 'Dharma' that is so fundamental to Buddhist philosophy. Of its manifold meanings, three clearly stand out:

First, in its transcendental sense, Dharma stands for the ultimate reality, the absolute, which is eternal, uncreated and unmanifest. It is also known as Dharmakāya, often rendered in English as Buddha-mind or Buddha-nature.

Secondly, Dharma manifests itself in the world as an Enlightened One (the Buddha), whom the Mahāyāna Buddhists call the Nirmāṇakāya (created body). That is why Dharma is said to be the essence of the Buddhas. The Buddhas descend from and merge back into the Dharmakāya after fulfilling the purpose of their coming to the world.

Thirdly, in its practical sense, Dharma is said to be the means – the true or eternal way, or the path – which only the Enlightened Ones know and teach, and which naturally leads to the source, the transcendental reality, the Dharmakāya.

Thus, Dharma can be taken in three senses: the transcendental reality; its human embodiment as a Buddha; and the means or transporting power by which people are enabled to realize the goal of enlightenment.

The fact that the Dharma is the true nature or essence of the Buddha is indicated in the early Pali Canon, in which the Buddha himself states that he should not be mistaken for a mere human being. Being an embodiment of the Dharmakāya, Dharma is his true essence, as he says to his disciple Vakkali:

> What is there, Vakkali, in seeing this corruptible body? He who sees Dhamma, sees me; he who sees me, sees Dhamma. Seeing Dhamma, Vakkali, he sees me; seeing me, he sees Dhamma.[314]

In the later Mahāyāna text, the *Perfection of Wisdom Sūtra in Eight Thousand Lines* (*Ashṭasāhasrikā Prajñāpāramitā*), the Buddha says:

> The Dharma-body is the Buddha, the Lord. But, monks, you should not think that this individual body is my body. Monks, you should see me as the accomplishment of the Dharma-body.[315]

There is actually no difference between our own original state and that of the Buddha. The Dharma is our true essence and nature as well, but we do not know how to experience this truth. What we normally perceive as our self is not real. What we see as our personal history is just a temporary layer over our original state.

The Dharma or transcendental reality is considered non-dual. By merging into it the illusion of duality is dissolved, egoism is extinguished and all traces of 'mine' and 'yours' are erased. The last two lines of the following verse of the *Diamond Sūtra* (*Vajrachchhedikā Prajñāpāramitā*) indicate that the Dharma can be realized only by going beyond our familiar framework of duality – subject-object or knower-known:

> From the Dharma one should see the Buddhas;
> from the Dharma body comes their guidance.
> Yet Dharma's true nature cannot be discerned,
> and no one can be conscious of it as an object.[316]

D. T. Suzuki points out that the Buddha must descend to the physical level from the absolute reality, Dharmakāya, for the sake of liberating the people of the world. In terms of Western ideas, Suzuki points out a parallel with Christianity:

> We may regard the Dharmakāya as corresponding to the Christian idea of Godhead.... The essence of Buddhahood is the Dharmakāya, but as long as the Buddha remains such, there is no hope for the salvation of a world of particulars. The Buddha has to abandon his original abode, and must take upon himself such forms as are conceivable and acceptable to the inhabitants of this earth. The Holy Spirit emanates, as it were, from Absolute Buddhahood and is seen by those who are prepared by their previous karma to see him.[317]

The historical Buddha was an embodiment of the transcendental Dharmakāya. He descended from it, realized his true nature as Dharma, taught others to realize that same reality and then merged back into the Dharmakāya. The Buddha came to the world simply to liberate people, as he declares:

> I am the Tathāgata, the Blessed One, the Unconquerable. I have taken birth in this world for the sake of saving others.[318]

According to early Buddhism, the Buddhas who came before Gautama Buddha did the same. Mahāyāna Buddhism speaks of innumerable Buddhas emerging from the Dharmakāya out of compassion for the suffering beings of the world, and merging back into the Dharmakāya after completing their mission of mercy and compassion.

Since all the Buddhas or enlightened teachers emerge from the same absolute reality, they are essentially one and the same. Hence, by taking refuge in the Buddha of one's time, one takes refuge in all the Buddhas. That is why, while taking refuge in his own teacher, Shāntideva says that he is taking refuge in all the Buddhas:

> On this very day, I take refuge in the Conquerors
> [the Buddhas], the mighty Lords of the Universe,
> The destroyers of all fears,
> who are ready to save the world.[319]

It may also be noted here that the Buddha was not an inventor of a new Dharma, but a discoverer and propagator of the ancient and eternal Dharma. Truth is always the same and the path leading to it cannot but always be the same. Although the Dharma did not originate from or depend upon the Buddha who came to the earth as Siddhārtha Gautama, the revelation of the Dharma certainly depended on him. He was a channel through which the Dharma was made known to people who were drawn to him. We need a Buddha or bodhisattva* to reveal and teach the Dharma, and the Dharma needs a Buddha or bodhisattva in order to be revealed.

In the early Pali Canon the Buddha points out that the Dharma is "difficult to see and comprehend", because it is beyond ordinary

---

* A bodhisattva (Pali: bodhisatta), 'enlightened being', is the name given to anyone who, motivated by great compassion, has generated the spontaneous wish to attain Buddhahood for the benefit of all living beings. They have vowed that they will not step out of the cycle of birth and death until all other sentient beings are enlightened.

perception and reason. But he states that it is only on the basis of his own direct realization of the Dharma that he teaches it to others:

> This other [transcendental] Dhamma is profound, difficult to see and comprehend, serene, excellent, beyond reason, subtle and comprehensible only by the wise, which the Tathāgata teaches only after having himself known and realized it.[320]

Those who wish to reach the goal of enlightenment, and thus fulfil the purpose of human life, must find and take refuge in an enlightened teacher of their time, as Anaṅgavajra, an eighth-century Mahāsiddha, says in *The Attainment of the Realization of Wisdom and Means* (*Prajñopāyaviniścayasiddhi*):

> So a wise man must resort to a good master, for without him the truth cannot be found even in millions of ages. And if truth is not found, the final goal can never be reached, just as without a seed a plant will not grow even in the best and clearest field. So when in the course of life one comes upon masters with this truth, those who are teachers of Wisdom-Means, firm in line of succession, wondrous as a wish-granting gem ... and established in the path that is free from querulous thought, one should honour them to the best of one's ability if final perfection of the self is really one's aim. It is by means of their splendour that the bliss of infinite enlightenment is gained which is the highest goal possible for all beings in this triple world of moving and motionless things.[321]

It is great good fortune to encounter an enlightened teacher, to be initiated or ordained by him into the true spiritual discipline, and another good fortune to work earnestly to put the spiritual master's teachings into practice. In this way the potential of human life is truly fulfilled. Shāntideva, a noted exponent of

Mahāyāna Buddhism, indicates that initiation signifies a new birth into the Buddha's spiritual family as his son or daughter:

> Now my life is blessed,
> since I have obtained a human birth.
> Today I am reborn in the Buddha's family
> and am now the Buddha's son.
> Now I should conduct myself
> in a manner befitting my family,
> So that I may not bring dishonour
> to my immaculate family.[322]

In *Secrets on Cultivating the Mind*, Sŏn master Chinul quotes from the verse *Wan chu-yin* of Master Tan-hsia Tzu-ch'un (1064–1117), who writes that the Dharma, our Buddha-nature and our essence, is realized within our self, within our physical body:

> If you want to become a Buddha, understand that Buddha is the mind.* How can you search for the mind in the far distance? It is not outside the body. The physical body is a phantom, for it is subject to birth and death; the true mind is like space, for it neither ends nor changes. Therefore it is said, "These hundred bones will crumble and return to fire and wind. But One Thing is eternally numinous and covers heaven and earth."
>
> It is tragic. People have been deluded for so long. They do not recognize that their own minds are the true Buddhas. They do not recognize that their own natures are the true dharma. They want to search for the dharma, yet they still look far away for holy ones. They want to search for the Buddha, yet they will not observe their own minds.... If you will only leave behind false conditioning, you

* 'Mind' here refers to the unchanging Essence, not to the changing mind-body from where our thinking arises.

> will be "such" as the Buddha.... Since this Buddha-nature exists in your body right now, why do you vainly search for it outside?[323]

It is not easy to achieve enlightenment, and it is only out of compassion that the fully enlightened teach us and show the way to the transcendental reality, enabling us to realize it or to be one with it. They point out that we are caught in the vicious cycle of birth and death. Hence, we suffer terribly as long as we remain ignorant of our true nature and fail to realize ultimate reality, from which we have come. The Tibetan Buddhist master Longchenpa (1308–1364) says:

> Just as a patient is in need of a physician,
> People of a ruler, a lonely traveller of an escort,
> A merchant of a guild-master, a boatman of a boat,
> So in order to calm the emotions,
> to make the evil harmless,
> To overcome birth and death ...
> you must rely on a teacher.[324]

The Wisdom-Teachings of the Ādi-Buddha, as set forth in *The Good-Wishes of the All-Good Buddha Samanta-Bhadra*, speak of the consequences of not attaining Buddhahood – of not becoming one with the foundation of all:

> The Foundation of all is uncreated [unmanifested], uncompounded, independent, beyond mental concept and verbal definition.... To realize It is to attain Buddhahood. Not to realize It is to wander in the saṁsāra....
>
> Not knowing the Foundation, beings aforetime erred. They were overwhelmed by the darkness of unconsciousness, whence sprang ignorance and error. Immersed in error and obscured by ignorance, the 'knower' became bewildered and afraid. Then

> arose the concepts 'I' and 'Others', together with hatred. When these had grown strong, there was born an unbroken current of saṁsāric evolution.[325]

According to Buddhism, we are caught in a snare of endless suffering. Yet we do not seek light. We have become so utterly blind and ignorant that we know not who we are, where we have come from or whither we have to go, although in our delusion, we may think of ourselves as intelligent and wise, able to work our way out. We are thus not only ignorant, but also ignorant of the fact that we are ignorant. Seeing the fire of worldly passions and the compounded state of our ignorance, the Buddha says:

> How can there be laughter, how can there be rejoicing,
> While this world is always burning?[326]
>
> This world is blinded; only a few can see here.[327]
>
> The ignorant one who is aware of his ignorance
> Is wise at least to that extent;
> But that ignorant one who thinks himself wise
> Is indeed truly ignorant.[328]

Utterly ignorant, groping in darkness and caught in the cycle of birth and death, how can we, by our own efforts, know our own nature or that of ultimate reality? Can we extricate ourselves from suffering and attain freedom or enlightenment without any help and guidance from an enlightened teacher?

Taking Refuge in the Buddha

It is well known that one enters the Buddhist order by taking refuge in the Buddha. Now, what is meant by taking refuge in the

Buddha? Taking refuge in the Buddha, or one's spiritual guide, means to have complete reliance on him and to be fully devoted to him. This is said to be of utmost importance in Buddhism. In Tibetan Buddhism it is known as 'the root of the path'. Explaining it, Pabongka Rinpoche says:

> [This is] most crucial to our practice. The words, 'the root of the path' tell us the following: All of a tree's leaves, fruit, and so on are the outcome of its roots. All insights and realizations similarly derive exclusively from one's devotion to a spiritual guide.... We will receive all realizations up to the unification when we have proper devotion for our spiritual guide. Thus, it is vital to devote ourselves to a spiritual guide at the outset.[329]

In the Buddhist tradition one takes refuge in what is known as the 'Three Jewels': the Buddha, the spiritual teacher; the Dharma, the teaching; and the saṅgha, the community of practitioners. Of these Three Jewels, the Buddha or the spiritual teacher is of paramount importance, since the remaining two are dependent on him. Patrul Rinpoche explains:

> Look upon your teacher, the spiritual friend who teaches you here and now what to do and what not to do, as the true Jewel of the Buddha.... Consider every word of your sublime teacher as the Jewel of the Dharma.... The Teacher is the main refuge.... Recognize him, therefore, as the quintessential union of the Three Jewels. Follow him with absolute trust and try to pray to him all the time. Remember that to displease him with anything you do, say or think is to renounce the entire refuge, so make every effort to please him all the time. No matter what happens to you, be it pleasant or unpleasant, good or bad, sickness or suffering, entrust yourself entirely to the Jewel of the Teacher.[330]

He adds:

> By simply taking refuge [in Him], you plant the seed of liberation within yourself.... Ultimately, it will lead you to the state of Buddhahood.[331]

It is thus evident that in Buddhism one cannot be released from the cycle of birth and death simply by one's own efforts, and that one must seek and take refuge in a wise and compassionate master in order to attain enlightenment.

The Indispensability of a Teacher

Spiritual adepts who have travelled through inner regions and reached the ultimate goal with the help of their teachers speak with authority that there are many challenges and pitfalls along the way of the inner spiritual journey, and that people are bound to lose their way unless a competent master is there to help and guide them.

Patrul Rinpoche presents the view of his master, Jigme Gyalwai Nyugu, regarding the necessity for a spiritual teacher:

> When it comes to following the path of liberation and omniscience, we are as confused as a blind person wandering alone in the middle of a deserted plain.[332]
>
> No sūtra, tantra [scripture] or shāstra [treatise] speaks of any being ever attaining perfect Buddhahood without having followed a spiritual teacher. We can see for ourselves that nobody has ever developed all the accomplishments of the stages and paths by relying on their own efforts and abilities alone.[333]

In his *Points to Watch in Practising the Way* (*Gakudō-yōjin-shu*), the Japanese master Eihei Dōgen Zenji (1200–1253) says that only a spiritual adept can lead practitioners to the Way that lies beyond the limitations of the mind:

> Practitioners! You must understand that the Buddhist Way lies beyond thinking, discrimination, viewing, contemplation, perception and intellection. If the Buddha Way were contained within these mental functions, why haven't you yet awakened, since you have always been living and playing within that domain? In practising the Way, you should not use thinking or discrimination. If you look at yourself, who is always influenced by such things as thinking, this will be as clear as looking into a bright mirror. The gate through which you can enter the Way can be pointed out only by a master who has attained the Dharma. Scholars of words and letters can not reach it.[334]

Let us then consider the necessity for a living guide to teach this Way from a common sense point of view. Even in ordinary worldly matters, we find that we have to depend on some guide, teacher or helper to acquire any knowledge or skill in our day-to-day life. In childhood we need the help of our parents, caretakers, friends and relatives to be able to learn how to eat, drink, speak and walk. As we grow and wish to learn to drive a car or fly an aeroplane, we again need the practical guidance of a teacher. Likewise, to be a doctor or an engineer we need practical training by a competent doctor or an engineer. Mere reading of books or remembering and praising well-known past drivers, pilots, doctors or engineers will not make us proficient in any field of our life in the world.

Now spirituality is a much more difficult and complex subject than all others, because we are dealing with ultimate reality, beyond the reach of the mind and ordinary senses. In matters of spirituality, we find ourselves completely blind and deaf, lost and confounded. It is impossible for us to find the right path, become free from the cycle of birth and death and attain enlightenment on our own without the help and guidance of a competent guide or spiritual adept.

Patrul Rinpoche emphasizes the necessity of a spiritual teacher or master with the help of some similes from our everyday life in the world. He says:

> Sick people put themselves in the care of a skilful doctor. Travellers on dangerous paths entrust themselves to a courageous bodyguard. People afraid of enemies, robbers or wild beasts look to a companion for protection. Merchants heading for lands across the ocean entrust themselves to a captain. Wayfarers taking the ferry to cross a river entrust themselves to a boatman. In the same way, to be protected from death, rebirth and negative emotions, we must follow a teacher, a spiritual friend.[335]

And:

> He [the teacher] is the great ship carrying us
> beyond the seas of saṁsāric existence,
> The true unfailing navigator of the sublime path,
> The rain of nectar quenching the inferno
> of emotions and actions,
> The sun and moon dispelling the darkness of ignorance.
> He is the earth, immensely patient,
> The wish-granting tree, source of help and happiness,
> The perfect vase containing the treasure of the Dharma.
> He provides all things, more than a wish-granting gem.
> He is a father and mother, loving all equally.[336]

The famous Indian teacher Atīsha of Vikramashilā (CE 982–1054), also known as Dīpaṅkara, who spent his last ten years in Tibet revitalizing Buddhist teachings there, was once asked:

"For someone to achieve liberation and complete omniscience, which is more important – the canonical scriptures and their commentaries, or the oral instructions of the teacher?"

"The teacher's instructions," Atīsha replied.

"Why?"

"Because when it comes to doing the practice – even if you can explain the whole *Tripiṭaka* from memory and are very skilled in metaphysics – without the teacher's practical guidance you and the Dharma will part company."[337]

First one must be accepted by the teacher of his time in order to engage fruitfully in spiritual practice according to the master's instructions. As Patrul Rinpoche states:

Even if you start practicing the Dharma, unless you have been accepted by a spiritual friend it will be of no use.[338]

According to the Buddhist yogi Saraha, one's spiritual practice is doomed without a guru, and all the spiritual texts and treatises are of no avail. He says:

Whoever does not drink their fill
from the guru's nectarine instruction,
Which coolly clears all pain,
Will die exhausted, tormented by thirst
In the sorrowful desert of many treatises.[339]

Pabongka Rinpoche, in his "Discourse on the Path to Enlightenment", reiterates the indispensability of the guru and the futility of the scriptures without him. He says:

Some people think they can know the path by reading books and not have a guru, but this is not good enough – you must rely on a qualified guru.[340]

> If you are not properly devoted to the guru, you will not develop even the slightest realization into the stages of the path, no matter what practice you cultivate.... But if you devote yourself properly, you will soon attain the state of unification even though this (normally) requires many aeons to achieve.[341]

He refers to the following assurance by Nāgārjuna:

> If you receive beneficial teachings
> Through the kindness of the guru,
> You will still be liberated,
> Though you think, 'I shall not be.'[342]

The *Dhammapada*, one of the most well-known texts of early Buddhism, considered to be the words of the Buddha himself, also indicates the futility of sacrificial practices in contrast to devotedly following the instructions of a master who has perfected himself:

> Better than offering thousands of sacrifices
> Month after month for a hundred years
> Is one moment spent honouring one
> Who has perfected himself.[343]

Here, honouring the perfected one means devotedly following the instructions of a true or perfect master.

Thus, according to Buddhism it is absolutely essential to find a wise and compassionate guru and to follow his instructions most devotedly in order to avoid the dangers and pitfalls of the inner journey and safely reach the goal. That is why Gampopa lays stress on the following as "indispensable things":

> A guru capable of guiding thee on the Path of Emancipation is indispensable....

> Special instructions (by a wise guru) which will enable one to avoid misleading paths, temptations, pitfalls and dangers are indispensable.[344]

When we are sick we must go to a competent doctor who is available to us now. No past doctors, however competent they may have been, can treat us today. Likewise, no past Buddha can treat our spiritual sickness today. As Patrul Rinpoche puts it:

> When people are seriously ill, they go to consult a good doctor. They follow the doctor's advice, take whatever medicine he prescribes, and do all they can to overcome the disease and get well. In the same way, you should cure yourself of the diseases of karma, negative emotions and suffering by following the prescriptions of that experienced doctor, the authentic teacher, and by taking the medicine of the Dharma.[345]

He cites the following quotation from the *Sūtra Arranged like a Tree*:

> Noble one, you should think of yourself
>   as someone who is sick,
> Of the Dharma as the remedy,
> Of your spiritual friend as a skillful doctor
> And of diligent practice as the way to recovery.[346]

In a similar way Pabongka Rinpoche also says:

> We are most afraid if we are sick and the illness has already lasted a month or two. But we have suffered under the disease of delusion in beginningless saṁsāra until the present. It is impossible for us to recover from this disease until we manage to achieve liberation from cyclic existence.

Thus, the wise who strongly wish
to seek holy enlightenment
Should completely subjugate their pride.
Just as patients in order to be cured depend on doctors,
So should the seeker depend steadfastly
on a spiritual guide.[347]

In the *Lotus Sūtra* the Buddha is depicted as a great physician who appears in the world to provide the panacea for the chronic illness of ignorance, which is so widespread in this world:

> The all-knowing and kind-hearted Tathāgata, the unsurpassed One, appears as a great physician in the world, which is deluded by utter ignorance.[348]

The Necessity of a Living Teacher

When we speak of the indispensability of a spiritual teacher, we mean the indispensability of a living teacher, i.e., a master of our own time. We have already seen that Buddhas descend from the Dharmakāya and merge back into the same reality after they leave their body. They then become one with the supreme reality from which they have come. Their only purpose in coming to this world in the human form is to be accessible to the people of their time and to teach them the way to attain freedom from the vicious cycle of birth and death and to merge back into that reality. After completing their mission of mercy and compassion, these masters are no longer available to us to help and guide us. Hence, we need a living master, a spiritual guide of our time.

Only a human being can effectively communicate with another human being and help him or her understand the deep secrets of spirituality. Only a burning lamp can light another lamp.

In Buddhism it is clear that only a living guide can be a person's true protector, teacher and saviour. The necessity of practising with a living teacher of one's time is explained by Zen master Bassui, who was asked about an exemplary practitioner named Jizō, a famous bodhisattva primarily revered in East Asian Buddhism who is mentioned in the Buddhist scriptures:

> "In the sūtra of Jizō Bodhisattva it is written: 'The bodhisattva [Jizō] rises early each day and enters various meditations and various hells to free ordinary people from their suffering in the eras without a Buddha.' If these words mean that this is his skillful means for beings immersed in the six realms, those who wholeheartedly appeal to this bodhisattva will not fall into evil paths. But why would they seek enlightenment? People would simply appeal to Jizō for guidance. What do you think of this reasoning?"
>
> Bassui responded: "What is your purpose asking this question?"
>
> "For the sake of understanding the great matter of life and death."
>
> "Then why don't you ask Jizō Bodhisattva?"
>
> "I have only heard his name and seen his picture and statue. I have never seen his real body. How can I ask him?"
>
> "If he can't teach you of the great matter of life and death now, he is not the right teacher for this world today. If he isn't a good teacher for this present world, how can he guide you after you leave it?"[349]

Some people doubt or deny the necessity of a living master on the ground that the ultimate reality or God or the formless Dharmakāya Buddha can himself serve the purpose of a living teacher. Others hold the view that one of the past masters will continue to guide them for all times. And still others regard one of the scriptures or holy books to be their master. Buddhist masters try to extricate people from all these misleading beliefs.

If a past master who has attained Nirvāṇa (liberation) and merged back into the supreme reality and is thus inaccessible to us could help and guide us today, then we might as well depend directly on that inaccessible reality itself. In that case, there would have been no need for any master at any time. But if ever there was a need for a master in the past, and a master descended into the human form to fulfil that need, a similar need certainly exists in the present also. It would be absurd to think that the natural law has changed, and that a master will not appear today to fulfil the need of the present seekers. If a master is needed once, he is always needed.

In other words, if we deny the need for a contemporary master, we shall be compelled to deny the need for the advent of all masters of all times. But we cannot do so, because it is a fact that many masters have come, and Buddhist teachers emphasize that the transcendental Dharmakāya can be realized only by following the path shown and guided by a living Buddha or enlightened teacher.

The Buddha in human form can come only at a particular time and place. In our state of ignorance, however, we tend to remain fascinated with past masters and undermine the value of the present ones, though they are all essentially one and the same. It is no doubt true that the past teachers, as embodiments of the supreme reality, were most qualified to teach and guide the people of their own time, and that their lives were highly inspiring. But after merging back into the ultimate reality, they are not available *now* to teach and guide us.

The scriptures, which provide accounts of the life of the Buddha or other enlightened masters and contain their moral or spiritual teachings, cannot assume the role of a living teacher or be a substitute for him. It is only the compassionate living master who provides a concrete example for his disciples, responds to their queries and questions and provides them direct guidance and support. Scriptures or holy books certainly are helpful inasmuch as they arouse interest in spirituality and stimulate the desire to hear and know more about moral and spiritual teachings. One may get some moral guidance and inspiration from them, but being inanimate they cannot interact directly with people and respond to their present concerns and problems.

A picture or a statue, being lifeless, cannot guide us. Only living human beings can relate to, communicate with, teach and guide others. No relationship, including that of master and disciple, can be established between a dead and a living person. We can vaguely imagine past masters, but we can have no meaningful contact or communication with them because we are incapable of seeing and hearing them directly.

Pabongka Rinpoche explains that the Enlightened Ones descend now to the level of those who were not fortunate enough to receive instructions from Gautama Buddha during his lifetime and who seek spiritual instruction. He points out:

> Buddha manifested his body for us (in the supreme Nirmāṇakāya form) but we were not fortunate enough to receive Dharma teachings from him (in that aspect). We therefore need an enlightened body suited to our level of good fortune to teach us Dharma. Thus, the Victorious Ones in the ten directions emanate themselves as gurus for our sakes.[350]

Speaking of the fruit of relying on one's living guide, he gives the following quotation from the *Essence of Nectar*:

> When you properly rely on your spiritual guide,
> you will soon be liberated from cyclic existence.[351]

The Buddhas know this and are pleased when we properly devote ourselves to our gurus – the root of all health and happiness and the only means to free ourselves from the sufferings of saṁsāra [the cycle of birth and death] and the lower realms.[352]

Patrul Rinpoche also explains:

> The spiritual teacher is like the Buddha himself. He brings us the transmission of the Buddhas of the past, embodies for us the Buddhas of the present, and, through his teaching, is the source of the Buddhas of the future.[353]

People often have a strong sense of relationship with a past teacher. To help us to go beyond this tendency, Pabongka Rinpoche gives the example of Sadāprarudita, an eminent bodhisattva of the recent past who, until he met his own Guru, Dharmodgata, had no satisfaction even after meeting innumerable Buddhas in his inner visions. As Pabongka Rinpoche says:

> If we were to meet a Buddha, say, we would think, This Buddha is higher than my guru. This is a natural reaction, but Sadāprarudita saw countless Buddhas and was not satisfied; instead he searched for a guru [his own guru]. This is a vital point. If we do not meet a guru with whom we have a karmic relationship… we have missed the most beneficial thing of all.[354]

If we do not try to meet a master during our lifetime, we miss the rarest opportunity that human life offers and incur an incalculable loss.

Masters Are Always Present in the World

According to Buddhist tradition, many Buddhas and bodhisattvas are said to have come to this world at different times to help the people of their time realize their spiritual goal. If only one Buddha or bodhisattva could have helped all the human beings seeking enlightenment through the ages, there would have been no reason for a second Buddha or bodhisattva to come to this world. We know that patients of today cannot receive treatment from past physicians, however proficient they may have been. Likewise, the spiritual seekers of different times can obtain help and guidance only from the Buddha or bodhisattva of their own time.

People always need practical training in the discipline and active guidance in their spiritual practice. All this necessitates a continuous chain of living teachers and disciples. As Patrul Rinpoche says:

> Every meditation practice and training for the mind is passed on from teacher to student, and then internalized till it becomes an integral part of that person's experience. A truly qualified spiritual teacher must have actually attained realization.... This lineage has been passed on unbroken, from one realized teacher to the next, until the present day.[355]

Buddhism clearly indicates that the spiritual path or Dharma is not the invention or creation of a particular Buddha. The Dharma is ancient and eternal. Shākyamuni (Gautama Buddha) only discovered it and then taught it to others so that, by following it, they also could realize what he himself had realized. Many Buddhas came before him and many will come in the future. Thus, the spiritual path or Dharma is not dependent on any particular master, and no master claims to create or invent a new path or Dharma. The Buddha clearly says:

> I have, monks, seen an ancient path, an ancient way travelled by Enlightened Ones of former times.[356]

> It is by following this path that men crossed the ocean of existence in the past, cross it now and will cross it in the future.[357]

Indicating that this path is not dependent on him, the Buddha says:

> Whether the Buddha preaches the Dhamma to his disciples or does not preach it, it remains the same.[358]

That is why, referring to the *lam-rim* (steps on the path to enlightenment), Pabongka Rinpoche traces its origin to the lineage of illustrious masters starting with the Buddha himself. He says:

> Now, the *lam-rim* was not invented by Je Rinpoche (Lama Tsongkhapa), Atīsha, etc. Its lineage stems from the completely perfect Buddha himself.[359]

In the Buddhist tradition, great teachers, masters and Enlightened Ones are known to have emerged from time to time. Whilst humbly disclaiming the title of Buddha for themselves, many such teachers have been recognised by their disciples as enlightened masters. Many of these enlightened teachers or 'Buddhas' are said to have come to this world to help the people of their time realize their spiritual goal. All patients need the physician of their own time. Likewise, the spiritual seekers of different times can obtain help and guidance only from the enlightened guide or true teacher of their own time, and the world is never without these guides.

The Unbroken Chain of Living Teachers

In this imperfect world, no one can become perfect unless united with the Perfect One, the ultimate reality, the foundation of all. Some Buddhist masters call this Perfect One the 'Primordial Buddha' (Ādi-Buddha) or 'All-Goodness' (Samanta-Bhadra). In other traditions people use the term 'God' for this same highest reality. In different languages and traditions, different names are used, but this transcendental reality is ultimately beyond all thought and speech.

According to this Buddhist interpretation, the Primordial Buddha, who is all goodness, the storehouse of infinite compassion and the foundation of all, precedes all the Buddhas, including Gautama Buddha. All the Buddhas are said to have descended from the one Primordial Buddha. Hence, they are considered the embodiments of the Primordial Buddha.

W. Y. Evans-Wentz points out that the radiating love and compassion of an enlightened master brings benefit to the whole world:

> Even as the sun ripens the corn and the fruits of the earth, so do the Enlightened Ones, by emitting upon the saṁsāra the radiances of their all-embracing Love and Compassion, cause the growth and maturity of the Bodhic essence which is implanted in all living things.[360]

Since all true Buddhas have realized the same reality, they are all considered essentially one – the same Supreme Being. The *Lotus Sūtra* says:

> He [the Buddha] always keeps coming to the world and conducts himself according to the circumstances. He indeed is the Supreme Lord, the Lord of Dharma, and also Lord among the greatest of the world.[361]

Speaking of the true spiritual teacher, Patrul Rinpoche explains:

> The spiritual teacher is like the Buddha Himself. He brings us the transmission of the Buddhas of the past, embodies for us the Buddhas of the present and, through his teaching, is the source of the Buddhas of the future.[362]

> This teacher in whom all the attributes are complete is the embodiment of the compassionate wisdom of all Buddhas of the ten directions, appearing in the form of an ordinary human simply to benefit beings.... A teacher with all these qualities is like a great ship in which to cross the ocean of saṁsāra. Like a navigator, he unfailingly charts out for us the route to liberation and omniscience. Like a downpour of nectar, he extinguishes the blaze of negative actions and emotions. Like the sun and moon, he radiates the light of Dharma and disperses the thick darkness of ignorance. Like the earth, he patiently bears all ingratitude and discouragement, and encompasses in the breadth of his mind the vastness of view and action. Like the wish-granting tree, he is the source of all help in this life and all happiness in the next.[363]

Pabongka Rinpoche also says:

> He is by nature all Buddhas. You must become convinced that the guru is an entity that includes all the Buddhas' primal wisdom embodied in the one physical form.[364]

And for this reason he says:

> You must therefore rely on a fully qualified spiritual guide.[365]

Since a Buddha is one with the supreme reality, he is considered the greatest being. None can exceed his powers. In the early Pali Canon, Shāriputra, a highly accomplished disciple of the Buddha, spoke of the greatness of the Buddha in his very presence in the following way:

> I have such conviction in the Exalted One that I think that there never was, nor would ever be, nor is now a recluse or

> brahmin who may excel the Exalted One in respect of higher knowledge.[366]

The Buddha asked Shāriputra how, without knowing all the past, present and future masters, he could make such a grand and bold statement. Shāriputra explained this by comparing the highest knowledge with a king's fortress which has only one door, so that anyone entering it must use the same door, and reach the same fortress.[367] Thus, the way and the goal being the same, there may be equals of a perfect master, but none can be superior to him at any time. The Buddha approved of Shāriputra's explanation.[368]

The statement that one must seek a true spiritual teacher of his time can be meaningful only if such teachers are always present in the world. This is exactly the case according to Buddhism.

In the *Lotus Sūtra*, the Buddha explains that he himself had to undergo training previously under many past masters, aside from those in his present life:

> Formerly, in the company of many Buddhas, I have followed the course which is profound, subtle, difficult to know and difficult to see.[369]

Then speaking of the endless succession of masters who shall "follow one another in regular succession", the Buddha declares:

> Moved by benevolence and compassion they shall in succession foretell each other's destiny, saying, "This one is to be my immediate successor, and he is to command the world as I do at present."[370]

Patrul Rinpoche notes that the teacher-disciple relationship has continued unbroken from the earliest time to the present day.[371] And he reiterates this point, saying:

> In fact, each century (including the present one) and each generation has produced its share of spiritual giants.[372]

Thus, the path to freedom is always made available to sincere seekers. Gampopa points out:

> The fact that there are Those who have attained Bodhic Enlightenment and are able to return to the world as Divine Incarnations and work for the deliverance of mankind and of all living things till the time of the dissolution of the physical universe showeth the virtue of the Holy Dharma....
>
> It is great joy to realize that the Path to Freedom which all the Buddhas have trodden is ever-existent, ever unchanged, and ever open to those who are ready to enter upon it.[373]

According to Buddhism at least one master is always present in the world. As Pabongka Rinpoche points out:

> There must be (at least) one emanation of the Buddha among them [the people of the world].[374]

An important point should be noted here: since a true master is not limited to his physical body, he continues to provide protection to his disciples even after his physical death, as is illustrated by the Buddha's words to his devoted disciple Ānanda.

The Buddha was seriously ill three months before his death. When he recovered, Ānanda told him that he had been so worried and upset due to the Buddha's illness that he could not take interest even in the Dhamma (spiritual practice). Thereupon the Buddha said:

> What, Ānanda, does the order of monks expect of me? The Dhamma has been taught by me, Ānanda, without making any

> distinction between exoteric and esoteric.... Surely, Ānanda, if there were anyone who were to harbour the thought that he should lead the order or that the order is dependent on him, he would indeed give guidance on anything concerning the order. But the Tathāgata thinks that he is not that one.... Therefore, Ānanda, live with the lamp kindled unto yourself, take refuge unto yourself and seek no other refuge. Hold fast to the Dhamma as a lamp, the Dhamma as a refuge and no other refuge.[375]

Here the Buddha indicates that those who have been accepted by him as his disciples should have no worry. They have no need to take refuge in any other teacher. They should only practise most intently the Dharma taught by him and try to kindle light within themselves.

At the time of his passing away, the Buddha again exhorts his disciples to rely fully on his teachings and follow them most faithfully, because his teachings alone will serve as their guide. As he says to Ānanda:

> It may be, Ānanda, that after my passing away you might think: "Gone is the utterance of my master; we have no master anymore." But you should not think so, Ānanda, for the doctrine [*dhamma*] and discipline [*vinaya*] which I have taught to you and prescribed for you will be your master [guide] after my death.[376]

The Teacher's Responsibility

The responsibility that a true master takes on is indeed very serious. He and he alone is capable of undertaking and fulfilling such a serious responsibility. He lovingly takes upon himself the charge of liberating his disciples from the vicious cycle of birth and death. In fact, it is precisely for this purpose that he, in his wisdom and compassion, descends to this world of suffering from his blissful abode. As we have noted, the Buddha stated the purpose for which he came to the world:

> I am the Tathāgata, the Blessed One, the Unconquerable. I have taken birth in this world for the sake of saving others.[377]

Pabongka Rinpoche points out the compassion with which the Buddhas perform their mission:

> The Buddhas unmistakably know the situation of all sentient beings, love them even more than a mother loves her only child and always do their utmost to carry out good works. How could they not be working for our sakes with present times the way they are?... All the Buddhas would not callously abandon us by not working for our sakes. They most surely do so.[378]

The *Lotus Sūtra* offers a parable to explain the mission of a master. In this story the Buddha explains that he descended from his blissful abode to this world in human form in search of his son, who, not knowing his father and his glorious origin, is lost here. The son is wandering in this world, working as a menial servant and living in a wretched condition. The Buddha, depicted here as a fabulously wealthy man, comes to meet his son in the guise of an ordinary labourer and gradually wins his confidence and respect.

In the course of time, he inculcates in his son all the necessary virtues and finally encourages him to come to his splendorous palace. To the utter amazement of the son, he discovers that his labourer friend is no other than the owner of the palace, which is full of treasures. He is amazed to see that he is being warmly welcomed as the wealthy man's own son and is the inheritor of all his treasure.[379]

A true master teaches us the way to liberation and exhorts us to follow his teachings most faithfully. When we follow the teachings in earnest, we are led to liberation. It is through the practice of the master's teachings, which he gives to others on the basis of his own inner experience, that disciples are liberated. Masters apply no force, display no public miracle and adopt no other means. As Pabongka Rinpoche explains:

> The Great Ones do not wash away sin with water;
> They do not rid beings of suffering
> with the touch of their hands;
> They do not transfer their realizations of Suchness [the ultimate reality] onto others.
> They liberate by teaching the truth of Suchness.[380]

True teachers do not make public displays of their powers, as is evident from the following story. Once a person named Sunakshatra, who had recently joined the order of the Buddha, came to inform the Buddha that he was no longer following the noble path because the Buddha was not displaying any supernatural miracles. The Buddha asked if he had requested that Sunakshatra join the order, or if he had promised to display some miracles if the latter joined the order. Sunakshatra naturally replied 'no' to both questions. Then the Buddha further asked if Sunakshatra had ever said that he was joining the Buddha's order to witness miracles. Again, Sunakshatra said 'no' to the Buddha. Finally, the Buddha asked Sunakshatra if the accomplishment of the purpose of the noble path had anything to do with the Buddha's displaying or not displaying supernatural miracles. Sunakshatra replied 'no' to this final question as well. Thereupon the Buddha remarked:

> Why should I then display any miracle if the purpose of the noble path leading to complete cessation of suffering is fully accomplished whether or not I display any miracle?[381]

The true miracle – if it is to be called a miracle – is that the Buddha opens the eyes of a disciple to a path which, if practised diligently and faithfully, leads to complete cessation of suffering. In addition, the Tathāgata, the true master who has undertaken the responsibility of liberating his disciples, will be with them at the most crucial hour of their life, namely, death. He appears before them and takes them to Sukhāvatī, his Blissful Abode. As the Buddha, in the *Larger Sukhāvatī-Vyūha*, explains to his close attendant and disciple Ānanda:

> And before the eyes of those beings, O Ānanda, who again and again think of the Tathāgata reverently, and who make the great and unmeasured stock of good works grow, turning their thought towards Bodhi, and who pray to be born in that world, Amitābha, the Tathāgata, holy and fully enlightened, when the time of their death has approached, will appear.... And then these beings, having seen the Bhagavat [Blessed One], their thoughts filled with joy, will, when they have died, be born in that world of Sukhāvatī.[382]

The responsibility that a master undertakes and fulfils is mostly incomprehensible to the unenlightened. Even to those disciples who have not yet been able to go within and see the help and support their master provides, and the mercy and compassion he showers upon them, it may seem incredible.

The Disciple's Attitude

The work of the enlightened teacher inspires inexpressible gratitude in his disciples. From his blissful abode the teacher comes down in a human form and lives on earth amidst all kinds of difficulties for his disciples' benefit. He has no selfish purpose of his own. He leaves no stone unturned to awaken, teach, guide and accompany his disciples, constantly protecting and showering his grace upon all through the inner regions up to his ultimate blissful abode. This is all out of his sheer love and compassion. Can anyone be a greater benefactor than the master?

Disciples might ask themselves this question: should we not do anything we can to facilitate the master's work, which he is doing precisely for our sake? Does it not behove us to do our part to the best of our ability, howsoever little we may be capable of contributing in our limitation? To practise the spiritual discipline enjoined upon us must be taken to be our necessary duty, and this indeed is of paramount concern to us as disciples. In this respect our attitude towards our teacher and his teachings is crucial.

The master untiringly imparts his teachings to his disciples all his life, exhorting them to put his teachings into practice, for the sole purpose of enabling them to attain their salvation. It is the disciple's sacred duty to carry on the spiritual practice as prescribed by the master with utmost sincerity. This is the real worship of a revered master. In the Buddha's last words to his close disciple Ānanda, when the Buddha was being honoured with flowers and sandalwood powder at the time of his passing away, this is precisely what the Buddha said:

> Although, Ānanda, all these offerings are made in honour of the Tathāgata, it is not thus that the Tathāgata is rightly honoured, venerated, revered and worshipped. If monks, nuns, and lay disciples were to live in accordance with my teachings and strictly follow my teachings, they would be honouring me and venerating me rightly, and paying me true respect and true reverence. Therefore, Ānanda, you should act according to my teaching, following all the instructions, and it should be so taught to others. This would be the highest worship, which would please me most.[383]

For the spiritual practice to be fruitful, it is essential to develop proper devotion for the guide. This is why Pabongka Rinpoche says:

> The best means of pleasing your spiritual guide is to offer him your practice of his instructions.[384]

> First you should devote yourself properly to a spiritual guide and put into practice the instructions he gives you.[385]

Since the disciple is ignorant and the teacher is wise, the disciple is weak and the teacher is all-powerful, the disciple is lost and the teacher can guide, it is essential to approach the guide with utmost humility and follow his instructions with faith and devotion, without which the disciple can make no progress. Gampopa points out:

> It is useless to have lived, even for a very long time, with a spiritual preceptor if one be lacking in humility and devotion and thus be unable to develop spiritually....
>
> For him whose humility and faith with respect to his guru are unshakeable, it is the same whether he dwell with his guru or not.[386]

Longchenpa says:

> Seeing your guru as a Buddha should be your primary path; without any other approach, the signs of success and auspicious circumstances on the path will be subverted.[387]

It is indeed a regrettable mistake to look upon an enlightened teacher as a mere human being. As Patrul Rinpoche points out:

> To meet a perfect teacher
> Is more valuable than gaining a kingdom.

Look how those with no devotion
Treat the teacher as their equal![388]

Presenting the teaching of Nāropa, the renowned Tibetan Buddhist master of the eleventh century, Herbert Guenther states:

It is a maxim of the guru-disciple relation that the guru must never be conceived of in mere human form.[389]

A hallmark of all disciples' experience of their teacher is that at some point they experience the living master as more than a mere human being, and the attitude of reverence then arises spontaneously. We have already noted how the brahmin Droṇa was awe-struck at the very sight of the Buddha. The legend of the adoption of the Buddha's noble path by the notorious robber Aṅgulimāla offers another striking example of the sublime power of the physical presence of the Buddha.

Aṅgulimāla – 'one who wears a garland of fingers' – was a notorious robber and murderer who was called by this name because he used to wear a garland of the fingers of people whom he had killed. He created great havoc in the kingdom of King Prasenjit during the time the Buddha stayed near the capital of that kingdom. One day the Buddha set out along the path which led towards the dangerous area inhabited by Aṅgulimāla, and many of those who saw the Buddha going that way tried repeatedly to dissuade him from proceeding along that path. But the Buddha continued. The *Majjhima Nikāya* narrates this episode in detail, and we give here a gist of the incident by quoting a few passages:

The robber Aṅgulimāla saw the Blessed One coming in the distance. On seeing him, it occurred to him: "Indeed it is wonderful, indeed it is marvellous. This is a road along which ten or twenty or thirty or forty or fifty men set out only after they have formed organized groups, and even then they fall victim to me. And now this recluse is coming along undauntedly without a companion. Surely, I shall take away his life."

The robber Aṅgulimāla, having taken up his sword and shield, and having armed himself with bow and quiver, followed close after the Blessed One.

Then the Blessed One made such a wondrous display of power that the robber Aṅgulimāla, although running with all his strength, was not able to catch up with the Blessed One, who was walking at a normal pace. The robber Aṅgulimāla thought: "Indeed it is wonderful, indeed it is marvellous. Although formerly I could attack and seize a running elephant ... a running horse ... a running chariot ... yet now I am not able to catch up with this recluse who is walking at a normal pace." Standing still, he shouted at the Blessed One: "Stand still, recluse; stand still, recluse." The Buddha, while continuing to walk, said: "I am standing still, Aṅgulimāla; you too stand still." ...

Then the robber Aṅgulimāla spoke out thus to the Blessed One: "While you are walking, recluse, you say, 'I am standing still' and you tell me, who am standing still, that I am not standing still! I ask you, recluse, about this matter. How is it that you are standing still, yet I am not standing still?" The Buddha explained: "I am always standing still, Aṅgulimāla, having laid aside the stick against all beings. But you are unrestrained towards living beings. Therefore, I am standing still [at peace]; you are not standing still [not at peace]."[390]

The Buddha's simple and yet piercing words penetrated Aṅgulimāla's heart. He threw away his sword and other weapons, prostrated himself at the Buddha's feet, and begged to be accepted as his disciple. Later, King Prasenjit was astonished when he visited the Buddha and saw Aṅgulimāla sitting near him as an obedient disciple. He exclaimed in amazement:

> It is wonderful, Lord, it is marvellous, Lord, how the Lord tames the untamed, calms the uncalmed.... The one whom I could not control, Lord, with rod or weapon, the same has been controlled by the Lord without rod or weapon![391]

Such was the graceful yet powerful influence of the Buddha. The Buddha, if he so wished, could prevail even upon the most confused or violent human beings and bring them into his fold.

The Disciple's Duty

Longchenpa advises that it is essential to devote oneself both to the teacher and to the spiritual practice:

> Six pieces of advice are given on what is entirely sufficient:
>
> One lifetime is entirely sufficient – make that decision here and now.
> One means of spiritual development is entirely sufficient – treat your guru as a Buddha.
> One activity is entirely sufficient – practise focusing on your guru as a Buddha.
> One kind of training is entirely sufficient – give up activities that are not spiritual.
> One means of direct introduction is entirely sufficient – receive introduction to the true nature of mental activity.
> One practical method is entirely sufficient – maintain an ongoing awareness of Suchness itself.
>
> If you heed this advice, supreme bliss will swiftly be yours.[392]

A master is immensely pleased to see that his disciples are doing their duty with utmost sincerity and earnestness. If a disciple takes one step towards him, he takes many steps towards the disciple. No master will suddenly launch his disciples to the highest heaven. The disciples must participate in the process of purification by doing their part. The master says: There is a channel to give and a channel to receive. His teaching, guidance and the continuous showering of his grace and blessings constitute his way or channel of giving. Listening to his teachings intently; practising the prescribed disciplines faithfully; remembering him constantly with devotion; realizing who he really is; remaining in complete obedience to him; and rendering service with utmost dedication in thought, word and deed constitute the disciple's way or channel of receiving his grace and bounty.

In the course of an unimaginably long chain of lives in various forms of species, a person collects heavy layers of karmic burden. These layers are removed with the help of regular and devoted spiritual practice as prescribed by the master. When the disciple is thus gradually purified, and the vessel of his heart is clean and pure, the guru will automatically pour into it his purest and rarest gift. The guru's help and protection are always there, and without this assistance, no one could ever purify himself.

A true teacher and guide is a perfect being. He never delays, falters or fails in fulfilling his responsibilities and granting his gifts. It is only we who, weak and imperfect as we are, become slack, falter and fail many a time. Yet he does not give up on us. He lifts us and helps us resume our way. Much emphasis is laid on the necessity for us to make our best efforts to do our duty, while at the same time realizing that the mountain is moved not so much by our limited efforts as by the guru's unbounded grace and blessings.

Explaining to a brahmin why some of the Buddha's disciples succeed in attaining Nirvāṇa in this very life, whereas others fall short of reaching the goal, the Buddha points out to him that this is so because some disciples are ever vigilant and earnest, while others are slack and slothful in their spiritual practice. He says:

> Nibbāna is the same, the same is the path leading to Nibbāna, and the same also am I, the teacher. Yet, some of my disciples put my teachings into practice with proper earnestness and dedication and attain Nibbāna, while others don't do so. What can I do, O Brahmin? The Tathāgata is only the guide, O Brahmin [who can only assist the traveller on the path].[393]

Spirituality is cultivated by practice, and one cannot have it without sincere efforts. A disciple who is slack or negligent in attending to his spiritual duties may find fault with the guru or the path, but he has none but himself to blame. Patrul Rinpoche explains this point:

> The Dharma is nobody's property. It belongs to whoever is the most interested. The Buddha himself obtained the teachings at the price of hundreds of hardships.[394]

Some people, he says, mistakenly think:

> The teacher, in his compassion, will toss them up into the heavenly realms as if he were throwing a pebble. But when we speak of the teacher holding us with his compassion, what this really means is that he has lovingly accepted us as disciples, and that he gives us his profound instructions, opens our eyes to what to do and what not to do, and shows us the way to liberation taught by the Conqueror. What greater compassion could there be? It is up to us whether or not we take advantage of this compassion and actually pursue the path of liberation.... It is crucial that we choose between saṁsāra and Nirvāṇa once and for all and put the instructions of our teacher into practice.[395]

He continues:

> Following a teacher without doing what he says is like disobeying your doctor, which leaves him no chance of treating your illness. Not taking the medicine of the Dharma – that is to say, not putting it into practice – is like having innumerable medications and prescriptions beside your bed but never touching them. That will never cure your disease.[396]

As the *Samādhirāja Sūtra* reminds us:

> Yet the patient does not take this most wholesome
> And precious medicine, the potential cure.
> Do not blame the doctor;
> The medicine's not at fault.
> Rather, the patient himself is to blame.[397]

And Pabongka Rinpoche therefore concludes:

> It is entirely up to you whether you practise your guru's instructions and teachings. You should strive to make your optimum human rebirth something meaningful and integrate the Dharma into your life right to the very end.[398]

Dharma is no small matter. In Buddhism it is considered 'the great matter of life and death'. Finding a master is not enough. The disciple also has to set his priorities according to the Dharma. Zen Master Bassui Tokushō teaches:

> An ancient [the ninth-century Zen master Sozan Honjaku] said: "To care for this matter as your own, be like a man who, passing through a village that has been infected with destructive rice worms, will not even wet his throat with a drop of water – then you will attain it."[399]

Practising the teachings with an attitude of acceptance and receptivity towards the teacher and his teachings is crucial. Dōgen Zenji says in *Points to Watch in Practicing the Way* (*Gakudō-yōjin-shu*):

> Clarifying the dharma and attaining the Way comes about by the power gained from practice under an enlightened teacher; just listen to his words without twisting them to fit your own views. As long as you base your interpretation of your teacher's words on your own views, your teacher's dharma will be beyond reach. When you practice with a teacher and receive instructions on the dharma, purify your body and mind, open your ears and eyes. Just listen to your teacher's dharma and accept it without judging it by your sentiments. Your body and mind must be one; [receive the teacher's dharma] as if pouring water [from one vessel] to another. If you are like this, you will not fail to attain his dharma.[400]

And in the *Shōbōgenzō-Zuimonki*, Dōgen Zenji emphasizes the same idea:

> Many people in the world say that though they listen to the words of their teachers, they are not in accord with their thinking. This attitude is a mistake. I don't understand how they can say such things. Do they say it is because the principles in the sacred teachings do not agree with what they think, and believe the teachings to be wrong? If so, they are utterly foolish. Or is it that what the teacher says does not agree with their own preferences? If so, why do they ask the teacher in the first place? Or do they say it on the basis of their own ordinary discriminating thoughts? If so, this is illusionary thought from the beginningless beginning. The vital attitude in learning the Way is to give up and reform your egotistical views. Even if they go against

> your own preferences, if they are your teacher's words or statements from the sacred scriptures, you must follow them completely. This is an essential point you should be careful about in learning the Way.[401]

The disciple is to accept the teacher's actions and words – and take no offence at the master's scoldings or admonitions. Patrul Rinpoche says:

> If your teacher appears angry,
> conclude that he has seen a fault in you,
> Ripe for correction with his rebukes.
> Confess and vow never to repeat it.
> Thus, be wise and do not fall under the power
> of Māra [the Tempter].[402]

Drogön Tsangpa Gyare also says:

> A hard scolding is like a wrathful mantra
> That removes every hindrance.[403]

We have already noted that Pabongka Rinpoche calls this devotion to one's spiritual guide "the root of the path", and considers it "vital to devote ourselves to our spiritual guide at the outset".[404] Love and devotion for the guru are essential for success in the spiritual practice.

Atīsha, the reputed Indian master who made great impact on the development of Tibetan Buddhism, used to say that any good qualities he had were due to his guru. Commenting on this statement of Atīsha, Pabongka Rinpoche says:

> He meant that we obtain all our good qualities through the guru's kindness.[405]

One is able to develop perfection in wisdom only through devotion to the guru, which in turn evokes the guru's grace and blessings. As Patrul Rinpoche puts it:

> All the ways in which wisdom develops in the perfection phase depend only on the power of your devotion to your teacher and of his blessings.[406]

Geshe Kharak Gomchung says that all study of scriptures is useless without devotion to the master:

> You may know the whole Tripiṭaka, but without devotion to your teacher that will be of no use to you.[407]

When one's devotion to the guru becomes intense and deep, it purifies the devotee's heart, so much so that the devotee imbibes the qualities of the guru. This is known as 'Guru Yoga'. As Patrul Rinpoche states:

> Finally comes the Guru Yoga, uniting one's mind with the mind of the teacher ... where the purity of the link between teacher and disciple is of paramount importance.[408]

> The devotional practice of Guru Yoga is the only way to awaken within you the realization of the uncontrived natural state. No other method will work.[409]

> The Guru Yoga is the essence of all paths.... Total openness and devotion to a realized teacher is the most sure and rapid way to progress.[410]

In Mahāyāna Buddhism, the guru is sometimes referred to as Kalyāṇa-Mitra, which means 'that friend (*mitra*) who secures our ultimate good or salvation (*kalyāṇa*)'. Without his grace and guidance, it is impossible to gain success in completing the spiritual journey and fulfilling the unique opportunity of human life. That is why Shāntideva in his *Bodhicharyāvatāra* says:

> Even for the sake of one's life, one should
> never abandon one's Kalyāṇa-Mitra.[411]

Concerning obedience to the master, Patrul Rinpoche repeatedly emphasizes this point. He says:

> The teacher whom you have met by the power of your past actions, and whose kindness you have received, is the most important of all.... Obey him in all things and disregard all hardships, heat, cold, hunger, thirst and so on. Pray to him with faith and devotion. Ask his advice on whatever you may be doing. Whatever he tells you, put it into practice, relying on him totally.[412]

> You should obey his every instruction, praying to him from the very depths of your heart and considering him to be a real Buddha.[413]

Again he emphasizes the importance of obedience:

> Consider every word of your sublime teacher as the Jewel of the Dharma. Accept everything he says without disobeying a single point.[414]

> There is no greater Dharma practice than obeying one's teacher. The benefits are immense, as we can see here. On the other hand, to disobey him, even a little, is an extremely grave fault.[415]

Disciples do well to emulate their teacher in practising the same unshakeable determination which the Buddha exhibited in trying to achieve his spiritual goal. If disciples maintain their determination, they are sure to attain success, as did the Buddha. The firm resolve with which the Buddha sat in meditation under the peepal tree is described in the *Lalitavistara* in these words ascribed to him:

> My body may dry up, my skin, bones and flesh may be totally destroyed, yet my body shall not move from this posture without attaining enlightenment, so hard to attain even in many aeons.[416]

Explaining how determined disciples should act in serving their spiritual teacher, and the result of their obedience, Patrul Rinpoche says:

> A courageous disciple, armoured with the determination never to displease his teacher even at the cost of his life, stable-minded enough not to be shaken by immediate circumstances, who serves his teacher without caring about his own health or survival and obeys his every command without sparing himself at all – such a person will be liberated simply through his devotion to the teacher.[417]

The best service to one's teacher consists in putting his teachings into practice. But disciples also please their master by rendering service to him through body, mind and wealth. Patrul Rinpoche outlines the three levels of service:

> There are three ways to please the teacher and serve him. The best way is known as the offering of practice, and consists of putting whatever he teaches into practice with determination, disregarding all hardship. The middling way is known as service with body and speech, and involves serving him and doing whatever he needs you to do whether physically, verbally or mentally. The lowest way is by material offerings, which means

to please your teacher by giving him material goods, food, money and so forth.[418]

Patrul Rinpoche says that by serving the teacher most sincerely in these three ways, the disciples bring their mind in unison with their master's. He urges us therefore to try our best to do this:

> While we have him here in person, we must try our best to do whatever he says and to unite our minds with his through the three kinds of service.[419]

The master is the all in all for true disciples, and hence disciples should be prepared to offer or surrender their all to him. As Patrul Rinpoche says:

> You should be so generous that you can give the teacher whatever you possess.[420]

Discrimination in Finding a Fully Enlightened Master

Dōgen Zenji speaks of the importance of finding a true teacher: in his *Points to Watch in Practicing the Way* (*Gakudō-yōjin-shu*):

> The practice of the Way depends solely upon whether your teacher is true or false. A practitioner is a piece of good timber, while a teacher is a carpenter. The beauty of a piece of fine timber will not come out without good craftsmanship. Even warped timber manifests its own usefulness when worked out by skilled hands. It should be clear through this analogy that whether you truly attain realization or not depends upon if your teacher is right or wrong.[421]

Only a true master can extricate people from the cycle of birth and death. A seeker of truth needs to guard against imposters who assume the role of enlightened teachers due to their own misconceptions, or to gain respect and honour, or to satisfy their greed for wealth and power. The ninth-century root teacher of the lineage of Patrul Rinpoche, Padmasambhāvā, also known as Guru Rinpoche, describes the challenge for those who seek liberation:

> In the future, when the dark age of degeneration arrives, some people who claim to be practitioners will desire to teach others without having received permission. Without having practised themselves they will instruct others in meditation. Without being liberated themselves they will pretend to give instructions for liberation. Without being devoid of self-interest they will instruct others to cast away their fetters of attachment and be generous. Without the slightest understanding of the good or evil of their own actions they will spout clairvoyant statements about good or evil fare of others. Having no stability themselves they will claim to be benefiting other beings. I think there will be many who will pretend, be hypocritical, cheat, and deceive in the name of the Dharma. All people of future generations who wish to practise the Dharma, read this written testament of the mendicant Padmakara and examine yourself![422]

It is wise to be cautious in selecting one's master, because true teachers are rare and hard to find, while imposters are many and easily found. While it is essential to find a true master, one cannot afford to act in haste, because the stakes are very high. A true master alone will lead his disciples to the supreme state of blessedness.

Indicating the disastrous consequences of following a false master and the happy outcome of having a true master, the Buddha compares a false or unenlightened teacher with a foolish cowherd who, while taking his cattle across the flooded river, drowns them in midstream; whereas an enlightened master is like a competent cowherd who, knowing the right place to ford, takes his cattle safely across. The Buddha then adds:

> Whoever thinks the incompetent recluses or brahmins are worth hearing and worth placing faith in, that will be for their woe and suffering for a long time.... Contrariwise, whoever thinks the competent recluses or brahmins* are worth listening to and worth believing in, that will be for their welfare and happiness for a long time.[423]

Zen master Bassui Tokushō speaks of the challenge of finding a true master in *Mud and Water*:

> People searching for a master should first clearly discern whether his way is truly the way of the Buddha and also discern the truth or fallacy of his attainment. If the teacher is a person who has definitely understood the great Way, spare neither life nor fortune – go to him and receive his personal teaching. A truly good teacher, when speaking of the Dharma of karmic change, does not destroy people's sight. He points directly to their minds, showing them their true nature and inducing the attainment of Buddhahood.[424]
>
> Trying to perceive the great Dharma from one's narrow viewpoint is like a mosquito trying to bite an iron cow. Clearly, one who tries to discriminate between a teacher of false views and a true teacher through his own feelings is like one who tries to light up heaven with the light of a firefly. How can he ever come close to proper discernment? It is very difficult to teach one who

*This is what the Buddha means here by a brahmin: "Him I call a brahmin who is steeped in meditation, free from passions and steadfast in posture; who has accomplished what has to be accomplished, is free from blemishes and has attained the highest aim. (*Dhammapada* 386)

> has not yet clearly opened the eye of the Way, the difference between the fallacious and the authentic Buddhadharma or a good and a bad teacher. It's like trying to teach the difference between black and white to one who has been blind from birth. Even though one may say he understands the words to some extent, can he really be in complete agreement? If I may venture to say, however, the mind of the Buddha and ancestors has been passed down through the ages, so you should only believe persons who [are not self-proclaimed gurus but] receive the seal of transmission from a good teacher certified in his attainment. The true teacher is one who has seen into his own nature. One who gives sermons while not having seen into his own nature is a false teacher.[425]

Master Bassui then speaks of the great value and rarity of finding a true teacher:

> Bodhidharma* said: "He who makes practice and theory one is an ancestral teacher." Meeting a great master who is certified by a virtuous teacher, has coordinated body and mind, for whom meditation and precepts are equally understood ... who has attained the true Buddha Way, and in whom the gathering of disciples as numerous as the sands does not arouse pride, is as rare as the *udonge* flower,† which blossoms only once in three thousand years. You should risk all, even your life, searching for such a teacher.[426]

If someone deceives us in matters of the world, we may take the loss with some discomfort and may even be able to make up

* Bodhidharma (c. sixth century CE) was the Buddhist monk traditionally credited with bringing to China the teachings that came to be known as Ch'an (Zen).

† The *ficus racemosa*, also called the *udumbara* flower, is often mentioned in Buddhist writings. Because the flower of this plant is difficult to see, the myth arose that it bloomed so rarely.

for the loss. But if people are duped by a false master regarding the true path to liberation, they are deprived of the very rare opportunity of attaining the ultimate goal of enlightenment. That is why Patrul Rinpoche warns of imperfect teachers who try to impart the gift of Dharma to others. He says:

> It is quite difficult to really make the gift of Dharma to others. To expound a teaching to others without having experienced it oneself will not help them at all.[427]
>
> It is useless for a beginner with neither experience nor realization to try to help others with the Dharma. No blessings can be obtained from him, just as nothing can be poured out of an empty vessel.[428]

He then admonishes these imperfect teachers:

> To be the guide and teacher of others,
> Not having yourself reached liberation's shore,
> Is as contradictory as giving your hand to someone drowning,
> While you yourself are being swept away by the flood.[429]

He goes on to warn seekers against relying on false masters, which he calls a "fatal mistake":

> To rely on a false spiritual friend without having examined him properly is to waste the merits you have spent your whole life accumulating, and to throw away the good fortune of having obtained the freedoms and advantages of a human existence. It is a fatal mistake.[430]

It is therefore of crucial importance that a seeker uses discrimination and makes a thorough examination of a master and his teachings before taking him for his master. The Buddha himself gives some suggestions for examining a master and his teachings. He advises that a seeker, who has no capacity to know another's mind, should examine the Tathāgata in two ways, namely, by means of seeing and hearing.

One should ascertain that the Tathāgata is not seen or heard to have impure or even partially impure conduct, but is found to have only pure conduct. Then he should examine further whether he has been so for a long time past or only recently. After he is satisfied from what he has seen and heard that the Tathāgata has long been endowed with pure conduct, he should further enquire if he is uniformly so, despite his reputation or fame, for blemishes are likely to arise when a monk gains fame and reputation.

Then he should further investigate whether he has taken to holy life out of fear and attachment or because of being freed from them. Then one should approach a teacher in order to listen to his doctrines. Then, as he listens to the noble and excellent doctrines being explained in a clear way, he gains more and more confidence in the doctrine. When he realizes the truth of some of the teachings in the light of his own higher knowledge, his faith in that teacher is firmly fixed.[431]

Speaking to the people of Kalama, the Buddha says:

> Do not go by revelation; do not go by tradition; do not go by hearsay; do not go on the authority of sacred texts; do not go on the grounds of pure logic; do not go by a view that seems rational; do not go by reflecting on mere appearances; do not go along with a considered view because you agree with it; do not go along on the grounds that the person is competent; do not go along because [you think] 'the recluse is our teacher'. Kalamas, when you yourselves know: 'These things are unwholesome; these things are blameworthy; these things are censured by the wise; and when observed and undertaken, these things lead to

> harm and ill, abandon them.... Kalamas, when you know for yourselves: These are wholesome; these things are not blameworthy; these things are praised by the wise; these things, when observed and undertaken, lead to benefit and happiness; having undertaken them, abide in them.[432]

The great adept Atīsha took a long journey of thirteen months to Indonesia to make a personal enquiry into the master Suvarṇadvīpī, about whom he had heard in India. He made a thorough examination of the life of that Guru before accepting him as his master. Referring to Atīsha's critical and careful attitude, Pabongka Rinpoche remarks:

> He [Atīsha] was setting us an example: we must properly investigate a guru first.[433]

Patrul Rinpoche indicates the consequence of not carefully investigating a spiritual teacher:

> By not examining a teacher with great care,
> The faithful waste their gathered merit.
> Like taking for the shadow of a tree a vicious snake,
> Beguiled, they lose the freedom
> they at last had found.[434]

We must do our best to assess a master before committing ourselves to a practice, but it is not easy to do so because there are so many so-called masters in the world with glamorous and attractive displays of apparent spirituality. Moreover, as the Buddha points out, we can examine only to a certain extent in terms of what we can see and hear externally. We cannot discern a true master fully at the outset of the journey. We shall be able to know him more and more as we continue to make progress in attaining higher knowledge. In actuality, only a true master can properly perceive another true master.

Indicating our limitations in discerning a true master, Patrul Rinpoche says:

> For ordinary people like us, however, no amount of careful examination can reveal to us the extraordinary qualities of those sublime beings who hide their true nature. Meanwhile, charlatans pretending to be saints abound, skilled in the art of deception.[435]

Referring to the gradual deepening of our knowledge of the master, Pabongka Rinpoche says:

> At the moment we are beginners and (to us) our gurus are ordinary people. When we achieve the continuous Dharma single-pointed concentration, we shall meet the supreme Nirmāṇakāya, when on the first bodhisattva level, we shall meet Sambhogakāya, and so on.[436]

He adds:

> You are not fortunate enough to see the guru as a real Buddha because you do not have the mind-stream of a person fortunate enough to do so. That is, you do not have the valid cognition that permits seeing the guru in that way.... Only Buddhas themselves perceive one another's Dharmakāya [truth-body].[437]

In *The Essence of Nectar*, it is said:

> As long as you are not free
> Of the veil of karma and obscurations,
> Even if all the Buddhas actually came to you,

You would not have the good fortune to see
Their supreme bodies adorned
with the marks and signs.[438]

Truly speaking, as ordinary human beings, we are so limited that we can examine and know a true teacher only superficially. It is really the pull of our past karmas which brings us to a true master, who enables us to feel contented with him. As Patrul Rinpoche says:

> The greatest of all teachers is the one with whom we are linked from former lives.... For without the right conditions created by your past actions, you would never have had the good fortune of meeting an excellent teacher....
>
> In the beginning, skilfully examine the teacher;
> In the middle, skilfully follow him;
> In the end, skilfully emulate his realization and action.
> A disciple who does that is on the authentic path.[439]

Faith and Devotion

We have seen in the preceding section that Dharma, the impersonal ultimate reality, manifests itself in the form of a fully enlightened master who helps the seeker to realize ultimate reality and thereby attain enlightenment. We have also indicated that devotion and love for the master are essential for realizing the spiritual goal.

Why should we have devotion and love for a master? A master, who manifests the supreme reality and is endowed with unbounded wisdom, love and compassion, comes down from his blissful abode to this dark world and works relentlessly, disregarding all his troubles and discomforts, for the sole purpose of liberating seekers. It is only natural and necessary, therefore, for people to be immensely grateful to and have tremendous reverence, adoration, faith, devotion and love for such a selfless spiritual benefactor. And this attitude of faith, love and devotion on the part of a disciple towards his master is essential for realizing the ultimate spiritual goal.

We shall now explore the role of faith, love and devotion. In early Buddhist teachings, as the Pali Canon reveals, the Buddha lays great emphasis on faith and love, saying:

> Those who have sufficient faith in me and love for me are all bound for heaven.[440]

He points out:

> If the noble disciple, Ānanda, is possessed of faith in the Buddha ... if he is possessed of faith in the Dhamma ... and if he is possessed of faith in the order, then that noble disciple may, if he should so desire, foretell his own future: "Hell is destroyed for me; as also rebirth as an animal or a ghost, or in any place of woe. I am a *srotāpanna* [one who has plunged into the spiritual current], never liable to be reborn in a state of suffering, and am assured of finally attaining enlightenment."[441]

In the Pali Canon, the words, faith (*saddhā* in Pali, *shraddhā* in Sanskrit), and love (*pema*) frequently occur. It has been said by the Buddha that faith is humanity's best wealth in this world,[442] and through faith one is said to cross the flood of the world.[443] It is the first of the five-fold requisites leading to the cessation of suffering.[444]

In early Buddhism faith is regarded as the first indispensable requisite, without which no progress in the Dharma can be made. Faith is actually the very foundation of devotion (*bhakti*), for when faith becomes deep-rooted and firmly fixed, it then automatically transforms into love and devotion. Finally it develops into full-fledged devotion.

In order for seekers to succeed in their spiritual pursuit, they must have full faith and trust in their teacher, and with this attitude they take refuge (*sharaṇa*) in the master, relying fully on his doctrines and disciplines. A spiritual aspirant is required to take refuge in the Buddha, his Dharma and his spiritual community while embarking on the spiritual journey. To take refuge in the enlightened teacher means to surrender oneself to him, to erase one's self or ego, and to follow his instructions and discipline in their entirety. It means to be obedient to his teachings and entrust one's life and spiritual welfare to his hands.

In the Pali work *Milindapañhā*, King Milinda asks the renowned monk Nāgasena how a person of evil conduct could be saved by the Buddha simply on the ground that he has taken refuge in him and has unwavering faith in him. Nāgasena gave the following answer:

> A stone, however small, will sink into the water, but even a stone weighing hundreds of tons, if put on a ship, will float [go across].[445]

Now, it may be understood that the spiritual seeker who takes refuge (*sharaṇa*) in the Buddha is not taking refuge in a human being. The Buddha, the Enlightened One, is the Dharmakāya or the Tathāgata made manifest – the supreme reality in human form. He has the power to make others realize his true nature, his Buddha-nature, which is the seeker's own essence as well. Only a being who is one with the Dharmakāya is worthy of a disciple's faith and love.

However, lest a devotee – in his reverence, faith and love – begin to worship the human form of the Enlightened One, the Buddha discourages veneration of the physical form. At the time of his death, when flowers and sandalwood powder were being offered to him, the Buddha told Ānanda the true way to worship him:

> Although, Ānanda, all these offerings are made in honour of the Tathāgata, it is not thus that the Tathāgata is rightly honoured, venerated, revered and worshipped. If monks, nuns, and lay disciples were to live in accordance with my teachings and strictly follow my teachings, they would be honouring me and venerating me rightly, and paying me true respect and true reverence. Therefore, Ānanda, you should act according to my teaching, following all the instructions, and it should be so taught to others. This would be the highest worship, which would please me most.[446]

The faith that is greatly emphasized by the Buddha is not blind or irrational, but is based on a close observation of the teacher and a careful understanding of his teachings. Faith is quite compatible with free enquiry and critical examination.[447] Doubts in regard to the teacher, the doctrine and the order are the first three of the five obstacles to progress,[448] which must be resolved through practice of the teachings and gradually replaced by faith.

We may here bring out these elements of faith and devotion found in abundance in various schools of Mahāyāna Buddhism. In the famous Mahāyāna text, the *Lalitavistara*, for example, the Blessed One (the Buddha) himself assures his disciple Ānanda:

> Whosoever, Ānanda, will have faith in me, I shall save him. Since they have taken refuge in me, they will be as my friends.[449]

Emphasizing the pivotal importance of taking refuge in one's master and its enormous benefit, Patrul Rinpoche says:

> Taking refuge is the foundation of all practices. By simply taking refuge you plant the seed of liberation within yourself. You distance yourself from all the evil you have accumulated and develop more and more positive actions. Taking refuge is the support for all vows, the source of all good qualities. Ultimately, it will lead you to the state of Buddhahood.[450]

It is important once again to remember that in Mahāyāna Buddhism the Buddha or the Tathāgata is considered the all-pervading reality. If this reality could manifest itself in the form of Gautama Buddha in the sixth century BCE for the good and happiness of many, there is no reason why this reality should not be able to find instruments to manifest itself at all times for the same purpose. For living faith and devotion to grow and thrive, one needs a living reality one can adore and love. This need is well fulfilled in Mahāyāna Buddhism, as Edward Conze points out:

> The Mahāyāna greatly developed this idea [of the all-pervading reality giving rise to various manifestations] and filled the entire universe ... with Buddhas and Bodhisattvas who were alive and thus could be loved and treasured.[451]

It is the Buddha who dwells within all beings, as Edward Conze puts it:

> The Mahāyāna came to the conclusion that it is really the Buddha in us who does the seeking and that it is the Buddha-nature in us which seeks Buddhahood.[452]

This Mahāyāna idea as explained by Conze reminds us of the Indian theistic view that the soul, the particle of God within us, has a natural pull towards God, its source. As it works off its karmic burden, it is automatically pulled toward its source.

Unless the impersonal Dharmakāya, the Absolute, appears in human form as a guide or master, it is not possible for a seeker to listen to his spiritual teachings and to offer his love and reverence to him. Any meaningful love and devotion can only begin between people who are able to see and communicate with one another. As Edward Conze says:

> In this context, *love* in the sense of *bhakti* means a personal relationship with a person whom one not only cherishes and adores, but whom one wishes to be with, whom one does not want to let go, whom one wants to persist.[453]

This Buddhist view, that a seeker needs to see and have personal contact with the one whom he loves and adores, is also considered essential in the theistic Indian tradition. Whether the impersonal Absolute is called the Tathāgata, the Dharmakāya or God, the supreme reality, it must manifest itself to earthly beings in the form of an enlightened teacher, a guru or a master. Without coming into contact with this manifested form of Dharmakāya, the Supreme Divinity, it is impossible to attain the imperishable or immortal state. Without seeing, having love for or being devoted to a true master or a guru, one cannot realize the spiritual goal. As Pabongka Rinpoche states:

> If you are not properly devoted to the guru, you will not develop even the slightest realization into the stages of the path, no matter what practice you cultivate.... But if you devote yourself properly, you will soon obtain the state of unification, even though this (normally) requires many aeons to achieve.[454]

He then points out:

> So, Buddhas emanate as ordinary beings so that sentient beings are fortunate enough to see them.[455]

The path of devotion, of taking refuge in the teacher, came to be recognized as the 'easy' way as against the more difficult way of knowledge or wisdom. Referring to Nāgārjuna, the famous exponent of Mahāyāna, Edward Conze says:

> Nāgārjuna distinguishes the easy way of Faith [or devotion, *bhakti*] from the hard and difficult way of Wisdom.[456]

With the means of knowledge or wisdom, one travels as if on foot to a far-off destination, whereas with the means of faith or devotion, one travels as if aboard a ship that regularly voyages to that destination.

Since the Buddha is hidden within all without distinction, the path of faith and devotion is open to all who seek Buddhahood, regardless of whether they had been virtuous or sinful. In Japanese Buddhism, the Compassionate One is worshipped as Amida (Amita), 'the one endowed with infinite light', and hence the widely prevalent devotional school of Japan is labelled by English authors as Amida- or Amita-pietism. Speaking of this devotional school of Buddhism, Edward Conze says:

> All men, whether honest or criminal, are, without distinction, admitted to Amida's Paradise. Faith in Amida's grace is the one and only condition of admission. We are all equally sinful, and Amida is a God of compassionate love.[457]

One must not, however, think that faith in Amida (Amita) is only a superficial formality. As Junjirō Takakusu points out:

> The faith in Amita was simply the outcome of a far-reaching contemplation of the Buddha-nature.[458]

The *Lotus Sūtra* (*Saddharmapuṇḍarīka*) in this respect bears a striking resemblance to the well-known Hindu devotional work, the *Bhagavadgītā*. The very form and atmosphere in which the Buddha appears in the *Lotus Sūtra* is celestial. Like the cosmic form of Krishṇa in the *Bhagavadgītā*, he is depicted as shedding resplendent light, dazzling the enormous space from hell to the eighteen thousand regions of the Buddhas.[459] Innumerable gods and angels are contained within him and flowers are constantly showered on him from heaven. Again, as in the *Bhagavadgītā*, even a sinful person is said to be saved by seeking refuge in the Compassionate One. The Lord is said to protect his devotees and is greatly pleased by their various acts of piety and worship.[460]

A true devotee, out of his utter humility, submits himself to his master and calls himself a slave, ignorant and deluded. Relying on his master's mercy and compassion, he surrenders to him, takes refuge in him, and dedicates himself to serve him. Earnest and intense faith and devotion, absolute and unwavering dedication and surrender to the Buddhas and the bodhisattvas (manifest forms of the same reality, the Dharmakāya or the Tathāgata), and unqualified and full trust in and reliance on one's master are some of the characteristic features of Mahāyāna Buddhism. A few quotations from the famous Mahāyāna work *Bodhicharyāvatāra* may exemplify these elements of Buddhist devotion. Shāntideva, the author of this work, says:

> I have no virtue; I am utterly poor;
> I have nothing to offer for your worship.
> O Lords, having come on the mission
> of doing good to others, pray, accept me
> by your own [gracious] power.
> To the Jinas [the Buddhas, the Conquerors]
> and the bodhisattvas I surrender myself
> completely in every way.

> Accept me, O embodiments of supreme benevolence;
> with utmost devotion
> I offer myself as a slave to you.[461]

Apprehensive of the terrible situation he would have to face at the time of death without protection from the Buddhas, Shāntideva again says:

> When I am caught by the fierce messengers of death,
> overpowered by the fever of great fear,
> besmeared with urine and faeces,
> Looking pitifully in all the four directions
> for some one to come to rescue me
> from this tremendously frightful situation,
> what saint will come to my rescue?
> Seeing none in any direction to rescue me,
> and having fallen faint again, what shall I then do
> in that place of overwhelming fear?
> Realizing this, today itself I take refuge in the Conquerers
> [the Buddhas], the mighty Lords of the universe,
> the destroyers of all fears,
> who are ready to save the world.[462]

Having been himself helped by the Buddha and thereby having understood the value of helping others, Shāntideva dedicates himself to doing good to others and serving them with utmost fortitude. As he puts it:

> For the sake of worshipping the Tathāgata,
> I offer myself today as a slave of the world.
> A multitude of people may kick me in the head
> and beat me, but may the Lord of the universe
> be pleased with me.

There is no doubt regarding the fact that
the merciful Lords have graciously
become one with the entire universe.
It is indeed they who are visible
in the forms of various beings.
How can there be any dishonour in serving them?[463]

The fruit of deep meditation is that one becomes aware of the Buddha's presence both inside and outside of himself. Realizing that this same Lord dwells in all beings, the disciple is ready to serve all people like a slave, regardless of being dishonoured and insulted by them. For him to serve others is to serve and worship the all-pervading Tathāgata.

Again, since all the Buddhas and bodhisattvas are the manifest forms of the same Tathāgata or Dharmakāya, a devout Buddhist thinks that by offering devotion to the one who happens to be present in his time, he is offering devotion to all; just as by bathing at any one place in the sea, one knows that he is bathing in the same sea which reaches across the world.

This point is well expressed in the Tibetan Buddhist tradition, particularly in the concept of Guru Yoga. Guru Yoga signifies such an intense devotion to the guru that it establishes a close rapport between the guru and the disciple. Referring to this yoga, Patrul Rinpoche says:

> In particular, the Guru Yoga is the essence of all paths.... Total openness and devotion to a realized teacher is the most sure and rapid way to progress.... The spiritual teacher is like the Buddha himself. He brings us the transmission of the Buddhas of the past, embodies for us the Buddhas of the present, and, through his teachings, is the source of the Buddhas of the future.[464]

He further adds:

So absolute unwavering trust, arising from extraordinary faith and devotion, is indispensible.[465]

In Japan the most widespread form of Buddhism is Amita-pietism. As Junjirō Takakusu says:

Now Amita-pietism with all its kindred schools taken together has more than one-half of the Japanese population as adherents.... One should rely exclusively and absolutely on Amita, faith alone being the cause of salvation.... Even the believing thought itself is the grace of the Buddha, and one's remembrance or repetition of the name of the Buddha is simply a token of free thanksgiving shown towards the Buddha.[466]

We may note here the brief reason given by Edward Conze for why the technique of repetition of the name is so potent and valuable. He says:

Since the name contains the power of the Buddhas and the Bodhisattvas, its invocation is an act of the highest virtue.[467]

He then adds:

One should train the visual imagination to see the Buddhas and Bodhisattvas, and the senses of sound, sight and smell to perceive the sensory beauty of the Buddha-lands.[468]

These elements of Amita-pietism are found in many other schools of Mahāyāna Buddhism prevalent in other countries.

Since faith or devotion is greatly emphasized in several Mahāyāna texts, the adherents of the Mahāyāna faith in many countries regard faith or devotion as the favourite means of attaining salvation or securing a place in the Blissful Abode (Sukhāvatī).

Edward Conze explains why faith or devotion (*bhakti*) is the best and most effective means to efface egotism and the conceit of separate selfhood, the most formidable barrier in the way of salvation. He says:

> The bhaktic trend eliminates, in faith, all reliance on *self-power*, all reliance in one's own ability to plan and control one's own life and salvation.... Surrender in faith involves a high degree of extinction of separate selfhood, partly because one does not rely on oneself, or one's own power, and partly because one sees the futility of all conscious and personal efforts and allows oneself to be 'carried' to salvation.... Elementary modesty lets us perceive that any merit we may claim compares as nothing with that of the Buddhas and Bodhisattvas, and with the power of their help.... All pride in our intellect, all pride in the purity of our heart, sets up a self against others. If the intellect is seen as futile, the heart as corrupt, that self is deflated. The grace of the Absolute alone can carry us across, and our own personal schemes and endeavours are quite trivial.[469]

In the light of what has been said above, it would seem that faith or devotion in one form or another is present in both early and later Buddhism, but in later Mahāyāna Buddhism, it is found in its full-fledged form, and it obviously plays a much more dominant and vital role.

8

THE ETERNAL PATH

PERSPECTIVES AND PRACTICES

Buddhism offers a comprehensive guide to the attitudes and actions essential to the pursuit of enlightenment. The teachings represent a way of life that addresses the fundamental questions and challenges that all seekers of truth must inevitably encounter within themselves or in the world. In this chapter we shall discuss some of these fundamentals.

Two basic conditions are essential for the pursuit of a spiritual path. The first is birth as a human being, and the second is finding and following an enlightened teacher. Human beings, unique amongst all the species, are endowed with the faculty of discrimination. Because of this capacity, we alone are capable of pursuing a spiritual life, and to pursue a spiritual life and attain its goal is indeed the very objective of obtaining a human birth. Therefore, once we obtain this invaluable human birth, it is in our highest interest to direct our lives towards the fulfilment of our ultimate spiritual goal as diligently as possible. It would be folly to ignore the rare opportunity of the human life. The Buddha remarks:

Vigilance takes one to immortality;
Negligence takes one to death.
Those who are vigilant do not die;
Those who are negligent are as if dead already.[470]

It is essential to work assiduously during our life to realize the goal – the complete cessation of suffering. In the *Bodhicharyāvatāra*, Shāntideva says:

Having obtained the boat of human life,
cross the dreadful river of suffering.
This is not the time to sleep, O fool; this boat
[human life] is hard to obtain again.[471]

The Three Jewels

In Buddhism, the Three Jewels (*triratna*), the essentials for those embarking on the spiritual path, are the Buddha, the Buddha's true teaching (Dharma), and the community of spiritual practitioners (saṅgha). Among the Three Jewels, a Buddha or true teacher is of paramount importance, since without him none can incorporate Dharma into one's life or form a community of spiritual practitioners. Of course, Dharma and saṅgha are vital as well, because when a Buddha imparts the teachings, seekers must then apply themselves to the practice of the Dharma, and the company of other spiritual practitioners is greatly conducive to this practice.

It might be helpful here to review briefly the Buddhist perspective on the importance of the true and living teacher. Patrul Rinpoche says:

The Teacher is the main refuge.... Recognize him, therefore, as the quintessential union of the Three Jewels.... Follow him with

> absolute trust and try to pray to him all the time. Remember that to displease him with anything you do, say, or think is to renounce the entire refuge, so make every effort to please him all the time.
>
> No matter what happens to you, be it pleasant or unpleasant, good or bad, sickness or suffering, entrust yourself entirely to the Jewel of the Teacher.[472]

Bodhidharma (CE 440–528) says:

> To find a buddha all you have to do is see your nature. Your nature is the buddha. And the buddha is the person who's free: free of plans, free of cares. If you don't see your nature and run all day around looking somewhere else, you'll never find a buddha. The truth is, there's nothing to find. But to reach such understanding you need a teacher and you need to struggle to make yourself understand. Life and death are important. Don't suffer them in vain. There's no advantage in deceiving yourself. Even if you have mountains of jewels and as many servants as the sand along the Ganges, you see them when your eyes are open. But what about when your eyes are shut? You should realize then that everything you see is like a dream or illusion.
>
> If you don't find a teacher soon, you'll live this life in vain. It's true you have the buddha-nature. But without the help of a teacher you'll never know it.[473]

True spiritual teachers are emanations of the absolute form of the Buddha, the Dharmakāya, and are thus essentially the Buddha himself. Being fully realized beings themselves, only they can help us realize our true nature. As Patrul Rinpoche points out:

> To follow the teacher, you should have so much confidence in him that you perceive him as a real Buddha.[474]

In essence, the Buddha and the bodhisattvas embody both the Dharma, the teachings, as well as the Dharmakāya, the supreme reality. Hence they alone are capable of imparting the Dharma that leads practitioners to the full realization of the Dharmakāya. Seekers take refuge in the human manifestations of the Buddha because they are embodiments of the Dharma – otherwise, there would be no rationale for one human being taking refuge in another.

Buddhist masters lay great emphasis on being absorbed in a master's presence and listening to his spiritual discourses most carefully and with single-minded attention. Quoting the famous Mahāyāna text, *Gaṇḍa-Vyūha*, Shāntideva in his *Shikshāsamuchchaya* emphasizes the great value of having the rare opportunity of seeing one's master:

> It is difficult, even in the course of
> hundreds of crores of aeons,
> To hear a Buddha preach;
> How much more to see him,
> His sight being the supreme remover of all hesitations.
> Good is the sight of the light of the world,
> Who has fully understood all Dharmas,
> Who is the ford to merit for the triple world,
> and who purifies all beings.[475]

Speaking of the great value of reverently attending the spiritual discourses of one's master, Shāntideva in his *Bodhicharyāvatāra* says:

> Mindfulness is easily generated in those
> who are blessed with their Guru's company
> And who remain in his obedience,
> holding him in awe and reverence.[476]

Being in the company of one's master and being receptive to his teachings are of great help to a spiritual practitioner. That is why Patrul Rinpoche says:

> Like a swan swimming on a perfect lake,
> Or a bee tasting the nectar of flowers,
> Never be tired of being with your teacher,
> But be inspired, and always receptive to him.
> Through such devotion you will experience
> all his qualities.[477]

The human form of the Buddha is as mortal as those of his disciples, but the Dharma that the Buddha embodies is immortal. At the time of ordination, therefore, a seeker takes refuge not only in the Buddha, but in the Dharma as well. Even if the master passes away, rendering the first refuge inaccessible, disciples should adhere to the Dharma, the second refuge, with renewed faith and determination. They will not need to take refuge in any other master after his passing from the physical form. Through their practice of the Dharma, they will continue to experience the compassion of the Buddha, and their reliance on the Dharma will take them to their ultimate goal. According to the Buddha, the best way to pay homage to him is to practise his teachings faithfully.

Regarding the third refuge of the saṅgha, the community of spiritual practitioners, the term should first be explained. As the Buddha continued to spread his teachings, many men and women were ordained as monks and nuns. When their number had substantially grown, the Buddha, and later his successors, laid down detailed codes of conduct for the community of monks and nuns. These codes of conduct were later collected in the canonical text, the *Vinaya* (Discipline). The main purpose of the codes was to maintain and promote harmonious living among the community of practitioners. All were required to have absolute respect for these codes as well as for those who lived by them. Allegiance and respect to both is what is meant by taking refuge in the saṅgha.

The saṅgha provides the most conducive surroundings and atmosphere for practitioners to carry on their spiritual practice. Of all living beings, humans have the greatest capacity to learn, understand and absorb. Accordingly, they are most influenced by the company they keep. In the purifying presence of a master, the entire atmosphere is charged with spirituality, and the enlightened teacher's discourses inspire and elevate the minds of seekers. The company of worldly people, on the other hand, is often not conducive to spiritual pursuits. That is why seekers of truth are advised to cultivate the company of the saṅgha.

Indicating how uplifting it is to be in the place where an enlightened person lives, and what a blessing it is to be part of his community, the Buddha says:

> That place is delightful where the enlightened dwell;
> Whether in a village or a deserted place,
> Whether on low or high land.[478]

> Pleasing is the advent of the Enlightened One,
> Pleasing is his discourse on the true Dhamma;
> Pleasing is the harmonious living in the saṅgha,
> And pleasing it is to carry on the spiritual practice
> Amidst the harmonious atmosphere of the saṅgha.[479]

On the other hand, the company of fools will only encourage negativity and suffering:

> To have the sight of the Noble Ones is good
> And to live in their company is always blissful.
> He will always be happy who does not see fools.
> He who lives in the company of fools

Grieves for a long time.
Association with fools,
Like with an enemy,
Is always productive of pain,
While association with the wise,
Like meeting with one's kinsfolk,
Is productive of happiness.[480]

Bodhichitta

The ultimate goal in Buddhism is to escape the wheel of birth and death and attain enlightenment, which in Buddhism is explained as seeing things as they are. In Mahāyāna Buddhism this intention is paired with the altruistic motivation to enable all sentient beings to become enlightened as well. This twofold intention is called *bodhichitta*, 'an awakening mind'.

Right motivation is motivation that is not linked to any impermanent, material or personal goal. If our motivation to walk the spiritual path is connected to a goal involving our limited selves, then that motivation will not last, since we as 'ourselves' will not last. Therefore it is necessary to connect with the eternal ultimate. In *Words of My Perfect Teacher* Patrul Rinpoche explains:

> Here again, "entering the Dharma" does not simply mean asking for some teaching and being given it. The starting point of the path of liberation is the conviction that the whole of *samsara* is meaningless and the genuine determination to be free from it. To travel the path of the Great Vehicle, the essential is to have genuinely aroused *bodhichitta*. The minimum is to have such unshakeable faith in the Three Precious Jewels that you could never renounce them, even to save your life. Without that, simply reciting prayers and wearing yellow robes is no proof that you entered the Dharma.[481]

The Buddha was practical – he did not ask his students to be perfect; he did not ask the impossible. He simply advised that they should have the sincere motivation to achieve liberation and to assist others in this pursuit. Intention is the foundation. Patrul Rinpoche says:

> What makes an action good or bad?
> Not how it looks, nor whether it is big or small,
> But the good or evil motivation behind it.[482]

All we have to do is to take full advantage of the teacher's instructions and seriously engage in the inner spiritual practice enjoined by the master. There is no need to be concerned about our shortcomings – we can accept them as our starting point.

It is the aim of the master to help us to see how things really are, to help us realize our true nature. Once we realize our true nature, we have accomplished our lives as human beings.

The Essential Practice of the Eightfold Path

The Eightfold Path, which constitutes the complete practice in Buddhism, consists of the following:

1. Right View
2. Right Resolve
3. Right Speech
4. Right Conduct
5. Right Livelihood
6. Right Effort
7. Right Mindfulness
8. Right Meditation[483]

These eight practices are grouped within three categories often known as the three *sampadās* or *khandhas*: good moral conduct (*sīla*), meditation (*samādhi*) and wisdom (*paññā*). The accomplished nun Dhammadinnā explains to the lay disciple Visākha:

> Friend Visākha, right speech, right conduct and right livelihood are included in *sīla*; right effort, right mindfulness and right meditation are included in *samādhi*; and right view and right resolve are included in *paññā*.[484]

All of the practices of the Eightfold Path are essential to the life that leads to liberation; however, we might single out here the seventh practice of right mindfulness. This practice is at the heart of living the Buddhist teachings. Thich Nhat Hanh says: "To cultivate mindfulness … is to cultivate the Buddha within, to cultivate the Holy Spirit."[485] Mindfulness is the practice of becoming conscious at ever-expanding levels, until, finally, a seeker becomes one with transcendent consciousness, the true Buddha.

The capacity of attention (*manaskāra*) is innate in all human beings, but we are always focusing our attention on one thing or another. The question for seekers of enlightenment is how to focus the attention appropriately – how to cultivate attention in such a way that we awaken to Truth. The practice of mindfulness means establishing one's attention fully in the present moment, cultivating a mind that is open and alive to that which simply is, in the here and now – in our body, our feelings, our mind and the objects of our mind.[486]

Mindfulness supports and is supported by all the other practices of the Eightfold Path, but it is the profound cultivation of mindfulness in particular that creates the foundation for meditation. Mindfulness directed inwardly leads ultimately to the experience of emptiness and stillness, and in this emptiness the consciousness comes to apprehend 'that which is as it is' – the true and eternal.

The highest wisdom leading to final liberation is attained through meditation, which in its turn requires purification of the mind by means of moral virtue and discipline. Thus, in Buddhism, virtue and discipline, mindfulness and meditation, highest insight and final liberation are all intimately interrelated, and they also represent the progressive stages of the path. Seekers cultivate moral virtue, then enter into concentration, through which knowledge and insight[487] are acquired. Having attained perfect wisdom, they experience final release.[488]

"Wisdom is adorned by conduct."[489] This intimate and essential relationship between virtue and knowledge is expressed in the Buddha's famous teaching:

> Wisdom is cleansed by virtue and virtue is cleansed by wisdom; where there is virtue there is wisdom and where there is wisdom there is virtue; the virtuous one has wisdom and the wise one has virtue; virtue and wisdom are reckoned in the world to be of utmost importance.[490]

The Eightfold Path of Buddhism represents a comprehensive and balanced spiritual practice, free of extremes. An aspirant has no reason to become complacent at any stage, but rather has every reason to maintain the determination to reach the highest attainment. The Buddha says:

> Do not rest content, O monks,
> Without reaching the destruction of defilements.[491]

> It may occur to you … 'this much is enough, accomplishing this much is enough, fulfilled is our holy life, nothing beyond is left to be done by us' and you may rest content. I declare to you, O monks, I instruct you, while following the holy life, do not stop

> with anything short of the goal of the holy life, leaving anything beyond to be done.[492]

A holy practitioner needs to remain aware of even the smallest unwholesome thoughts and actions.[493] The Buddha gives the simile of a man pierced by a poisoned arrow who, because the arrow has been taken out, moves carelessly without protecting his unhealed wound. As a result, he comes to grief.[494] On the other hand, the Buddha indicates that great power lies in pursuing the path resolutely, with utmost care and vigilance:

> A holy practitioner who delights in vigilance
> And looks with fear on negligence
> Moves along like a fire,
> Burning all fetters, great or small.[495]

The Five Essential Precepts or Abstentions

To embark on the spiritual path is the true task of human beings, but it is also a deeply challenging task. That is why seekers need to take refuge in an enlightened master. Once disciples take refuge in a master, they can then actually tread the path according to the teacher's instructions. We have seen the importance of developing *bodhichitta*, right motivation, and will now look at what the Buddha lays down as the basic prerequisites for treading the path.

Buddhist aspirants begin their spiritual practice by adhering to the Five Basic Precepts (*pañchashīla*), the five basic abstentions: abstinence from destroying life, abstinence from taking what is not given (not stealing), abstinence from indulging in lustful conduct, abstinence from uttering falsehood and abstinence from taking any intoxicants.[496] They are to be adhered to scrupulously by every spiritual aspirant. The violation of any one is considered an obstacle to spiritual progress.

The presupposition is that if the mind learns to live in accordance with these five precepts, it will smoothly follow what is right and virtuous. As the disciple proceeds on the path, his mind will become further purified. Then the mind will naturally be filled with nobility and compassion, and the disciple will begin to do good to others. Living by these precepts, however, is not enough to attain liberation. It is through meditation that the mind is gradually purified and one develops deeper knowledge and insight. This is why, after giving the five precepts, the Buddha adds:

> When the mind is concentrated, pure, cleansed, free from blemishes, purged of defilements, supple, pliant, steady and unperturbed, then one turns and directs his mind towards knowledge and insight.[497]

> Thus, having been set free, there arises the knowledge within him that he is emancipated; rebirth is destroyed; he has lived the holy life and has done whatever was to be done; and nothing further remains after this.[498]

According to Buddhism, it is meditation that brings about absolute purity, deep knowledge and insight, and final release from worldly bondage. The five precepts are the prerequisites for entering upon the path, while meditation, along with ongoing adherence to the five precepts, is the path. It is meditation that leads one to accomplish all that is worth accomplishing.

It may be noted here that although the initial vows prescribed by Buddhism are expressed as seeming negatives – in that they are prohibitions – they nonetheless create the foundation for positive attainments. It is inaccurate to think that Buddhism emphasizes 'negative' virtues; it is by removing the negative that their positive counterparts develop. We may note the following verse of the Buddha:

Refraining from all evil,
Cultivating what is good
And purifying one's mind –
This is the teaching of the Buddhas.[499]

These basic vows or precepts of Buddhist discipline help spiritual practitioners to stay on the right track. Without following these precepts, meditation cannot be effective. It cannot produce spiritual knowledge, insight or liberation. But if meditation is practised with faith and devotion, supported by the techniques and precepts set by one's master, it will certainly bring the desired results. Master Bassui says:

> The precepts are the shortcut for entering the Buddha gate. They are the wall and moat that keep out the six rebels,* the fortress that protects the jeweled Dharma. If the fortress is not secure, it will be destroyed by the enemy: life and death. And you will be put to shame before the king of darkness while suffering limitless pain in the lowest chambers of hell. Moreover, the precepts set the standards for this world. When the rules for the Royal Way are followed, there is peace in the four seas. When humanity and justice are disregarded, quarreling will take place. When wind and rain follow their natural order, the country will be calm and peaceful. When the rules for farming are not followed, the five grains will not grow. How much more is this so in the house of the Buddha? Even when, for example, there is no enlightenment, if you earnestly follow the precepts and do not create a great deal of bad karma while doing good deeds, you will have the good fortune to be born in the world of humans or heavenly beings. It goes without saying that one who

*The six rebels are vision, hearing, taste, touch, smell and conceptualization, all of which arise as a function of the senses.

> outwardly keeps the precepts while inwardly seeking his own nature will attain the Buddha Way as surely as water combines with water.[500]

The first precept, refraining from killing living beings, reflects both the importance in Buddhism of *ahimsa*, the avoidance of violence, and the notion that all life, not only human life, is very precious. For many Buddhists, this precept implies that we should refrain from eating animal flesh of any kind. Generally, people kill animals to eat or to sell the meat for others to eat. The teaching that we should not kill cuts at the very root of meat-eating – at both the killing and eating of flesh. However, some Buddhists interpret certain texts in the sūtras referring to the diet of begging monks at the time of the Buddha to mean that the Buddha's first requirement is not related to meat-eating. We shall discuss this point later in more detail.

It is not difficult to see that the second, third and fourth precepts of Buddhism – abstinence from stealing, lust and dishonesty – combine to constitute a sound foundation for a moral life. These three precepts constitute the rule that guides the actions of spiritual practitioners. The fifth precept is to refrain from taking any intoxicants. This is imperative for anyone who wishes to control and still the mind, for stillness of mind is the very crux of Buddhist practice. Fortified with adherence to the five foundational requirements, seekers can then dedicate themselves wholeheartedly to the most important requirement: practising meditation with steadfast resolve and faith.

The Chinese Mahāyāna *Sūtra of Perfect Enlightenment* says:

> Concentration is produced depending upon moral discipline; wisdom is produced depending on concentration – this is the order of practice. Concentration cannot be complete without moral discipline; wisdom cannot be manifested without concentration.[501]

Reverence for Life and Vegetarianism

Although the Buddha in his first precept speaks of "abstinence from destroying life", it is often argued that this does not imply refraining from eating meat. We will look at what the Buddha and Buddhist teachers say in this regard.

It should be borne in mind that meat-eating was not common during the Buddha's time in the part of India where the Buddha lived and preached. Indeed, vegetarianism has long been a tradition in India, and it still prevails there to a great extent. Naturally, therefore, it was considered taboo for a respectable householder to offer meat to a holy man, and much more so for the holy man knowingly to eat it.

This is reflected in the following dialogue between the Buddha and a nobleman named Jīvaka Komārabhachcha, who asks:

> This is what I have heard, revered sir: that they kill living creatures on purpose for the recluse Gautama, and that the recluse Gautama knowingly makes use of the meat of the killed living creatures on purpose and specially provided for him. Those who speak thus, revered sir, are they telling the truth or are they accusing you falsely for doing so?

The Buddha answers:

> Those who speak thus, Jīvaka, they are accusing me of what is not true, of what is not fact....
>
> Jīvaka, he who kills a living creature on purpose for a Tathāgata or a Tathāgata's disciple stores up much demerit in five ways: When he speaks thus: 'Go and fetch such and such a living creature' – in this first way he stores up much demerit. While this living creature is being fetched it experiences pain and distress because of the feeling of suffocation in its throat – in this second

way he stores up much demerit. When he speaks thus: 'Go and kill that living creature' – in this third way he stores up much demerit. While this living creature is being killed it experiences pain and distress – in this fourth way he stores up much demerit. If he serves that forbidden food to a Tathāgata or a Tathāgata's disciple, which is not allowable, in this fifth way he stores up much demerit. He who, Jīvaka, kills a living creature on purpose for a Tathāgata or a Tathāgata's disciple stores up much demerit in these five ways.[502]

The Buddha explains three things. First, we are morally responsible for an action that is intentional or volitional. He says that when one has intentionally [*sañchetanikaṁ*] done a deed by body, speech and mind, he will, according to his deed, experience pleasure, pain, or neither pain nor pleasure.[503]

Second, the Buddha leaves no room for a person endowed with the capacity of volition or intention to remain morally blameless if meat is knowingly eaten. Third, not only the person who kills a living creature, but also the person who causes the killing by creating the need for the supply of meat, is responsible for the act of killing.

The following statements by the Buddha provoke us to consider this issue deeply:

All fear punishment; all tremble at death.
Likening others to oneself,
One should neither kill nor cause to kill.[504]

He who, seeking his own happiness,
Inflicts pain on other beings,
Who [like his own self] are desirous of happiness,
Does not obtain happiness after death.[505]

In another book of the Pali Canon, the *Aṅguttara Nikāya*, the Buddha says:

> Monks, one possessed of three things is put into purgatory according to his deserts. What three? One who is a destroyer of life, another who encourages another to do the same, and a third who approves thereof.[506]

The Buddha then enumerates the forbidden means of livelihood:

> These five trades are forbidden as unrighteous means of livelihood: The trade of 1) selling of arms, 2) selling animals or human beings, 3) selling flesh or meat, 4) selling intoxicating drinks, and 5) selling poison.[507]

The Buddha reminds people to reflect on the consequences of killing living creatures;

> A noble disciple reflects thus: 'I am leading the holy life to get rid of and be free from those fetters which are caused by killing living creatures. If I were to kill living creatures again, my own conscience would bite me; the wise, also, after proper scrutiny would reproach me; and as a result of killing living creatures, at the disintegration of my body, after my death, a terrible destiny would await me. This killing of living creatures is indeed a fetter. This is indeed a hindrance.... But for one who refrains from killing living creatures, there would be no such destructive and oppressive cankers.[508]

The Buddha reminds a group of brahmins:

> Like unto a mother, a father, a brother and other relatives, cows are our best friends from which medicines are produced. They give food and they give strength; they likewise give a good complexion and happiness; knowing all this to be so, they [the brahmins of old times] did not kill cows.[509]

In chapter three of the *Sutta Nipāta*, the Buddha explains that what makes somebody a true brahmin is determined by action (not by birth). In this context the Buddha explains that a brahmin does not only refrain from killing, but also refrains from causing others to kill, saying:

> Whoever, having laid aside violence in respect for all beings, those that tremble and those who are still and strong, who does not kill or cause to kill, him I call a [true] brahmin.[510]

Some people still justify meat-eating by saying that the Buddha knowingly ate pork (*sūkara maṁsa*) at his last meal. In support of their view, they say that Chunda served pork to the Buddha on his express wish. But according to the account, when Chunda invited the Buddha and his accompanying monks to his house, he had a wide variety of excellent food prepared, including delicious milk-rice, *sūkara maddava*. The Buddha asked Chunda to serve him only the *sūkara maddava*.[511]

The interpretation that the Buddha's last meal consisted of pork hinges on the words '*sūkara maddava*' and '*sūkara maṁsa*'. The former means a delicious soft food especially prepared for vigour and strength and made from tasty rice and a large quantity of milk. '*Sūkara maddava*', however, is sometimes mistakenly taken as a synonym for '*sūkara maṁsa*', which is pork.*

We find repeated references to holy men, Buddhist and non-Buddhist, being served milk-rice and other sweet dishes, but nowhere is there record of meat being served to them in that part of India where the Buddha took his last meal. Thus this portrayal of the Buddha as a non-vegetarian is unfounded. We have seen that the Buddha clearly forbade householders to deliberately serve

---

*T. W. Rhys Davids, the translator of the *Dīgha Nikāya*, in which the Pali word *sūkara-maddava* occurs, adds a note suggesting two possible meanings of this word: a root called *sūkara-kanda*, or *bhatta* (cooked rice). Both are vegetarian foods. (*Dialogues of the Buddha*, vol.2, p.137)

meat to monks, and monks to knowingly eat meat. Would the Buddha, who had prescribed non-violence as the first precept of morality, then ask to be served animal flesh?

Eating of meat is denounced in the famous Mahāyāna text, the *Laṅkāvatāra Sūtra*. The Buddha explains his views to the Bodhisattva Mahāmati. A few excerpts follow:

> The Blessed One said this to him: For innumerable reasons, Mahāmati, the Bodhisattva, whose nature is compassion, is not to eat any meat; I will explain them.
>
> Mahāmati, in this long course of transmigration here, there is not one living being that, having assumed the form of a living being, has not been your mother, or father, or brother, or sister, or son, or daughter … and when acquiring another form of life may live as a beast, as a domestic animal, as a bird, or as a womb-born, or as something standing in some relationship to you; (this being so) how can the Bodhisattva-Mahāsattva, who desires to approach all living beings as if they were himself and to practise the Buddha-truths, eat the flesh of any living being that is of the same nature as himself?… Even in exceptional cases, it is not (compassionate) of a Bodhisattva of good standing to eat meat.… The food of the wise, Mahāmati, is what is eaten by the rishis [ancient sages]; it does not consist of meat and blood. Therefore, Mahāmati, let the Bodhisattva refrain from eating meat.…
>
> Now, Mahāmati, the food I have permitted (my disciples to take) is gratifying to all wise people but is avoided by the unwise; it is productive of many merits; it keeps away many evils; and it has been prescribed by the ancient rishis. It comprises rice, barley, wheat, kidney beans, beans, lentils, etc., clarified butter, oil, honey, molasses, treacle, sugar cane, coarse sugar, etc.; food prepared with these is proper food. Mahāmati, there may be some irrational people in the future who will differentiate themselves and establish new rules of moral discipline, and who, under the influence of the habit-energy belonging to the carnivorous

races, will greedily desire the taste (of meat): it is not for these people that the above food is prescribed. Mahāmati, this is the food I urge for the Bodhisattva-Mahāsattvas.

Again, Mahāmati, there may be some unwitting people in the future time who ... being under the influence of the thirst for [meat-] taste, ... will string together in various ways some sophistic arguments to defend meat-eating.... But, Mahāmati, nowhere in the sūtras is meat permitted as something enjoyable, nor is it referred to as proper among the foods prescribed.

Further, a tenfold prohibition is given as regards the flesh of animals found dead by themselves. But in the present sūtra all (meat-eating) in any form, in any manner, and in any place, is unconditionally and once for all prohibited for all. Thus, Mahāmati, meat-eating I have not permitted to anyone, I do not permit, I will not permit. Meat-eating, I tell you, Mahāmati, is not proper for homeless monks. There may be some, Mahāmati, who would say that meat was eaten by the Tathāgata thinking this would slander him. Such ignorant people as these, Mahāmati, will follow the evil course of their own karma-hindrance, and will fall into such regions where long nights are passed without profit and without happiness....

(Meat-eating) is forbidden by me everywhere and all the time for those who are abiding in compassion; (he who eats meat) will be born in the same place as the lion, tiger, wolf, etc.

Therefore, do not eat meat, because it hinders the truth of emancipation; not to eat meat – this is the mark of the wise.[512]

Following these extracts from both Pali and Sanskrit texts, we conclude with quotations from Tibetan Buddhist masters on the subject of meat-eating. Patrul Rinpoche says:

Taking life means doing anything intentionally to end the life of another being, whether human, animal or any other living creature.... Some of us, thinking only of the specific act of killing with our own hands, might imagine that we are innocent of ever taking life....

So all of us humans, in fact, spend our entire time taking life, like ogres. Indeed – considering how we slaughter our cattle to enjoy their flesh and blood when they have spent their whole lives serving us and feeding us with their milk as if they are our mothers – we are worse than any ogre.[513]

Similarly, Pabongka Rinpoche says:

In Tibet, I believe ordained people are making others slaughter cattle for them, claiming, 'They are our serfs'. But the slaughterer and the person who made him do it, each commits the sin of taking a life.... We may think that we do not acquire the sin of actually killing a living being, but we *do*, because it is also a great sin to make others kill for us.[514]

Showing that the Great Compassion is the Root of the Mahāyāna Path ... you must contemplate the way the sheep dies.... Its eyes are full of tears and it stares into the butcher's face.[515]

His Holiness the XIV Dalai Lama declares:

Of all the various species of animals on the planet, human beings are the biggest troublemakers. That is clear. I imagine that if there were no longer any humans on the planet, the planet itself would be safer! Certainly millions of fish, chicken and other small animals might enjoy some sort of genuine liberation![516]

The principle of non-violence or non-injury, which is central to Buddhist ethics, necessitates strict adherence to the vow of abstaining from meat and flesh in any shape or form.

Control of the Mind

The mind is said to be the greatest impediment to following the spiritual path. But we have no understanding of what the mind is. How can we then bring it under control, win its friendship and turn it into a helper? The mind is so unknown to us, yet so near; so restless and unwieldy, yet essentially so serene and capable of calm. It creates so much turbulence and misery, yet is originally so pure and blissful. It is our worst enemy, yet our best friend. The mind has two diametrically opposed states. In its original, pure state, it is positive. In its acquired and impure state, it is negative. The *Vimalakīrti Nirdesha* says:

> The mind is originally luminous [*chittaṁ prabhāsvaram*], but it can be defiled by passions or liberated from passions.[517]

In the *Saṁyutta Nikāya* of the Pali Canon, the Buddha says:

> For a long, long time this mind has been defiled by lust, anger and delusion. By a defiled mind, O monks, beings are defiled. By a pure mind, beings are made pure.[518]

In another volume of the *Saṁyutta Nikāya*, the tremendous power of the mind is indicated in these words:

> By the mind is the world led, by the mind directed;
> it is the mind which brings all under its sway.[519]

The *Aṅguttara Nikāya* of the Pali Canon says:

> Whatever is of evil, connected with evil, belonging to evil [likewise whatever is related to good] – all of it issues from the mind.[520]

Regarding the restlessness of the mind, the *Saṁyutta Nikāya* says:

> Just as a monkey, playing in a forest or wood, seizes a branch, then lets it go and seizes another one, so this mind arises and disappears, continually changing like day and night.[521]

In the two opening verses of the *Dhammapada*, the Buddha says:

> The mind precedes all [actions];
> The mind is the chief;
> All [actions] are mind-made.
> If a person speaks or acts with an impure mind,
> Sorrow follows him even as the wheel
> Follows the hoof of the one who draws [the cart].
> But if a person speaks or acts with a pure mind,
> Happiness follows him even as a shadow
> That never leaves him.[522]

The Buddha elaborates on controlling the mind in other verses of the *Dhammapada*:

> Just as an archer straightens his arrow,
> A wise person straightens
> His restless and unsteady mind,
> Which is difficult to guard and control....
>
> It is good to restrain the mind,
> Which is difficult to control.
> It is fickle and wanders at will;
> A tamed mind is the bearer of happiness....
>
> If a person's mind is not steadfast,
> If it does not know the true Dhamma,

If the serenity of the mind is troubled,
His wisdom is not perfected....

Knowing that this body is fragile like a clay pot,
Let one make this mind firm like a fortress,
And fight with Māra with the weapon of his wisdom,
Protecting what has been conquered
Without being attached to it....

Whatever someone may do to one he despises,
Whatever someone may do to his enemy,
An ill-directed mind may do one greater harm.

Whatever a mother or a father
Or any other relative can do for a person,
Greater good than that
Does a well-directed mind do for him.[523]

Conquest of the mind is essential for spiritual aspirants. In the *Bodhicharyāvatāra*, Shāntideva says:

If this unruly elephant, the mind, is bound
    from all sides by the rope of mindfulness,
One may be assured that all fears have ended
    and all good has come....

It is the proclamation of the knower
    of the Truth [the Buddha]
That all fears and immeasurable sufferings
    arise only from the mind....

Where can I find enough leather
    to cover the whole earth?
But with just enough leather for a pair of shoes,
    I can cover the whole earth.

Likewise, I cannot prevent external circumstances;
I shall only guard my mind –
What have I to do with preventing anything else?[524]

In Buddhism, great emphasis is laid on control of the mind, for if this is done, all else is easily done. If it is not done, nothing of worth can be accomplished.

Detachment

All teachers lay emphasis on detaching the mind from the external world by turning it within and rendering it fully concentrated. They advise us to live in the world but not to be of the world. So long as our mind is attached to and engrossed in the pursuit of worldly objects and their false, transient pleasures, we cannot attain liberation.

The Noble Eightfold Path prescribed by the Buddha is directed towards complete control of the mind, its gradual purification, and eradication of all attachments. When the mind is fully controlled, purged of impurity and freed from attachment, seekers are able to complete the spiritual journey and attain the ultimate goal.

Having achieved complete detachment, the Buddha lives and moves in the world totally uncontaminated:

> Just as, monks, a dark-blue or white lotus, born and developed in the water, rises above the water and stands untouched by the water, even so, monks, the Tathāgata, born and developed in the world, transcends the world and moves about detached from or uncontaminated by the world.[525]

In the first sutta of the *Majjhima Nikāya*, the Buddha points out that the Enlightened One, freed from all defilements and having truly realized the nature of all things in all respects, becomes detached from the world and its objects and thus achieves awakening.[526]

> Having seen thus, O monks, the instructed noble disciple finds estrangement in corporeality, in feeling, in perception, in volitions and in empirical consciousness. Being estranged, he is detached. Being detached, he is freed. Being freed, the knowledge arises in him that he is free. 'Exhausted is rebirth, fulfilled is the holy life, done what was to be done, nothing other is beyond this' – thus he knows.[527]

Only when we rise above our desires, the root of all attachments, can we be detached from the world. Our desires bind us to this world, and our desires know no bounds. The *Great Play Sūtra* says:

> O king, if someone were to receive
> All celestial pleasures,
> All human pleasures,
> It would not be enough;
> He would seek even more.[528]

If we rise above our desires, we are automatically liberated:

> It is due to desire that one is bound, and it is by surmounting the very same desire that one is liberated.[529]

Musō Kokushi speaks of utilizing the difficult situations of life to encourage us to develop detachment:

> When people are unsympathetic to you and the world does not go as you wish, this should be a help to detachment of feelings from the repetitious cycle of becoming and decay, gaining and losing.[530]

> For those who know the nature of the world, lack of complete satisfaction or fulfillment in things of the world is in itself advice to cultivate detachment.[531]

THE MEDITATION PRACTICE – DYING WHILE LIVING

The state of complete detachment from the external world – including detaching from the body – is sometimes called 'dying while living', because the process of the withdrawal of consciousness from the body at the time of meditation is the same as that of physical death. At death, the consciousness never returns to the body, but the spiritual practitioner's consciousness returns to the body after meditation.

In the Pali Canon, the account of the Buddha's deep meditation serves as a vivid illustration of dying while living. It is said that once while the Buddha was deeply absorbed in meditation in his dwelling near a village, there was a heavy downpour of torrential rain. Lightning flashed. Nearby, two peasant brothers were ploughing the field with four oxen, and all were killed by a lightning bolt. A multitude from the village assembled. The Buddha, having finished his meditation, came outside and was walking up and down his veranda. Seeing the Buddha, a man entered into a dialogue with him about the event:

> "Where, Lord, were you then?"
> "I, noble man, have been here all the while."
> "But, Lord, did you see it?"
> "I, noble man, saw nothing."
> "But, Lord, did you hear it?"
> "I, noble man, heard nothing."
> "Were you then, Lord, asleep?"
> "I, noble man, was not asleep."
> "Were you then conscious, Lord?"
> "Yes, I was, noble man."
> "So you, Lord, being conscious and awake, neither saw the accident nor heard the sound thereof, while the rain went on

beating and splashing, and the lightning was flashing, and the thunderbolts were crashing!"

"That is so, noble man."[532]

During deep meditation, the Buddha's attention was completely cut off from the external world. He was dead to the world, but fully alive to the world within. The eleventh-century Indian mystic Nāropa, who made a significant contribution to Tibetan Buddhism, calls this 'the emptying of consciousness':

> The actual practice of the light as the path is the emptying of consciousness from every content. Outwardly this is a process of dying, while inwardly it is an increase and gathering of light, passing through the non-effulgent state of unknowing into the radiant light which cannot be predicated in any way ... provided one is fully aware of the various phases in this process.
>
> The attainment of the goal is an access to a sphere of life larger and more powerful and divinely inspired than the normal conscious life. Not only does it make us happy, it also sheds its light through us on others who, awakened by it, may also follow its path.[533]

Nāropa explains that in order to approach the stage of dying while living we must first 'close' the nine outgoing openings of the body – the two eyes, two ears, two nostrils, the mouth and the two lower apertures:

> The nine openings open on samsara
> But one opening opens up to Mahāmudrā.*
> Close the nine openings and open up the one;
> Do not doubt that it leads to liberation.[534]

---

* A state of deep meditation.

A true spiritual practitioner dies daily and thus becomes fearless in the face of physical death. Marpa, a Tibetan master and disciple of Nāropa, says:

> I might die an ordinary death, but I need not worry;
> Familiarity has given me perfect confidence.[535]

Edward Conze points out that we must, through meditation, withdraw our attention from our present tainted state of being in order to attain enlightenment.

> The pure heart is the pure heart of our own nature, the natural heart which is identical with the Buddha heart.*
>
> Fundamentally our true heart is pure and infinite, like the moon clear in the blue sky. At some distant time past our knowing, it was tainted by passion and became the impure heart, something not our real selves but which came afterwards. But this which came afterwards becomes predominant and sets at naught the true heart, just as the concubine sets at naught the real wife.
>
> Just in this way we entrust ourselves to the operations of the deluded and passion-ridden heart, so that the real master, the Buddha heart, cannot even show its face. The thoughts of the impure heart are topsy-turvy, for it sees reality as upside down.... The essential thing is resolutely to take a leap into death, to give up one's body and life itself. It means to cut off at the root and source, all our discriminating fancies. If we really cut them off at the root, then of itself the freedom from thought will come, which means that our own true nature appears, and this is called enlightenment.[536]

---

*The pure heart could be likened to the soul; the Buddha heart to the essence of the Divine.

As we have learned from the previous chapters, we have to do this under the guidance of a true master. Especially in Vajrayāna (Mantrayāna), the guru gives his student a set of sounds or words called a mantra to repeat in order to concentrate the mind and connect it with spiritual qualities instead of remembering the impressions one has received through the senses or by repeated thoughts. Speaking of the application of the mantra practice, W. Y. Evans-Wentz says:

> In Mantra Yoga ... the yogin's aim is to establish telepathic and even more intimate communication with the deities that he invokes to assist him in his yogic endeavours.[537]

In his *Bodhicharyāvatāra*, Shāntideva says that one who carries on the repetition of the name of Lord Avalokiteshvara has none to fear. Lord Avalokiteshvara is known as the Lord of Compassion, as he is the 'one who sees' with compassion the sufferings of all beings. Edward Conze explains:

> The word Avalokiteshvara is a compound of the word *Īshvara* – Lord or Sovereign – and of *avalokita*, which means 'he who looks down with compassion', i.e., on beings suffering in this world. Avalokiteshvara personifies compassion.[538]

Speaking of the esoteric interpretation of the name Avalokiteshvara, W. Y. Evans-Wentz, the editor of *Tibetan Yoga and Secret Doctrines*, says that the esoteric interpretation of the word Avalokiteshvara, as given by his friend, Mr E. T. Sturdy [translator of the *Nārada Sūtra*], is as follows: Avalokita – seen, and Īshvara – Lord, so that Avalokiteshvara is the Lord who is seen within.[539]

As 'the Lord who is seen', Lord Avalokiteshvara can thus represent an inner form of the transcendent creative power. Speaking of the power of his name, Shāntideva says:

> Lord Avalokiteshvara has charged his name
> with so much power that through it
> His devotee is freed from the fear of appearing
> in any assembly [of questioners or debaters].[540]

Warning against any wrong use of the mantra, which is meant strictly for spiritual purposes, Pabongka Rinpoche says:

> Some people wanting to practise Dharma, but not knowing how to do so, may go to some lonely place and recite a few mantras, make a few prayers or even manage to achieve a few of the mental states (leading to mental quiescence), but they will not know how to do anything else.... You may think you will receive the power to subdue evil spirits by reciting the mantra, and so forth; or you may think you will subdue sicknesses or spirits, achieve wealth, acquire power, etc. Others, no matter how many teachings they have received, treat Dharma as if it were, for example, capital to start a business.... To exploit such teachings for worldly ends is equal to forcing a king off his throne and making him sweep the floor.[541]

One should also bear in mind that the Buddha enjoins his disciples to maintain secrecy and not to divulge the mantra to others:

> Men of wise understanding guard the word, guard the mystery, and do not reveal it to living beings.[542]

The mantra imparted by a true master to a seeker who is accepted as a disciple contains the power of that master. This power is manifested when the disciple repeats the mantra and contemplates on the inner form of the Buddha. Edward Conze says:

> One should think of the Buddha while repeatedly pronouncing his name. Since the name contains the power of the Buddhas

and Bodhisattvas, its invocation is an act of the highest virtue.... One should train the visual imagination to see the Buddhas and Bodhisattvas.[543]

The practice of the visualization or contemplation of one's guru as the Buddha is explained in the Tibetan text *The Epitome of the Great Symbol*:

Meditate upon thy Guru as being seated upon the crown of thy head. Regard him, as being in reality, the Buddha.[544]

Emphasizing the great importance of this meditation or contemplation on the guru, Pabongka Rinpoche quotes the authority of the mystic Atīsha:

Atīsha said that the truly precious meditation was meditation on the guru.[545]

Indicating how to visualize the guru's form, he says:

Imagine the guru is actually Bhagavān Shākyamuni [the Buddha]. Each of you must clearly imagine the visualization according to your guru's description.[546]

Pabongka Rinpoche explains how this visualization will not be clear at first, but the clarity will come with increasing concentration. As he puts it:

At first this visualization will not be clear, but it is not yet necessary to achieve clarity. All that will appear may be, for example, a flickering yellow blob or just some part of him, such as the head, feet, hands, etc. Do not let these slip from your memory; tighten your retention and do not allow the mind to become distracted. This system of nurturing your recollection alone will be all that is needed to interrupt dullness or excitement. This is why this supreme instruction of the great adepts is something to hold in your heart.... You must definitely achieve single-pointed concentration with the two features: great clarity together with some stability, and a tight image retention.[547]

Shāntideva explains the attitude that a spiritual practitioner should have when keeping his guru in mind. He says:

Mindfulness is easily generated in those
who are blessed with their Guru's company
And who remain in his obedience,
holding him in awe and reverence.

Buddhas' and bodhisattvas' vision
extends everywhere.
All is right before them, and I am sitting
in their very presence.

One should contemplate thus [on the guru,
the embodiment of all the Buddhas],
With a sense of unworthiness, awe and reverence;
one should repeatedly contemplate in this way.

When the inner vision appears,
it will never disappear again.
It stands for [the disciple's] protection
at the inner door.[548]

The sight of the inner form of the guru is so overwhelmingly blissful and purifying that one is said to be free from all blemishes and suffering. As Shāntideva says in his *Shikshāsamuchchaya*, quoting the Mahāyāna text, *Gaṇḍa-Vyūha*:

Annulled are all the sufferings,
When one has seen the Jina [the Conqueror],
the Lord of the world,
And it becomes possible to enter on gnosis,
The sphere of the supreme Buddhas.
One extinguishes all coverings
When one has seen the Buddha, best of men;
One heaps up infinite merit,
Which helps to win enlightenment.[549]

There are many invaluable benefits of the repetition of a mantra given by the master and enshrining within oneself the inner form of the master who imparted the secret instructions. By contemplating on a master who has perfected himself in the Buddha Dharma, aspirants acquire the same merit that they would acquire by contemplating on Lord Buddha himself. This is illustrated by the example of Lord Avalokiteshvara. The *Lotus Sūtra* says:

> One should remember Avalokiteshvara, whose sound is like the cloud and the drum, who thunders like a rain cloud and has a beautiful voice like that of Brahma, and who has attained perfection in the sound of all inner spheres [*svaramaṇḍala-pāramiṁgataḥ*]. Remember Avalokiteshvara, that pure being, again and again, and never doubt that he who takes refuge in him is protected and saved at the time of death, disaster and calamity.[550]

> Those who adore the Bodhisattva Avalokiteshvara, the great Being, will derive unfailing benefit.... One who adores a great number of Lord Buddhas many times and cherishes their names within oneself, and another who adores Bodhisattva Avalokiteshvara, the great Being, and cherishes his name within – both will have an equal acquisition of spiritual merit. Both these acquisitions of spiritual merit are difficult to destroy, even in hundreds

of thousands of myriads of crores of aeons. Incomprehensible is the measure of the spiritual merit accruing from cherishing the name of Bodhisattva Avalokiteshvara, the great Being.[551]

In the same chapter of the *Lotus Sūtra* the Buddha declares:

All those who in this world are subjected to suffering, if they hear the name of the Bodhisattva Avalokiteshvara, the Great Being, they all will be released from that mass of suffering. If those who keep the name of the Bodhisattva Avalokiteshvara, the Great Being, fall into a great mass of fire, they will be saved by virtue of the radiance of the Bodhisattva Avalokiteshvara, the Great Being.[552]

The process of repetition of the mantra given by our teacher and contemplation on the inner form of the teacher helps us achieve stillness and liberation from suffering. We stop rushing around and scattering our attention. Without mincing words, Ch'an master Lin-Chi (d. 866) explains:

Fellow believers, you lug your alms bag and this sack of shit that is your body and you rush off on side roads, looking for Buddhas, looking for the Dharma. Right now, all this dashing and searching you're doing – do you know what you're looking for? It is vibrantly alive, yet has no root or stem. You can't gather it up, you can't scatter it in the winds. The more you search for it the farther away it gets. But don't search for it and it's right before your eyes, its miraculous sound always in your ears. But if you don't have faith, you'll spend a hundred years in wasted labour.[553]

As we empty our minds and die while living, we come to that vibrant and unfathomable state with its "miraculous sound always in our ears". In the next chapter, we will discuss further this miraculous sound.

9

Inner Experiences of Sound and Light

It has already been indicated that Buddhism brushes aside needless metaphysical speculations. It basically presents a practical path which leads one to experience reality as it is in itself: the profound emptiness of Nirvāṇa. This reality is beyond the reach of thought and speech. Clinging to all that one experiences – via the six senses, the conceptualizing mind and one's habitual tendencies – gets in the way of true realization. One has to free oneself of these obstructions and look inwards, not outwards, to find reality as it is. The Buddhas come to this world to teach the Way. They teach us how to remove the ignorance that prevents us from experiencing the true nature that is the ground of our being and that of the whole creation.

Buddhism, like other mystic traditions of the world, points out that mystic light and sound pervade all and that an adept practitioner experiences light and sound while travelling on the inner path. Engagement with this inner experience is key to the path of enlightenment, so we shall now explore how several Buddhist texts speak of inner light and sound.

All Is Sound and Light

According to Buddhist teachings, all is manifested from emptiness through sound, and all is pervaded by sound. The Tibetan Buddhist Lama Thubten Yeshe (1935–1984) says:

> Actually, the Buddhist scientific experience is that everything – form, colour, smell, water, fire – has sound energy.[554]

Chogyal Namkhai Norbu (1938–), one of the foremost contemporary Dzogchen* masters, says about the sound of emptiness:

> Why then is sound important? Because when we speak of our real nature, the source of everything is how sound manifests from emptiness. What we firstly manifest is sound and sound manifests light and rays. These three are called our primordial potentiality. Sound doesn't mean ordinary sound, what we hear with our ears. When we speak of sound immediately we think of that. That is outer sound, which we can hear with our ears.
>
> There is also inner sound we can feel only through vibrations; we don't need ears for hearing or discovering inner sound.
>
> Still more important is secret sound. Secret sound we discover only when we discover our real nature. When we discover our real nature and how it is related with this energy and how it manifests, then we discover secret sound.[555]

The Zen poet Takuan Sōhō (1573–1654) writes about the sound of emptiness:

*Dzogchen, 'The Great Perfection', also called Atiyoga, is the most profound yoga practice within the Nyingma School of Tibetan Buddhism and involves direct transmission from teacher to student. Only in the last few decades have Dzogchen teachings been made partially available to non-initiates.

Vibrating within
The ear are many voices
But their origin
Has a source which may be called
The sound of no sound.[556]

Zen Buddhism makes explicit mention of the inner sound, which is regarded as the ultimate reality. Soyen Shaku, a Zen Buddhist master, for example, speaks of Kannon (the Japanese name for Avalokiteshvara). The name 'Kannon' is an abbreviated form of 'Kan-ze-on', which means one who perceives (*kwan*) the world-sound (*ze-on*). Soyen Shaku says:

> There is but one reality and we can call it by any name.... You may call it God or reason or life or suchness or love ... but Buddhism has called it 'Sound' ... and declares that all things are of one Sound in which every discordant note is eternally synthesized.[557]

> The one who hears the world-sound is no more nor less than he whose spiritual insight has gone deep into the very foundation of existence, whose knowledge comprehends everything and understands the reason for things, why they are so and not otherwise, and whose life and thought are in perfect harmony with the mind [consciousness] that controls the destiny of the universe. He has gone, as we say, to the other shore, he is a Buddha, the enlightened.[558]

Indicating that sound is the source of all, and is the unifying power or force of the universe, he says:

> Not only the wind that blows, waves that roar, the flute that whistles, but the mountains, rivers, oceans, suns, heavens, and

> everything that exists, are no more than so many vibrations of the Sound, eternal, ultimate and unifying.[559]

Sound, according to Edward Conze, an acknowledged Buddhist writer and translator, is the essence of that power or force which moves the world:

> Sound comes much nearer to the essence of a force than anything else. Each word can be analyzed into its syllables, and ... different syllables not only correspond to different spiritual forces or deities, but a syllable, or letter, can be used to conjure up a deity, and therefore it can, in a sense, be called the 'germ' [seed] of the deity, just as a grain of wheat contains the plant in itself.[560]

In the famous Mahāyāna text *Sukhāvatī-Vyūha*, the Buddha mentions sound and light in describing the bliss and beauty of Sukhāvatī, the Land of Bliss. He says to Ānanda:

> In that world Sukhāvatī, O Ānanda, there flow different kinds of rivers.... All these rivers are delightful, carrying water of ... various gems, resounding with sweet ... sound which is deep, unknown, incomprehensible, clear, pleasant to the ear, touching the heart, beloved, sweet, delightful, never tiring, never disagreeable [and always] pleasant to hear....
>
> Having heard such sounds, everyone feels the highest delight and pleasure accompanied by retirement, passionlessness, quiet, cessation, law [Dharma] and a stock of merit leading to the perfect knowledge.[561]

The Buddha's Enlightenment: An Experience of Light and Sound

In the early stages of the Buddha's spiritual search, he applied various methods to control his mind including fasting and austerities.

But it was only when he adopted the right course of meditation that his eye of wisdom opened and light appeared. After this experience, says the Buddha, he remained securely on the path:

> By inconceivable good karmas,
> I have rid myself of delusions
> And have achieved various lights.
>
> By all kinds of [virtuous] practices,
> I abide securely in the Buddha's path.[562]

The Buddha refers to the experience of light while describing to a brahmin what he experienced at the time of his enlightenment:

> In the last watch of the night, Brahmin, I attained the third true knowledge: Ignorance is destroyed, wisdom is arisen; darkness is dispelled and light is arisen.[563]

Speaking of the emergence of light during the time of the Buddha's meditation, the *Lotus Sūtra* (*Saddharmapuṇḍarīka*) says:

> His body was motionless and his mind had reached perfect tranquillity. And as soon as the Lord had entered upon his meditation, there fell a great rain of divine flowers ... And at that moment there issued a ray of light from within the point between the eyebrows of the Lord. It extended over eighteen hundred thousand Buddha-fields ... so that all those Buddha-fields appeared wholly illumined by its radiance.[564]

Then, indicating the marvellous state of the Buddha's enlightenment, marked by splendorous light and sound, the *Lalitavistara* says:

> All the universes were illuminated by a splendorous light.... They became resonant, greatly resonant and resonant all

> around, and a divine sound resounded, resounded majestically, and resounded all around.[565]

The *Lotus Sūtra* also gives an account of the Buddha's enlightenment in terms of resounding music:

> Now, monks, while the Lord was just on the summit of the terrace of enlightenment, the gods of paradise prepared for him a magnificent royal throne … and no sooner had the Lord occupied the seat of enlightenment than the Brahmakāyika gods* scattered a rain of flowers all around the seat of enlightenment … and the divine drums of the gods resounded … and the celestial musical instruments were played ceaselessly.[566]

The Buddha's enlightenment marked the turning point in his life. Having become a veritable fountain of wisdom and endowed with boundless compassion, he undertook a mission of imparting the same wisdom to suffering humanity. When he was on his way to Vārāṇasī (Kāshī) to begin rotating the wheel of the Dharma – to deliver his discourse on the Dharma for the first time – he met a naked ascetic named Upaka, who enquired of the Buddha about his mission. At this the Buddha replied:

> I shall go to Vārāṇasī,
> And having gone there to the city of Kāshī,
> I shall kindle the incomparable Light
> For people lost in blindness.
> And I shall beat the drum of deathlessness
> For people devoid of *shabd* [inner sound].[567]

---

* Gods who belong to Brahma's world.

The Transcendent Voice of the Buddha

In an important early Buddhist text, the *Mahāvastu*, a reference is made to the unique qualities of the word of the Buddha that pervades everywhere as sound.

> The voice of the Excellent Man [the Buddha] pervades everywhere with a sweet musical sound. The Sugata's [the Buddha's] voice is like the sound of the lute and the fife. It is like a swan's song. The voice of the eminently Wise One is like the roar of the thunder-cloud, yet sweet like the cuckoo's call. It is like the rattle of chariot wheels, like the booming of the ocean, like the cry of a water-bird ... a rain-bird ... like the trumpeting of an elephant and like the lion's roar.
>
> The voice of him who is pre-eminent among men and the gods is deep like the sound of drums; it is like the rustling of the wind-swept forest, and like the rumbling of an earthquake.
>
> The voice of the Jina [Conqueror, the Buddha] pervades everywhere; it sounds like the mighty playing of the five instruments. It is low like the gentle note of the duck, and of the red-lipped, slender-tongued peacock. It is like the sound of the lapping of waves, and it is not rendered confused by distance.
>
> The voice of him who is the foremost among beings, both in heaven and on earth, is like the merry tinkling of bells, yet full; it is like the rustling of a net of gold, and like the jingling of jewels.
>
> The voice of those who have attained perfection is to be recognized and acknowledged as deep and awe-inspiring, yet good to hear, and always reaching the heart.
>
> The voice of all the meritorious Ones, who have gathered a rich store of goodness, whose glory is unending, is pleasant to the ear like an Indian lute.[568]

Chandrakīrti (600–c.650) in the *Prasannapadā*, his famous commentary on Nāgārjuna's *Madhyamakashāstra* (*Treatise on the Middle Way*), explains with a simile how, by one resounding sound, the diverse discourses of the Buddha flow automatically:

> Just as a mechanically operated musical instrument, the 'tūrya', is automatically blown by the gusts of wind without anyone blowing it, so also utterances issue forth automatically from the Buddha.[569]

As the Buddha points out to Mahā Kāshyapa, one of his leading disciples:

> Like unto a great cloud coming up, the Tathāgata appears and raises his voice [*svara*] and issues forth his resounding sound [*ghosha*]. . . . I am he, Kāshyapa, who, knowing the Dharma that is of one essence, that is, the essence of deliverance, ever peaceful, ending in Nirvāṇa of eternal rest . . . does not suddenly reveal to all the knowledge of the all-knowing. . . . You are astonished and amazed, Kāshyapa, that you cannot fathom the veiled and esoteric utterance of the Tathāgata. Why is it so? Because, difficult it is, Kāshyapa, to understand the veiled and esoteric utterance [*sandhā-bhāshitam*] of the Tathāgata, the Arhat and the fully Enlightened One.[570]

Chandrakīrti quotes from the *Guhyasamāja-Tantra*, where a response is given to the question of how the Blessed One delivers diverse discourses without actually uttering a single word:

> All his discourses issue forth from just a moment's resounding voice of his which captivates the mind of all, which brings delight to the intellect of a multitude of listeners, which dries up the vast ocean of the cycle of birth and death and which emits rays of great light like the soothing full moon of autumn, extending over the entire expanse of the sevenfold universe.[571]

The *Samādhirāja Sūtra* (*King of Samādhi Sūtra*) makes a similar statement:

> From the one word of yours, O benefactor of the world, diverse words spring forth for the sake of the deliverance of many.[572]

In the *Lotus Sūtra* the Buddha declares: "I speak the Dharma with one voice" (*svareṇa chaiken vadāmi dharmaṁ*).[573] Edward Conze adds the following note to this declaration of the Buddha:

> An adequate translation seems impossible. The sentence refers to the doctrine of the Mahāsaṅghikas* according to which the Buddha by one single sound reveals the entire range of dharmic world. He speaks one word only and all beings hear the Dharma in a fashion adapted to their own nature, and as capable of removing the defilement peculiar to each one of them. By one single sound the Buddha can proclaim the entire Dharma, and his listeners will understand its meaning, be it gross or subtle, according to their own particular aptitude.[574]

Also, in the *Lotus Sūtra* the Buddha, foretelling Ānanda's attainment of Buddhahood, says:

> He shall be a Jina [Buddha] endowed with great spiritual power and his sound [*shabd*] shall resound in all the ten directions of the world.[575]

It is remarkable to note that even the names of many of the Tathāgatas referred to in the *Lotus Sūtra* suggest that they are embodiments of sound or light. A few examples include:

---

*One of the early Buddhist schools in ancient India which is now extinct.

Simha-ghosha	He whose sound is like a lion's roar
Dundubhi-svara-rāja	King of the sound of the drum
Megha-svara-rāja	King of the sound of the cloud
Megha-dundubhi-svara-rāja	King of the sounds of the drum and the cloud
Jaladhara-garjita-ghosha-susvara-nakshatra-rāja-saṅkusumitābhijña	He who has the sweet voice like the thundering sound of the cloud, who has the brilliance of the king of the heavenly stars and whose higher knowledge is in full bloom.[576]

Experiencing the Transcendent Form of the Buddha

We have seen that the Buddha in his real form, the Dharmakāya, is everlasting. But out of compassion for suffering beings, he assumes many physical or created bodies (Nirmāṇakāya), and thereby helps people to attain salvation. In addition, the Buddha in his transcendent form appears to the practitioner who is engaged in inner practice.

> My real body has existed unchanged in thousands of crores of regions, and I have been teaching the Dharma to beings through unthinkable aeons. To an undaunted devotee who proclaims this sūtra after I have passed away, I will send many of my created forms.... And when he is living alone, engaged in repetition in a lonely place, in the forest or the hills, then I will show him my luminous body and enable him to remember the lesson he forgot.[577]

A Buddha or true master never dies for his disciples, and he appears before them if and when he, in his wisdom and compassion, feels the need to do so. The disciple is naturally thrilled to see the inner form of the Buddha. In a description of bodhisattvas having a vision of the Buddha, the *Lotus Sūtra* says:

> At this sight [of the Lord Shākyamuni] they felt struck with wonder, amazement, and rapture. And they heard a voice [*ghosha*] from the sky calling… "There the Tathāgata called Shākyamuni, the Arhat, is just now revealing to the bodhisattvas the Dharmaparyāya [gate of truth, esoteric secret] of the Lotus of the True Dharma…. Accept it joyfully with all your heart, and do homage to the Lord Shākyamuni, the Tathāgata."[578]

Indicating that a master reveals the Dharmakāya to his devoted disciples after his passing, the *Lotus Sūtra* assures:

> The bodhisattva who, after the passing away [Parinirvāṇa] of the Tathāgata, holds him in mind, teaches, writes, and reads this Dharmaparyāya… will hear the pure sound of the Dharma [*shabdaṁ shriṇute vishuddhaṁ*] which the Buddha… reveals to all the world, and he catches what the Buddha speaks.[579]

The Buddha also indicates that a devoted disciple sees the Buddha and hears his voice even in the dream state:

> He sees in his dream the Tathāgata, the Lord of golden colour, preaching the Dharma to innumerable beings with a lovely voice and emitting thousands of rays.[580]

Here a practitioner describes his experiences in deep meditation as well as in dream:

> Again, he sees his own person meditating on the Dharma in mountain caves, and by meditating he attains the very nature of the Dharma, and obtaining complete absorption, sees the Jina

> [Buddha]. After seeing in his dream the golden-coloured one, endowed with a hundred hallowed signs, he hears the Dharma.[581]

Lastly, we must bear in mind that a Buddha does not reveal his Dharmakāya to those who have no yearning to see the master. The Buddha says:

> I see how beings are afflicted, but I do not show them my true being. Let them first have an aspiration to see me. Then I will reveal to them the true Dharma.[582]

Experiencing Light and Sound in Meditation Practice

When we look to the different Buddhist schools and their texts, we find that in spite of their variety, hearing inner sound and seeing inner light as a result of single-minded focus is often mentioned, and that looking and listening within can be part of a meditation practice.

In the well-known *Shūraṅgama Sūtra*, Mañjushrī, the Buddha of Wisdom, explains that the meditation of Avalokiteshvara is the easiest and best method for people of all kinds. While there are a few different meditation practices associated with Avalokiteshvara, the one described by Mañjushrī is a method based on hearing the inner sound. Mañjushrī says to the Buddha, the World-Honoured One:

> I now submit to the World-Honoured One
> That all Buddhas in this world appear
> To teach the most appropriate method,
> Which consists in using pervasive sound.
> The state of Samadhi can be
> Realized by means of hearing.
> Thus was Avalokiteshvara freed from suffering.[583]

Inner stillness, concentration and purity bring the attention inward and enable the practitioner to experience inner sound. In the *Dīgha Nikāya* of the Pali Canon, the Buddha explains to King Ajātashatru of Magadha that whatever a practitioner is to attain will come through practice, and this practice is inner:

> When one's mind is thus concentrated, pure, cleansed, free from blemishes, purged of adventitious defilements, supple, pliant, steady and unperturbed, then he applies and directs his mind to the divine ear. With that clear divine ear, surpassing the ear of men, he hears both human and divine sounds, whether far or near.
>
> His knowledge would be clear and distinct, O King, just as if a man were on the high road and were to hear the sound of a kettledrum or a tabor or the sound of a conch or of a drum, he would know: 'This is the sound of a kettledrum, this is the sound of a tabor, this of a conch, and this of a drum.'[584]

The *Platform Sūtra*, which presents the life and work of the Sixth Patriarch of Zen, Hui-neng, likewise expresses the importance of looking into oneself through spiritual practice. It says that one day the Fifth Patriarch suddenly called all of his disciples together. After they had assembled, he said:

> I've told you that the greatest concern for a human being is life and death. But you disciples spend your days making offerings, just looking for ways to reap merit and not for a way out of the bitter Sea of Saṁsāra. If you're blind to your own nature, how can you find the doorway to merit? Go back to your rooms and look into yourselves.[585]

It is by entering within oneself that one can experience the esoteric, as Soyen Shaku, a Zen Buddhist master, says:

> Do not think that this is too hidden and esoteric: Only train yourself in meditation… and you come to realize the truth of my statement.[586]

Speaking of the discipline of Zen Buddhism, the noted Japanese scholar of Buddhism, Junjirō Takakusu (1866–1945), also says:

> We can say without hesitation that it [Zen] requires training to hear a voice in silence.[587]

Hsüan-sha Shih-pei (835–908) also indicates the importance of looking – and listening – within:

> "How can I enter Ch'an?"
> "Do you hear the murmuring of the stream?"
> "Yes."
> "Therein you may enter."[588]

This dialogue between master and disciple may indicate that although the sound – such as the murmuring of the stream – which a disciple hears in the early stages of concentration is weak and unclear, yet one can enter the realm of inner experience by being attentive to it.

Guru Padmasambhāvā explores the inner practice that leads to "Clear Light":

> And when you look inward at your own mind
> inside yourself,
> If there exists no projectionist who projects thoughts
> by thinking them,
> Then your own subtle mind will become lucidly clear
> without anything projected.

Since the Clear Light of your own intrinsic awareness
  is empty, it is the Dharmakaya;
And this is like the sun rising in a cloudless illuminated sky.
Even though (this light cannot be said) to possess a particular
  shape or form, nevertheless it fully can be known.
The meaning of this, whether it is understood or not,
  is especially significant.[589]

Lama Thubten Yeshe also talks about Tibetan lamas hearing inner sound as well as having inner visions:

If you listen carefully there is always sound in your brain; for me there is always so much sound in there.

Sometimes from space [inside] you can hear incredibly beautiful music; it's natural. Really!... Actually, there are lamas who have visions, and they hear tunes. It is a very esoteric sound. It is not like when an ordinary person makes up a tune. When these lamas meditate, they hear the sound of the tune.[590]

Indicating the saving power of Avalokiteshvara, the embodiment of limitless compassion, Mañjushrī says:

O you, who (have achieved) the sound profound,
The seer of sound, of sound the purifier,
Who, unfailing as the sound of ocean tides,
  saves all beings in the world,
Make them secure [and] ensure their liberation and
  attainment of eternity.
Reverently I declare to the Tathāgata
What Avalokiteshvara said:
When one dwells in quietude,
Rolls of drums from ten directions
Simultaneously are heard,

So hearing is complete and perfect.
The eyes cannot pierce a screen,
But neither can mouth nor nose,
Body only feels when it is touched.
Mind's thoughts are confused and unconnected,
(But) voice whether near or far
At all times can be heard.[591]

Mañjushrī states that it is the practice or method of attuning to the inner sound which all the Buddhas of the past, present and future adopt:

> Ānanda and all you who listen here should inward turn your faculty of hearing to hear your own nature. Which alone achieves Supreme Bodhi....
>
> All past Tathāgatas have achieved this method. All Bodhisattvas now enter this perfection. All who practice in the future on this Dharma should rely. Avalokitesvara did not practice it alone, because through it I [Mañjushrī] also passed.... Blessed be coming generations so that they have faith in this easy expedient.[592]

In book twelve of the *Avataṁsaka Sūtra*, Mañjushrī asks the enlightened being, Chief in Goodness, to "expound the supreme virtues of practical application" of the "purifying practices cultivated by the Buddhas in the past". He replies:

There is a supreme concentration called peace and bliss
Which can universally save and liberate
all sentient beings,
Radiating a great light, inconceivable,
Causing those who see it to all be pacified.
This light emanated is called 'good manifestation' –

If any sentient beings encounter this light,
It will cause them to benefit, without fail:
By this way they can attain unsurpassed knowledge....

It also emanates a light called 'tranquillity':
This light can awaken the scatter-minded,
Causing them to detach from greed, anger, and folly,
With their minds unstirring and properly stabilized.
Abandoning all bad associates,
Meaningless talk and impure action,
Praising meditation and solitude:
Thus is this Light produced.

It also radiates a light called 'wondrous sound':
This light can awaken enlightening beings
And cause all voices heard in the world
To be to the hearer the voice of Buddha.
Praising the Buddha out loud,
And presenting music like bells and chimes,
And causing all creatures to hear the sound of Buddha
Is how this light can be made.[593]

The Buddha explains what kind of practice is necessary to be able to see the light as well as to hear the sound. He says if one practises concentration with the aim of seeing the heavenly sights and hearing the heavenly sounds, he will both see and hear because of the nature of his concentration.[594]

The practice of attuning oneself to the inner sound may seem arduous and ineffective in the early years. In the *Dīgha Nikāya* of the Pali Canon, a prince named Oṭṭhaddha Lichchhavi reports to the Buddha what he heard from Sunakkhatta, a disciple of the Buddha who is disappointed with the results of his efforts:

> [Sunakkhatta has stated:] It is for three long years that I have been practising the holy discipline under the Buddha. I can see divine forms, pleasant to behold, pacifying my desires and captivating my mind, but I cannot hear divine sounds like that.
>
> [Prince Oṭṭhaddha asks the Buddha about what Sunakkhatta has said:] Now, Sir, [is Sunakkhatta right, and] are there such divine sounds, which he could not hear, or do no such divine sounds exist?
>
> [The Buddha replies:] Certainly there are divine sounds, pleasant to hear, pacifying the desires and captivating the mind....
>
> [Prince Oṭṭhaddha responds:] Then, Lord, what is the cause, what is the reason why Sunakkhatta cannot hear them?
>
> [The Buddha explains:] In one case a monk ... goes into one-sided samadhi and sees heavenly sights, pleasant, delightful, enticing ... but does not hear heavenly sounds. By means of this one-sided samadhi he sees heavenly sights but does not hear heavenly sounds. Why is this? Because this samadhi only leads to the seeing of heavenly sights, but not to the hearing of heavenly sounds.... In another case, a monk ... hears heavenly sounds but does not see heavenly sights.... In another case, a monk ... goes into two-sided samadhi and both sees pleasant, delightful and enticing heavenly sights and hears heavenly sounds. Why is this? Because this two-sided samadhi leads to both the seeing of heavenly sights and the hearing of heavenly sounds.[595]

In different realms light and sound are experienced in different ways. The *Avataṁsaka Sūtra* speaks of many different regions where the "lightning in the clouds" in each region has different colours, defining it very specifically – saying it's like sunlight, like moonlight, like rose gold, like the colour of jade-like snow, like the colours of a mine of jewels.[596] And regarding sound it says that there is thunder like the sound of great drums, like the sound of singing, the sound of pipes. It explains that among simple people the thunder of inner regions is "like the sound of the surf".[597] It says:

> In the heaven of access to others' enjoyments,
> thunder is like a voice of Brahma;
> In the heaven of enjoyment of emanations,
> it's like the sound of great drums;
> In the heaven of happiness
> it's like the sound of singing;
> In the heaven of timely portion
> it's like the voices of goddesses;
> In the heaven of thirty-three celestial regions
> it's like the various sounds of Kinnaras;*
> In the heaven of four world-guarding kings
> it's like the sounds produced by Gandharvas;
> In the ocean it sounds like mountains crashing together;
> Among the Kinnaras, it's the sound of pipes;
> In the castles of the dragons, it sounds like
> the call of *kalavinka* birds;
> In the *yakshas*' abode it's like the voice
> of dragon maidens;
> Among the titans, it sounds like a celestial drum.
> Among humans, it's like the sound of the surf.[598]

The following lines mark the point where the Buddha, as the perceiver of light, starts to emanate light and sound himself, being merged with the realm of actionless action, the realm of emptiness. We may best comprehend this turning point through the metaphor of a superlative dancer who, becoming one with the dance, becomes the dance – yes, *is* the dance. In other words, the

---

*Kinnaras and Gandharvas are inhabitants of heavenly planets; the *kalavinka* bird is said to have the sweetest voice of all the birds in paradise; *yakshas* are attendants of a beneficent being.

practitioner merges with what he was focusing on and becomes one with it. Thus, duality is dissolved. It is through securely abiding in the Buddhist path that a practitioner joins the same dance as the Buddha and eventually meets the Buddha within and becomes one with him. As one merges with the Buddha's dance, light and sound emanate from the Buddha-nature that one is becoming. As the Mahāyāna *Mahāratnakūṭa Sūtra* says:

> By the wisdom of emptiness and non-action,
> I emanate intermingled lights.
>
> Empty, egoless, inactive,
> And devoid of thought
> Are external things; and yet
> They can manifest different forms.
>
> Empty, egoless, and inactive
> Is the body [is its nature], and yet
> It can produce various sounds.[599]

The true Buddha can only be found in the human body. It is this that is being expressed in the lines above. The manifestation of intermingled lights, different forms and various sounds are all inner experiences of practitioners on their spiritual journey after they take refuge in the Buddha's path and free themselves from delusion.

In Pure Land Buddhism it is said that practitioners who are pursuing their spiritual practice most arduously and progressing along their spiritual journey reach Sukhāvatī, the region of supreme bliss, a stage of non-returning, from which one can attain Nirvāṇa.

The *Sukhāvatī-Vyūha* indicates the bliss and beauty of this realm with its sonorous sound and sublime light:

> In that world Sukhāvatī, O Ānanda, there flow different kinds of rivers ... carrying water of different sweet odour, carrying bunches of flowers adorned with various gems, resounding with sweet voices ... the sound of which is deep, unknown, incomprehensible, clear, pleasant to the ear, touching the heart, beloved, sweet, delightful, never tiring, never disagreeable [and always] pleasant to hear....
>
> Having heard these sounds, everybody feels the highest delight and pleasure accompanied by retirement, passionlessness, quiet, cessation, law, and a stock of merit leading to the perfect knowledge....
>
> Being elevated in knowledge ... imperturbable in thought, they are like the ocean; they surpass the light of the sun and moon, by the light of wisdom, and by the whiteness, brilliancy, purity, and beauty of their knowledge.[600]

The *Avataṁsaka Sūtra* (*The Flower Ornament Scripture*) speaks of the joy of entering the "ocean of sound" of the Buddha:

> The far-reaching sound of the Buddhas
> Is heard throughout the cosmos;
> Enlightening beings can understand,
> And enter the ocean of sound.[601]

And the *Lotus Sūtra* also speaks of this profound sound:

> Now I hear the Buddha's soft and gentle sound,
> profound, far-reaching, very subtle and wonderful,
> expounding and discoursing on the pure Law [Dharma],
> and my mind is filled with great joy.
> My doubts and regrets are forever ended,
> I will rest and abide in true wisdom.[602]

In this chapter we have seen that many important texts of Buddhism teach that inner sound and light is the enrapturing and uplifting Buddha-nature that resides within everyone – and is, in fact, our own true nature. Again the words of Soyen Shaku:

> There is but one reality and we can call it by any name.... You may call it God or reason or life or suchness or love... but Buddhism has called it 'Sound'... and declares that all things are of one Sound in which every discordant note is eternally synthesized.[603]

It is through the experience of this inexpressible sound and light that practitioners progress on the inner path with renewed hope and encouragement, and finally attain the ultimate goal of enlightenment.

10

The Futility of Austerities, Rituals and the Caste System

The Buddha as a pragmatic teacher gave out his teachings in response to the particular situation of those whom he was teaching. He taught people in language they could understand and gave metaphors that they could relate to. He gave specific teachings to ascetics and brahmins, to the learned and the householder. While doing so, he addressed particular social practices that were widely accepted at the time and that were obstacles to enlightenment: austerities, rituals and caste prejudices.

Futility of Rituals

In Buddhism it is the Eightfold Path that leads to the cessation of suffering and the attainment of Nirvāṇa. This is a path which avoids empty ritual and the extremes of self-indulgence and self-mortification. It is for this reason that Buddhism is often referred to as the Middle Path or Middle Way. In the first discourse the Buddha gave, the Dhammachakkappavattana Sutta from the *Saṁyutta Nikāya*, also popularly known as the Wheel of Dhamma Discourse, the Buddha points out:

> The two extremes, monks, are not to be followed. What are the two? To give oneself up to indulgence in sensual pleasure, which is base, common, vulgar, unholy and unprofitable; or to give oneself up to self-mortification, which is painful, unholy and unprofitable. Avoiding both these extremes, the Tathāgata has shown the Middle Path, which is to seek insight and knowledge, leading to peace, discernment, enlightenment or Nibbāna. What, monks, is that Middle Path? It is the very same Noble Eightfold Path.[604]

Advocating a middle way between sense indulgence and sense mortification, the Buddha outlined practices that would lead to meditation, the focusing of the attention within. Buddhism does not advocate external practices such as austerity, outer display and rituals, because it is the inner control of the mind that is important. In the *Dhammapada*, the Buddha says:

> Neither wandering naked, nor having matted hair,
> Nor covering the body with mud,
> Nor fasting, nor sleeping on the bare ground,
> Nor besmearing the body with ashes,
> Nor squatting for long periods
> Can purify a mortal who is not yet free from doubt.[605]

Similarly, in the *Majjhima Nikāya*, the Buddha declares:

> I, monks, do not say that being a recluse consists in wearing a mere outer cloak, or … in remaining naked, or … in rubbing ash or dust on the body, or … in remaining standing in water, or … in living at the root of a tree, or … in living always in the open, or … in always remaining standing, or … in eating after certain days of fasting, or … in meditating on mantras for casting spells, or … in having matted hair.[606]

The Buddha rejects such austere practices since they do not calm the restless mind. One cannot, he says, obtain true knowledge by performing penance in the forest, living on its roots and fruits.[607]

In India during the time of the Buddha, renouncing household life and wearing particular robes was considered the first step towards a holy life. There are frequent references in the Pali Canon to hundreds of renunciates leading holy lives under the tutelage of their gurus. Following this tradition, Siddhārtha Gautama left his life as a prince, put on the robe of an ascetic and went in search of a true master to learn meditation. After attaining enlightenment, he continued to live as a recluse, wearing a yellow robe. But he makes it clear that one does not become a genuinely spiritual person either by renouncing household life, by becoming a recluse, or by wearing a robe of a certain colour. The Buddha denounces the behaviour of monks who seemingly renounce the world but do not actually practise a holy life. He points out that the outer appearance of a monk – shaving the head, wearing a yellow robe, going about with a begging bowl – are not the marks of a true recluse. The real recluse is one who has subdued his mind:

> One who remains undisciplined and utters falsehood
> Does not become a recluse merely by shaving his head.
> How can one be a recluse
> When he is full of desire and greed?
>
> He who wholly subdues evil deeds,
> Both small and great,
> Is called a recluse because he has subdued evil.
>
> One does not become a monk [*bhikkhu*]
> By begging from others.
> By adopting evil ways, one cannot become a monk.

> He who has abandoned virtue and vice
> And is possessed of holiness,
> Who moves about with enlightenment in the world,
> He indeed is called a monk.[608]

He adds:

> There are many wearing yellow robes
> Who are uncontrolled and of evil conduct.
> Such wicked ones, on account of their evil deeds,
> Are born in hell.[609]

Referring to such pretenders, the Buddha says:

> Just as, O monks, there was a double-edged Maṭaja weapon [dagger], sharp and poisoned, covered and wrapped by an outer robe, like unto this do I declare the life of such a monk as a recluse.[610]

Monks are taught by the Buddha to live up to their ideals and fulfil the purpose of renunciation. If they do that, they will purify themselves and bring merit to alms-givers as well. The Buddha accepts the fact that begging is the lowest means of obtaining a livelihood, but points out that it is considered conducive to the attainment of the highest goal. He warns that those who fail to justify their life as recluses and remain negligent and slothful in their spiritual practice are really good for nothing:

> Begging, O monks, is the meanest way of making one's living. It is a curse, O monks, in the world to hear, "You scrap-gatherer! With bowl in hand you roam about." But this way of life, O monks, the clansmen resort to with a purpose in view … so that they may realize the end of this entire mass of suffering. That is why, O monks,

a clansman adopts the life of a recluse. But if he turns out to be covetous, acutely given to sensuous pleasures, malevolent in mind, evil in resolve, corrupt in mindfulness, thoughtless, uncomposed, distracted in mind and unsubdued in senses, then I deem him like unto a firebrand from a funeral pyre which is lit at both ends and smeared with filth in the middle, serving no purpose as fuel, either in the village or in the forest, for he lacks household pleasures and yet does not fulfil the purpose of the life of a recluse.[611]

He declares:

It is better to swallow a red-hot iron ball
Like a flame of fire
Than to eat the alms food of the land
And remain immoral and uncontrolled.[612]

The Buddha says that the food and clothes of a disciple should remain simple and practical – what is needed to keep his body fit and protected – so that he can dedicate his life to his practice:

The noble disciple takes food reflecting carefully, not for enjoyment, not for adornment nor for beautification, but only for the sake of maintaining his body and keeping it going, for keeping it unharmed and for the promotion of the holy life.[613]

Whatever robe has been prescribed by me, that is only for the sake of guarding against cold, heat, wasps, mosquitoes, wind, sunstroke, reptiles and to cover nakedness.[614]

Can householders attain the highest knowledge as well as recluses? The Buddha answers this question in a dispassionate way. A brahmin student named Subha asks the Buddha:

> The brahmins, O Gautama, speak thus: "A householder is capable of obtaining the wholesome state of knowledge and not a recluse." Now, what does Venerable Gautama think about this?[615]

The Buddha replies:

> Here, student, I am one who speaks after making an analysis; I do not speak one-sidedly. I do not praise the wrong way of practice either of a householder or one gone forth; for whether it be a householder or one gone forth, one who has entered on the wrong way of practice, by reason of his wrong way of practice, is not accomplishing the true way, the Dhamma that is wholesome. I praise the right way of practice on the part either of a householder or one gone forth; for whether it be a householder or one gone forth, one who has entered on the right way of practice, by reason of his right way of practice, is accomplishing the true way, the Dhamma that is wholesome.[616]

The belief that a householder is incapable of attaining as high a spiritual state as a recluse was also shown to be false by Vimalakīrti, the householder of Vaishālī, who exposed the shortcomings of the most illustrious recluses.[617]

Since the main emphasis of practitioners is on controlling the mind and absorbing themselves in deep meditation, their teachers show no concern about outer dress, though they do prefer that their followers wear clothes in accord with social norms, decency and decorum. But they have no respect for hypocrites who display ascetic robes while remaining crooked and deceitful. The Buddha denounces this vain display of religiosity.

The Buddha considers outer rituals also as futile and fruitless. In the *Majjhima Nikāya*, the Buddha declares that ablutions in so-called holy rivers are futile. Asked by Sundarika Bhāradvāja if the Buddha bathes in Bāhukā, a holy river, to wash away sins, the Buddha replies, including other holy bathing places in his answer:

In the Bāhukā, and at Adhikakkā,
At Gayā, and in the Sundarikā,
In the Sarassatī, and at Prayāga,
Then in the river Bāhumatī,
The fool may bathe every day,
But he cannot wash away his sins.

What can the Sundarikā do,
What Prayāga, what the Bāhukā river?
They do not cleanse the sins of a sinful person
Engaged in evil deeds.

For the pure, every day is auspicious;
For the pure, every day is holy.
For the pure one of good conduct
All holy observances are ever complete.

Bathe here within yourself, O Brahmin,
And make all creatures secure.[618]

The Buddha considers fire rituals also as futile:

I pile no firewood on altars; I kindle a flame only within myself. This flame is ever bright and splendorous. I, as an *arahant* [a liberated one], ever live the pure and holy life.[619]

Patrul Rinpoche says:

Absolute *bodhichitta* is attained by the power of meditation and does not depend on rituals.[620]

In his *Dohākosha* (*The Royal Song*), Saraha criticizes sacred recitation, fire worship and smearing the body with ashes:

> The brahmins who do not know the truth
> Vainly recite the *Vedas* four.
>
> With earth and water and kusha-grass
> they make preparations,
> And seated at home they kindle fire,
> And from the senseless offerings that they make,
> They burn their eyes with the pungent smoke.
>
> With ashes these masters smear their bodies,
> And on their heads they have matted hair.
> Seated within the house they kindle lamps;
> Seated in a corner they tinkle bells.[621]

Mere rituals turn our attention outward, whereas the Buddha wants us to turn our attention inward. Going on pilgrimages and bathing in so-called sacred rivers are futile, since purity is attained by diving within oneself:

> Here [within the body] is the sacred Yamunā
> and here the River Ganges;
> Here are Prayāga and Benares;
> here are Sun and Moon.
>
> I have visited in my wanderings shrines
> and other places of pilgrimage,
> But I have not seen another shrine blissful
> like my own body.[622]

Zen master Bassui says:

> Ordinary people, who mistakenly seek the Dharma outside their own minds, not knowing that their own selves are the true Buddha, are like deluded children who have forgotten their father.[623]

Even after acquiring supernatural powers, one is instructed not to make a display of them, for talking about one's own attainments will inflate one's ego and bring about a downfall. The example of Devadatta clearly demonstrates this law. Devadatta was the cousin and an accomplished disciple of the Buddha, and through meditation he had acquired some miraculous powers, but desired honour and respect. Assuming the form of a young boy in a girdle of snakes, he appeared in the lap of Prince Ajātashatru, who was terrified. Devadatta then appeared before him as a monk and asked why the prince was startled. The prince marvelled at Devadatta's great power. With more miracles, Devadatta completely won the prince over. Many monks and followers of the Buddha also began to admire Devadatta. Some of the monks reported this to the Buddha, at which the Buddha responded:

> Do not, monks, envy Devadatta's gains, honour and fame.... Devadatta's psychic powers may be expected to decline, not to grow.[624]

Devadatta lost all his powers. Masters therefore impress upon their disciples that they are to keep their inner attainments and spiritual experiences to themselves. Pabongka Rinpoche emphatically says:

> You should only develop insight and improve your mind: do not make any outward display; nor should anyone know you have made great progress.... You meet with many hindrances when you advertise yourself: it is like boasting to others about your wish-granting gem.[625]

Futility of Caste Distinctions

The Indian society in which the Buddha lived and preached was divided during his time into four classes: brahmins (the priestly class), kshatriyas (the rulers and warriors), vaishyas (those devoted to agriculture, commerce, etc.) and shūdras (those who served others with their hands). This fourfold division may have been based on occupation in the beginning, but by the Buddha's time it had become hereditary. It is this classification of society which the Buddha condemned and denounced. This classification later became further subdivided into various other branches, called 'castes' in the typical sense, and insofar as all of them are considered hereditary, the Buddha's criticisms are equally applicable to both – the class system of his time and the caste system that developed later.

The Buddha in unmistakable language asserts the biological unity of humankind and makes a radical departure from the traditional concept of hereditary divisions of society. The Buddha taught that all human beings are potential Buddhas.

In the *Majjhima Nikāya* the Buddha explains at great length that there are no different species among human beings, such as are found between different species of plant and animal life.[626] The divisions assigned to people are but nominal and artificial divisions (*samaññā*). The *Sutta Nipāta*, a text from the *Khuddaka Nikāya*, says:

> Not as regards their hair, head, ears, eyes, mouth, nose, lips, brows... nor as regards their hands, feet, fingers, nails, calves, thighs, colour or voice are there marks constituting species, as in the case of other species. Difference there is among other embodied beings, but amongst human beings, this is not the case; the difference amongst human beings is merely nominal.[627]

> Not by birth does one become a brahmin, not by birth does one become a non-brahmin. By work one becomes a brahmin and by work one becomes a non-brahmin. By work one becomes a peasant and by work one becomes an artisan. By work one becomes a merchant and by work one becomes a servant.[628]

Buddhism cuts at the roots of all so-called fundamental distinctions based on ancestry. The fourfold division of society is not fundamental or divine in origin. People are not inherently different at birth but can be distinguished later on the basis of their actions and the occupations they choose. These distinctions are by no means divine, but are merely the result of convention (*samaññā*).

The Buddha makes no compromise with traditional views of fixed social hierarchies. Not only does he open the door of enlightenment to all, regardless of class or creed, but he also emphasizes the inherent equality of all, considering caste prejudice to be an obstacle to the path of enlightenment. It was a great departure on the Buddha's part to challenge the brahminical orthodoxy of that period, and the brahmin priests were greatly disturbed to learn that "the recluse Gautama proclaims the purity of all the four castes".[629] In a debate with a brahmin, the Buddha asks:

> What do you think, O brahmin, can only a brahmin, by taking soap and going to the river, wash away his dirt, but not a kshatriya, a vaishya or a shūdra?[630]

The brahmin naturally replies that it is not so, to which the Buddha says:

> Similarly, O brahmin, a person from a kshatriya family, a brahmin family, a vaishya family as well as a shūdra family, having

adopted the doctrine and discipline preached by the Tathāgata, obtains the knowledge of the noble doctrine.[631]

The king of Kosala pointedly questions the Buddha about his teaching of equality:

There are these four castes, Sir, the kshatriya, the brahmin, the vaishya and the shūdra. Let us suppose that they all possessed the five forms of strenuous exertion for attaining salvation. In this case, would there be any distinction, Sir, any difference among them?[632]

In a simile of fire he often employs,[633] the Buddha replies:

Here also, Sire, I do not admit any difference whatsoever in regard to the nature of their salvation. Just as if, Sire, a person were to kindle a fire with dry herbs, and another with dry *sāla* wood, and a third with dry mango wood, and a fourth with dry fig wood – what think you, Sire, would these diverse fires kindled with diverse woods show any difference whatsoever in respect of their flame, hue and brilliance?[634]

The king naturally says that there would be no difference at all. Buddha then concludes:

Even so, Sire, is the inward illumination that is kindled by effort and nursed by strenuous exertion. I declare that there is no difference whatsoever herein with regard to their salvation.[635]

According to Saraha, the distinctions between high and low castes – between brahmins and shūdras – are invalid:

> When the mind goes to rest,
> And the bonds of the body are destroyed,
> Then the one flavour of the Innate pours forth,
> And there is neither outcast nor brahmin.[636]

All people, irrespective of caste, stand as equals before the moral law. Reward or punishment is meted out in accordance with positive or negative conduct, not according to caste. People are born in a heaven or hell after they die, simply according to their meritorious or unmeritorious deeds.[637] Everyone is capable of moral and spiritual development and everyone "can develop within himself loving thoughts towards all beings free from hatred and ill-will".[638] There is only one criterion for a person's true 'status', and that is the criterion of moral and spiritual progress. Such progress is open to all equally, and thus there can be no reality to classifications of worth created by human beings. A person is always capable of transformation.

The Buddha speaks of prejudice of caste or clan as a spiritual obstacle:

> Whosoever, Ambaṭṭha,* is bound by caste-prejudices or clan-prejudices ... is far removed from the way of the highest salvation. By casting aside the bond of caste-prejudices or clan-prejudices, Ambaṭṭha, the highest salvation is realized.[639]

Many still hesitate, however, to discard the old system of caste distinction. The following quotation from the Tibetan Buddhist text *The Ocean of Delight for the Wise* admonishes people to utilize their discrimination:

---

* Here Buddha addresses a young Brahmin by the name of his clan, which is considered to be aristocratic by its own members.

Relinquish an evil custom even though it be
of thy fathers and ancestors;
Adopt a good custom even though it be
established among thine enemies:
Poison is not to be taken even though offered
by one's mother;
But gold [spiritual wealth] is acceptable even from
one who is inimical.[640]

Since there is no valid ground for caste distinctions, Buddhism rejects these anachronistic customs without reservation, imparting teachings that preach the unity and equality of all people.

Conclusion

Buddhism offers a pragmatic and achievable path to final liberation from suffering. The Buddha dived deep into the core of reality and emerged with the rare gem of eternal wisdom. Like all Buddhas before and after him, he relied upon direct and personal experience of Dharma, of Truth – not on hearsay, reasoning or speculation. Out of their mercy and compassion, all Buddhas reveal and unfold the Dharma for the good and happiness of people beset with ignorance and suffering. Since their insight and inspiration comes from the same one source within, all have the same fundamental message to convey, regardless of the time and place in which they are born.

Once Siddhārtha Gautama came to see the suffering and impermanence of life, he dedicated himself to the search for permanent release from suffering. With this purpose he went from one teacher to another to realize his spiritual goal. He tried various rigorous austerities, but external methods proved to be of no avail. Through the inner practice of meditation, he discovered the way to attain Nirvāṇa, the state of liberation from suffering.

When, after attaining Nirvāṇa, the Buddha was reflecting on whether or not to teach the profound Truth to a world lost in ignorance and delusion, Sahampati Brahmā, a god from the Pure Abodes, came to urge him to teach. Brahmā realized that the world could not sustain itself if it were to remain deprived of the Buddha's teaching of the Dharma. Sahampati Brahmā said:

> If the mind of the Tathāgata, the Exalted One, were to remain disinclined to preach the noble Dhamma to the world, the world would indeed be destroyed. It would be ruined.[641]

Sahampati Brahmā implored the Buddha:

> Lord, let the Blessed One teach the Dhamma, let the Sublime One teach the Dhamma. Among beings there are some with just a little dust in their eyes. Not hearing the Dhamma, they are languishing; if taught, they will see the truth.[642]

It is out of their compassion that Buddhas or true masters descend to the world and, not sparing themselves, teach the Dharma to suffering human beings. Sincere seekers can be truly benefited by an enlightened master who, having himself attained full realization of Truth, is willing and ready to help others. It is the company of an enlightened teacher that enables a seeker to distinguish false from real. And it is only through the technique of meditation imparted by a master that seekers can go within and gradually realize what is true. Since there is an essential oneness among the teachings of true masters, there is never a need to lament the unavailability of a Buddha of earlier times. Instead we can find a Buddha of our own time and dedicate ourselves to practising his teachings.

Spiritual teachers use reason and language to convey their message; but being well aware of the limitations of reason and intellect, they do not rely on the mind or words as the tool for discovering Truth. Reason and intellect can generate great feats of exploration in the outer world, enabling people to dive deep down to the bottom of the ocean or to fly to great heights in outer space. But it is a different aspect of our nature, our transcendent consciousness, which leads us within and frees us from suffering. Thus the Buddha taught that there is a means of awakening to this transcendent consciousness and gave us a practical path that leads to Nirvāṇa.

It is to encourage the realization of this goal that the Buddha exhorts us to make utmost effort, saying:

> Vigilance takes one to immortality;
> Negligence takes one to death.
> Those who are vigilant do not die;
> Those who are negligent are as if dead already.[643]

Urging aspirants to continue their practice till their goal is reached, he again says:

> It may occur to you ... 'this much is enough, accomplishing this much is enough'.... I declare to you, O monks, I instruct you, while following the holy life, do not stop with anything short of the goal of the holy life, leaving anything beyond to be done.[644]

If freedom from the vicious cycle of birth and death and attainment of eternal bliss is the goal, those who are blessed with the invaluable gift of human life cannot afford to ignore the compassionate call of the Buddha.

There is no doubt that all enlightened teachers proclaim one truth and one path leading to the realization of the ultimate goal. The Buddha was once asked, "Why do others put forward diverse theories? Are truths many and various?" The Buddha replied, "Truths, indeed, are not many."[645] He asserts simply: "Truth is one without a second."[646] This truth or reality is nothing other than Nibbāna, the final release, the absolute cessation of suffering.[647] Let no one, therefore, misconstrue and misinterpret the teachings of the Buddhas to create different sects and creeds, to divide humanity in the name of different masters and religions, or disregard their essential unity.

It may be remembered that it is human beings who create religions. We do this to remind ourselves of our true nature and to recall the one reality that embraces us all, so we can transcend the pain of the human condition. Religions were never founded for the purpose of dividing humankind or creating conflict, but to unite and promote peace and harmony among all. We can examine the spiritual core of our own religion, whatever it may be, and try to understand this: all religions, founded on the teachings of enlightened teachers, have propounded essentially the same truth. It is then for us to step onto the path to Nirvāṇa and extinguish the illusory flame of our self or ego so that we too can become enlightened.

Appendix

Texts Included in the Pali Canon (*Tipiṭaka*)

The Pali Canon includes three groups or 'baskets' of texts: 1) *Sutta Piṭaka* – Basket of Discourses; 2) *Vinaya Piṭaka* – Basket of Discipline; 3) *Abhidhamma Piṭaka* – Basket of the Higher Teachings.

1) The *Sutta Piṭaka* is divided into five *nikāyas* or collections:

   a. *Dīgha Nikāya* – Collection of Long Discourses
   b. *Majjhima Nikāya* – Collection of Middle-Length Discourses
   c. *Saṁyutta Nikāya* – Collection of Kindred Discourses
   d. *Aṅguttara Nikāya* – Collection of Numerical Discourses
   e. *Khuddaka Nikāya* – Collection of Short Texts. The *Khuddaka Nikāya* is subdivided into fifteen to eighteen texts, depending on the country:

      1. *Khuddaka Pāṭha* – Short Texts
      2. *Dhammapada* – Path of Truth
      3. *Udāna* – Inspired Exclamations
      4. *Itivuttaka* – "Thus Said" Discourses
      5. *Sutta Nipāta* – Collected Discourses
      6. *Vimana Vatthu* – Stories of Celestial Mansions
      7. *Peta Vatthu* – Stories of Petas
      8. *Theragāthā* – Verses of the Elder Monks
      9. *Therīgāthā* – Verses of the Elder Nuns
      10. *Jātaka* – Birth Stories

11. *Niddesa* – Expositions
12. *Paṭisambhidā Magga* – Path of Discrimination
13. *Apadāna* – Lives of Arahants
14. *Buddhavaṁsa* – The History of the Buddha
15. *Chariyā Piṭaka* – Proper Conduct
16. *Milindapañhā* – Questions of Milinda (Burmese Canon)
17. *Nettipakaraṇa* – Book of Guidance (Burmese and Sinhalese Canon)
18. *Peṭakopadesa* – *Piṭaka* Disclosure (Burmese and Sinhalese Canon)

2) The *Vinaya Piṭaka* consists of three books.

3) The *Abhidhamma Piṭaka* consists of seven books.

ENDNOTES

See below for a key to abbreviations for texts often quoted in this book. When scriptures are cited with no page numbers, the citations are standard references. Thus *Dham* 11:151 refers to chapter 11, verse 151 of the *Dhammapada*. When quoting the *Nikāyas*, the volume numbers are given as lower-case roman numerals, and the page numbers refer to the Pali edition published by the Pali Text Society; these page numbers are generally referenced in English translations. Thus *MN.i*, p.510 refers to volume 1 of the *Majjhima Nikāya*, page 510 in the Pali edition of the Pali Text Society publication. Page numbers for the *Lalitavistara* and other scriptures refer to the Sanskrit or Pali edition unless a particular translation is cited.

KEY TO ABBREVIATIONS OF TEXTS QUOTED

AN	*Aṅguttara Nikāya*
BCH	*Buddhacharita*
BG	*Bhagavadgītā*
BIE	Edward Conze, *Buddhism: Its Essence and Development*
BOD	*Bodhicharyāvatāra*
BRU	*Brihadāraṇyaka Upanishad*
BTA	Edward Conze, *Buddhist Texts through the Ages*
BWB	Edward Conze, *Buddhist Wisdom Books*
DCB	Musō Kokushi, *Dream Conversations on Buddhism and Zen*
Dham	*Dhammapada*

DN	*Dīgha Nikāya*
EBP	Junjirō Takakusu, *The Essentials of Buddhist Philosophy*
KAZ	Chinul, *The Korean Approach to Zen*
Lal	*Lalitavistara*
LAN	*The Laṅkāvatāra Sūtra*, tr. D. T. Suzuki
LPH	Pabongka Rinpoche, *Liberation in the Palm of Your Hand*
MN	*Majjhima Nikāya*
Sadd	*Saddharmapuṇḍarīka*
SBA	Soyen Shaku, *Sermons of a Buddhist Abbot*
SLS	D. T. Suzuki, *Studies in the Laṅkāvatāra Sūtra*
SN	*Saṁyutta Nikāya*
TYD	W. Y. Evans-Wentz, *Tibetan Yoga and Secret Doctrines*
WPT	Patrul Rinpoche, *Words of My Perfect Teacher*

1. *Mahāyānaviṁshikā* 1.
2. *MN.i*, p.510.
3. *SN.ii*, p.106.
4. *MN.i*, p.168.
5. P. Harvey, *An Introduction to Buddhism*, p.3.
6. P. Williams and A. Tribe, *Buddhist Thought*, p.193.
7. Many Buddhist terms such as Dharma have a range of meanings depending on the context in which they are used. See the Glossary for a discussion of various facets of the terms and their subtle differences of meaning.
8. *Gambhīrā duddasā duranubodhā santā paṇītā atakkāvacharā nipuṇā paṇḍitavedanīyā*, *DN.i*, p.12.
9. *bhagavā tuṇhī ahosi*, *SN.iv*, p.400; *mā h'evaṁ*, *AN.ii*, p.161; *na kallo pañho*, *SN.ii*, p.60–61.
10. *DN.ii*, p.100.
11. *SN.v*, p.438.
12. *MN.iii*, p.234.
13. *MN.ii*, p.240.
14. *The Power of Compassion*, p.113.
15. *The Power of Compassion*, p.128.
16. *BIE*, p.95.
17. *SN.ii*, p.106; see also *SN.v*, p.168.
18. *DN.ii*, p.144.
19. Mention is made in the *Dīgha* and *Saṁyutta Nikāyas*; see L. M. Joshi, *Brahmanism, Buddhism and Hinduism*, p.52:150–151.
20. *Sadd* 2:70.
21. *DN.iii*, p.84.
22. *SN.iii*, p.120.
23. *Vajrachchhedikā Prajñāpāramitā* 26b. See *BWB*, p.63.
24. *WPT*, p.xxxii.
25. *TYD*, p.50.
26. In *TYD*, p.99.
27. *bahujana hitāya bahujana sukhāya lokānukampāya*, *AN.ii*, p.34–35.

28. *Tathāgato sayaṁ abhiññā sachchhikatvā pavedeti, DN.i*, p.12; see also "that [reality] I know and see" (*tam ahaṁ jānāmi passāmi*), *MN.i*, p.329.
29. *Dham* 11:151.
30. *SN.ii*, p.106.
31. *SN.v*, p.168.
32. For a detailed discussion on the subject see K.N. Upadhyaya, *Early Buddhism and the Bhagavadgītā*, p.31–39.
33. *Encyclopedia of Buddhism*, ed. D. Keown, p.700.
34. *Encyclopedia of Buddhiṣm*, ed. R. E. Buswell, Jr., vol.1, p.295.
35. P. Harvey, *An Introduction to Buddhism*, p.14–15.
36. *An Introduction to Buddhism*, p.15–16; *DN.ii*, p.76.
37. *Lal* 12, p.136.
38. *BCH* 3:36–37.
39. *BCH* 3:40.
40. *BCH* 3:46–47.
41. *BCH* 3:61–62.
42. *BCH* 4:85–87, 89, 96–98.
43. *BCH* 5:18–19.
44. *BCH* 5:30, 32–33.
45. *Lal* 15:596–600, p.190.
46. *BCH* 5:37–38.
47. E. J. Thomas, *The Life of the Buddha as Legend and History*, p.54.
48. *Lal* 15:674, p.210.
49. *Middle Length Discourses of the Buddha* 100:9, tr. B. *Ñāṇamoli*, p.821.
50. *Middle Length Discourses of the Buddha* 99:4, tr. B. *Ñāṇamoli*, p.808.
51. *The Vimalakīrti Nirdeṣa Sūtra*, tr. C. Luk, p.15.
52. *BCH* 6:15–16, 18, 21–22.
53. *BCH* 6:43–46, 48, 50–52.
54. *Lal* 15, p.214.
55. *BCH* 8:86–9:6.
56. *BCH* 9:68–69.
57. *Lal* 19:907.
58. This is based on the Tibetan Records, as stated in *The Life of the Buddha and the Early History of His Order*, tr. W. W. Rockhill, p.31.
59. *DN.i*, p.76.
60. *DN.i*, p.76–77.
61. *BCH* 14:87.
62. *MN.i*, p.23; *SN.ii*, p.51; *SN.iv*, p.66.
63. *MN.i*, p.167–168.
64. *MN.i*, p.169.
65. *Lal* 25:1394.
66. *MN.i*, p.169–170.
67. *Lal* 25:1394.
68. *MN.i*, p.169.
69. *Lal* 26:1422–1424.
70. *MN.i*, p.171.
71. *Sadd* 2:3.
72. *Sadd* 8:32.
73. *MN.i*, p.171; see also *Lal*, p.26.
74. *MN.i*, p.172.
75. *Jātaka* 485, iv.282; see also E. J. Thomas, *The Life of the Buddha as Legend and History*, p.101.
76. *DN.ii*, p.96.
77. *DN.ii*, p.99.
78. *DN.ii*, p.100.
79. *DN.ii*, p.118.
80. *DN.ii*, p.120.
81. *DN.ii*, p.137.
82. *DN.ii*, p.138.
83. *DN.ii*, p.154.
84. *DN.ii*, p.154–155.
85. *DN.ii*, p.156.
86. *SN.iii*, p.120.
87. *AN*.ii, p.37–39.

88. *EBP*, p.133.
89. *EBP*, p.133.
90. *MN.i*, p.326–331.
91. *Aṣṭasāhasrikā Prajñāpāramitā* 4:94, tr. E. Conze, p.35.
92. *Aṣṭasāhasrikā Prajñāpāramitā* 31:512–513, cf tr. E. Conze, p.216.
93. *The Zen Teaching of Huang Po on the Transmission of Mind*, p.29–30.
94. *Vajrachchhedikā Prajñāpāramitā* 17c, in *BWB*, p.58.
95. *Vajrachchhedikā Prajñāpāramitā* 29 in *BWB*, p.64.
96. *Sadd* ch.15, in *BTA*, p.142–143; see also *Saddharmapuṇḍarīka Sūtra*, tr. R. Das, p.322.
97. *LAN*, p.13.
98. *Saddharmapuṇḍarīka Sūtra*, tr. R. Das, p.5.
99. *The Larger Sukhāvatī-Vyūha*, in *Buddhist Mahāyāna Texts*, tr. F. M. Müller, p.33–41.
100. See *BTA*, p.14.
101. *bahujana hitāya bahujana sukhāya lokānukampāya*, *AN.ii*, p.34–35.
102. *Aṣṭasāhasrikā Prajñāpāramitā*, tr. E. Conze, p.25.
103. *Sadd* 5:19.
104. *The Flower Ornament Scripture*, tr. T. Cleary, p.102.
105. *SLS*, p.308.
106. *SLS*, p.310.
107. *The Realization of the Certitude of Appreciative Awareness and Ethical Action* (*Prajñopayavi-niscayasiddhi*), ch.2, in *BTA*, p.242–243.
108. *Asaṁskrita prabhāvitā hi ārya pudgalāḥ*, *Vajrachchhedikā Prajñāpāramitā* 7, in *BWB*, p.36.
109. *BWB*, p.39.
110. *DN.iii*, p.136–137.
111. *Mud and Water*, p.110.
112. *Mud and Water*, p.110.
113. *MN.iii*, p.169.
114. *BOD* 4:20.
115. *LPH*, p.320.
116. *WPT*, p.379, n34.
117. *Dham* 14:182.
118. *BOD* 7:14.
119. *WPT*, p.17–18.
120. *LPH*, p.25.
121. *Zenshū* 1:2, in *Great Fool*, p.242.
122. *Zen Mind, Beginners Mind*, p.26.
123. *Pachchattaṁ veditabbo viññūhī*, *MN.i*, p.37.
124. *SN.i*, p.62; *AN.ii*, p.48.
125. *LAN*, p.10.
126. *Dewdrops on a Lotus Leaf*, p.81.
127. *DCB*, p.6.
128. *Dohākosha* 47, 48, 68, 89, in *BTA*, p.230, 233, 236.
129. Quoted in *WPT*, p.10.
130. Quoted in *KAZ*, p.102.
131. *The Platform Sūtra*, p.30.
132. *Dham* 3:41, 4:48, 4:46.
133. *Dham* 11:148, 20:277.
134. *BOD* 2:58, 2:61; 8:20.
135. *BOD* 7:5, 34.
136. *WPT*, p.53.
137. *WPT*. p.42.
138. *The Supreme Path, the Rosary of Precious Gems*, in *TYD*, p.86.
139. *Dham* 2:21, 8:114–115, 9:116.
140. *Dham* 5:75, 9:126.
141. *BOD* 1:10.
142. *BOD* 5:13.
143. *LPH*, p.80.
144. *LPH*, p.26.
145. *LPH*, p.32.
146. *DCB*, p.5.
147. *KAZ*, p.155.

148. *WPT*, p.35.
149. *Dham* 24:355.
150. *Dham* 19:264, 22:307.
151. *BOD* 7:36.
152. *Path to Enlightenment in Tibetan Buddhism*, p.209, 216.
153. *LPH*, p.348.
154. *The Supreme Path, the Rosary of Precious Gems*, in *TYD*, p.76.
155. In *TYD*, p.67–68.
156. In *TYD*, p.73.
157. *KAZ*, p.157.
158. *WPT*, p.37.
159. *Dham* 20:277–279.
160. *AN*.iv, p.137.
161. *MN.iii*, p.280.
162. *MN.ii*, p.261–262.
163. *MN.ii*, p.263.
164. *LPH*, p.346.
165. *LPH*, p.347.
166. *LPH*, p.485–486.
167. *LPH*, p.355.
168. *LPH*, p.338.
169. *Buddhist Thought in India*, p.35.
170. *Dham* 11:146.
171. *Dham* 15:202–203.
172. *MN.i*, p.365.
173. *MN.i*, p.364.
174. *MN.i*, p.506.
175. Quoted in *LPH*, p.492.
176. Quoted in *LPH*, p.493.
177. Quoted in *LPH*. p.483.
178. Quoted in *LPH*. p.476.
179. *taṁ kiṁ maññasi ... rūpaṁ nichchaṁ vā anichchaṁ vāti*, *MN.i*, p.232–233; *SN.iii*, p.88, 118.
180. *SN.ii*, p.124–126.
181. *SN.iii*, p.46.
182. *SN.iii*, p.46.
183. *SN.iii*, p.68.
184. *Dham* 20:279.
185. *Udāna* 1.3, p.2.
186. *The Heart of the Buddha's Teaching*, p.221.
187. *DN.ii*, p.55.
188. *Katamo eko dhammo pahātabbo? Asmimāno-ayaṁ eko dhammo pahātabbo. DN.iii*, p.273.
189. *MN.i*, p.137.
190. *SN.ii*, p.253.
191. *SN.iii*, p.130.
192. *SN.iii*, p.131.
193. *SN.iii*, p.131.
194. *DN.i*, p.202; *SN.i*, p.135.
195. *DCB*, p.74.
196. *MN.i*, p.232–233; *SN.iii*, p.88, 118.
197. *SN.iii*, p.46.
198. *atthattā'ti, natthattā'ti, Bhagavā tuṇhī ahosi*, *SN.iv*, p.400.
199. *SN.iv*, p.400–401.
200. *BG* 2:71.
201. *BG* 12:13–4.
202. *BG* 18:53.
203. *LAN*, p.69.
204. *Ratnagotravibhāga* 40, in *BTA*, p.181.
205. *Buddhist Thought in India*, p.45.
206. *Dohākosha* 89, 105, in *BTA*, p.236, 238.
207. *DCB*, p.40–41.
208. *TYD*, p.5.
209. *Chhāndogya Upanishad* 8:12:1.
210. *Maitrī Upanishad* 2:5.
211. *BG* 15:7, tr. S. Radhakrishnan, p.328.
212. *MN.i*, p.431.
213. *MN.i*, p.426.
214. *DN.ii*, p.332–333.
215. *DN.ii*, p.334.
216. *DN.ii*, p.329.
217. *Itivuttaka*, p.37.
218. *Udāna* 8.3, p.80.

219. *pachchattaṁ veditabbo viññūhī*, *MN.i*, p.37.
220. *DN.i*, p.223.
221. *MN.i*, p.487–8; *SN.iii*, p.107–8, 111–2, 118–9, 122–4.
222. *māro pāpimā... viññāṇaṁ samanvesati*, *SN.i*, p.122; *SN.iii*, p.124.
223. *appatiṭṭhitena... viññāṇena... parinibbuto ti*, *SN.i*, p.122; *SN.iii*, p.124.
224. *anantam apāraṁ vijñāna-ghan eva*, *BRU* 2:4:12.
225. *anantash chātmā vishva-rūpo*, *Shvetāshvatara Upanishad* 1:9.
226. *anantā rashmayas tasya dīpavad yaḥ sthito hridi*, *Maitrī Upanishad* 6:30.
227. *BRU* 4:5.6.
228. *atha kho aññataro satto āyukkhayā vā puññakkhayā vā ābhassarakāyā chavitvā suññaṁ brahma-vimānaṁ upapajjati*, *DN.i*, p.17.
229. *DN.i*, p.18.
230. *DN.i*, p.18.
231. *AN.i*, p.173–174.
232. *Jātaka.v*, p.238.
233. *Jātaka.vi*, p.208.
234. *DN.i*, p.220–223.
235. *DN.iii*, p.28–34.
236. *MN.i*, p.326–330.
237. *DN.i*, p.168; *DN.ii*, p.157; *DN.ii*, p.226–227.
238. *MN.iii*, p.101–102.
239. *Shvetāshvatara Upanishad* 6:16; *Kaṭha Upanishad* 6:1.
240. *Muṇḍaka Upanishad* 1:1:1.
241. *BRU* 2:4:14; 4:5:15; *Taittirīya Upanishad* 2:7; *Kaṭha Upanishad* 3:15, 6:12.
242. *BG* 3:15.
243. *garīyase brahmaṇo'pyādikartre*, *BG* 11:37.
244. *BG* 11:5.
245. *Ābrahma-bhuvanāl lokāḥ punar āvartino 'rjuna.* (Along with the region of Brahmā downwards, all the worlds are subject to return to rebirth, O Arjuna) *BG* 8:16.
246. *BG* 4:6–7, 9:17–18, 11:43, 14:3–4.
247. *SN.ii*, p.178.
248. *MN.ii*, p.31–32.
249. *Sutta Nipāta* 654, p.120.
250. *BRU* 4:4:5.
251. *BG* 14:16.
252. *Chhāndogya Upanishad* 8:1:6.
253. *BG* 3:27.
254. *BG* 3:5.
255. *MN.i*, p.390.
256. *AN.i*, p.174.
257. *Īsha Upanishad* 2.
258. *svakarmaṇātam abhyarchya siddhiṁ vindati mānavah*, *BG* 18:46.
259. *BG* 2:47.
260. *Chhāndogya Upanishad* 4:14:3.
261. *Kena Upanishad* 1:5–6.
262. *Shvetāshvatara Upanishad* 6:11.
263. *Shvetāshvatara Upanishad* 3:20.
264. *Īsha Upanishad* 7.
265. *BG* 5:15.
266. *Shvetāshvatara Upanishad* 6:16; *Kaṭha Upanishad* 6:1.
267. *BRU* 2:4:14, 4:5:15, *Taittirīya Upanishad* 2:9, *Kaṭha Upanishad* 3:15, 6:12.
268. *BRU* 2:3:6, 4:2:4, 4:4:22, 4:5:15.
269. *Taittirīya Upanishad* 2:4:1; 2:9:1.
270. *BRU* 1:4:10.
271. *BRU* 3:9:28.
272. *Chhāndogya Upanishad* 3:14:1; *Maitrī Upanishad* 4:6.
273. *BG* 2:7.

274. *BG* 13:12.
275. *Udāna* 8.1, p.80.
276. *Udāna* 1.10, p.9.
277. *Milindapañhā*, p.316–317.
278. *So … nibbuto … brahmabhūtena attanā viharati*, *MN.ii*, p.159.
279. *SN.iii*, p.83.
280. *MN.i*, p.386.
281. *Tathāgatassa hetaṁ … adhivachanaṁ dhammakāyo iti pi, brahmakāyo iti pi, dhammabhūto iti pi, brahmabhūto iti pi. DN.iii*, p.84.
282. *Bhagavā … Dhammabhūto, Brahmabhūto*, *MN.iii*, p.195, 224, etc.
283. *MN.iii*, p.195, 224.
284. *imass' eva kho … ariyassa aṭṭhaṅgikassa maggassa adhivachanaṁbrahmayānaṁ iti pi, dhammayānaṁ iti pi*, *SN.v*, p.5.
285. *Brahmunā saddhiṁ saṁvasati … dhammena saddhiṁ saṁvasati*, *AN.i*, p.207–208.
286. *Tathāgato … Brahmachakkaṁ pavatteti*, *SN.ii*, p.27; *bhagavatā … dhammachakkaṁ pavattitaṁ*, *SN.v*, p.423.
287. *Bodhiḥ Buddhatvaṁ … dharmakāyākhyaṁ paramārtha-tattvam-uchyate. Bodhicharyāvatāra of Shāntideva*, ed. P.L. Vaidya, p.208.
288. *Māṇḍūkya Upanishad* 7.
289. *Dohākosha* 58, in *BTA*, p.232.
290. *Dohākosha* 88, in *BTA*, p.236.
291. Quoted in *DCB*, p.64.
292. *Dohākosha* 90, in *BTA*, p.236.
293. *EBP*, p.34, 41.
294. *EBP*, p.33.
295. *EBP*, p.109–110.
296. *SLS*, p.308.
297. *SLS*, p.310.
298. *Sadd* 4:60.
299. *Sadd* 15:21.
300. *Saddharmapuṇḍarīka*, tr. H. Kern, p.xxvi–xxvii.
301. In *You Are the Eyes of the World*, p.38.
302. *BIE*, p.43.
303. *BG* 11:38.
304. In *TYD*, p.vi.
305. *The Flower Ornament Scripture*, p.450.
306. *BIE*, p.147.
307. *BRU* 3:9:28.
308. *Taittirīya Upanishad* 2:1:1.
309. *Nrisimhottara-tapanīya Upanishad* 7.
310. In V. Mackenzie, *Reincarnation: The Boy Lama*, p.22.
311. *Sadd* ch.6.
312. *SLS*, p.310.
313. *Ehipassiko … pachchattaṁ veditabbo viññūhī'ti. MN.i*, p.37.
314. *SN.iii*, p.120.
315. *Aṣṭasāhasrikā Prajñāpāramitā*, tr. E. Conze, p.25, 35.
316. *Vajrachchhedikā Prajñāpāramitā* 26b, see *BWB*, p.63.
317. *SLS*, p.308, 310.
318. *Sadd* 5:19.
319. *BOD* 2:48.
320. *DN.i*, p.12.
321. *Prajñopāyaviniścayasiddhi* 2:189, in *BTA*, p.242–243.
322. *BOD* 3:25–26.
323. Quoted in *KAZ*, p.140–141.
324. *Kindly Bent to Ease Us*, vol.1, p.78.
325. In *TYD*, p.vi.
326. *Dham* 11:146.
327. *Dham* 13:174.

328. *Dham* 5:63.
329. *LPH*, p.130.
330. *WPT*, p.183–184.
331. *WPT*, p.187.
332. *WPT*, p.137.
333. *WPT*, p.137.
334. Quoted in E. Dōgen, *Dōgen Zen*, p.25.
335. *WPT*, p.143.
336. *WPT*, p.143.
337. Quoted in *WPT*, p.28–29.
338. *WPT*, p.28.
339. *Dohākosha of Saraha*, quoted in Dalai Lama XIV, *Universal Responsibility*, p.99.
340. *LPH*, p.252.
341. *LPH*, p.253–254.
342. Quoted in *LPH*, p.255.
343. *Dham*, 8:106.
344. *The Supreme Path, the Rosary of Precious Gems*, in *TYD*, p.79–80.
345. *WPT*, p.16.
346. Quoted in *WPT*, p.16.
347. *LPH*, p.106–107.
348. *Sadd* 5:60.
349. *Mud and Water*, p.55.
350. *LPH*, p.257.
351. Quoted in *LPH*, p.257.
352. *LPH*, p.257.
353. *WPT*, p.xxxviii.
354. *LPH*, p.254.
355. *WPT*, p.xxxii.
356. *SN.ii*, p.106.
357. *SN.v*, p.168.
358. *MN.i*, p.331.
359. *LPH*, p.38.
360. *TYD*, p.18.
361. *Sadd* 4:60.
362. *WPT*, p.xxxviii.
363. *WPT*, p.141–142.
364. *LPH*, p.190.
365. *LPH*, p.272.
366. *DN.ii*, p.82; *DN.iii*, p.99.
367. *DN.ii*, p.83; *DN.iii*, p.101.
368. *DN.iii*, p.115.
369. *Sadd* 2:3.
370. *Sadd* 8:32.
371. *WPT*, p.xxxii.
372. *WPT*, p.xxxviii.
373. *The Supreme Path, the Rosary of Precious Gems*, in *TYD*, p.95, 99.
374. *LPH*, p.278.
375. *DN.ii*, p.100.
376. *DN.ii*, p.154.
377. *Sadd* 5:19.
378. *LPH*, p.281.
379. *The Lotus Sūtra* ch.4, tr. B. Watson, p.61–64.
380. *LPH*, p.281.
381. *DN.iii*, p.4.
382. *The Larger Sukhāvatī-Vyūha* in *Buddhist Mahāyāna Texts*, tr. F. M. Müller, p.45.
383. *DN.ii*, p.138.
384. *LPH*, p.300.
385. *LPH*, p.718.
386. *The Supreme Path, the Rosary of Precious Gems*, in *TYD*, p.82, 91.
387. *The Precious Treasury of Pith Instructions*, p.91.
388. *WPT*, p.35.
389. *The Life and Teaching of Nāropa*, p.xiv.
390. *MN.ii*, p.98–99.
391. *MN.ii*, p.102.
392. *The Precious Treasury of Pith Instructions*, p.108.
393. *MN.iii*, p.6.
394. *WPT*, p.13.
395. *WPT*, p.17.
396. *WPT*, p.16–17.
397. Quoted in *LPH*, p.324.
398. *LPH*, p.325.
399. *Mud and Water*, p.152.

400. Quoted in E. Dōgen, *Dōgen Zen*, p.24.
401. Quoted in E. Dōgen, *Dōgen Zen*, p.29–30, n.18.
402. *WPT*, p.148.
403. Quoted in *LPH*, p.262.
404. *LPH*, p.130.
405. *LPH*, p.293.
406. *WPT*, p.150.
407. Quoted in *WPT*, p.310.
408. *WPT*, p.xxxvi.
409. *WPT*, p.312.
410. *WPT*, p.xxxvii.
411. *BOD* 5:102.
412. *WPT*, p.153.
413. *WPT*, p.309.
414. *WPT*, p.183.
415. *WPT*, p.159.
416. *Lal* 19:907.
417. *WPT*, p.144.
418. *WPT*, p.145.
419. *WPT*, p.151.
420. *WPT*, p.144.
421. Quoted in E. Dōgen, *Dōgen Zen*, p.17.
422. *Dakini Teachings*, p.150.
423. *MN.i*, p.225–226.
424. *Mud and Water*, p.59.
425. *Mud and Water*, p.62–63.
426. *Mud and Water*, p.66.
427. *WPT*, p.238.
428. *WPT*, p.237.
429. *WPT*, p.353.
430. *WPT*, p.141.
431. *MN.i*, p.318–320.
432. *AN.i*, p.188–193.
433. *LPH*, p.56.
434. *WPT*, p.141.
435. *WPT*, p.152.
436. *LPH*, p.277.
437. *LPH*, p.284–285.
438. Quoted in *LPH*, p.285.
439. *WPT*, p.152–153.
440. *yesaṁ mayi saddhāmattaṁ pemamattaṁ sabbe te saggaparāyanā ti*, *MN.i*, p.142.
441. *DN.ii*, p.93–94.
442. *saddhīdha vittaṁ purisassa seṭṭham*, *SN.i*, p.42, 214.
443. *saddhāya tarati ogham*, *SN.i*, p.214.
444. *pañchimāni padhāniyaṅgāni… sammādukkhakkhaya gāminiyā*, *MN.ii*, p.95.
445. Quoted in *EBP*, p.174; see also *Milindapañhā*, Hindi tr. Jagdish Kāshyap, p.296.
446. *DN.ii*, p.138.
447. For details, see K. N. Upadhyaya, *Early Buddhism and the Bhagavadgītā*, p.251–272.
448. *MN.i*, p.101.
449. *Lal* 7, Hindi tr. S.B. Shāstrī, p.189.
450. *WPT*, p.187.
451. *BIE*, p.153.
452. *BIE*, p.149.
453. *BIE*, p.152.
454. *LPH*, p.253–254.
455. *LPH*, p.280.
456. *BIE*, p.144; see also *EBP*, p.174.
457. *BIE*, p.206.
458. *EBP*, p.175.
459. Compare *BG* 11:9–50 with *Sadd* 1:1–56.
460. Compare *BG* 9:22–34 with *Sadd* 2:77–98.
461. *BOD* 2:7–8.
462. *BOD* 2:44–48.
463. *BOD* 6:125–126.
464. *WPT*, p.xxxvii–xxxviii.
465. *WPT*, p.176.
466. *EBP*, p.183–185.
467. *BIE*, p.158.

468. *BIE*, p.158.
469. *BIE*, p.159.
470. *Dham* 2:21.
471. *BOD* 7:14.
472. *WPT*, p.183–184.
473. *The Zen Teaching of Bodhidharma*, p.23.
474. *WPT*, p.144.
475. *Shikshāsamuchchaya* 310, in *BTA*, p.188.
476. *BOD* 5:30.
477. *WPT*, p.149.
478. *Dham* 7:98.
479. *Dham* 14:194.
480. *Dham* 15:206–207.
481. *WPT*, p.32.
482. *WPT*, p.7.
483. *MN.i*, p.300.
484. *MN.i*, p.301.
485. *The Heart of the Buddha's Teaching*, p.64.
486. The four objects for the practice of mindfulness described by the Budhha in the *Satipaṭṭhāna Sutta*, *MN.i*, p.55–62.
487. *sīlasampadaṁ ārādheti*, *MN.i*, p.200; *samādhi sampadaṁ ārādheti*, *MN.i*, p.201; *ñāṇadassanam ārādheti*, *MN.i*, p.202.
488. *sammāñāṇassa sammāvimutti pahoti*, *MN.iii*, p.76.
489. *apadāne sobhati paññā*, *AN.i*, p.102.
490. *DN.i*, p.124.
491. *Bhikkhu Vissāsam āpādi appatto āsavakkhayam*, *Dham* 19:272.
492. *MN.i*, p.271–272.
493. *aṇumattesu vajjesu bhayadassāvī*, *DN.i*, p.63; *DN.iii*, p.78.
494. *MN.iii*, p.256–257.
495. *Dham* 2:31.
496. *DN.i*, p.63–64; *DN.i*, p.146.
497. *DN.i*, p.76; *DN.i*, p.147.
498. *DN.i*, p.84; see also *DN.i*, p.147; *MN.i*, p.23; *SN.ii*, p.51; *SN.iv*, p.66.
499. *Dham* 14:183.
500. *Mud and Water*, p.52–53.
501. *The Sutra of Perfect Enlightenment*, tr. A. C. Muller, p.104.
502. *MN.i*, p.368, 371.
503. *MN.iii*, p.209.
504. *Dham* 10:129.
505. *Dham* 10:131.
506. *AN.i*, p.296.
507. *AN.iii*, p.208.
508. *MN.i*, p.361.
509. *Sutta Nipāta* 295–296. See tr. V. Fausböll, p.50.
510. *Sutta Nipāta* 629.
511. *DN.ii*, p.127.
512. *LAN*, ch.7, p.212–221.
513. *WPT*, p.102–103.
514. *LPH*, p.444.
515. *LPH*, p.580–581.
516. *The Four Noble Truths*, p.132.
517. In *The Teaching of Vimalakīrti* (*Vimalakīrtinirdeṣa*), tr. Sara Boin, p.lxxv.
518. *SN.iii*, p.151.
519. *SN.i*, p.39.
520. *AN.i*, p.8.
521. *SN.ii*, p.95.
522. *Dham* 1:1–2.
523. *Dham* 3:33, 35, 38, 40, 42, 43.
524. *BOD* 5:3, 6, 13, 14.
525. *viharati anupalitto lokenā'ti*, *SN.iii*, p.140.
526. *MN.i*, p.5–6.
527. *N.iii*, p.68, 90; see also *SN.iv*, p.65–66.

528. Quoted in *LPH*, p.479.
529. *SN.i*, p.40.
530. *DCB*, p.4.
531. *DCB*, p.34.
532. *DN.ii*, p.132.
533. Quoted in *The Life and Teaching of Nāropa*, tr. H. Guenther, p.196–197.
534. Quoted in *WPT*, p.356.
535. Quoted in *WPT*, p.356.
536. *Buddhist Scriptures*, p.139, 141.
537. *TYD*, p.29.
538. *BIE*, p.147.
539. *TYD*, p.233, fn.2.
540. *BOD* 8:118.
541. *LPH*, p.35–37.
542. *Sadd* 5:2, tr. H. Kern, p.122.
543. *BIE*, p.158.
544. In *TYD*, p.122.
545. *LPH*, p.156.
546. *LPH*, p.711–712.
547. *LPH*, p.666–667.
548. *BOD* 5:30–33.
549. *Shikshāsamuchchaya* 311, in *BTA*, p.189.
550. *Sadd*, 24:24–26; see *Saddharmapuṇḍarīka*, tr. H. Kern, p.415–416.
551. *Sadd* 24 prose.
552. *Sadd* 24 prose.
553. *The Zen Teachings of Master Lin-chi*, p.58.
554. *Becoming the Compassion Buddha*, p.107.
555. "Working with Circumstances", *The Mirror*, December, 2001.
556. Quoted in S. Addiss, *The Art of Zen*, p.29.
557. *SBA*, p.163.
558. *SBA*, p.162.
559. *SBA*, p.163.
560. *BIE*, p.186.
561. *The Larger Sukhāvatī-Vyūha*, in *Buddhist Mahāyāna Texts*, tr. F. M. Müller, p.36–38.
562. *Mahāratnakūṭa Sūtra*, in *A Treasury of Mahāyāna Sūtras*, tr. The Buddhist Association of the United States, p.192.
563. *MN.i*, p.23.
564. *Sadd* 1 prose.
565. *Lal* 22 prose, tr. Shānti Bhikshu Shāstrī, p.663.
566. *Sadd* 7 prose; see *Saddharmapuṇḍarīka*, tr. H. Kern, p.156–157.
567. *Lal* 26:1423–1424, tr. Shānti Bhikshu Shāstrī, p.770.
568. *The Mahāvastu*, vol.1, tr. J. Jones, p.134–136.
569. *Chandrakīrti's Prasannapadā on Nāgārjuna's Madhyamakashāstra*, p.155, commenting on 18:7.
570. *Sadd* 5 prose.
571. *Chandrakīrti's Prasannapadā on Nāgārjuna's Madhyamakashāstra*, p.155.
572. *Samādhirāja Sūtra* 14.87; quoted in *Chandrakīrti's Prasannapadā on Nāgārjuna's Madhyamakashāstra*, p.156.
573. *Sadd* 5:21.
574. *Thirty Years of Buddhist Studies*, p.110.
575. *Sadd* 9:3; see *Saddharmapuṇḍarīka*, tr. H. Kern, p.207.
576. Transliterated names from the romanized text of the *Saddharmapuṇḍarīka*, ed. U. Wogihara: 1. *siṁha-ghosha* (p.164) 2. *dundubhi-svara-rāja*

(p.321) 3. *megha-svara-rāja* (p.322) 4. *megha-dundubhi-svara-rāja* (p.357) 5. *jaladhara-garjita-ghosha-usvara-nakshatra-rāja-saṅku-umita-abhijñā* (ch. 25).
577. *Sadd* 10:26, 27, 30, 31.
578. *Sadd* 20 prose.
579. *Sadd* 18 prose, 71.
580. *Sadd* 13:62.
581. *Sadd* 13:67–68.
582. *Sadd* 15:9; see *Saddharmapuṇḍarīka*, tr. H. Kern, p.308.
583. *The Śūraṅgama Sūtra*, tr. C. Luk, p.142.
584. *DN.i*, p.79; see also *MN.i*, p.34, 69.
585. Hui-neng, *The Platform Sūtra*, tr. Red Pine, p.5.
586. *SBA*, p.163.
587. *EBP*, p.173.
588. Quoted in *Original Teachings of Ch'an Buddhism*, p.viii.
589. *Self-Liberation through Seeing with Naked Awareness*, no. 12, p.16.
590. *Becoming the Compassion Buddha*, p.128.
591. *The Śūraṅgama Sūtra*, tr. C. Luk, p.146–147.
592. *The Śūraṅgama Sūtra*, tr. C. Luk, p.149.
593. *The Flower Ornament Scripture*, tr. T. Cleary, p.346, 349, 351.
594. *DN.i*, p.155.
595. *DN.i*, p.152–155.
596. *The Flower Ornament Scripture*, tr. T. Cleary, p.364–365.
597. *The Flower Ornament Scripture*, tr. T. Cleary, p.365.
598. *The Flower Ornament Scripture*, tr. T. Cleary, p.365.
599. *Mahāratnakūṭa Sūtra*, in *A Treasury of Mahāyāna Sūtras*, tr. The Buddhist Association of the United States, p.192.
600. *The Larger Sukhāvatī-Vyūha*, in *Buddhist Mahāyāna Texts*, excerpted, tr. F. M. Müller, p.37–38, 40, 56.
601. *The Flower Ornament Scripture*, p.169.
602. *The Lotus Sūtra*, tr. B. Watson ch.3, p.51.
603. *SBA*, p.163.
604. *ayam eva ariyo aṭṭhaṅgiko maggo*, *SN.v*, p.421.
605. *Dham* 10:141.
606. *MN.i*, p.281–282.
607. *DN.i*, p.102.
608. *Dham* 19:264–267.
609. *Dham* 22:307; see also *Dham* 1:9.
610. *MN.i*, p.281.
611. *SN.iii*, p.93.
612. *Dham* 22:308.
613. *MN.i*, p.355; see also *DN.iii*, p.130; *MN.i*, p.273.
614. *DN.iii*, p.130.
615. *MN.ii*, p.197.
616. *MN.ii*, p.197.
617. *The Teaching of Vimalakīrti* (*Vimalakīrtinirdeṣa*), tr. S. Boin, p.v.
618. *MN.i*, p.39.
619. *SN.i*, p.169.
620. *WPT*, p.220.
621. *Dohākosha* 1, 2, 4, in *BTA*, p.224–225.
622. *Dohākosha* 47, 48, in *BTA*, p.230.
623. *Mud and Water*, p.44–45.
624. *Vinaya Piṭaka.ii*, p.185. Kullavagga 7:2:5.
625. *LPH*, p.619.
626. *MN.ii*, p.196.

627. *Sutta Nipāta* 608–611, p.115.
628. *Sutta Nipāta* 650–651, p.120.
629. *samaṇo Gotamo chātuvaṇṇiṁ suddhiṁ paññāpeti*, *MN.ii*, p.147–148.
630. *MN.ii*, p.182.
631. *MN.ii*, p.183.
632. *MN.ii*, p.129.
633. *MN.ii*, p.129–130, 152, 183.
634. *MN.ii*, p.130.
635. *MN.ii*, p.130.
636. *Dohākosha* 46, in *BTA*, p.230.
637. *MN.ii*, p.149–150.
638. *MN.ii*, p.151.
639. *DN.i*, p.99–100.
640. Verses 73–76. Quoted in *TYD*, p.64.
641. *MN.i*, p.168.
642. *MN.i*, p.168.
643. *Dham* 2:21.
644. *MN.i*, p.271–272.
645. *Sutta Nipāta* 885–886, p.173.
646. *ekaṁ hi sachchaṁ na dutiyam atthi*, *Sutta Nipāta* 884, p.172.
647. *MN.iii*, p.245.
648. *M.i*, p.168.
649. *Sadd*, ch.12.
650. *MN.ii*, p.21.
651. *Questions of King Milinda*, tr. T. W. Rhys Davids, p.xlviii.

GLOSSARY

Most terms are listed under their Sanskrit spellings in this Glossary, except where the Pali spelling is specific to a particular term. Note that the sound generally represented by *ṣ* or *ś* in many diacritical systems is represented by *sh* in this glossary, and the sound generally represented by *c* is represented by *ch* for ease of pronunciation for readers not familiar with these symbols.

Abhidhamma Piṭaka (Pali; Skt: *Abhidharma Piṭaka* – Basket of the Higher Teachings) The third of three sections of the Tipiṭaka in the Pali Canon, the *Abhidhamma Piṭaka* consists of a detailed analysis of doctrine and philosophy based on the Buddha's discourses. It standardized the teachings by summarizing and listing key doctrines regarded as the core of Buddhist thought and practice. Although legend has it that the Buddha formulated these teachings during his meditations and taught them to beings in heavenly realms, most scholars believe the *Abhidhamma* was recorded by monks around the third century BCE. *See also* Pali Canon, Tipiṭaka.

Ādi-Buddha The Primordial Buddha. Unborn and present before all else existed, Ādi-Buddha is absolute reality and the ultimate 'ground of being' – the foundation of all. Ādi-Buddha is synonymous with Samanta-Bhadra (he whose beneficence is everywhere) in Tibetan Buddhism. *See also* Dharmakāya.

Amida/Amita *See* Amitābha.

Amitābha (Skt; also Amida, Amita) Literally, infinite light. A Buddha revered in Mahāyāna tradition, Amitābha symbolizes the vast mercy and pure discriminating awareness developed through meditation. According to Mahāyāna teachings, he was a king who became a monk and acquired infinite merit from his good deeds over countless past lives as a bodhisattva named Dharmakāra. Amitābha is the centre of worship of the Pure Land schools of Chinese and Japanese Buddhism. He is the ruler of Sukhāvatī, his 'Pure Land' or paradise, where one can be reborn through loving recitation of his name and prescribed meditation practices, and thereafter continue to pursue enlightenment without having to be reborn in this world. *See also* Pure Land, Sukhāvatī.

Ānanda One of the Buddha's ten principle disciples, Ānanda was also the Buddha's cousin and personal attendant. Because of his extraordinary memory, his mastery of the sequential structure of the teachings and his steadfast study, Ānanda was able to retain the Buddha's discourses. His exposition of the discourses provided the basis for the codification of the *Sutta Piṭaka*, one of the three sections of the Pali Canon. Hailed by the Buddha as the Guardian of the Dhamma, Ānanda is also known for his role in the establishment of the order of Buddhist nuns. *See also* Pali Canon, Tipiṭaka.

anātman *See* anattā.

anattā (Pali; Skt: *anātman*) Literally, non-self, non-ego. One of the central teachings of Buddhism, the *anattā* doctrine asserts that no 'self' or 'I-ness' truly exists in any living being in the sense of a permanent and independent entity. The self (*attā*) is regarded as a transient phenomenon that manifests as a function of the interplay of five physical and mental constituents (*skandhas*) of a human being. Anattā is also the third of the three marks or characteristics of the phenomenal world. *See also* ātman, attā, skandhas, three marks.

Aṅguttara Nikāya (Collection of Numerical Discourses) The *Aṅguttara Nikāya* is the fourth collection within the *Sutta Piṭaka* in the Pali Canon. It consists of suttas (sūtras) arranged in eleven sections according to the number of elements referenced in them. For example, the first section (*Book of the Ones*) contains suttas concerning a single topic; the second section (*Book of the Twos*) contains suttas concerning pairs of things, for example, two people, and the discussion that one can never adequately repay one's parents. *See also* Pali Canon, Tipiṭaka.

anitya Impermanence; the first of the three marks or characteristics of the phenomenal world. *See also* three marks.

arahant (Pali; Skt: *arhat*) Literally, worthy one. In Theravāda teachings, an *arahant* is one who has attained the goal of complete awakening. Having extinguished all defilements, an *arahant* will not be reborn in the cycle of rebirth. While arahantship is the focus of earlier schools of Buddhism, the focus of the Mahāyāna tradition is to attain enlightenment and instead of stepping out of the cycle of birth and death, to be reborn in order to assist all suffering beings. In the Pali Canon, *arahant* is sometimes synonymous with Tathāgata. *See also* bodhichitta, bodhisattva, Tathāgata.

arhat *See* arahant.

Arjuna Literally, bright, shining; white or silver. The warrior hero of the *Mahābhārata*, a major Sanskrit epic of ancient India, Arjuna was a friend and disciple of Krishṇa. He received spiritual instruction on the battlefield of Kurukshetra in India, where Krishṇa served as his charioteer. He exemplifies the spiritual seeker through whom God instructs all humanity. The account of his instruction is related in the *Bhagavadgītā*. *See also* Bhagavadgītā.

Ashṭasāhasrikā Prajñāpāramitā *See* Perfection of Wisdom Sūtras.

Ashvaghosha A well-known Indian poet, dramatist and philosopher of North India, Ashvaghosha lived in the first to second centuries CE. His works include the *Buddhacharita*, an account of the life of the Buddha, and the epic poem *Saudarananda-kāvya*, the story of the spiritual journey of the Buddha's half-brother, Nanda. *See also* Buddhacharita.

Atīsha [Dīpaṅkara] (c.980–1055) A Bengali prince who became a renowned Buddhist scholar, Atīsha was invited by the King of Guge in Western Tibet to teach at a monastery there and to assist in the re-establishment of Buddhist teachings, which were in decline due to persecution by the Tibetan King Langdarma in the ninth century. In his major work, *Bodhipathapradīpa* (*Lamp on the Way to Enlightenment*), Atīsha gave an overview of Mahāyāna Buddhism. *See also* Mahāyāna Buddhism.

ātman (Skt; Hind: *ātmā*) Literally, self; from the Indo-European root meaning breath. In the Hindu tradition, *ātman* denotes the soul, in the sense of an unchanging, undying spiritual self at the core of all living beings. According to Buddhist teachings, however, the five physical and mental components that constitute a human being (*skandhas*) are transient, and therefore empty of self as a substantial, lasting entity. *See also* anattā, attā, skandhas, soul.

attā Literally, self. In Buddhist teachings, *attā* denotes the transient self that manifests as a function of the interplay of the five physical and mental constituents (*skandhas*) of a person. This self is not regarded as a permanent and individual entity, and to regard it as such is considered a cause of misery and a form of attachment that distracts from the path to enlightenment. *See also* anattā, ātman, skandhas, soul.

Avalokiteshvara (Jap, Kannon; Tib: Chenrezig; Chin: Kuan-Yin) Literally, the lord who looks below. According to Mahāyāna teaching, Avalokiteshvara is the Bodhisattva of Compassion, who postponed his Buddhahood in order to assist all living beings to attain Nirvāṇa. Avalokiteshvara has had numerous manifestations, both male and female, wherever Buddhism has flourished, including Kuan-Yin, the Buddhist goddess of compassion in China (not related to Avalokiteshvara in Taoism) and Chenrezig, one of the protectors of Tibet. *See also* Dalai Lama.

Avataṁsaka Sūtra *See* Flower Ornament Scripture.

Bassui Tokushō (1327–1387) A Zen master whose teaching brought reform to the Zen school in Japan. He taught moderation between the extremes of too much ritual and too much informality, saying that enlightenment is possible for anyone who aspires to it. Bassui was an itinerant practitioner of meditation in hermitages throughout Japan until 1378, when he founded the Kogakan Temple in response to his great number of students. Bassui is said to have died sitting in meditation with his students immediately after imparting his teachings to them. *Mud and Water: The Collected Teachings of Zen Master Bassui* is a translation of his teachings.

Bhagavadgītā Literally, sung by the Lord. A Sanskrit text written probably between the fifth century BCE and the second century CE, the *Bhagavadgītā* embodies the teachings of Lord Krishna. Written as a dialogue between Krishna and Arjuna on the battlefield of Mahābhārata, it emphasizes knowledge of the soul, devotion to God and the detached performance of one's duties. The *Bhagavadgītā* is one of the most popular books of Hindu philosophy.

Bhagavat Amitābha *See* Amitābha.

bhakti Devotion, worship, adoration, obeisance; a spiritual discipline undertaken to please God, a deity or a revered being. By following a path of love and spiritual discipline in accordance with the instructions of one's spiritual teacher or guru, an aspirant realizes enlightenment and inner union with the beloved. *See also* Guru Yoga.

Blissful Abode *See* Sukhāvatī.

bodhi *See* enlightenment.

Bodhicharyāvatāra (Entering the Path of Enlightenment) A well-known Mahāyāna text by Shāntideva, composed around 700 CE, the *Bodhicharyāvatāra* describes the steps to be followed on the bodhisattva path. The *Bodhicharyāvatāra* states the benefits of the desire to attain enlightenment, and then goes on to describe the method of practising the Six Perfections described in the *Lotus Sūtra* – generosity, ethics, patience, effort, concentration and wisdom – in order to attain enlightenment as well as relieve the suffering of all living beings. *See also* bodhisattva, Lotus Sūtra, Shāntideva.

bodhichitta Literally, enlightenment (*bodhi*) mind (*chitta*); 'awakening mind' or thought of enlightenment. *Bodhichitta* is the aspiration and firm resolve to attain enlightenment and to enable all beings to achieve Buddhahood as well. The term implies a delicate balance between limitless compassion for all beings and at the same time detachment from all – as well as from the illusion of an individual self. *See also* bodhisattva, enlightenment.

Bodhidharma An Indian prince in the early sixth century CE who became a Buddhist master, Bodhidharma (originally named Bodhidhana) is credited with bringing to China the teachings that came to be known as Ch'an (Zen). Bodhidharma is known as the Twenty-Eighth Patriarch of Buddhism as well as the First Patriarch of the Chinese Zen lineage. *See also* Ch'an, Zen.

bodhisattva Literally, one whose essence is enlightenment; the name given to anyone who, after having developed *bodhichitta*, seeks or has attained enlightenment in order to benefit all living beings suffering in the cycle of rebirth. In pure compassion and wisdom, fully-awakened bodhisattvas serve as true spiritual teachers or masters who guide their students outwardly and inwardly to perfect awakening and tranquillity. In Mahāyāna teaching, the bodhisattva ideal replaced the earlier ideal of the *arahant*, whose goal is the attainment of personal liberation. *See also* bodhichitta, guru, Mahāyāna.

Brahmā Sahampati Literally, mighty lord. Brahmā Sahampati is a god from the 'Pure Abodes' who attended upon the Buddha when he attained enlightenment, and soon after pleaded with him to teach the Dharma to those "with just a little dust in their eyes",[648] so that they might achieve enlightenment as well. The encounters of the Buddha and Brahmā Sahampati, believed to be the Brahmā closest to the Buddha, are related in the *Saṁyutta Nikāya* of the Pali Canon.

Brahmā A deity or superhuman being in Buddhist cosmology. Early Buddhist texts describe several Brahmās, some of whom consider themselves creators of the universe. The term 'Brahmā' in Buddhist teachings is to be distinguished from Brahman, the absolute reality or Supreme Being of the *Upanishads* and the *Vedas*, the earliest Hindu scriptures. In the Indian traditions, Brahmā is the creator-god, the first deity of the sacred Hindu trinity that also includes Vishnu (the preserver) and Shiva (the destroyer). *See also* Brahman.

Brahman The Sanskrit term in the *Upanishads* and the *Bhagavadgītā* denoting the Supreme Being, the indescribable, absolute and imperishable reality.

brahmin The class of priests and scholars, the highest among the four classes in the Hindu social hierarchy of the Buddha's time. A substantial number of the Buddha's disciples were brahmin by birth. The Buddha denied hereditary superiority, however, saying that one becomes a brahmin by one's actions alone. In Buddhist texts, the term is also synonymous with *arahant*, one who has attained enlightenment. *See also* caste, class.

Brihadāraṇyaka Upanishad Literally, extensive teachings by sages of forests. One of the older *Upanishads*, of pre-Buddhist origin, written between the eighth and fifth centuries BCE, the *Brihadāraṇyaka Upanishad* contains many philosophical reflections, including elementary teachings regarding the soul – *jīva* or *ātman*. *See also* ātman, jīva, Upanishads.

Buddha Literally, the enlightened or awakened one; one who through spiritual practice has attained final Nirvāṇa and has been released from the cycle of birth and death. A Buddha has eliminated all inner obstacles to Truth and has achieved absolute liberation from desires, cravings and attachments. Some Buddhas are *samyaksambuddhas*, those who have attained enlightenment and lead others to Nirvāṇa; others are *pratyekabuddhas*, those who have attained Nirvāṇa but do not teach aspirants. The epithet 'Buddha' usually refers to Shākyamuni Buddha or Gautama Buddha, the historical Buddha, though as a generic epithet, it may be applied to anyone who attains Buddhahood. Those who aspire to enlightenment take refuge in the Three Jewels of Buddhism: the Buddha, his teaching (Dharma) and the spiritual community (saṅgha). *See also* Shākyamuni, Siddhārtha Gautama, Three Jewels, triple body.

Buddhacharita (Life of the Buddha) The first complete account of the Buddha's life from birth to his enlightenment, written by the second-century Indian philosopher-poet Ashvaghosha. The complete version of the Sanskrit epic of twenty-eight cantos is preserved in Tibetan and Chinese translations. *See also* Ashvaghosha.

Buddha-field *See* Pure Land.

Buddha-nature Refers to the pure, eternal, knowing and luminous innate nature of all living beings. Buddha-nature is identical with the true nature of the Buddha, or ultimate reality. Illusion and defilements obscure one's Buddha-nature, which is unknowable by the mind; but adherence to the Buddhist path leads one beyond these limitations to the realization of the Absolute. Buddha-nature is used synonymously with Dharmakāya and Tathāgata-garbha. *See also* Dharmakāya, Tathāgata-garbha.

caste One of four principle divisions in the hierarchy of Hindu society that evolved from the hereditary system of four classes existing in the Buddha's time. The divisions were: 1) brahmins – priests and scholars whose duty was to maintain the Vedic tradition; 2) kshatriyas – warriors and rulers who were to maintain the social order; 3) vaishyas – professionals and farmers whose role was to generate wealth;

4) shūdras – labourers whose duty was to serve the other three classes. The caste system was originally intended to define individual responsibility and stabilize the social structure, but eventually it became a system of inherited power and oppression. The Buddha repudiated the notion that one's class status has any relationship to moral or spiritual status. *See also* brahmin, class.

Ch'an (Chin; Kor: Sŏn / Seon; Jap: Zen) A major Mahāyāna Buddhist school established in China, Ch'an derives its name from the Sanskrit word *dhyāna*, meaning meditation. The Ch'an school emphasized a practical approach over intellectual understanding of scriptures on the spiritual path. Meditation and the relationship between master and student play a central role in Ch'an, as they are the foundation of the 'mind-to-mind transmission' of the Dharma that occurs 'beyond words and letters'. This transmission passed through twenty-eight generations of 'patriarchs' to Bodhidharma, an Indian Buddhist master who then brought these teachings to China in the early sixth century CE and became the first Chinese patriarch. The Ch'an school spread in the same century to Korea (as Sŏn), Vietnam (as Thiên) and Japan (as Zen). *See also* Bodhidharma, Zen.

Chhāndogya Upanishad One of the primary and oldest *Upanishads*, dating before the first millennium BCE, the *Chhāndogya Upanishad* contains the principal mystic fundamentals of the *Vedas*, the earliest Hindu scriptures. *See also* Upanishads.

Chinese Buddhism It is generally assumed that Buddhism spread eastward along the Silk Road, the network of trade routes between northern India and China, by the first century CE, when rules for translating sacred texts from Sanskrit to Chinese were already in place. Buddhism in China has been shaped by interaction with the indigenous Taoism, a path of religious traditions and philosophical concepts that emerged in East Asia two millennia ago. Both paths mutually absorbed and integrated concepts and terms, since both focused on metaphysics and meditation practices. From the sixth century onward, 'five doors' to enlightenment via Buddhism were introduced in China: the Ch'an School, the Discipline School, the Teaching School, the Pure Land School and the Yoga School. The most well-known of these schools is Ch'an, thought to have originated with teachings brought to China by the Indian master Bodhidharma circa 526 CE. *See also* Ch'an.

Chinul (1158–1210) One of the most influential masters of Korean Buddhism (Sŏn), Chinul reformed the monastic community that had become commercialized, re-establishing discipline and pure-mindedness. He emphasized that one's innate nature is pure and taught that the search for enlightenment is essentially an inward journey, which he called 'observing the radiance'. According to Chinul one can perceive how things really are via three gates of meditation: *samādhi* (concentration), *prajñā* (wisdom) and the gate of complete and 'sudden awakening', which is based on understanding and faith. According to Chinul, the third gate provides the swiftest way to realization because it is a kind of meditation that helps to pierce illusion created by the mind. He shared this method only with those he considered spiritually mature. *See also* Zen.

chitta Literally, mind; state of mind or mind-set. Early Buddhism considered *chitta* to be virtually the same as consciousness; later schools, however, distinguished it as an underlying ground of consciousness that influences all conscious thought.

class A class was one of four principle divisions in the hierarchy of Indian society in the time of the Buddha, and these divisions became the foundation for the caste system that developed later. The Buddha regarded inherited class as irrelevant to moral or spiritual practice. *See also* brahmin, caste.

Conze, Edward (1904–1979) An important scholar and practitioner of Buddhism, Conze was one of the twentieth century's foremost Western translators of Buddhist texts. Born in London of mixed French, German and Dutch ancestry, Conze taught psychology, philosophy and comparative religion at the University of Oxford and the University of London. Conze translated and edited more than thirty texts that comprise the *Perfection of Wisdom Sūtras*, a group of Mahāyāna sūtras that discuss the perfection of spiritual wisdom or insight. His translations include the *Diamond Sūtra* and the *Heart Sūtra*, which contains the well-known mantra 'Gone wholly beyond – enlightenment, hail!' In addition, Conze wrote *Buddhism: Its Essence and Development* and the *Sanskrit-English Dictionary*. *See also* Perfection of Wisdom Sūtras.

cycle of birth and death *See* saṁsāra.

Dalai Lama, XIV (1935–) Literally, teacher whose wisdom is as great as the ocean. Dalai Lama is an honorary title denoting the lineage of Dalai Lamas who have served as spiritual leaders in Tibet from the sixteenth century onward and as titular heads of state from the mid-eighteenth century. Each successive Dalai Lama is considered to be an incarnation of the Bodhisattva of Compassion, Chenrezig. His Holiness, the XIV Dalai Lama, Tenzin Gyatso, left Tibet in 1959 following the assumption of control of the government of Tibet by the People's Republic of China in 1950 and now lives in Dharamsala, India. He received the Nobel Peace Prize in 1989.

Deer Park Deer Park is the site where the Buddha 'set in motion the wheel of Dharma' – where he first taught the Dharma after attaining enlightenment. Deer Park is an area within Rishipatana (now Sāranātha), one of the four main places of pilgrimage for Buddhists. It is located near Varanasi in Uttar Pradesh, India. *See also* Dharma.

dependent origination/interdependent co-arising Dependent origination is a core insight and teaching of the Buddha: all phenomena 'arise' out of each other in a vast and totally interdependent web of cause and effect that spans past, present and future; therefore no phenomenon is independent or permanent in its origin or existence. The Vietnamese monk Thich Nhat Hanh explains: "According to the teaching of Interdependent Co-Arising, cause and effect co-arise (*samutpāda*) and everything is a result of multiple causes and conditions. The egg is in the chicken, and the chicken is in the egg. Chicken and egg arise in mutual dependence.... 'The one contains the all.'" The doctrines of non-self (*anattā*) and emptiness (*shūnyatā*) are inter-related with dependent origination. *See also* anattā, emptiness.

Devadatta The Buddha's cousin and one of his disciples, Devadatta committed the grave offense of trying to have the Buddha killed several times. He also tried to create his own saṅgha. After his followers returned to the saṅgha of the Buddha, he felt remorse, but when he entered the monastery to apologize to the Buddha, the earth opened and he fell into a deep hell. However, according to the Lotus Sūtra, the Buddha reported that in a past life Devadatta was his teacher, and that after aeons Devadatta will also achieve Buddhahood and become a great teacher.[649] *See also* Buddha, Siddhārtha Gautama.

Dhamma *See* Dharma.

Dhammapada (Pali; Skt: Dharmapada) Literally, truth (*dhamma*) path (*pada*). One of the best-known and popular texts of the Pali Canon, the *Dhammapada* is a scripture in verse that contains discourses ascribed to the Buddha. The *Dhammapada* is the second text of the *Khuddaka Nikāya*, a 'collection' within the *Sutta Piṭaka* of the Pali Canon. It contains 423 stanzas arranged in 26 chapters and also appears in somewhat different versions in Prakrit, Sanskrit and Chinese. More than half of the verses also appear in other canonical texts. *See also* Khuddaka Nikāya, Pali Canon, Sutta Piṭaka.

Dharma (Skt; Pali: Dhamma) From the Sanskrit root *dhr*, which means to carry, bear, sustain, support. Dharma is the underlying law of all things and also the way to act in harmony with this law. Dharma has a wide range of meanings, but it can be defined from three essential perspectives: 1) the Truth or Law – ultimate reality that is absolute, eternal and the underlying power that orders the cosmos; 2) the teaching of the Buddha, who embodies Dharma in the world; 3) the path that leads to Truth and enlightenment – the Eightfold Path. One becomes a Buddhist and follows the path to enlightenment by taking refuge in the Three Jewels: the Buddha, the Dharma and the saṅgha (the spiritual community). *See also* Dharmakāya, Three Jewels.

Dharma-body *See* Dharmakāya.

Dharmakāya Literally, truth body; the true form of the Buddha that is identical with ultimate reality. The highest of the 'three bodies' or forms of the Buddha (*trikāya*), the Dharmakāya is formless, unchanging, transcendental and inconceivable. Dharmakāya is the essence of all living beings as well – the innate Buddha-nature within. Dharmakāya can also refer to the teachings expounded by the Buddha. *See also* Nirmāṇakāya, Sambhogakāya, triple body.

Diamond Sūtra (Vajrachchhedikā Prajñāpāramitā) Literally, sūtra of the diamond-cutter of supreme wisdom, the diamond of transcendent wisdom. The *Diamond Sūtra* states that according to the Buddha it should be so named because its teaching cuts like a diamond blade through worldly illusion in order to illuminate what is real and everlasting. The *Diamond Sūtra* gained great importance in East Asian Buddhism; it was translated into Chinese around 400 CE and printed there some time later. A copy of the book from 868 CE, which is kept in the British Library, is the oldest existing dated printed book in the world. *See also* Buddha-nature, sūtra.

Dīgha Nikāya (Collection of Long Discourses) The first of the five *nikāyas* (collections) in the *Sutta Piṭaka*, which is one of the three 'baskets' that constitute the Pali Canon, the *Dīgha Nikāya* consists of thirty-four discourses divided into three groups: the Division concerning Morality (*Silakkhandha-vagga*), suttas 1–13; the Great Division (*Mahavagga*), suttas 14–23; and the Patika Division (*Patikavagga*), suttas 24–34. *See also* Pali Canon, Sutta Piṭaka.

dukkha (Pali; Skt: *duḥkha*) A term derived from the Pali *dus-kha* denoting suffering, both mental and physical. In its fuller sense, *dukkha* means the underlying uneasiness and disquietude of life. That life itself is *dukkha* is the first of the Four Noble Truths taught by the Buddha. In Sanskrit lore, *dukkha* is likened to a potter's wheel that moves with difficulty and screeches as it turns; and the Chinese imagery for *dukkha* is that of a cart with a broken wheel that jostles the rider. *Dukkha* is also one of the three marks or basic characteristics of all things and beings that exist, the other two being impermanence and the absence of self. *See also* Four Noble Truths, skandhas, three marks.

Dzogchen Literally, the great perfection. Dzogchen is the central yoga practice of the Nyingma school of Tibetan Buddhism. The goal of this practice is not to develop but rather to reveal the Buddha-nature – innately pure, luminous and eternal – within all living beings. The method of Dzogchen practice is to cultivate observation of the movements of the mind without preference or judgement. In addition to verbal teaching, this practice also involves mind-to-mind transmission from guru to student. Dzogchen texts have only recently been made partially available to non-initiates. *See also* Longchenpa, Nyingma, Tibetan Buddhism.

Eightfold Path (Pali: *ariya-aṭṭhaṅgika-magga*; Skt: *ārya-ashṭāṅgika-mārga*) The Noble Eightfold Path is the last of the Four Noble Truths taught by the Buddha. It explains the all-encompassing practical path that leads an aspirant from saṁsāra to Nirvāṇa, from suffering in the cycle of rebirth to perfect tranquillity and oneness with the Absolute. The eight elements are: 1) right view: discernment based on an understanding of the Four Noble Truths; 2) right resolve: including right thought, right intent and right aspiration; 3) right speech: honest speaking, as well as avoidance of falsehood, slander, abuse and idle talk; 4) right conduct: acting in ways beneficial to all and abstaining from negative actions, gross as well as subtle; 5) right livelihood: engaging in professions that are honest and beneficial to all beings; 6) right effort: overcoming negativity in one's life and pursuing the way of truth; 7) right mindfulness: ongoing mindfulness of body, feelings, thoughts and the objects of thought; 8) right meditation: profound mindfulness directed inwardly that leads to the experience of stillness, emptiness and finally the Absolute. It is important to note that walking the Eightfold Path is not linear in the sense that one passes from one step to the next, but it is a process in which all eight elements are practised simultaneously. *See also* Four Noble Truths, Middle Path.

Eihei Dōgen Zenji (1200–1253) A Japanese Buddhist master and founder of the Sōtō school of Zen Buddhism, Dōgen Zenji taught that people inherently possess Buddhahood within themselves and that the means to realizing this is *shikan taza*, or 'nothing but precisely sitting' – with alert attention, free of thoughts and objectives. Dōgen Zenji also emphasized the need for a master. His writings include the *Treasury of the Eye of the True Dharma* (*Shōbōgenzō*), which contains ninety-five chapters of philosophical writings, and *Points to Watch in Practising the Way* (*Gakudō-yōjin-shu*), which gives ten rules for beginners on the path of Zen. *See also* Zen.

emptiness From the Sanskrit *shūnyatā*, meaning emptiness or void; a central doctrine of Buddhism that describes the phenomenal world as 'empty'. While different schools emphasize different aspects of this doctrine, the foundation for the concept of emptiness for all schools is the Buddha's teaching of dependent origination, the observation that all that manifests is nothing more than an ever-changing dynamic process and is therefore empty of a real or enduring identity. This does not mean that the phenomenal world is nonexistent, however. As the famous lines from the *Heart Sūtra* say: "Form is emptiness and emptiness itself is form." Worldly phenomena are simply empty of intrinsic reality. Thus the true nature of all things is emptiness, the realization of emptiness is enlightenment, and it is often interpreted that emptiness is ultimate reality or Nirvāṇa. *See also* anattā, dependent origination, Nāgārjuna, Suchness.

enlightenment The common English translation of the Sanskrit *bodhi*, meaning 'awakening'. Enlightenment is the culmination of Buddhist spiritual practice – awakening to the true nature of reality and the perfect tranquillity of Nirvāna – the same enlightenment experienced by the historical Buddha Siddhārtha Gautama. The experience of enlightenment is said to be achieved when the Four Noble Truths are fully apprehended. While there are different levels of enlightenment, Buddhas are those considered to have achieved perfect and complete enlightenment. *See also* Eightfold Path, Four Noble Truths, Nirvāṇa.

Evans-Wentz, W. Y. (1878–1965) An anthropologist who became a pioneer in the study of Tibetan Buddhism, Evans-Wentz was born in Trenton, New Jersey, USA. He travelled to India in 1919, where he first encountered Tibetan spiritual texts. Evans-Wentz is known for editing and compiling these texts, including some in the book *Tibetan Yoga and Secret Doctrines* and the compilation known as *The Tibetan Book of the Dead.* These texts were translated primarily by his spiritual teacher, the Tibetan Lama Kazi Dawa-Samdup.

Flower Ornament Scripture (Avataṁsaka Sūtra) The *Flower Ornament Scripture* is one of the most important compilations of Mahāyāna sūtras in East Asian Buddhism. The *Ten Stages Sūtra* (the twenty-sixth chapter) details the stages a bodhisattva must pass through to achieve enlightenment. Written in Sanskrit, it was translated into Chinese around the second century CE. Text was added in successive translations, such that it is now one of the largest sūtras in the Buddhist canon, with over forty chapters. Also rendered in English as *Flower Garland Sutra*.

Four Noble Truths (Pali: *cattāri ariyasaccāni*; Skt: *catvāri āryasatyāni*) In his first discourse after attaining enlightenment, the Buddha explained the Four Noble Truths that are the foundation of the Buddhist path – four principles that express the true nature of things and how to experience insight into this true nature. These truths are: 1) Life in the world is full of suffering (*dukkha*); 2) There is a cause of suffering; 3) It is possible to attain cessation from suffering; 4) There is a path that leads to cessation of suffering. Also known as the Four Ennobling Truths. *See also* dukkha, Eightfold Path.

Gampopa [Dvagpo-Lharje] (1079–1153) A Tibetan physician turned monk and student of Milarepa, one of Tibet's most famous yogis and poets, Gampopa introduced *lam-rim* (doctrinal manuals of Tibetan Buddhism) to his disciples as a way of developing the mind gradually. He wrote *The Jewel Ornament of Liberation* and *The Supreme Path, the Rosary of Precious Gems*, both of which are included in *Tibetan Yoga and Secret Doctrines. See also* lam-rim.

Gautama Buddha *See* Siddhārtha Gautama.

Gelugpa/Gelukpa *See* Tibetan Buddhism.

Gotama (Pali; Skt: Gautama) *See* Siddhārtha Gautama.

Guenther, Herbert V. (1917–2006) A German Buddhist philosopher and one of the leading Buddhist scholars of our time, Guenther taught in India from 1950 to 1964 at Lucknow and Sanskrit Universities, and studied with many prominent Tibetan and Mongolian lamas, including the XIV Dalai Lama. He is known for his outspoken views as well as his remarkable facility with languages; he learned Chinese and Sanskrit by the age of nineteen and soon added sixteen other languages to his repertoire. Guenther translated and wrote many books, including a translation of texts from Saraha, *Ecstatic Spontaneity: Saraha's Three Cycles of Dohā*; and *Kindly Bent to Ease Us*, a translation of a Dzogchen text by the thirteenth-century Nyingma master Longchenpa. *See also* Dzogchen.

guru Literally, destroyer (*ru*) of darkness (*gu*); one who destroys darkness and brings light; a spiritual teacher or master whose mission it is to guide others to enlightenment. In Buddhist traditions, the term 'guru' or 'lama', its Tibetan equivalent, may denote differing degrees of spiritual attainment. In the Theravāda tradition, the guru is regarded as a deeply-respected and honoured senior monk who inspires aspirants on the path to enlightenment. In the Vajrayāna tradition, the guru is seen to be identical with the Buddha, leading the disciple to enlightenment, with the ultimate guru being one's Buddha-nature. *See also* Guru Yoga, Three Jewels.

Guru Yoga A meditation practice within Mahāyāna that focuses on devotion to one's spiritual teacher or guru. The purpose of this meditation is to merge one's inner essence with the guru's, and thereby with the essence of the Buddha. The guru is available in the human form to guide and assist aspirants on the path to enlightenment. On a practical level, the guru is considered to be one with and to embody the Buddha, who cannot be contacted today on the physical plane. *See also* bhakti.

householder A lay disciple who is married and lives a family life. Householders who were spiritually accomplished came to be called 'married monks' and 'married nuns'. *See also* lay disciples, monk / nun.

Huang-Po [Hsi Yin] (d. 850) An influential Ch'an master born in Fujian, China, noted for his rigorous teaching method, Huang-Po was disdainful of traditional methods and emphasized learning from direct experience rather than from studying the sūtras. As Chinese Buddhism had done for two centuries before him, Huang-Po focused on the concept of 'mind' (Chinese: *hsin*), maintaining that the mind cannot seek the Mind. Many sayings are attributed to Huang-Po on this subject, such as: "To awaken suddenly to the fact that your own Mind is the Buddha, that there is nothing to be attained or a single action to be performed – this is the Supreme Way."

Hui-neng (638–713) One of the most important figures in the Ch'an tradition, Hui-neng was the sixth and last Patriarch of Ch'an Buddhism. Author of the *Platform Sūtra*, he rendered the Buddha's teachings within a Chinese context. The *Platform Sūtra* consists of a somewhat mythological autobiography followed by discourses on 'sudden enlightenment', direct perception of one's true nature, and attaining Buddhahood through right conduct, meditation and spiritual insight. This scripture was the basis for the Sudden Enlightenment School of Ch'an Buddhism. *See also* Ch'an.

Indra Literally, god of the firmament; the king of gods in the *Vedas*, the earliest Hindu scriptures. Buddhist texts refer to Indra as one of the twelve gods said to protect the world.

inner sound The primal sound that emanates from the ultimate reality and can be experienced through meditation. The Buddha spoke of listening to inner sound in the Mahāsakuludāyi Sutta: "I have proclaimed to my disciples the way whereby they hear both kinds of sounds, the divine and the human, with the divine ear, which is purified and surpasses the human.... And thereby many disciples of mine abide, having reached the consummation and perfection of direct knowledge."[650] Buddhist practices involving inner sound require one not to speak of inner experiences, and it is only in recent times that the subject of inner sound within these practices (particularly in Dzogchen) has been openly addressed.

interdependent co-arising *See* dependent origination.

Japanese Buddhism Buddhist teachings travelled from Korea to Japan beginning in the mid-sixth century CE, though some Buddhist texts had probably been brought to Japan from China in earlier years. From the late eighth century onward, Japanese Buddhism incorporated teachings from the Ch'an, Pure Land and Vajrayāna schools, as well as the belief in indigenous Japanese deities. In the late nineteenth century, intervention by the Japanese government as well as Japan's opening to Western influence had a great impact on further development of Buddhism there. One response was to present Buddhism as a more scientific religion, which resulted in the rapid development of modern Buddhist scholarship in the twentieth century by scholars such as D. T. Suzuki. Sects from the three major schools are active in Japan today, but the dominant practices are Zen, Pure Land and Nichiren Buddhism. *See also* Ch'an, Pure Land, Suzuki, Zen.

Jātakas (Birth Stories) Early Buddhist sūtras attributed to the Buddha and his chief disciples, the *Jātakas* recount stories of past lives of Shākyamuni, the historical Buddha. The 547 *Jātakas* are part of the *Khuddaka Nikāya*, one of the collections within the *Sutta Piṭaka* in the Pali Canon. Among other things, the stories illustrate the fact that the actions of past lives determine the course of one's present life according to the law of karma, or cause and effect. *See also* Pali Canon, Sutta Piṭaka, Tipiṭaka.

Jina Literally, conqueror; an epithet of the Buddhas. The title suggests that in achieving complete enlightenment a Buddha conquers all the negative forces that imprison beings in the cycle of birth and rebirth (saṁsāra).

jīva From the Sanskrit *jīv*, to breathe; the eternal essence of a living being. In the Pali Canon, *jīva* is synonymous with *ātman*. *See also* anattā, ātman.

Junjirō Takakusu *See* Takakusu, Junjirō.

kalpa A 'world period', a time unit denoting an inconceivably long time.

Kapilavastu (Pali: Kapilavatthu) The capital of the Shākya people. Buddha spent his childhood at Kapilavastu, which archaeologists assume was situated at Tilaurakot, Nepal, near the border of the Indian state Uttar Pradesh. The Shākya state was at that time a prosperous state under the larger kingdom of Kosala, ruled by King Prasenjit. *See also* Shākya.

karma (Skt; Pali: kamma) Literally, action; the law of cause and effect, or action and reaction, whereby people must face the consequences of all their actions throughout an ongoing cycle of incarnations. Karma governs the cycle of birth, rebirth and suffering (saṁsāra) that all beings must undergo until they attain liberation. In Buddhist teaching, the three roots of unwholesome karma (actions) are greed, hatred and delusion; the three roots of wholesome karma are unselfishness, goodwill and knowledge. *See also* saṁsāra.

Kāshyapa/Kassapa *See* Mahā Kāshyapa.

Khandhaka *See* Vinaya Piṭaka.

Khuddaka Nikāya (Collection of Short Texts) The fifth and last *nikāya* (collection) within the *Sutta Piṭaka* in the Pali Canon, the *Khuddaka Nikāya* consists of between fifteen and eighteen texts (depending on the edition of the Pali Canon) on various topics, attributed to the Buddha or his main disciples. The *Khuddaka Nikāya* contains both early and later materials that were not included in the four other *nikāyas*. The *Dhammapada*, *Udāna*, *Sutta Nipāta* and *Jātaka* are among the texts included in the *Khuddaka Nikāya*. *See also* Dhammapada, Jātakas, Sutta Nipāta, Udāna.

Korean Buddhism Brought to Korea from China in the fourth century CE, Korean Buddhism is considered the most ecumenical tradition in Asia and it retains many of the characteristics of ancient Chinese Buddhism. The primary focus of the various schools was initially either on the Mādhyamaka (Middle Way) philosophy, vinaya (moral discipline) or academic study of scriptures. Some centuries later, however, the Pure Land School became popular. Ch'an Buddhism (Korean: Sŏn), which emphasized practice over intellectual study, was introduced in the eighth century. *See also* Ch'an, Middle Way, Pure Land.

kshatriya The second of four castes in the hierarchy of Hindu society, that of warriors, princes and kings. The duty of this caste was the protection of the community. *See also* caste, class.

Lalitavistara (The Unfolding of the Play) Most likely from the third century CE, the *Lalitavistara* is a Mahāyāna sūtra that describes the 'play' (*lila*) or early life of Gautama Buddha. The present Sanskrit text is a compilation of works by various authors in both prose and verse and describes the events of the Buddha's life from his descent from the Tushita heaven in the form of a white elephant into his mother's womb up to his illumination and the preaching of his first sermon.

lama *See* guru.

lam-rim Literally, stages of the path. A group of doctrinal manuals of Tibetan Buddhist teaching, *lam-rim* describes the stages of the spiritual path and gives students an understanding of Buddhism from elementary tenets to the most profound realizations. The *Jewel Ornament of Liberation*, an early *lam-rim* text, was written by Gampopa (Dvagpo-Lharje). There are a number of *lam-rim* versions, which are all extensions of Atīsha's eleventh-century root text, *A Lamp on the Path to Englightenment.* The largest version is Tsongkapa's *Great Discourse on the Stages of the Path. See also* Atīsha, Gampopa, Tibetan Buddhism, Tsongkapa.

Laṅkāvatāra Sūtra (Sūtra on the Descent to Sri Lanka) Thought to have been composed in Sanskrit around 400 CE, the *Laṅkāvatāra Sūtra* is one of the few traditional Mahāyāna texts that have been influential in the development of East Asian Buddhism. The *Laṅkāvatāra Sūtra* explains that inner enlightenment dissolves duality and it contains a chapter concerning Chinese Buddhism's adherence to vegetarianism.

Larger Sukhāvatī-Vyūha *See* Pure Land Sūtra.

lay disciples The majority of practising Buddhists within the spiritual community, lay disciples are not ordained monks or nuns. Cultivating merit in order to develop one's spiritual growth was at the foundation of Buddhist life, and lay disciples traditionally cultivated merit in two ways: 1) by performing wholesome actions; 2) by giving food, clothing and services to the monastic community. In return for these 'acts of giving' the lay disciples received spiritual guidance and Dharma instruction from the monastics. The ethical conduct of the lay community was set forth in five vows: 1) to abstain from taking life, 2) to abstain from taking what has not been given to one, 3) to abstain from sexual misbehaviour, 4) to abstain from dishonest speech, 5) to abstain from intoxicants. *See also* monk/nun, saṅgha, Three Jewels.

Lin Chi (d. 866) Ch'an master Lin Chi was a student of Huang-po who founded one of the most influential schools of Buddhism in China. His teachings spread to Japan in the twelfth century and formed the Rinzai School of Buddhism. He is known in Japan as Master Rinzai Gigen. *See also* Ch'an, Huang-po.

Longchenpa [Longchen Rabjampa] (1308–1364) Considered one of the greatest masters of Tibetan Buddhism, Longchenpa elucidated Dzogchen, a central teaching of the Nyingma school, which holds that one's innate nature is perfect and enlightenment is a process of realizing this through meditation and direct transmission from teacher to student. Recognized as a manifestation of Mañjushrī, the Bodhisattva of Wisdom, Longchenpa wrote over two hundred works, amongst them being *Seven Treasuries*, a synthesis of the teachings of six hundred years of Buddhist thought, and *You Are the Eyes of the World*. *See also* Dzogchen, Nyingma.

Lotus Sūtra (Saddharmapuṇḍarīka Sūtra) Literally, Sūtra of the Lotus Blossom of the Marvellous Dharma. Thought to contain the complete teachings of the Buddha, the *Lotus Sūtra* offers essential Mahāyāna teachings: firstly, that the Buddha is Dharmakāya – the absolute reality and the oneness of all things; secondly, that the Dharmakāya is the essential nature of all beings, and therefore all beings have the potential to attain Buddhahood. The *Lotus Sūtra*, compiled in India probably in the first century BCE, was influential in the development of Buddhism in China and Japan. *See also* Dharmakāya, Mahāyāna.

Mādhyamaka *See* Middle Way.

Mahā Kāshyapa One of the Buddha's three principle disciples, Mahā Kāshyapa was renowned for his ascetic self-discipline and moral strictness. He assumed leadership of the Buddhist community after the death of the Buddha, heading the first council and selecting the five hundred monks who attended. Mahā Kāshyapa is also considered the first patriarch of Zen.

Mahāmudrā (Skt; Tib: Chagchen) Literally, Great Seal. Mahāmudrā is a central meditation practice in the Kagyu, Sakya and Gelug traditions of Tibetan Buddhism and has strong similarities with the Dzogchen practice of the Nyingma tradition, including the necessity of guidance by a master. This meditation practice focuses on various aspects of mental experience, culminating in non-conceptual realization of the nature of consciousness itself. *See also* Dzogchen, Tibetan Buddhism.

Mahāsiddha Literally, great perfection. A Mahāsiddha is a yogi who has mastered the practice of mantras, esoteric visualizations and rituals. In Tibetan Buddhism it is said that there were between eighty-four to eighty-eight Mahāsiddhas. Probably living between the eighth and twelfth centuries, the Mahāsiddhas were non-monastic and came from all walks of life (four were women). They taught that direct experience of the most sublime esoteric dimensions could be had while living ordinary lives. Their teachings were codified in texts called tantras, and some Mahāsiddhas are acknowledged as founders of Tibetan Buddhist lineages. *See also* Saraha, tantra, Tibetan Buddhism.

Mahāvastu Literally, great book. A comprehensive text of early Buddhism believed to have been compiled from the second century BCE through the fourth century CE, the *Mahāvastu* contained Sanskrit, Pali and Prakrit prose and verse related to the codes of conduct of Buddhism. Most of the text is comprised of stories about the earlier lives of the Buddha and a number of bodhisattvas as well as literature correlating the virtuous deeds of past lives with the events of subsequent lives.

Mahāyāna (Great Vehicle) Mahāyāna Buddhism is one of the two main groups of schools within Buddhism today (the other being Theravāda). Mahāyāna spread north from India to Tibet and then east to China and other East Asian countries and is practised mainly in East Asia and in Tibet (particularly in its Vajrayāna form). Its most prevalent branches include Ch'an/Zen/Sŏn and Pure Land Buddhism. The primary focus of Mahāyāna became the aspiration to achieve enlightenment for the benefit of all living beings (*bodhichitta*). Developed on the foundation of early Buddhist teachings in the first century CE, Mahāyāna made it possible for more people to practise Buddhism than in earlier times, when the practice was focused primarily on those who were able to live the monastic life – hence the name Mahāyāna, literally meaning 'the greater ox-cart'. *See also* bodhichitta, Ch'an, Pure Land, Theravāda, Tibetan Buddhism, Vajrayāna, Zen.

Majjhima Nikāya (Collection of Middle-Length Discourses) The second of five collections (*nikāyas*) within the *Sutta Piṭaka* in the Pali Canon, the *Majjhima Nikāya* consists of 152 discourses attributed to the Buddha and his principal disciples. According to tradition, this collection was recited by the Buddha's disciple Ānanda at the first Buddhist council shortly after the Buddha's death. *See also* Pali Canon, Tipiṭaka.

Mañjushrī The Bodhisattva of Wisdom in Mahāyāna teaching, Mañjushrī is depicted holding a flaming sword in his right hand, which symbolizes the severing of duality, and holding the *Prajñāpāramitā Sūtras* – teachings on emptiness and the perfection of wisdom – in his left hand. With these two tools he leads sentient beings to enlightenment, thus ending the cycle of birth, death and suffering. In the *Shurangama Sūtra*, one of the main Ch'an Buddhism texts, Mañjushrī speaks of meditation on the ever-present sound as the most appropriate method for realizing *samādhi* (pure concentration). *See also* Perfection of Wisdom Sūtras, Shurangama Sūtra.

Mantra Yoga The yogic path whose objective is to achieve union with Brahman by means of repetition of a mantra. *See also* mantra.

mantra Literally, tool for thinking; sacred sounds. A mantra is a sound, syllable, word or group of words imparted by a master and is considered capable of generating spiritual transformation when faithfully repeated. The power of mantras is said to reside in their sound or vibration, which may be experienced through repetition, chanting or preferably silent mental repetition. Repetition of mantras is a meditation practice in many Buddhist schools.

Mantrayāna *See* Vajrayāna.

Māra Literally, death or destruction; the force that misguides and turns beings away from the right path. Māra is the tempter in Buddhist cosmology, the personification of evil. A deva or celestial being often depicted with a hundred arms and riding an elephant, Māra symbolizes the passions that overwhelm human beings. Māra tries to obstruct those who seek enlightenment, which is beyond his grasp. He appeared to the Buddha several times, most notably just before the Buddha's enlightenment and before his death.

master *See* guru.

Middle Path (*majjhimā paṭipadā*) Buddhism is often referred to as the Middle Path or Middle Way because it avoids the extremes of sense-indulgence and self-mortification and encourages a well-balanced moderate path of self-discipline. More specifically, the Middle Path denotes the Eightfold Path, the last of the Four Noble Truths taught by the Buddha. The Eightfold Path sets forth an all-encompassing way of life and spiritual practice, free of extremes, which leads to enlightenment. After experiencing a life of indulgence as a prince, followed by years of renunciation as an ascetic, Siddhārtha Gautama realized that neither of these extremes was helpful in achieving enlightenment and he came to espouse a life of moderation. The Pali term *majjhimā paṭipadā* is sometimes translated as the Middle Way, which is not to be confused with the Middle Way referring to the Mādhyamaka philosophy. *See also* Eightfold Path, Four Noble Truths, Middle Way.

Middle Way (*mādhyamaka*) Expounded in the second or third century CE by the Buddhist philosopher Nāgārjuna, the Middle Way is the teaching of the Mādhyamaka school. This school emphasizes the centrality of the doctrine of dependent co-origination, steering clear of all extreme views and suggesting that reality is devoid of all phenomenal attributes. *See also* Nāgārjuna.

Milindapañhā (Questions of Milinda) A text dating from approximately 100 BCE included only in the Burmese edition of the *Khuddaka Nikāya*, the *Milindapañhā* records a dialogue said to have taken place between the Indo-Greek king Menander (Milinda in Pali) and the monk Nāgasena. King Milinda was a historical figure who ruled Bactria (a kingdom in current-day Afghanistan and Pakistan); Nāgasena is unknown except in this work. In the introduction to his translation, Rhys Davids called the *Milindapañhā* "the masterpiece of Indian prose".[651] *See also* Khuddaka Nikāya.

monk/nun The early Buddhist community (saṅgha) included monks, nuns, laymen and laywomen. Ordination, the act of entry into monastic life for monks and nuns, was preceded by stating the voluntary intention to be ordained as well as fulfilling some basic prerequisites. In early Theravāda ordination, men and women were ordained at two levels: 1) as novices, by repeating the formula for taking refuge in the Three Jewels and promising to uphold certain elements of the monastic discipline of the *Vinaya Piṭaka*; 2) as monks or nuns (after the age of twenty), a higher ordination with full responsibilities and rights within the monastic community. The act of renunciation – 'going forth' from home to homelessness – distinguished monastics from lay disciples, but as time passed the monastics began to settle permanently in monasteries, serving the lay disciples. *See also* lay disciples, saṅgha, Three Jewels, Vinaya Piṭaka.

Musō Kokushi [born Musō Soseki] (1275–1351) The most famous Japanese Zen master of his time, Musō Kokushi was raised by monks and devoted himself to the study of the sūtras. As abbot of a monastery in Kyoto, he was also a genius in landscape design and considered creating Zen gardens an integral part of spiritual practice. His works include the *Muchū-mondo*, which presents the principles of Zen in the form of questions and answers. Musō Kokushi is credited with establishing a Musō line of Rinzai Zen. This school emphasizes rigorous meditation and koans, a set of verbal riddles that defy reason and therefore encourage intuitive insight.

Nāgārjuna One of the most important Buddhist philosophers, Nāgārjuna is thought to have lived in southern India in the second or third century CE. His teaching on emptiness (*shūnyatā*) as the ultimate truth and his methodical process of rejecting all opposites established the foundation of the Middle Way of the Mādhyamaka school of Buddhism. Nāgārjuna developed the concept of emptiness or void from the Buddha's principle of dependent origination and established the notion of the "two truths", discriminating between a relative and an absolute level of truth in the teachings of the Buddha. *See also* dependent origination, emptiness.

Namkhai Norbu, Chogyal (1938–) Born in Eastern Tibet, Chogyal Namkhai Norbu was recognized before the age of five as an incarnation of two previous teachers of the Dzogchen philosophy, the core teaching of the Nyingma school of Tibetan Buddhism. He began his studies at a young age and followed a course of accelerated training with renowned Tibetan masters. Namkhai Norbu brought Dzogchen teachings to the West, beginning in Italy in 1976, and he went on to establish Dzogchen learning centres around the world. *See also* Dzogchen, Tibetan Buddhism.

Nāropa (1016–1100) Born a brahmin in Kashmir, Nāropa, the disciple of Tilopa, became a Buddhist monk and yogi. He systemized Vajrayāna teachings and developed a set of advanced yogic practices. Nāropa's student Marpa brought his teachings to Tibet in the eleventh century. These teachings emphasize the transmission of knowledge from master to student and form one of the central doctrines of Kagyu, one of the four main schools of Tibetan Buddhism. *See also* Tibetan Buddhism, Vajrayāna.

Nhat Hanh, Thich (1926–) A widely known and respected Zen master, poet and peace activist born in central Vietnam, Thich Nhat Hanh helped found the 'engaged Buddhism' movement during the Vietnam War, which merged the contemplative life with service in the world for those suffering the agonies of war. He was nominated for the Nobel Peace Prize in 1967. In exile in France in 1982, he founded Plum Village, a Buddhist community dedicated to alleviating the suffering of people from Vietnam and the Third World. He has published many titles, including *Call Me by My True Names*, *Peace Is Every Step*, *Being Peace*, *Living Buddha Living Christ*, *Teachings on Love* and *Old Path White Clouds*.

Nibbāna *See* Nirvāṇa.

Nirmāṇakāya Literally, emanation body. The third of the three 'bodies' or forms of the Buddha (*trikāya*), Nirmāṇakāya is the physical body that an Enlightened One assumes in the world in order to lead suffering beings to enlightenment. *See also* Dharmakāya, Sambhogakāya, triple body.

Nirvāṇa (Skt; Pali: Nibbāna) Literally, extinction; a state of total liberation and perfect tranquillity; oneness with the Absolute; enlightenment. The goal of spiritual practice in Buddhism, Nirvāṇa signifies liberation from all attachments to the illusory and freedom from suffering in the cycle of rebirth (saṁsāra). Nirvāṇa is the experience and the bliss of realizing absolute freedom. There are two types of

Nirvāṇa: Nirvāṇa with some conditionality, which can be achieved before death; and absolute Nirvāṇa, or Parinirvāṇa, usually attained at death. *See also* enlightenment, Parinirvāṇa, saṁsāra.

nun *See* monk/nun.

Nyingma Literally, ancient. The Nyingma tradition is the oldest of the four major schools of Tibetan Buddhism, tracing back to the Indian masters Padmasambhāvā and Shāntarakshita. The Dzogchen teachings of the Nyingma school are considered to be the essence and highest teachings of this school. *See also* Dzogchen, Longchenpa, Padmasambhāvā, Tibetan Buddhism.

Pabongka Rinpoche [Jampa Tenzin Trinlay Gyatso] (1878–1941) A renowned Tibetan Buddhist master of the Gelugpa school, Pabongka Rinpoche was born near Lhasa, Tibet, and became a disciple of Dagpo Lama Rinpoche. During a period of twenty-four days in 1921, he gave an exposition on the *lam-rim*, or 'stages of the path', which was translated into English and published as *Liberation in the Palm of Your Hand*. Pabongka Rinpoche was the Guru of Ling Rinpoche and Trijang Rinpoche, two tutors of the XIV (current) Dalai Lama.

Padmasambhāvā Literally, the lotus-born. Also known as Guru Rinpoche (Precious Guru), Padmasambhāvā was an eighth-century guru instrumental in introducing Buddhism into Tibet. He was particularly influential in the Nyingma school, the followers of which regard him as the 'second Buddha'. *See also* Nyingma, Tibetan Buddhism.

Pali An ancient Indian dialect in which the oldest complete canonical texts of the teachings of the Buddha are composed. Scholars believe that Pali derived from a blend of local dialects in which the Buddha's teachings were passed down orally before being written down. Some suggest that Pali is a variation of the Old Magadhi dialect, said to have been the language spoken by the Buddha.

Pali Canon The earliest complete set of Buddhist scriptures preserved intact in a single canonical language, the Pali Canon is largely attributed to the Buddha himself. It was written from oral tradition, probably around the first century CE, in the Pali language, a dialect related to Old Magadhi, the language the Buddha probably spoke. The Canon has three divisions, each called a basket (*piṭaka*), and it is therefore known as the *Tipiṭaka* (three baskets). *See also* Tipiṭaka.

paññā *See* prajñā.

Parinirvāṇa Literally, total extinction. Parinirvāṇa is the final state of Nirvāṇa, usually realized only at death. In the earliest Buddhist texts, Nirvāṇa and Parinirvāṇa are synonymous, denoting complete enlightenment. *See also* Nirvāṇa.

Patrul Rinpoche (1808–1887) A renowned Tibetan Buddhist master of the nineteenth century, Patrul Rinpoche was a prolific author whose writings include teachings, poems, songs of enlightenment and commentaries. He wrote a commentary on Shāntideva's *The Way of the Bodhisattva*, a commentary on Longchenpa's *Treasury of Precious Qualities* and *Words of My Perfect Teacher*, a transcription of his understanding of his master's teaching. His miscellaneous writings include *The Drama in the Lotus Garden*, written to console a young nobleman whose young bride had died in an epidemic. He broke with tradition by abolishing the custom of serving meat at certain gatherings.

perfect teacher *See* guru.

Perfection of Wisdom Sūtras/Prajñāpāramitā Sūtras The *Prajñāpāramitā* or *Perfection of Wisdom Sūtras* are a genre of Mahāyāna Buddhist scriptures dealing with the nature of emptiness (*shūnyatā*), the perfection of wisdom (spiritual insight) and the course of a bodhisattva. The earliest of the *Prajñāpāramitā Sūtras*, the *Perfection of Wisdom Sūtra in Eight Thousand Lines* (*Ashṭasāhasrikā Prajñāpāramitā*), probably dates from 100 BCE or earlier; later several versions of these sūtras, known collectively as the *Large Perfection of Wisdom Sūtras*, were expanded to up to a hundred thousand lines.

prajñā (Skt; Pali: *paññā*) Literally, wisdom. A central notion of Buddhism, often translated as wisdom, *prajñā* is closer in meaning to spiritual insight or heightened consciousness. Through *prajñā* insight is gained into the nature of existence, which is characterized by impermanence, suffering, and absence of self, as distinguished from true reality. Through *prajñā* all afflictions are extinguished; thus *prajñā* leads to enlightenment. In Mahāyāna Buddhism, *prajñāparamita*, the perfection of insight or wisdom, is the last of the six perfections realized by a bodhisattva in the journey to enlightenment. *See also* three marks.

Prajñāpāramitā Sūtras *See* Perfection of Wisdom Sūtras.

Primordial Buddha *See* Ādi-Buddha.

Pure Land According to early Mahāyāna teachings, a Pure Land, also called Buddha-land or Buddha-field, is a land of bliss, a paradise where a Buddha continues to exist beyond the cycle of rebirth in order to help those suffering in the world. The Pure Land Schools of East Asia, formally established in the fourth century CE, considered Pure Lands to be intermediate levels from which aspirants need not return to the world while working to attain Nirvāṇa. *See also* Amitābha, Sukhāvatī.

Pure Land Sūtra The *Pure Land Sūtra* (*Sukhāvatī-Vyūha*), one of the three main sūtras of the Pure Land schools of China and Japan, emphasizes faith in the Buddha Amitābha and loving recitation of his name with the goal of being reborn in Sukhāvatī, his Pure Land. It exists in two versions, the Shorter and the Larger. *See also* Amitābha, Sukhāvatī.

refuge *See* Three Jewels.

Rinpoche Literally, precious one. In Tibetan Buddhism, an honorary title bestowed upon highly respected lamas (gurus).

Ryokan (1758–1831) A Japanese monk whose Zen poetry is considered among the most beautiful in Asian literature. A monk of the Sōtō school, Ryokan set out on a spiritual pilgrimage through Japan after spending twelve years at a Zen monastery. After five years he settled at a hermitage, living as a recluse dedicated to writing simple, spontaneous poetry and calligraphy. Ryokan's poetry celebrates inner realization as well as a love of nature. Translations of his writings include *Dewdrops on a Lotus Leaf*; *One Robe, One Bowl: The Zen Poetry of Ryokan*; *Great Fool: Zen Master Ryokan: Poems, Letters, and Other Writings.*

Saddharmapuṇḍarīka Sūtra *See* Lotus Sūtra.

Sahampati Brahmā *See* Brahmā Sahampati.

samādhi Literally, the state of being firmly fixed; a state of intense, one-pointed stillness and concentration of the mind that results from meditative practice. *Samādhi* can denote either meditation or the final stage of pure concentration.

Samanta-Bhadra *See* Ādi-Buddha.

Sambhogakāya Literally, body of enjoyment; body of clear light. Sambhogakāya is the second of three 'bodies' (*trikāya*) or dimensions in which the Buddha manifests. The Sambhogakāya exists in heavenly realms and teaches the doctrine to the bodhisattvas and gods residing there. The Sambhogakāya includes Buddhas such as Amitabha and the Bodhisattvas Mañjushrī and Avalokiteshvara. Those skilled in meditation may gain access to the Sambhogakāya and receive direct transmission of teachings from those residing in this form. *See also* Dharmakāya, Nirmāṇakāya, triple body.

saṁsāra Literally, flowing on; journeying; transmigration. Saṁsāra is the cycle of repeated births and deaths in which living beings wander until they attain Nirvāṇa. Sentient beings are imprisoned in saṁsāra by karma, the law of cause and effect, according to which they must continuously be reborn to reap the effects of their previous actions. An underlying cause of captivity in saṁsāra is ignorance of the binding nature of one's actions, which gives rise to the delusion that one is free to act without consequences. Saṁsāra includes all phenomena that come into existence; they are conditioned by prior causes and will end when their current state of existence is dissolved. *See also* karma.

Saṁyutta Nikāya (Collection of Kindred Discourses) The third collection of the *Sutta Piṭaka* in the Pali Canon, the *Saṁyutta Nikāya* contains the Buddha's discourses and dialogues as well as numerous short texts relating incidents of the Buddha's life and teachings. *See also* Pali Canon, Sutta Piṭaka, Tipiṭaka.

saṅgha Literally, congregation; a community or fellowship of disciples. The saṅgha denotes the Buddhist community of monks, nuns, and novices; but in its wider sense, the saṅgha also includes the lay community of practitioners who strive for enlightenment. The saṅgha is one of the Three Jewels of Buddhism in which all practitioners take refuge, the other two being the Buddha and his teachings (Dharma). *See also* Three Jewels.

Sanskrit The ancient primary scriptural language of India for both Hinduism and Buddhism. According to some scholars, the classical form of Sanskrit was compiled during the third and fourth centuries BCE from different dialects and languages, and its use was originally restricted to the priestly caste. The *Vedas* are written in an early form of Sanskrit, and it is the language of many Mahāyāna texts.

Saraha A Buddhist mystic of the ninth century said to have been born in Eastern India, Saraha was a Mahāsiddha (a yogi who has mastered the practice of mantras, esoteric visualizations and rituals) and is considered to be one of the earliest practitioners of the Vajrayāna tradition of Buddhism. Saraha transmitted his teachings in a characteristic style of poetry known as *dohā*. *See also* Mahāsiddha.

sentient being A being endowed with consciousness. In Buddhism, animals, gods and human beings are examples of sentient beings. *See also* saṁsāra.

Shaku, Soyen (1859–1919) The first Zen Buddhist master to teach in the United States, Soyen Shaku was a Roshi (venerable teacher) of the Rinzai school, which focuses on lengthy meditation and introspection under the guidance of a teacher and the use of koans, a set of questions that are designed to stimulate abandonment of all mental activity that impedes the experience of illumination. He was abbot of the Kencho-ji and Engaku-ji temples in Kamkura, Japan. Soyen's English works include *Sermons of a Buddhist Abbot* and *Zen for Americans*.

Shākya A noble clan in the area of present-day southern Nepal that ruled one of the sixteen powerful states of northern India in the Buddha's time. The Buddha's father, Shuddhodana, was the ruler of the Shākya state. Shākyamuni Buddha (the Awakened One of the Shākya clan, the historical Buddha) was born in the capital, Kapilavastu. The Shākya clan was almost entirely destroyed by the dominant Kosala kingdom during the Buddha's lifetime. *See also* Kapilavastu, Shākyamuni.

Shākyamuni Literally, Awakened One of the Shākya clan; an epithet of Siddhārtha Gautama, the historical Buddha, who belonged to the Shākya clan of northern India. The name 'Shākyamuni' was given to Siddhārtha Gautama after he attained enlightenment. This epithet is often employed to distinguish the historical Buddha from other Buddhas. *See also* Buddha, Shākya, Siddhārtha Gautama.

Shāntideva (685–763) Shāntideva was a monk of the Mādhyamaka school of Mahāyāna Buddhism. This 'middle school' of Buddhist philosophy, founded by Nāgārjuna in the second century CE, claims to be faithful to the spirit of the Buddha's original teachings and advocates a middle course between all extreme views. According to legend, Shāntideva was a king's son from south India who studied at the monastic university Nālandā. He is the author of two surviving works: the *Shikshāsamuchchaya* (*Collection of Main Ingredients of Teachings*) and the *Bodhicharyāvatāra* (*Entering the Path of Enlightenment*). The latter is still used in Tibetan Buddhism as a teaching text. *See also* Bodhicharyāvatāra, Middle Path.

Shāriputra (Skt; Pali: Sāriputta) One of the three principal disciples of the Buddha, Shāriputra was born into a brahmin family in Nālandā. Shortly after the Buddha attained enlightenment, Shāriputra entered the Buddhist order and soon became renowned for his wisdom, expertise in analytical philosophy and his compassion, patience and humility. The Buddha declared him to be a perfect disciple, second only to himself in spiritual knowledge. Shāriputra often taught with the Buddha's approval.

shāstra Literally, instruction, textbook. In Buddhism, a shāstra is a philosophical analysis of and commentary on a sūtra. The shāstras are strongly didactic and form a large portion of the Chinese *Tripiṭaka*. *See also* sūtra, Tipiṭaka.

shīla (Skt; Pali: *sīla*) Literally, obligation, precept, noble conduct. *Shīla* means ethical discipline in thought, speech and action. *Shīla* often refers to several groups of precepts such as the Five, Eight and Ten Precepts or the numerous rules for monks and nuns. *Shīla* is considered a precondition for progress in meditation. Three practices of the Eightfold Path are included in *shīla*: right speech, right conduct and right livelihood. *See also* Eightfold Path.

shūdra One of the four castes in the hierarchy of Hindu society; members of the shūdra caste were manual labourers and servants to members of the other three castes. *See also* caste, class.

shūnya/shūnyatā *See* emptiness.

Shūraṅgama Sūtra (Sūtra of the Heroic One) The *Shūraṅgama Sūtra* greatly influenced the development of Mahāyāna Buddhism in China and explains the various methods of meditation on emptiness, through which individuals from all walks of life are said to be able to achieve enlightenment. The *Shūraṅgama Sūtra* is one of the main texts utilized in Ch'an Buddhism and is particularly well known in Zen Buddhism.

siddha Literally, perfect, complete; one who has achieved the supreme goal of spiritual enlightenment (such a being is also called a Mahāsiddha, a great siddha). The term may also refer to one who, through spiritual practice, has attained supernatural powers (*siddhis*) and the ability to perform miracles.

Siddhārtha Gautama (c.563–483 BCE) The historical Buddha, Siddhārtha (one whose aim is accomplished) Gautama was born in Lumbinī in the Rupandehi district of present-day Nepal, twenty-five kilometres outside Kapilavastu, at the time the capital of the Shākya people of which his father was the ruler. Prince Siddhārtha attained complete enlightenment, and his teachings are the foundation of Buddhism. He renounced family and kingship to set out in pursuit of spiritual truth. He sat for meditation under a peepal tree in Gayā, in Bihar, where he attained the Great Awakening when he was thirty-five. He subsequently began to travel from place to place teaching disciples the Dharma. Siddhārtha Gautama is recognized by Buddhists as the supreme Buddha of this time. *See also* Buddha, Dharma, Four Noble Truths, Kapilavastu, Shākyamuni.

sīla *See* shīla.

six realms The six categories of rebirth within the system of traditional Buddhist cosmology: hungry spirits, animals, fighting demi-gods, humans, gods, and beings in hells. These six realms include the entire range of life forms in the cycle of birth and rebirth. One's previous actions and thoughts determine which of the six realms one is reborn into.

skandhas The five psycho-physical components that constitute a person. The five *skandhas* are: 1) form (*rūpa*); 2) feelings or sensation (*vedanā*); 3) perception (*saññā*); 4) mental predispositions (*sañkhāra*); 5) consciousness (*viññāṇa*). The *skandhas* are often referred to as 'aggregates of attachment' because they are associated with craving or desire, which leads to suffering. Each of the *skandhas* bears the three marks or characteristics of all phenomena: impermanence, suffering, and absence of self. *See also* attā, dependent origination, emptiness, three marks.

skill in means (*upāya-kaushalya*) 'Skill in means' is the ability to adapt teachings and practices to the proclivities and capacities of trainees to bring these trainees closer to the spiritual goal. The Buddha was pragmatic and gave his teachings according to the needs and capacities of his audience, which varied according to background, culture and propensities. Buddhist teachers after him aspire to follow this use of the best means to teach and inspire their students through the means appropriate to their dispositions.

Sŏn/Seon *See* Ch'an.

soul The immortal essence of a living being, commonly thought to be distinct from and to exist independently of the physical body. In the Western world the concept of soul has differed through the ages; in this text it is used synonymously with *ātman* or *ātmā*. *See also* anattā, ātman, attā.

Suchness (Skt: *Tathatā*) The way things are in actuality; the absolute. A fundamental concept of Mahāyāna teaching, 'Suchness' or 'Thusness' refers to the true nature of all phenomena and the original state of things. A Buddha is regarded as one who observes things exactly as they are and perceives the true nature of all things. *See also* Dharmakāya, emptiness, Tathāgata.

suffering *See* dukkha.

Sukhāvatī Literally, the blissful. The western paradise or Pure Land of the Buddha Amitābha, Sukhāvatī is one of the most important Buddha-fields (spheres of influence and activity of a Buddha) of Mahāyāna teaching. Sukhāvatī was formed by Buddha Amitābha from the merit generated by his practices, and it is a Pure Land where those who invoke his name with faith and devotion may be reborn into a life of bliss until they attain final Nirvāṇa. Rebirth in this heavenly realm became the focus of the Pure Land Schools of East Asia. *See also* Amitābha, Pure Land.

Sukhāvatī-Vyūha *See* Pure Land Sūtra.

sūtra (Skt; Pali: sutta) Literally, thread; a discourse ascribed to the Buddha or derived from his teachings. The first sūtras were written around 300–200 BCE. Before that time the Buddha's teachings were exclusively committed to memory by his disciples and passed down from generation to generation. Oral transmission and memorization of sūtras is still an important practice of Buddhism today. The Buddha's sūtras are largely collected in the *Sutta Piṭaka* (Basket of the Teachings), one of the three sections of the *Tipiṭaka*. The early sūtras have been preserved in Pali and Sanskrit, as well as in Chinese and Tibetan translations. In addition, a great number of later Mahāyāna sūtras have been preserved, originally composed in Sanskrit and primarily existing now only in original Sanskrit and Chinese or Tibetan translations. *See also* Pali Canon, Tipiṭaka.

Sutta Piṭaka (Pali; Skt: *Sūtra Piṭaka* – Basket of Discourses) One of the three sections of the Pali Canon, the *Sutta Pitaka* is largely attributed to the Buddha himself. It is divided into five collections (*nikāyas*): the *Dīgha Nikāya* (*Collection of Long Discourses*), containing 34 lengthy suttas (sūtras), including some of the most important doctrinal expositions; the *Majjhima Nikāya* (*Collection of Middle-Length Discourses*), containing 152 suttas dealing with a variety of subjects; the *Saṁyutta Nikāya* (*Collection of Kindred Discourses*), with more than 7,000 suttas arranged according to subject; the *Aṅguttara Nikāya* (*Collection of Numerical Discourses*), 9,557 terse suttas arranged numerically for purposes of memorization; and the *Khuddaka Nikāya* (*Collection of Short Texts*). *See also* Aṅguttara Nikāya, Dīgha Nikāya, Khuddaka Nikāya, Majjhima Nikāya, Pali Canon, Saṁyutta Nikāya, Tipiṭaka.

sutta *See* sūtra.

Suzuki, Daisetsu Teitaro (1870–1966) A Japanese Buddhist scholar, D. T. Suzuki was one of the best-known modern interpreters of Zen in the West and was instrumental in bringing Zen Buddhism to Europe and America in the first half of the twentieth century. A lay student of Master Soyen Shaku, he focused primarily on the intellectual interpretation of the Zen teachings. Suzuki founded (together with his wife) the Eastern Buddhist Society in Japan, which publishes the English journal *Eastern Buddhist.* He published more than a hundred books, many in an informal style suited to the general reader, including *Essays in Buddhism*, translations and studies of the *Laṅkāvatāra Sūtra* and other classic texts.

Takakusu, Junjirō (1866–1945) A leading Japanese Buddhist scholar born in Hiroshima Prefecture, Takakusu studied Sanskrit at Oxford University, and after receiving his doctorate continued his studies in France and Germany. He founded the Musashino Girls' School in 1924, based on the concept of 'Buddhist-based human education', and the school eventually became Musashino Women's University. In collaboration with other scholars, Takakusu collected, edited and published the *Taisho Tripiṭaka*, the definitive edition of the Chinese and East Asian Buddhist canon of the twentieth century, including Japanese commentaries.

tantra Literally, weave, denoting continuity. Tantra refers to a range of inner and outer practices through which the practitioner seeks to channel the divine energy that flows through the universe to achieve spiritual and/or material goals. A tantra is also a core Vajrayāna text, and it is in this sense that tantra is used in this book. *See also* Mahāsiddha, Vajrayāna.

Tathāgata Literally, 'thus gone or thus come one'; an epithet of the Buddha, who, having become one with the eternal Absolute, neither comes from anywhere nor goes anywhere. *See also* Dharmakāya, Suchness.

Tathāgata-garbha A term analogous to the notion of *ātman* or soul, Tathāgata-garbha is the Buddha-nature present within every living being. It is the state of the Tathāgata, or ultimate reality, that is fully realized when one attains enlightenment. The *Laṅkāvatāra Sūtra* speaks of the Tathāgata-garbha as the presence of the Tathāgata, distinguishing it from the transitory ego-self. *See also* Buddha-nature, Dharmakāya, Tathāgata.

Tathatā *See* Suchness.

Theravāda (Teaching of the Elders) Theravāda is one of the major schools of Buddhism today (the others being Mahāyāna and Vajrayāna), and it is the only form of the earliest Buddhist schools to have survived to the present. The dominant form of Buddhism in Sri Lanka, Burma, Thailand, and Cambodia, Theravāda adheres to the texts and practices of the early Pali Canon, laying emphasis on monastic life. The Theravāda school accepts the Pali *Tipiṭaka* as the true teachings of the Buddha, as distinct from the later Mahāyāna sūtras. *See also* Mahāyāna, Pali Canon, Tipiṭaka, Vajrayāna.

Thich Nhat Hanh *See* Nhat Hanh, Thich.

Three Jewels (*triratna*) Taking refuge in the Three Jewels is the foundation of the Buddhist practice that culminates in enlightenment – the complete realization of one's Buddha-nature. The Three Jewels are: 1) the Buddha – both the historical Buddha and, in some interpretations, a teacher who has fully realized his Buddha-nature; 2) the Dharma – the scriptures or teachings of the Buddha; 3) the saṅgha – the community of practising Buddhists. Also known as the Three Refuges, the Three Treasures or Triple Gems, called thus because of their precious or invaluable nature. *See also* Buddha, Buddha-nature, Dharma, saṅgha.

three marks (*trilakshana*) According to the Buddha, there are three characteristics or marks of all phenomena: impermanence (*anitya*), suffering (*dukkha*), and the absence of self (*anattā*). Everything is conditioned and influenced by everything else, because all things and beings are intertwined in the vast net of cause and effect. The three marks are interrelated since things that are impermanent can have no enduring self or identity and it is attachment to the impermanent that is the cause of suffering. *See also* anattā, dukkha.

three worlds (*triloka*) Planes of existence in which all beings are born while they undergo the repeated cycle of birth and rebirth. These realms include: 1) the world of desire, in which 'hell beings', 'hungry spirits', animals, human beings, gods and demi-gods are living; 2) the world of form, inhabited by beings largely free of base desires but having subtle body forms, in which the gods of the form-world dwell; 3) the world of formlessness, which is a mainly spiritual continuum consisting of four heavens inhabited by the formless gods.

Thubten Yeshe, Lama *See* Yeshe, Lama Thubten

Thusness *See* Suchness.

Tibetan Buddhism Practised mainly in Tibet and neighbouring Himalayan regions, Tibetan Buddhism is derived primarily from Mahāyāna and Vajrayāna teachings. The four main schools of Tibetan Buddhism are: 1) Nyingma (school of the ancients), the oldest school, founded in the eighth century by Padmasambhāvā and Shantarakshita; 2) Kagyu (oral transmission lineage), teachings brought from India to Tibet in the eleventh century by Marpa, a student of Nāropa; 3) Sakya (gray earth), founded in the eleventh century by Khön Konchog Gyalpo; 4) Gelugpa (school of the virtuous), founded in the early fifteenth century by Tsongkapa. The Nyingma school lays emphasis on the practice of Dzogchen and the Kagyu school on the practice of Mahāmudrā. *See also* Dzogchen, lamrim, Mahāmudrā, Mahāyāna, Nāropa, Nyingma, Padmasambhāvā, Tsongkapa, Vajrayāna.

Tibetan Yoga and Secret Doctrines A collection of seven Tibetan yoga texts translated into English by the Tibetan Buddhist Kazi Dawa-Samdup and edited with commentary by his disciple, W. Y. Evans-Wentz. The book contains some of the principal types of meditation taught by Tibetan gurus and philosophers in pursuit of 'right knowledge' and enlightenment. These seven texts present a comprehensive view of some of the spiritual teachings at the foundation of the life and culture of the East. *See also* Evans-Wentz, W. Y.

Tipiṭaka (Pali; Skt: *Tripiṭaka*) Literally, three baskets. *Tipiṭaka* is the collective title of the three 'baskets' or divisions of the Pali Canon, the oldest complete canon of Buddhist scriptures. The three divisions include: 1) *Sutta Piṭaka*, the Buddha's discourses arranged into five collections (*Dīgha Nikāya*, *Majjhima Nikāya*, *Saṁyutta Nikāya*, *Aṅguttara Nikāya*, and *Khuddaka Nikāya*); 2) *Vinaya Piṭaka*, or monastic code; and 3) *Abhidhamma Piṭaka*, a compilation of analyses of Buddhist doctrine and philosophy. There are significant differences between the Theravāda and the Mahāyāna *Tipiṭaka*, as each of the eighteen early schools of Buddhism preserved their own version. The only *Tipiṭaka* to have survived intact in an Indian language is the Pali Canon of the Theravāda school. *See also* Abhidhamma Piṭaka, Pali, Pali Canon, sūtra, Sutta Piṭaka, Vinaya Piṭaka.

Tokushō, Bassui *See* Bassui Tokushō.

trikāya *See* triple body

Tripiṭaka *See* Tipiṭaka.

triple body (*trikāya*) According to Mahāyāna teaching, the Buddha, who is one with the Absolute, manifests in three 'bodies': 1) Dharmakāya (truth body), the formless, limitless true nature of the Buddha that is identical with ultimate reality; 2) Sambhogakāya (body of bliss), the subtle body that manifests in paradises or Pure Lands or can be perceived through advanced meditative faculties; 3) Nirmāṇakāya (emanated body), the physical body that Buddhas assume in the material world to guide sentient beings to liberation. The disciple encounters the three forms in ascending order as he or she becomes more spiritually receptive. *See also* Dharmakāya, Nirmāṇakāya, and Sambhogakāya.

triple world *See* three worlds.

Tsongkapa [Je Rinpoche, Losang Dragpa] (1357–1419) A renowned reformer and scholar born in northeast Tibet, Tsongkapa founded the Gelugpa school of Tibetan Buddhism. He studied with a number of masters of the major Tibetan Buddhist traditions and emphasized the development of renunciation, compassion and insight as a basis for Vajrayāna practice. Tsongkapa attempted to systematize what he believed were the authentic teachings of Indian Buddhism through his extensive writings, including the *Great Discourse on the Stages of the Path* (*Lam-rim Chenmo*) and the *Great Discourse on the Secret Mantra* (*Ngagrim Chenmo*). He established a following of students who – due to Tsongkapa's emphasis on pure monastic discipline – became known as the 'Virtuous Ones' (*gelugpa*). *See also* Tibetan Buddhism.

Tushita Literally, contented ones. The home of the 'contented gods', Tushita is considered the most beautiful of all the celestial heavens where bodhisattvas are reborn before their final return to earth in order to work through their remaining karma and attain enlightenment. Tushita Heaven is considered the residence of Bodhisattva Maitreya, who it is believed will one day incarnate on earth as the successor to Gautama Buddha.

Udāna (Inspired Exclamations) The third book of the *Khuddaka Nikāya*, the *Udāna* is a collection of eighty short discourses, each of which includes a prose section followed by a verse. At the end of each prose section, this text is given: "Then, on realizing the significance of that, the Blessed One exclaimed ...". This is followed by the verse, or 'exclamation'.

Upanishads The last section of the *Vedas* (the four earliest scriptures of Hinduism), the *Upanishads* contain philosophical and mystical teachings. *Upanishad* literally means 'to sit near or close to the teacher (Truth)'. These teachings were so named because their esoteric secrets and mysteries are directly imparted to the disciple by the teacher. The *Upanishads* are concerned with the nature of ultimate reality and the way to realize the oneness of the soul with that reality through meditation. *See also* Vedas.

Vajrayāna (Diamond Vehicle) One of the major traditions of Buddhism practised mainly in Japan and Tibet and its neighbouring Himalayan regions, Vajrayāna developed in northern India around the middle of the first millennium primarily from the Mahāyāna tradition. Vajrayāna emphasizes the use of esoteric visualizations, postures, rituals and mantras after initiation by and under the guidance of a master as the central approach to enlightenment. Because of the use of repetition of sacred syllables or mantras, Vajrayāna is also referred to as Mantrayāna, Esoteric Buddhism and Tantrayāna. *See also* Mahāyāna, Nāropa, Theravāda, Tibetan Buddhism.

Vārāṇasī Also known as Banāras or Benares, Vārāṇasī is an ancient pilgrimage city situated on the banks of the River Ganges in the present-day Indian state of Uttar Pradesh.

Vedas Literally, knowledge. The four earliest scriptures of Hinduism (*Rig Veda*, *Sām Veda*, *Yajur Veda*, *Atharva Veda*), the *Vedas* are said to have been directly revealed rather than of human origin. The *Vedas* deal with spiritual matters, the divine powers of gods, sacred formulas (mantras) and the problems of life in the world. The term also refers to Vedic literature in general, including the *Upanishads* and various interpretive texts. *See also* Upanishads.

vijñāna *See* viññāṇa.

Vimalakīrti A wealthy Buddhist of Vaishālī at the time of the Buddha. In the famous work *The Vimalakīrti Nirdesha Sūtra*, Vimalakīrti is depicted as refuting the views held by such prominent disciples of the Buddha as Shāriputra and offering Mahāyāna doctrines based on his understanding of non-duality and emptiness. *See also* emptiness.

Vinaya Piṭaka (Pali; Skt: *Vinaya Piṭaka* – Basket of Discipline) Literally, leading out; education; discipline. One of the three sections of the Pali Canon, the *Vinaya Piṭaka* primarily contains codes of monastic discipline believed to have originated with Gautama Buddha. The *Vinaya* consists of: 1) *Suttavibhanga*, a commentary on the rules of the community; 2) *Khandhaka*, a series of twenty-two pieces relating to admission to the order, monastic ceremonies, rules governing daily life and procedures for handling conflicts and disputes; it also includes accounts of the awakening of the Buddha and his disciples, his first sermons and the establishment of the community of Buddhist nuns; 3) *Parivara*, summaries and analyses of the rules of the first two sections organized in different ways for instructional purposes. *See also* Pali Canon, Tipitaka.

viññāṇa (Pali; Skt: *vijñāna*) Literally, consciousness, mental awareness. *Viññāṇa* sometimes refers to infinite consciousness, the highest state of spiritual realization that is identical with ultimate reality. At other times *viññāṇa* refers to the consciousness of daily human life. As such, it is the fifth of the five components (*skandhas*) that constitute a human being's experience of mind and body. *See also* skandhas.

Yeshe, Lama Thubten (1935–1984) A Tibetan lama known for his unconventional manner of teaching, Lama Thubten Yeshe was sent to a monastery in Lhasa at the age of six and was ordained at twenty-eight in the Gelugpa tradition. He taught that reality and consciousness 'embrace' each other and that all things have sound energy. Lama Yeshe created the Foundation for the Preservation of the Mahāyāna Tradition (FPMT) in 1975, during his years of exile in Nepal. It was reported that when asked why he refused the prestigious *geshe* degree for which he had studied, Lama Yeshe laughed and said, "And be Geshe Yeshe?" *See also* Tibetan Buddhism.

yoga From the Sanskrit *yuj*, meaning 'to yoke or join'; union. One of the six systems of Indian philosophy, yoga is believed to have been founded by the sage Yājñavalkya and later codified by Patañjali in his *Yoga Sūtras*. It is a form of control of mental states, a systematic discipline of ancient Indian origin meant to lead the human being to attain union with God. Early Buddhist techniques of meditation, including awareness of inhalation and exhalation, are similar to those codified in the *Yoga Sūtras*, written in the second and third century CE.

Zen (Jap; Chin: Ch'an; Kor: Sŏn) A Japanese school of Mahāyāna Buddhism that originated in China as Ch'an in the sixth century CE and spread from there to Vietnam, Korea and Japan. Zen, the Japanese pronunciation of Ch'an, encompasses various Japanese schools as well as their international counterparts. While there are differences among Zen, Ch'an and Sŏn Buddhism and the schools within each group, in general their philosophy and approach to practice are quite similar. *See also* Ch'an.

Bibliography

Note: This bibliography is divided into sections. English translations are first divided into four sections: Pali Buddhist Canon texts, Chinese scriptures, Sanskrit scriptures, and biographies and works of Buddhist teachers. Then all English books are listed, and finally Pali and Sanskrit/Hindi texts. Scriptures without an author are listed under their Pali or Sanskrit names if the Pali or Sanskrit name is given in the text. All other books are listed under the author's name.

English Translations of Pali Buddhist Canon Texts

Aṅguttara Nikāya (Collection of Numerical Discourses). *The Book of the Gradual Sayings (Anguttara-Nikāya), or, More-Numbered Suttas.* Pali Text Society Translation Series 22, 24, 25, 26, 27. Translated by F. L. Woodward and E. M. Hare. London: Oxford University Press for Pali Text Society, 1932–1936.

Āryasūra (Garland of Birth Stories). *The Gātakamālā or Garland of Birth Stories.* Translated by J. S. Speyer. Reprint (original 1895). Delhi: Motilal Banarsidass Publishers Pvt Ltd, 1980.

Dhammapada (The Path of Truth). *The Dhammapada.* Translated by S. Radhakrishnan. London: Oxford University Press, 1950.

———. *The Dhammapada: A Collection of Verses; Being One of the Canonical Books of the Buddhists.* Translated by F. Max Müller. Sacred Books of the East 10, part 1. Oxford: The Clarendon Press, 1881.

Dīgha Nikāya (Collection of Long Discourses). *Dialogues of the Buddha.* Sacred Books of the Buddhists 2, 3, 4. Edited and translated by

T. W. Rhys Davids. Reprint (original 1899–1921). Oxford: Pali Text Society, 1995.

Jātaka (Stories of the Buddha's Former Births). *The Jātaka or Stories of the Buddha's Former Births*. 7 vols. Translated by various hands under the editorship of E. B. Cowell. Cambridge: University Press, 1895–1913.

Majjhima Nikāya (Collection of Middle-Length Discourses). *The Collection of the Middle Length Sayings (Majjhima Nikāya)*. Pali Text Society Translation Series 29, 30, 31. Translated by Isaline B Horner. London: Luzac for Pali Text Society, 1954–1959.

———. *Middle Length Discourses of the Buddha: A New Translation of the Majjhima Nikāya*. Original translation by Bhikkhu Ñāṇamoli, Translation edited and revised by Bhikkhu Bodhi. Somerville, Massachusetts: Wisdom Publications, 2001.

———. *Further Dialogues of the Buddha*. Sacred Books of the Buddhists 5, 6. Edited and translated by Robert Chalmers. London: Pali Text Society, 1898–1899.

Milindapañhā (Questions of Milinda). *The Questions of King Milinda*. Sacred Books of the East 35, 36. Translated by T. W. Rhys Davids. Oxford, The Clarendon Press, 1898.

Saṁyutta Nikāya (Collection of Kindred Discourses). *The Book of the Kindred Sayings (Samyutta-nikāya) or Grouped Suttas*. Pali Text Society Translation Series 7, 10, 13, 14, 16. Translated by C. A. F. Rhys Davids, Sūriyagoda Sumangala Thera and F. L. Woodward, London: Oxford University Press for Pali Text Society, 1917–1930.

Sutta Nipāta (Collection of Discourses). *The Sutta-Nipāta, a Collection of Discourses*. Sacred Books of the East 10, part 2. Translated by V. Fausböll. Oxford: The Clarendon Press, 1881.

Vinaya Piṭaka (The Book of the Discipline). *Vinaya Texts*. Sacred Books of the East 13, 17, 20. Translated by T. W. Rhys Davids and Hermann Oldenberg. Oxford: The Clarendon Press, 1881–1885.

English Translations of Chinese Scriptures

Avataṁsaka Sūtra (The Flower Ornament Scripture). *The Flower Ornament Scripture: A Translation of the Avatamsaka Sūtra*. Reprint (original 1984). Translated by Thomas Cleary. Boston: Shambhala, 1993.

Bodhidharma. *The Zen Teaching of Bodhidharma*. Translated by Red Pine. Reprint (original 1987). New York: North Point Press, 1989.

The Flower Ornament Scripture. *See* Avataṁsaka Sūtra.

The Heart Sūtra. *See* Prajñāpāramitāhridaya.

Hsüan-sha Shih-pei. *See* Shih-pei, Hsüan-sha.

Huang-po. *The Zen Teaching of Huang Po on the Transmission of Mind; Being the Teaching of the Zen Master Huang Po as Recorded by the Scholar P'ei Hsiu of the T'ang Dynasty*. Translated by John Blofeld (Chu Ch'an). 2nd ed. New York: Grove Press, 1958.

Hui-neng. *The Platform Sutra: The Zen Teaching of Hui-neng*. Translation and commentary by Red Pine. Emeryville, CA: Shoemaker & Hoard, 2006.

Lin-chi Lu. *See* Yixuan.

Lotus Sūtra. *See* Saddharmapuṇḍarīka.

Mahāratnakūṭa Sūtra (Treasury Sūtra/Great Jewel-Heap Sūtra). *A Treasury of Mahāyāna Sūtras: Selections from the Mahāratnakūṭa Sūtra*. Translated by The Buddhist Association of the United States. Edited by Garma C. C. Chang. Reprint (1st Indian ed. 1991). New Delhi: Motilal Banarsidass Publishers Pvt Ltd, 2002.

The Platform Sūtra. *See* Hui-neng.

Prajñāpāramitāhridaya (The Heart Sūtra). *The Heart Sutra: The Womb of Buddhas*. Translated with commentary by Red Pine. Washington: Shoemaker & Hoard, 2004.

Saddharmapuṇḍarīka (The Lotus Sūtra). *The Lotus Sutra*. Bibliotheca Indo-Buddhica Series 202. Translated by Burton Watson. Reprint (original 1993). Delhi: Sri Satguru Publications, 1999.

———. *The Lotus Sutra*. Translations from the Asian Classics Series. Translated by Burton Watson. New York: Columbia University Press, 1993.

Shih-pei, Hsüan-sha. In *Original Teachings of Ch'an Buddhism: Selected from "The Transmission of the Lamp"*. Compiled by Shi Daoyuan. Translated with introductions by Chang Chung-Yuan. Reprint (original 1969). New York: Vintage Books, 1971.

Shūraṅgama Sūtra (The Method of a Brave Person). *The Śūraṅgama Sūtra (Leng Yen Ching)*. Translated by Charles Luk (Upāsaka Lu K'uan Yu). Commentary (abridged) by Ch'an Master Han Shan. Reprint (original 1966). New Delhi: Munshiram Manoharlal Publishers Pvt Ltd, 2003.

Sūtra of Perfect Enlightenment. *The Sutra of Perfect Enlightenment: Korean Buddhism's Guide to Meditation; with Commentary by the Sŏn Monk Kihwa*. SUNY Series in Korean Studies. Translated by A. Charles Muller. Albany: State University of New York Press, 1999.

Vimalakīrti Nirdesha Sūtra (Teachings of Vimalakīrti). *The Vimalakīrti Nirdeśa Sūtra*. Clear Light Series. Translated by Upāsaka Lu K'uan Yu (Charles Luk). Berkeley: Shambala Press, 1972.

Yixuan. *The Zen Teachings of Master Lin-chi: A Translation of the Lin-chi Lu*. Shambhala Dragon Editions. Translated by Burton Watson. Boston and London: Shambhala, 1993.

The Zen Teachings of Master Lin-chi. *See* Yixuan.

English Translations of Sanskrit Scriptures

Ashvaghosha. The Buddha-karita *of Asvaghosha*. In *Buddhist Mahāyāna Texts*. Sacred Books of the East 49, part 1. Translated by E. B. Cowell. Oxford: The Clarendon Press, 1894.

———. *The Buddhacarita: Or, Acts of the Buddha*. Panjab University Oriental Publications 31, 32. Edited and translated by E. H. Johnston. Calcutta: Baptist Mission Press, 1935–1936.

Ashṭasāhasrikā Prajñāpāramitā (The Perfection of Wisdom in Eight Thousand Lines). *Aṣṭasāhasrikā Prajñāpāramitā*. Bibliotheca Indica Series 284. Translated by Edward Conze. Calcutta: Asiatic Society, 1958.

Buddhacharita (Acts of the Buddha). *See* Ashvaghosha.

Conze, Edward. *Buddhist Wisdom Books: Containing the Diamond Sutra and the Heart Sutra*. Translated and explained by Edward Conze. London: George Allen & Unwin, 1958.

The Diamond Sūtra. *See* Vajrachchhedikā Prajñāpāramitā.

The Heart Sūtra. *See* Prajñāpāramitāhridaya.

Lalitavistara (The Unfolding of the Play). *Lalitavistara: English Translation with Notes*. Translated by Bijoya Goswami, Kolkata: The Asiatic Society, 2001.

Laṅkāvatāra Sūtra (Sūtra on the Descent to Sri Lanka). *The Laṅkāvatāra Sūtra: A Mahayana Text*. Ataka Buddhist Library Series 4. Translated by D. T. Suzuki. Reprint (original 1932). London: Routledge & Kegan Paul, 1968.

———. *Studies in the Laṅkāvatāra Sūtra*. *See* Suzuki, Daisetz Teitaro.

The Large Sūtra on Perfect Wisdom. *See* Pañchaviṁshatisāhasrikā Prajñāpāramitā.

The Larger Sukhāvatī-vyūha (The Larger Pure Land Sūtra). In *Buddhist Mahāyāna Texts*. Sacred Books of the East 49, part 2. Translated by F. Max Müller. Oxford: Clarendon Press, 1894.

Lotus Sūtra. *See* Saddharmapuṇḍarīka.

Mahāvastu (Great Book). *The Mahāvastu*. Sacred Books of the Buddhists 16, 18, 19. Translated by J. J. Jones. London: Pali Text Society, 1949–1956.

———. *The Mahāvastu*. Reprint. (original 1949–1956). Translated by J. J. Jones. London: Pali Text Society, 1973–1978.

Nāgārjuna. *Mahāyānaviṁshikā of Nāgārjuna*. In *Minor Buddhist Texts*. Serie Orientale Roma 9. Edited by G. Tucci. Rome: Instituto Italiano per il Medio ed Estremo Oriente, 1956.

Pañchaviṁshatisāhasrikā Prajñāpāramitā (The Perfection of Wisdom in Twenty-five Thousand Lines). *The Large Sūtra on Perfect Wisdom, with the Divisions of the Abhisamayālaṅkāra*. Translated and edited by Edward Conze. Berkeley and Los Angeles: University of California Press, 1975.

Prajñāpāramitāhridaya (The Heart Sūtra). In *Buddhist Wisdom Books, Containing the Diamond Sutra and the Heart Sutra*. Translated and explained by Edward Conze. Reprint (original 1958). London: Harper & Row Publishers, 1972.

———. *The Heart Sutra: The Womb of Buddhas*. Translated with commentary by Red Pine. Washington: Shoemaker & Hoard, 2004.

Prajñopāyavinishchayasiddhi. *The Realization of the Certitude of Appreciative Awareness and Ethical Action*. In *Buddhist Texts through the Ages*. Translated by Edward Conze. Edited by Edward Conze, I. B. Horner, D. Snellgrove and A. Waley. Oxford: Bruno Cassirer, 1954.

Ratnagotravibhāga of Sāramati. In *Buddhist Texts through the Ages*. Translated by Edward Conze. Oxford: Bruno Cassirer, 1954.

Saddharmapuṇḍarīka (The Lotus Sūtra). *The Saddharma-Pundarīka: Or, the Lotus of the True Law*. Sacred Books of the East 21. Translated by H. Kern. Edited by F. Max Müller. Oxford: The Clarendon Press, 1884.

Sukhāvatīvyūha (Pure Land Sūtra). In *Buddhist Mahāyāna Texts*. Sacred Books of the East 49, part 2. Edited and translated by F. Max

Mueller. Reprint (original 1894). Delhi: Motilal Banarsidass Publishers Pvt Ltd, 1985.

Suzuki, Daisetz Teitaro. *Studies in the Lankavatara Sutra: One of the Most Important Texts of Mahayana Buddhism, in which Almost All Its Principal Tenets are Presented, Including the Teaching of Zen.* Reprint. (original 1930). London: Routledge & Kegan Paul, 1968.

Vajrachchhedikā Prajñāpāramitā (The Diamond Sūtra). In *Buddhist Wisdom Books, Containing the Diamond Sūtra and the Heart Sūtra.* Translated and explained by Edward Conze. London: George Allen & Unwin, 1958.

Vimalakīrti Sūtra. *See* Vimalakīrti Nirdesha Sūtra.

Vimalakīrti Nirdesha Sūtra (Teachings of Vimalakīrti). *The Teaching of Vimalakīrti (Vimalakīrtinirdeśa).* Sacred Books of the Buddhists 32. UNESCO Collection of Representative Works. Translated by Sara Boin from the French translation by Étienne Lamotte. London: Pali Text Society, 1976.

TRANSLATED BIOGRAPHIES AND WORKS OF BUDDHIST TEACHERS

Japanese

Bassui Tokushō. *See* Tokushō, Bassui.

Dōgen Eihei. *Dōgen Zen.* Translated by Shohaku Okumura. Reprint (original 1988). Tokyo, Japan: Sōtō-shū Shūmuchō, 1998.

Eihei, Dōgen. *See* Dōgen Eihei.

Kokushi, Musō. *Dream Conversations on Buddhism and Zen.* Translated and edited by Thomas Cleary. Reprint (original 1994). Boston and London: Shambala Publications, 1996.

Ryōkan. *Dewdrops on a Lotus Leaf: Zen Poetry of Ryōkan.* Centaur Editions Series. Translated by John Stevens. Boston: Shambala Publications, 1996.

———. *Great Fool: Zen Master Ryōkan: Poems, Letters, and Other Writings.* Translated by Ryūichi Abé and Peter Haskel. Honolulu: University of Hawaii Press, 1996.

Shaku, Soyen. *Sermons of a Buddhist Abbot: Addresses on Religious Subjects.* Translated by Daisetz Teitaro Suzuki. Chicago: Open Court Publishing Company, 1906.

Soyen Shaku. *See* Shaku, Soyen.

Tokushō, Bassui. *Mud and Water: The Collected Teachings of Zen Master Bassui*. Translated by Arthur Braverman. Somerville, MA: Wisdom Publications, 2002.

Korean

Chinul. *The Korean Approach to Zen: The Collected Works of Chinul.* Translated with an introduction by Robert E. Buswell, Jr. Honolulu: University of Hawaii Press, 1983.

———. *Tracing Back the Radiance: Chinul's Korean Way of Zen.* Classics in East Asian Buddhism. Translated by Robert E. Buswell. University of Hawaii Press, 1991.

Muller, A. Charles, tr. *The Sutra of Perfect Enlightenment: Korean Buddhism's Guide to Meditation; with Commentary by the Sŏn Monk Kihwa.* SUNY Series in Korean Studies. Albany: State University of New York Press, 1999.

Tibetan

Chogyal Namkhai Norbu. *See* Norbu, Chogyal Namkhai.

Dalai Lama, XIV. *The Four Noble Truths: Fundamentals of the Buddhist Teachings*. Translated by Geshe Thupten Jinpa. Edited by Dominique Side. 2nd ed. (1st ed. 1977). New Delhi: HarperCollins Publishers India, 1998.

———. *The Power of Compassion: A Collection of Lectures by His Holiness the XIV Dalai Lama.* Translated by Geshe Thupten Jinpa. Reprint (original 1995). New Delhi: HarperCollins Publishers India, 1999.

———. *Universal Responsibility, a Collection of Essays.* Edited by Ramesh C. Tewari and Krishna Nath. New Delhi: Foundation for Universal Responsibility, 1996.

Geshe Kelsang Gyatso. *See* Gyatso, Geshe Kelsang.

Guenther, Herbert V., tr. *The Life and Teaching of Nāropa.* UNESCO Collection of Representative Works. Tibetan Series. Translation and commentary by Herbert V. Guenther. Reprint (original 1963). Boston: Shambhala South Asia Editions, 1999.

Gyatso, Geshe Kelsang. *Buddhism in the Tibetan Tradition: A Guide.* Translated by Tenzin P. Phunrabpa. Edited by R. F. Lister and M. R. Lister. London; New York: Routledge & K. Paul, 1984.

Kelsang Gyatso, Geshe. *See* Gyatso, Geshe Kelsang.

Longchenpa [Longchen Rabjam]. *You Are the Eyes of the World*. Copper Mountain Series. Translated by Kennard Lipman and Merrill Peterson. Ithaca: Snow Lion Publications, 2000.

———. *Kindly Bent to Ease Us: Part One: Mind*. Translated by Herbert V. Günther. Berkeley: Dharma Publishing, 1975.

———. *The Precious Treasury of Pith Instructions*. The Seven Treasuries Series. Translated by Richard Barron. Junction City: Padma Publishing, 2006.

Namkhai Norbu. *See* Norbu, Chogyal Namkhai.

Nāropa. In *The Life and Teaching of Nāropa*. UNESCO Collection of Representative Works. Tibetan Series. Translation and commentary by Herbert V. Guenther. Reprint (original 1963). Boston: Shambhala South Asia Editions, 1999.

Norbu, Chogyal Namkhai. "Working with Circumstances", *The Mirror: Newspaper of the International Dzogchen Community*. Edited by Liz Granger and Naomi Zeitz. Available at http://www.tsegyalgar.org/teachings/dec_2001.html.

Pabongka Rinpoche. *Liberation in the Palm of Your Hand: A Concise Discourse on the Path to Enlightenment*. Edited by Trijang Rinpoche. Translated by Michael Richards. Revised (original 1991). Boston: Wisdom Publications, 1997.

Padmasambhava. *Self-Liberation through Seeing with Naked Awareness: Being an Introduction to the Nature of One's Own Mind from the Profound Teaching of Self-Liberation in the Primordial State of the Peaceful and Wrathful Deities*. Edited and translated by John Myrdhin Reynolds. Ithaca: Snow Lions Publications, 2000.

———. *Dakini Teachings: Padmasambhava's Oral Instructions to Lady Tsogyal. From the Revelations of Nyang Ral Nyima Ozer, Sangye Lingpa and Dorje Lingpa*. Edited by Marcia Binder Schmidt. Translated by Erik Pema Kunsang (Eric Hein Schmidt). 2nd ed. (1st ed. 1990). Hong Kong: Rangjung Yeshe Publications, 1999.

Patrul Rinpoche. *The Words of My Perfect Teacher/ Kunzang Lama'i Shelung (Sacred Literature)*. The Sacred Literature Series of the International Sacred Literature Trust. Translated by The Padmakara Translation Group. Edited by Kerry Brown and Sima Sharma. Reprint (original 1994). New Delhi: HarperCollins Publishers India, 1998.

Rabjam, Longchen. *See* Longchenpa.

Thubten Loden, Geshe Acharya. *Path to Enlightenment in Tibetan Buddhism*. Melbourne: Tushita Publications, 1993.

Thubten Yeshe, Lama. *Becoming the Compassion Buddha: Tantric Mahamudra for Everyday Life: A Commentary on the Guru Yoga Practice Called the Inseparability of the Spiritual Master and Avalokiteshvara: A Source of All Powerful Attainments*. Edited by Robina Courtin. Somerville, MA: Wisdom Publications, 2003.

Tibetan Yoga and Secret Doctrines, or, Seven Books of Wisdom of the Great Path, According to the Late Lāma Kazi Dawa-Samdup's English Rendering. Reprint (original 1935). Edited and commentary by W. Y. Evans-Wentz. Translated by Lāma Kazi Dawa-Samdup. Delhi: Pilgrims Book, 1999.

Vietnamese

Nhat Hanh, Thich. *The Heart of the Buddha's Teaching: Transforming Suffering into Peace, Joy & Liberation: the Four Noble Truths, the Noble Eightfold Path, and Other Basic Buddhist Teachings*. London: Rider, 1999.

All English Texts and Translations

Aṅguttara Nikāya (Collection of Numerical Discourses). *The Book of the Gradual Sayings (Anguttara-Nikāya), or, More-Numbered Suttas*. Pali Text Society Translation Series 22, 24, 25, 26, 27. Translated by F. L. Woodward and E. M. Hare. London: Oxford University Press for Pali Text Society, 1932–1936.

Addiss, Stephen. *The Art of Zen: Paintings and Calligraphy by Japanese Monks 1600–1925*. Reprint (original 1989). New York: Harry N. Abrams, 1998.

Āryasūra (Garland of Birth Stories). *The Gātakamālā or Garland of Birth Stories*. Translated by J. S. Speyer. Reprint (original 1895). Delhi: Motilal Banarsidass Publishers Pvt Ltd, 1980.

Ashṭasāhasrikā Prajñāpāramitā (The Perfection of Wisdom in Eight Thousand Lines). *Aṣṭasāhasrikā Prajñāpāramitā*. Bibliotheca Indica Series 284. Translated by Edward Conze. Calcutta: Asiatic Society, 1958.

Ashvaghosha. The Buddha-karita *of Asvaghosha*. In *Buddhist Mahāyāna Texts*. Sacred Books of the East 49, part 1. Translated by E. B. Cowell. Oxford: The Clarendon Press, 1894.

———. *The Buddhacarita: Or, Acts of the Buddha*. Panjab University Oriental Publications 31, 32. Edited and translated by E. H. Johnston. Calcutta: Baptist Mission Press, 1935–1936.

Avataṁsaka Sūtra (The Flower Ornament Scripture). *The Flower Ornament Scripture: A Translation of the Avatamsaka Sūtra*. Reprint (original 1984). Translated by Thomas Cleary. Boston: Shambhala, 1993.

Banerjee, Anukul Chandra. *The Splendour of Buddhism*. New Delhi: Munshiram Manoharlal Publishers Pvt Ltd, 1991.

Bapat, P. V. *2500 years of Buddhism*. New Delhi: Publications Division, Ministry of Information and Broadcasting, Government of India, 1956.

Bassui Tokushō. *See* Tokushō, Bassui.

Bhagavadgītā (Song of the Lord). *The Bhagavadgītā*. Edited and translated by S. Radhakrishnan. Reprint (original 1948). London: George Allen & Unwin Ltd, 1960.

———. *The Bhagavadgītā with Sanatsugātīya and the Anugītā*. Sacred Books of the East 8. 2nd ed. (1st ed. 1882). Translated by Kāshināth Trimbak Telang. Oxford: Clarendon Press, 1898.

Bhattacharya, Vidushekhara. *The Basic Conception of Buddhism*. Adharchandra Mookerjee Lectures Series, 1932. Calcutta: University of Calcutta, 1934.

Bodhidharma. *The Zen Teaching of Bodhidharma*. Translated by Red Pine. Reprint (original 1987). New York: North Point Press, 1989.

Buddha, Gautama. *The Living Thoughts of Gotama, the Buddha*. Living Thoughts Library Series 26. Presented by Ananda K. Coomaraswamy and I. B. Horner. London: Cassell, 1948.

Buddhacharita (Acts of the Buddha). *See* Ashvaghosha.

Buswell, Robert E., Jr, ed. *Encyclopedia of Buddhism*. 2 vols. New York: Macmillan, USA/Thomson Gale, 2004.

Chinul. *The Korean Approach to Zen: The Collected Works of Chinul*. Translated with an introduction by Robert E. Buswell, Jr. Honolulu: University of Hawaii Press, 1983.

———. *Tracing Back the Radiance: Chinul's Korean Way of Zen*. Classics in East Asian Buddhism. Translated by Robert E. Buswell. University of Hawaii Press, 1991.

Chogyal Namkhai Norbu. *See* Norbu, Chogyal Namkhai.

Conze, Edward. *Buddhism: Its Essence and Development.* Harper Torchbooks Series. Reprint (original 1951). New York: Harper and Row Publishers, 1965.

———. *Buddhist Meditation.* Ethical and Religious Classics of East and West Series 13. London: Allen & Unwin, 1956.

———. *Buddhist Scriptures.* The Penguin Classics and UNESCO Collection of Representative Works. Selected and translated by Edward Conze. Harmondsworth: Penguin Books, 1959.

———. *Buddhist Scriptures: A Bibliography.* Garland Reference Library of the Humanities 113. Edited and revised by Lewis Lancaster. New York: Garland Publishing, 1982.

———. *Buddhist Texts through the Ages.* Translated by Edward Conze. Edited by Edward Conze, I. B. Horner, D. Snellgrove and A. Waley. Oxford: Bruno Cassirer, 1954.

———. *Buddhist Thought in India: Three Phases of Buddhist Philosophy.* Ann Arbor Paperbacks. Ann Arbor: The University of Michigan Press, 1967.

———. *Thirty Years of Buddhist Studies.* Oxford: Bruno Cassirer, 1967.

———. *Buddhist Wisdom Books: Containing the Diamond Sutra and the Heart Sutra.* Translated and explained by Edward Conze. London: George Allen & Unwin, 1958.

Coomaraswamy, Ananda K. *Hinduism and Buddhism.* Reprint (original 1943). New Delhi: Munshiram Manoharlal Publishers Pvt Ltd, 1986.

Dalai Lama, XIV. *The Four Noble Truths: Fundamentals of the Buddhist Teachings.* Translated by Geshe Thupten Jinpa. Edited by Dominique Side. 2nd ed. (1st ed. 1977). New Delhi: HarperCollins Publishers India, 1998.

———. *The Power of Compassion: A Collection of Lectures by His Holiness the XIV Dalai Lama.* Translated by Geshe Thupten Jinpa. Reprint (original 1995). New Delhi: HarperCollins Publishers India, 1999.

———. *Universal Responsibility, a Collection of Essays.* Edited by Ramesh C. Tewari and Krishna Nath. New Delhi: Foundation for Universal Responsibility, 1996.

Dhammapada (The Path of Truth). *The Dhammapada.* Translated by S. Radhakrishnan. London: Oxford University Press, 1950.

———. *The Dhammapada: A Collection of Verses; Being One of the Canonical Books of the Buddhists.* Translated by F. Max Müller.

Sacred Books of the East 10, part 1. Oxford: The Clarendon Press, 1881.

The Diamond Sūtra. *See* Vajrachchhedikā Prajñāpāramitā.

Dīgha Nikāya (Collection of Long Discourses). *Dialogues of the Buddha*. Sacred Books of the Buddhists 2, 3, 4. Edited and translated by T. W. Rhys Davids. Reprint (original 1899–1921). Oxford: Pali Text Society, 1995.

Dōgen Eihei. *Dōgen Zen*. Translated by Shohaku Okumura. Reprint (original 1988). Tokyo, Japan: Sōtō-shū Shūmuchō, 1998.

Eihei, Dōgen. *See* Dōgen Eihei.

Eliot, Sir Charles. *Buddhism and Hinduism: An Historical Sketch*. 3 vols. Reprint (original 1921). Delhi: Sri Satguru Publications, 1988.

———. *Buddhism and Hinduism: An Historical Sketch*. 3 vols. Reprint (original 1921). Richmond: Curzon Press, 1998.

The Flower Ornament Scripture. *See* Avataṁsaka Sūtra.

Gautama Buddha. *See* Buddha, Gautama.

Geshe Kelsang Gyatso. *See* Gyatso, Geshe Kelsang.

Gethin, Rupert. *The Foundations of Buddhism*. Oxford University Press Series. Oxford: Oxford University Press, 1998.

Glasenapp, Helmuth von. *Vedānta and Buddhism: A Comparative Study*. The Wheel Publication No. 2. Reprint (original 1951). Kandy, Ceylon: Wheel Publications, 1958.

Grimm, George. *The Doctrine of the Buddha: the Religion of Reason and Meditation*. Edited by M. Keller-Grimm and Max Hoppe. Reprint (original 1926). Delhi: Motilal Banarsidass Publishers Pvt Ltd, 1982.

Guenther, Herbert V., tr. *The Life and Teaching of Nāropa*. UNESCO Collection of Representative Works. Tibetan Series. Translation and commentary by Herbert V. Guenther. Reprint (original 1963). Boston: Shambhala South Asia Editions, 1999.

Gyatso, Geshe Kelsang. *Buddhism in the Tibetan Tradition: A Guide*. Translated by Tenzin P. Phunrabpa. Edited by R. F. Lister and M. R. Lister. London; New York: Routledge & K. Paul, 1984.

———. *Introduction to Buddhism: An Explanation of the Buddhist Way of Life*. London: Tharpa Publications, 1992.

Hanh, Thich Nhat. *See* Nhat Hanh, Thich.

Harvey, Peter. *An Introduction to Buddhism: Teachings, History and Practices*. Cambridge: Cambridge University Press, 1990.

The Heart Sūtra. *See* Prajñāpāramitāhridaya.

Hsüan-sha Shih-pei. *See* Shih-pei, Hsüan-sha.

Huang-po. *The Zen Teaching of Huang Po on the Transmission of Mind; Being the Teaching of the Zen Master Huang Po as Recorded by the Scholar P'ei Hsiu of the T'ang Dynasty.* Translated by John Blofeld (Chu Ch'an). 2nd ed. New York: Grove Press, 1958.

Hui-neng. *The Platform Sutra: The Zen Teaching of Hui-neng.* Translation and commentary by Red Pine. Emeryville, CA: Shoemaker & Hoard, 2006.

Jacob, George Adolphus. *A Concordance to the Principal Upanishads and the Bhagavadgītā.* Reprint (original 1891). Delhi: Motilal Banarsidass Publishers Pvt Ltd, 1963.

Jātaka (Stories of the Buddha's Former Births). *The Jātaka or Stories of the Buddha's Former Births.* 7 vols. Translated by various hands under the editorship of E. B. Cowell. Cambridge: University Press, 1895–1913.

Jayatilleke, Kulatissa Nanda. *Early Buddhist Theory of Knowledge.* London: G. Allen & Unwin, 1963.

Joshi, Lal Mani. *Brahmanism, Buddhism and Hinduism: An Essay on Their Origins and Interactions.* Wheel Publication Series 150/151. Kandy, Ceylon: Buddhist Publication Society, 1970.

———. *Discerning the Buddha: A Study of Buddhism and the Brahmanical Hindu Attitude to It.* New Delhi: Munshiram Manoharlal Publishers Pvt Ltd, 1983.

———. *Studies in the Buddhistic Culture of India during the 7th and 8th centuries A.D.* Reprint (original 1967). Delhi: Motilal Banarsidass Publishers Pvt Ltd, 1987.

Kelsang Gyatso, Geshe. *See* Gyatso, Geshe Kelsang.

Keown, Damien, ed. *Encyclopedia of Buddhism.* London: Routledge, 2007.

Kokushi, Musō. *Dream Conversations on Buddhism and Zen.* Translated and edited by Thomas Cleary. Reprint (original 1994). Boston and London: Shambala Publications, 1996.

Lalitavistara (The Unfolding of the Play). *Lalitavistara: English Translation with Notes.* Translated by Bijoya Goswami, Kolkata: The Asiatic Society, 2001.

Laṅkāvatāra Sūtra (Sūtra on the Descent to Sri Lanka). *The Laṅkāvatāra Sūtra: a Mahayana Text.* Ataka Buddhist Library Series 4. Translated by D. T. Suzuki. Reprint (original 1932). London: Routledge & Kegan Paul, 1968.

———. *Studies in the Laṅkāvatāra Sūtra*. *See* Suzuki, Daisetz Teitaro.
The Large Sūtra on Perfect Wisdom. *See* Pañchaviṁshatisāhasrikā Prajñāpāramitā.
The Larger Sukhāvatī-vyūha (The Larger Pure Land Sūtra). In *Buddhist Mahāyāna Texts*. Sacred Books of the East 49, part 2. Translated by F. Max Müller. Oxford: Clarendon Press, 1894.
Law, Bimala Churn. *Buddhistic Studies*. Edited by Bimala Churn Law. Calcutta and Simla: Thacker, Spink & Co., 1931.
Lin-chi Lu. *See* Yixuan.
Longchenpa [Longchen Rabjam]. *You Are the Eyes of the World*. Copper Mountain Series. Translated by Kennard Lipman and Merrill Peterson. Ithaca: Snow Lion Publications, 2000.
———. *Kindly Bent to Ease Us: Part One: Mind*. Translated by Herbert V. Günther. Berkeley: Dharma Publishing, 1975.
———. *The Precious Treasury of Pith Instructions*. The Seven Treasuries Series. Translated by Richard Barron. Junction City: Padma Publishing, 2006.
Lotus Sūtra. *See* Saddharmapuṇḍarīka.
Mackenzie, Vicki. *Reincarnation: The Boy Lama*. New Delhi: Time Books International, 1988.
Mahābhārata. *The Mahabharata*. 12 vols. Translated by Pratap Chandra Roy. Calcutta: Oriental Publishing Co., 1955–61.
Mahāratnakūṭa Sūtra (Treasury Sūtra/Great Jewel-Heap Sūtra). *A Treasury of Mahāyāna Sūtras: Selections from the Mahāratnakūṭa Sūtra*. Translated by The Buddhist Association of the United States. Edited by Garma C. C. Chang. Reprint (1st Indian ed. 1991). New Delhi: Motilal Banarsidass Publishers Pvt Ltd, 2002.
Mahathera, Nārada. *Buddhism in a Nutshell*. Reprint (original 1933). New York: N.p., 1959.
Mahāvastu (Great Book). *The Mahāvastu*. Sacred Books of the Buddhists 16, 18, 19. Translated by J. J. Jones. London: Pali Text Society, 1949–1956.
———. *The Mahāvastu*. Reprint. (original 1949–1956). Translated by J. J. Jones. London: Pali Text Society, 1973–1978.
Majjhima Nikāya (Collection of Middle-Length Discourses). *The Collection of the Middle Length Sayings (Majjhima Nikāya)*. Pali Text Society Translation Series 29, 30, 31. Translated by Isaline B Horner. London: Luzac for Pali Text Society, 1954–1959.

———. *Middle Length Discourses of the Buddha: A New Translation of the Majjhima Nikāya*. Original translation by Bhikkhu Ñāṇamoli, Translation edited and revised by Bhikkhu Bodhi. Somerville, Massachusetts: Wisdom Publications, 2001.

———. *Further Dialogues of the Buddha*. Sacred Books of the Buddhists 5, 6. Edited and translated by Robert Chalmers. London: Pali Text Society, 1898–1899.

McGovern, William Montgomery. *An Introduction to Mahāyāna Buddhism: With Especial Reference to Chinese and Japanese Phases*. Reprint (original 1922). New Delhi: Munshiram Manoharlal Publishers Pvt Ltd, 1997.

Milindapañhā (Questions of Milinda). *The Questions of King Milinda*. Sacred Books of the East 35, 36. Translated by T. W. Rhys Davids. Oxford, The Clarendon Press, 1898.

Misra, G. S. P. *Development of Buddhist Ethics*. 2nd ed. (1st ed. 1984). New Delhi: Munshiram Manoharlal Publishers Pvt Ltd, 1995.

Monier-Williams, Monier. *Buddhism: In Its Connexion with Brāhmanism and Hindūism and in Its Contrast with Christianity*. Reprint (original 1889). New Delhi: Munshiram Manoharlal Publishers Pvt Ltd, 1995.

Murti, T. R. V. *The Central Philosophy of Buddhism: A Study of the Mādhyamika System*. London: Allen & Unwin, 1955.

Nāgārjuna. *Mahāyānaviṁshikā of Nāgārjuna*. In *Minor Buddhist Texts*. Serie Orientale Roma 9. Edited by G. Tucci. Rome: Instituto Italiano per il Medio ed Estremo Oriente, 1956.

Namkhai Norbu. *See* Norbu, Chogyal Namkhai.

Nāropa. In *The Life and Teaching of Nāropa*. UNESCO Collection of Representative Works. Tibetan Series. Translation and commentary by Herbert V. Guenther. Reprint (original 1963). Boston: Shambhala South Asia Editions, 1999.

Nhat Hanh, Thich. *The Heart of the Buddha's Teaching: Transforming Suffering into Peace, Joy & Liberation: the Four Noble Truths, the Noble Eightfold Path, and Other Basic Buddhist Teachings*. London: Rider, 1999.

Norbu, Chogyal Namkhai. "Working with Circumstances", *The Mirror: Newspaper of the International Dzogchen Community*. Edited by Liz Granger and Naomi Zeitz. Available at http://www.tsegyalgar.org/teachings/dec_2001.html.

Pabongka Rinpoche. *Liberation in the Palm of Your Hand: A Concise Discourse on the Path to Enlightenment*. Edited by Trijang Rinpoche. Translated by Michael Richards. Revised (original 1991). Boston: Wisdom Publications, 1997.

Padmasambhava. *Self-Liberation through Seeing with Naked Awareness: Being an Introduction to the Nature of One's Own Mind from the Profound Teaching of Self-Liberation in the Primordial State of the Peaceful and Wrathful Deities*. Edited and translated by John Myrdhin Reynolds. Ithaca: Snow Lions Publications, 2000.

———. *Dakini Teachings: Padmasambhava's Oral Instructions to Lady Tsogyal. From the Revelations of Nyang Ral Nyima Ozer, Sangye Lingpa and Dorje Lingpa*. Edited by Marcia Binder Schmidt. Translated by Erik Pema Kunsang (Eric Hein Schmidt). 2nd ed. (1st ed. 1990). Hong Kong: Rangjung Yeshe Publications, 1999.

Pañchaviṁshatisāhasrikā Prajñāpāramitā (The Perfection of Wisdom in Twenty-five Thousand Lines). *The Large Sūtra on Perfect Wisdom, with the Divisions of the Abhisamayālaṅkāra*. Translated and edited by Edward Conze. Berkeley and Los Angeles: University of California Press, 1975.

Patañjali. *The Science of Yoga: The Yoga Sūtras of Patañjali in the Light of Modern Thought*. Translated by I. K. Taimni. Adyar, Madras and London: The Theosophical Publishing House, 1961.

Patrul Rinpoche. *The Words of My Perfect Teacher/ Kunzang Lama'i Shelung (Sacred Literature)*. The Sacred Literature Series of the International Sacred Literature Trust. Translated by The Padmakara Translation Group. Edited by Kerry Brown and Sima Sharma. Reprint (original 1994). New Delhi: HarperCollins Publishers India, 1998.

The Platform Sūtra. *See* Hui-neng.

Prajñāpāramitāhridaya (The Heart Sūtra). In *Buddhist Wisdom Books, Containing the Diamond Sutra and the Heart Sutra*. Translated and explained by Edward Conze. Reprint (original 1958). London: Harper & Row Publishers, 1972.

———. *The Heart Sutra: The Womb of Buddhas*. Translated with commentary by Red Pine. Washington: Shoemaker & Hoard, 2004.

Prajñopāyavinishchayasiddhi. *The Realization of the Certitude of Appreciative Awareness and Ethical Action*. In *Buddhist Texts through the Ages*. Translated by Edward Conze. Edited by Edward Conze, I. B. Horner, D. Snellgrove and A. Waley. Oxford: Bruno Cassirer, 1954.

Rabjam, Longchen. *See* Longchenpa.

Rahula, Walpola Sri. *What the Buddha Taught.* New York: Grove Weidenfeld, 1959.

Ratnagotravibhāga of Sāramati. In *Buddhist Texts through the Ages.* Translated by Edward Conze. Oxford: Bruno Cassirer, 1954.

Rockhill, W. Woodville, tr. *The Life of the Buddha and the Early History of His Order: Derived from Tibetan Works in the Bkah-hgyur and Bstanhgyur. Followed by Notices on the Early History of Tibet and Khoten.* Reprint. (original 1884.) Varanasi: Orientalia Indica, 1972.

Ryōkan. *Dewdrops on a Lotus Leaf: Zen Poetry of Ryōkan.* Centaur Editions Series. Translated by John Stevens. Boston: Shambala Publications, 1996.

———. *Great Fool: Zen Master Ryōkan: Poems, Letters, and Other Writings.* Translated by Ryūichi Abé and Peter Haskel. Honolulu: University of Hawaii Press, 1996.

Sadānand. *Vedānta Sāra of Sadānand.* Translated by Swami Nikhilananda. Mayavati: Advaita Ashram, 1949.

Saddharmapuṇḍarīka (Lotus Sūtra). *The Saddharma-Pundarīka: Or, the Lotus of the True Law.* Sacred Books of the East 21. Translated by H. Kern. Edited by F. Max Müller. Oxford: The Clarendon Press, 1884.

———. *The Lotus Sutra.* Bibliotheca Indo-Buddhica Series 202. Translated by Burton Watson. Reprint (original 1993). Delhi: Sri Satguru Publications, 1999.

———. *The Lotus Sutra.* Translations from the Asian Classics Series. Translated by Burton Watson. New York: Columbia University Press, 1993.

Sangharakshita, Bhikshu. *The Three Jewels: An Introduction to Buddhism.* London: Rider & Company, 1967.

Saṁyutta Nikāya (Collection of Kindred Discourses). *The Book of the Kindred Sayings (Samyutta-nikāya) or Grouped Suttas.* Pali Text Society Translation Series 7, 10, 13, 14, 16. Translated by C. A. F. Rhys Davids, Sūriyagoda Sumangala Thera and F. L. Woodward, London: Oxford University Press for Pali Text Society, 1917–30.

Shaku, Soyen. *Sermons of a Buddhist Abbot: Addresses on Religious Subjects.* Translated by Daisetz Teitaro Suzuki. Chicago: Open Court Publishing Company, 1906.

Shi Daoyuan, *See* Daoyuan, Shi.

Shih-pei, Hsüan-sha. In *Original Teachings of Ch'an Buddhism: Selected from "The Transmission of the Lamp"*. Compiled by Shi Daoyuan. Translated with introductions by Chang Chung-Yuan. Reprint (original 1969). New York: Vintage Books, 1971.

Shūraṅgama Sūtra (The Method of a Brave Person). *The Śūraṅgama Sūtra (Leng Yen Ching)*. Translated by Charles Luk (Upāsaka Lu K'uan Yu). Commentary (abridged) by Ch'an Master Han Shan. Reprint (original 1966). New Delhi: Munshiram Manoharlal Publishers Pvt Ltd, 2003.

Singh, Amar. *The Heart of Buddhist Philosophy, Dinnaga and Dharmakīrti*. New Delhi: Munshiram Manoharlal Publishers Pvt Ltd, 1984.

Soyen Shaku. *See* Shaku, Soyen.

Sukhāvatīvyūha (Pure Land Sūtra). In *Buddhist Mahāyāna Texts*. Sacred Books of the East 49, part 2. Edited and translated by F. Max Mueller. Reprint (original 1894). Delhi: Motilal Banarsidass Publishers Pvt Ltd, 1985.

Sūtra of Perfect Enlightenment. *The Sutra of Perfect Enlightenment: Korean Buddhism's Guide to Meditation; with Commentary by the Sŏn Monk Kihwa*. SUNY Series in Korean Studies. Translated by A. Charles Muller. Albany: State University of New York Press, 1999.

Sutta Nipāta (Collection of Discourses). *The Sutta-Nipāta, a Collection of Discourses*. Sacred Books of the East 10, part 2. Translated by V. Fausböll. Oxford: The Clarendon Press, 1881.

Suzuki, Daisetz Teitaro. *Studies in the Lankavatara Sutra: One of the Most Important Texts of Mahayana Buddhism, in which Almost All Its Principal Tenets are Presented, Including the Teaching of Zen*. Reprint. (original 1930). London: Routledge & Kegan Paul, 1968.

Suzuki, Shunryū. *Zen Mind, Beginners Mind*. Edited by Trudy Dixon. Boston: Shambala Publications, 2006.

Swāmī Vivekānanda. *See* Vivekānanda, Swāmī.

Takakusu, Junjirō. *The Essentials of Buddhist Philosophy*. Edited by Wing-tsit Chan and Charles A. Moore. Reprint (original 1947). New Delhi: Oriental Books Reprint Corporation, 1975.

Thich Nhat Hanh. *See* Nhat Hanh, Thich.

Thomas, Edward J. *The Life of the Buddha as Legend and History*. 3rd ed. (1st ed. 1927). London: Routledge & Kegan Paul, 1949.

Thubten Loden, Geshe Acharya. *Path to Enlightenment in Tibetan Buddhism*. Melbourne: Tushita Publications, 1993.

Thubten Yeshe, Lama. *Becoming the Compassion Buddha: Tantric Mahamudra for Everyday Life: A Commentary on the Guru Yoga Practice Called the Inseparability of the Spiritual Master and Avalokiteshvara: A Source of All Powerful Attainments.* Edited by Robina Courtin. Somerville, MA: Wisdom Publications, 2003.

Tibetan Yoga and Secret Doctrines, or, Seven Books of Wisdom of the Great Path, According to the Late Lāma Kazi Dawa-Samdup's English Rendering. Reprint (original 1935). Translated by Lāma Kazi Dawa-Samdup. Edited and commentary by W. Y. Evans-Wentz. Delhi: Pilgrims Book, 1999.

Tokushō, Bassui. *Mud and Water: The Collected Teachings of Zen Master Bassui.* Translated by Arthur Braverman. Somerville, MA: Wisdom Publications, 2002.

Upadhyaya, K. N. *Early Buddhism and the Bhagavadgītā.* Delhi: Motilal Banarsidass Publishers Pvt Ltd, 1971.

Upanishads. *The Principal Upanishads.* Translation, introduction, and editing by S. Radhakrishnan. London: George Allen & Unwin, 1953.

———. *The Upanishads Part I.* Sacred Books of the East 1. Translated by F. Max Müller. Oxford: Clarendon Press, 1879.

Vajrachchhedikā Prajñāpāramitā (The Diamond Sūtra). In *Buddhist Wisdom Books, Containing the Diamond Sūtra and the Heart Sūtra.* Translated and explained by Edward Conze. London: George Allen & Unwin, 1958.

The Vedāntic Buddhism of the Buddha: A Collection of Historical Texts. Edited and translated by J. G. Jennings. London: Oxford University Press, 1947.

Vimalakīrti Nirdesha Sūtra (Teachings of Vimalakīrti). *The Vimalakīrti Nirdeśa Sūtra.* Clear Light Series. Translated by Upāsaka Lu K'uan Yu (Charles Luk). Berkeley: Shambala Press, 1972.

———. *The Teaching of Vimalakīrti (Vimalakīrtinirdeśa).* Sacred Books of the Buddhists 32. UNESCO Collection of Representative Works. Translated by Sara Boin from the French translation by Étienne Lamotte. London: Pali Text Society, 1976.

Vinaya Piṭaka (The Book of the Discipline). *Vinaya Texts.* Sacred Books of the East 13, 17, 20. Translated by T. W. Rhys Davids and Hermann Oldenberg. Oxford: The Clarendon Press, 1881–1885.

Vivekānanda, Swāmī. *The Complete Works of Swāmī Vivekānanda.* 8 vols. 6th ed. (1st ed. 1907). Calcutta: Advaita Ashrama, 1964–1968.

Von Glasenapp, Helmuth. *See* Glasenapp, Helmuth von.

Walshe, Maurice O'Connell and Thera Nyanaponika. *Pathways of Buddhist Thought: Essays from 'The Wheel'*. Edited by Nyanaponika Mahathera and selected by Maurice O'Connell Walshe. London: George Allen & Unwin, 1971.

Warder, A. K. *Indian Buddhism*. 2nd revised ed. (1st ed. 1970). Delhi: Motilal Banarsidass Publishers Pvt Ltd, 1980.

Williams, Paul and Anthony Tribe. *Buddhist Thought: A Complete Introduction to the Indian Tradition*. London: Routledge, 2000.

Yixuan. *The Zen Teachings of Master Lin-chi: A Translation of the Lin-chi Lu*. Shambhala Dragon Editions. Translated by Burton Watson. Boston and London: Shambhala, 1993.

The Zen Teachings of Master Lin-chi. *See* Yixuan.

PALI TEXTS

Aṅguttara Nikāya. *The Aṅguttara-Nikāya*. 6 vols. Edited by R. Morris and E. Hardy. London: H. Frowde for Pali Text Society, 1888–1910.

Buddhaghosa. *Manorathapūraṇī: Buddhaghosa's Commentary on the Aṅguttara Nikāya*. 5 vols. Edited by Max Walleser and Herman Kopp. London: Pali Text Society, 1924–1957.

———. *Papañcasudani Majjhimanikayatthakatha of Buddhaghosācariya*. Pali Text Society Series 91, 107, 115, 125, 126. Edited by James Haughton Woods, Damodar Dharmanand Kosambi and I. B. Horner. London: Oxford University Press for Pali Text Society, 1922–1938.

———. *Sāratthappakāsinī: Buddhaghosa's Commentary on the Saṁyutta Nikāya*. Pali Text Society Series 118, 119, 120. Edited by F. L. Woodward. London: Humphrey Milford, Oxford University Press for Pali Text Society, 1929–1937.

———. *The Sumaṅgala-vilāsinī: Buddhaghosa's Commentary on the Dīgha Nikāya*. 3 vols. Edited by T. W. Rhys Davids, J. E. Carpenter and W. Stede. London: Henry Frowde, Oxford University Press Warehouse for Pali Text Society, 1886–1932.

———. *The Visuddhi-magga of Buddhaghosa*. 2 vols. Edited by C. A. F. Rhys Davids. London: Pali Text Society, 1920.

Dhammapada. *The Dhammapada*. Edited by Sūriyagoda Sumaṅgala Thera. London: Humphrey Milford, Oxford University Press for Pali Text Society, 1914.

Dīgha Nikāya. *The Dīgha-nikāya*. Pali Text Society Series 33, 34, 35. Edited by T. W. Rhys Davids and J. Estlin Carpenter. London: H. Frowde for Pali Text Society, 1889–1910.

Itivuttaka. *Iti-vuttaka*. Pali Text Society 26. Edited by Ernst Windisch. London: H. Frowde for Pali Text Society, 1889.

Jātaka. *Jātaka: Together with Its Commentary, Being Tales of the Anterior Births of Gotama Buddha*. 7 vols. Edited by V. Fausböll. London: Trubner & Co., 1875–1897.

Majjhima Nikāya. *Majjhima Nikāya*. 4 vols. Edited by V. Trenckner, Robert Chalmers and C. A. F. Rhys Davids. London: G. Cumberlege, Oxford University Press for Pali Text Society, 1948–1951.

Milindapañhā. *The Milindapañho: Being Dialogues between King Milinda and the Buddhist Sage Nagasena: The Pali Text*. James G. Forlong Fund Series vol. 5. Edited by V. Trenckner, London: Royal Asiatic Society, 1928.

Saṁyutta Nikāya. *The Saṁyutta-nikāya of the Sutta-Piṭaka*. 6 vols. Edited by Leon Feer. London: H. Frowde for Pali Text Society, 1884–1904.

Sutta Nipāta. *Sutta-nipāta*. Edited by Dines Anderson and H. Smith. Reprint (original 1913). London: H. Milford/Oxford University Press for Pali Text Society, 1948.

Udāna. *Udāna*. Edited by Paul Steinthal. Reprint (original 1885). London: G. Cumberlege, 1948.

Vinaya Piṭaka. *Vinaya Piṭaka*. 5 vols. Edited by Hermann Oldenberg. London: Pali Text Society, 1879–1883.

Visuddhimagga. *See* Buddhaghosa.

Sanskrit and Hindi Texts

Advayavajrasamgraha. *Advayavajrasaṁgraha*. Gaekwad's Oriental Series 40. Edited by Mahamahopadhyaya Haraprasāda Śhāstrī. Baroda: Oriental Institute, 1927.

Āryadeva. *Cittaviśuddhiprakaraṇa*. Viṣva-Bharati Studies 8. Edited by P. B. Patel. Santiniketan: Viṣva-Bharati, 1949.

Asaṅga. *Mahāyāna-sūtrālaṅkāra of Asaṅga*. Buddhist Sanskrit Texts 13. Edited by S. Bagchi. Dharbhanga: The Mithila Institute, 1958.

———. *Mahāyāna-sūtrālaṅkāra of Asaṅga*. Bauddha Bhāratī Series 19. Edited by Swami Dwarikadas Shāstrī, with Hindi trans. Vārānasī: Bauddha Bhāratī, 1985.

Ashṭasāhasrikā Prajñāpāramitā. *Aṣṭasāhasrikā Prajñāpāramitā*. Buddhist Sanskrit Texts 4. Edited by P. L. Vaidya. Dharbhanga: The Mithila Institute, 1960.

———. *Ashtasāhasrikā: A Collection of Discourses on the Metaphysics of the Mahāyāna School of the Buddhists*. Bibliotheca Indica (new series) 603, 620, 629, 645, 671, 690. Edited by Rājendralāla Mitra. Calcutta: Rouse, 1888.

Bhagavadgītā. *The Bhagavadgītā, with an Introductory Essay*. Sanskrit text [transliterated] and edited by S. Radhakrishnan. Gorakhapur: GītāPress, 1926.

Chandrakīrti. Prasannapadā of Chandrakīrti. *Chandrakīrti's Prasannapadā on Nāgārjuna's Madhyamakashāstra*. Bauddha Bhāratī Series 16. Edited by Swami Dwarikadas Shāstrī. Vārānasī: Bauddha Bhāratī, 1989.

———. In *Mūlamadhyamakakārikās (Mādhyamikasutrās) de Nāgārjuna, avec la Prasannapadā Commentaire de Candrakirti*. Bibliotheca Buddhica 4. Reprint (1st ed. 1903–1913). Edited by Louis de la Vallée-Poussin. Delhi, Motilal Banarsidass publishers, 1992.

Dhammapada. *Dhammapada*. Text and Hindi translation by Bikshu Dharmarakshita. Varanasi: Master Kheladilal, 1971.

Dohākosha of Saraha. *See* Saraha.

Gaṇḍavyūhasūtra. *Gaṇḍavyūhasūtram*. Buddhist Sanskrit Texts 5. Edited by P. L. Vaidya. Dharbhanga: The Mithila Institute, 1960.

Guhyasamājatantra. *Guhyasamāja Tantra, or, Tathāgataguhyaka*. Gaekwad's Oriental Series 53. Edited by Benoytosh Bhattacharyya. Baroda: Oriental Institute, 1931.

———. *Srī Guhyasamāja Tantra or Tathāgataguhyaka*. Buddhist Sanskrit Texts 9. Edited by S. Bagchi. Dharbhanga: The Mithila Institute, 1965.

———. *Guhyasamāja Tantra or Tathāgataguhyaka*. Bauddha Bhāratī Series 17. Hindi text edited by Swami Dwarikadas Shāstrī. Vārānasī: Bauddha Bhāratī, 1984.

Lalitavistara. *Lalitavistara*. Hindi translation by Shānti Bhikshu Shāstrī. Lucknow: Uttar Pradesh Hindu Sansthan, 1984.

———. *Lalita-vistara*. Buddhist Sanskrit Texts 1. Edited by P. L. Vaidya. Dharbhanga: The Mithila Institute, 1958.

Laṅkāvatāra Sūtra. *Lankāvatāra Sūtra*. Bibliotheca Otaniensis 1. Edited by Bunyiu Nanjio. Kyoto: Otani University Press, 1923.

Madhyamaka Shāshtra. *See* Nāgārjuna.

Mahābhārata. *Mahābhāratam*. 18 Parvas in 4 vols. Gorakhapur: GītāPress, 1956–1958.

Mahāvastu Avadānam. *Mahāvastu Avadānam*. Buddhist Sanskrit Texts 14, 15. 2 vols. Edited by S. Bagchi. Dharbhanga: The Mithila Institute, 1970.

Nāgārjuna. *Madhyamakaṣāstra of Nāgārjuna*. Buddhist Sanskrit Texts 10. Edited by P. L. Vaidya, Dharbhanga: The Mithila Institute, 1960.

———. *Mahāyānaviṁshikā of Nāgārjuna*. In *Minor Buddhist Texts*. Serie Orientale Roma 9. Edited by G. Tucci. Rome: Instituto Italiano per il Medio ed Estremo Oriente, 1956.

———. *Madhyamakaṣāstram (Madhyamika Karika) of Nāgārjuna*. Bauddha Bhāratī Series 16. Edited by Swami Dwarikadas Shāstrī, with Chandrakīrti's commentary. Vārānasī: Bauddha Bhāratī, 1989.

Pañchaviṁshatisāhasrikā Prajñāpāramitā. *Pañcaviṁṣatisāhasrikā Prajñāpāramitā*. Calcutta Oriental Series 28. Edited by N. Dutt. Calcutta: Thacker, Spink & Co., 1934.

———. *Pañcaviṁṣatisāhasrikā Prajñāpāramitā*. Selections from the Cambridge Manuscript Collection. Cambridge: Cambridge University Library.

Prajñāpāramitāhridaya. *Prajñāpāramitāhridaya*. Edited by Edward Conze. London: Journal of the Royal Asiatic Society, 1948.

Prajñopāyaviniṣchayasiddhi. In *Two Vajrāyana Works: Comprising Prajñopāyaviniṣcayasiddhi of Anaṅgavajra and Jñanasiddhi of Indrabhuti*. Gaekwad's Oriental Series 44. Edited by Benoytosh Bhattacharyya. Baroda: Oriental Institute, 1929.

Prasannapadā. *See* Chandrakīrti.

Saddharmapuṇḍarīka Sūtra. *Saddharmapuṇḍarīka Sūtram*. Edited by U. Wogihara and C. Tsuchida. Tokyo: The Seigo-Kenkyūkai, 1933–35.

———. Buddhist Sanskrit Texts no. 6, Edited by P. L. Vaidya. Dharbhanga: The Mithila Institute, 1960.

———. Revised. Bibliotheca Buddhica 10. Edited by H. Kern and B. Nanjio. St. Petersburg, 1909–1912.

———. Sanskrit text and Hindi translation. Ram Mohan Das. Patna: Bihar Rāshtrabhāshā Parishad, 1966.

Sādhanamālā. *Sādhanamālā*. Vol. 1. Gaekwad's Oriental Series 26. Edited by Benoytosh Bhattacharyya. Baroda: Central Library, 1925.

———. Vol. 2. Gaekwad's Oriental Series 41. Edited and introduction by Benoytosh Bhattacharyya. Baroda: Oriental Institute, 1928.

Samādhirāja Sūtra. *Samadhirājasūtra*. Buddhist Sanskrit Texts 2. Edited by P. L. Vaidya. Dharbhanga: The Mithila Institute, 1961.

Saraha. *Dohākoṣa: Apabhraṁśa Texts of the Sahajayāna School*. Calcutta Sanskrit College Research Series 25C. Edited by P. C. Bagchi. Calcutta: Metropolitan Printing and Publishing House, 1938.

———. *Les chants mystiques de Kāṇha et de Saraha: les Dohā-Koṣa et les Caryā*. Edited and translated by M. Shahidullah. Paris: Adrien-Maisonnueve, 1928.

Sāramati. *Ratnagotravibhāga of Sāramati*. Edited by E. H. Johnston and T. Chowdhury. Patna: Journal of Bihar Research Society, 36:1 (1950).

Shāntideva. *Bodhicaryavatara of Santideva with the Commentary Panjika of Prajnakaramati*. Buddhist Sanskrit Texts 12. Edited by P. L. Vaidya. Dharbhanga: The Mithila Institute, 1960.

———. *Bodhicharyāvatāra of Shāntideva with the Commentary Pañjikā of Prañākaramati*. Bauddha Bhāratī Series 21. Hindi translation by Ramniwas Tiwari. Vārānasī: Bauddha Bhāratī, 1993.

———. *Śikṣāsamuccaya of Śantideva*. Buddhist Sanskrit Texts 11. Edited by P. L. Vaidya. Dharbhanga: The Mithila Institute, 1961.

———. *Śikshāsamuccaya: A Compendium of Buddhistic Teaching Compiled by Śāntideva Chiefly from Earlier Mahāyāna-Sūtras*. Bibliotheca Buddhica 1. Reprint (original 1897–1902). Edited by Cecil Bendall. New Delhi: Motilal Banarsidass Publishers Pvt Ltd, 1992.

Shastri, Yaneshwar. *Mahāyāna Sūtrālaṅkāra – A Study in Vijnana-vada Buddhism*. Bibliotheca Indo-Buddhica Series 67. New Delhi: Sri Satguru Publications, 1989.

Shatasāhashrikā Prajñāpāramitā. *Ṣatasāhaṣrikāprajñāpāramitā*. Bibliotheca Indica 153. 2 vols. Edited by Pratap Chandra Ghosha. Calcutta: N.p., 1902–1913.

———. *Ṣatasāhaṣrikāprajñāpāramitā*. Selections from the Cambridge Manuscript Collection. Cambridge: Cambridge University Library.

Sthiramati. *Madhyāntavibhāgaṭīkā*. Edited by Susumi Yamaguchi. Nagoya: Librairie Hajinkaku, 1934–1937.

Index

Abhidhamma Piṭaka, 2
action(s), 129, 156, 215, 259, *see also* karma
  actionless, merging in, 261
  bring us towards or away from our goal, 89
  consequences of, 128, 129, 130
  desireless, 131
  determine a true brahmin, 225
  essential for enlightenment, 208
  intentional, responsibility for, 223
  mind precedes all, 230
  negative, 77, 88, 89, 91, 168
  past, determine if true teacher can be found, 196
  past, results of, 74, 88
  positive, 200
  power of positive and negative, 77
  responsibility for, 132
  right, 41, *see also* Noble Eightfold Path
  root in selfhood, 102
  three precepts guiding, 221
Ādi-Buddha
  affinities with primal God, 141
  wisdom teaching of, 152
ahimsa, *see* non-violence
Ajātashatru, 48
Ambapālī, 50
Ānanda, 53–57, 105, 111, 175
  distress at Buddha's approaching death, 51–53
  requests that women be ordained, 45
  told by Buddha to take refuge in Dharma, 51, 170–71
Anaṅgavajra, 70, 149
Anāthapiṇḍaka, 46–47
anātman, *see* anattā
anattā, *see also* non-self
  semantic confusion with anātman, 108
Aṅgulimāla, tamed by the Buddha's power, 177–79
anitya, *see* impermanence
Ārāḍa Kālāma, 30, 37
ariya-aṭṭhaṅgika-magga, *see* Noble Eightfold Path
ascetic(s)
  false, 89, 266
  taught according to their understanding, 265
  true, 190, 267, 270
Ashoka, 3
Ashṭasāhasrikā Prajñāpāramitā, see *Perfection of Wisdom Sutra in Eight Thousand Lines*
Ashvaghosha, 34
Atīsha of Vikramashilā, 156, 194
ātman, *see also* soul
  analogous to true essence, 110, 115
  beyond personal self, 111
  nature of, 120
  pure consciousness of, 120

attā, 110, *see also* self
attachment(s), *see also* detachment
  breaking chain of, 81, 232
  root of, 102, 233
  suffering as a result of, 97
  to 'I', 105, 107
  to worldly relationships, 82
attavādupādāna, *see* clinging
attention, *see also* mindfulness
  conditions for withdrawal of, 255
  focusing of, 211, 216
  turning within to experience true self, 114
  withdrawal of, 236
austerities, *see also* rituals
  avoidance of extremes, 40
  futility of, 279
  obstacles to enlightenment, 265
Avalokiteshvara
  compassion of, 142, 237
  meditation of, based on hearing inner sound, 254
  name of, 237–42
  refuge in, 241
  transcendent power of, 237, 257
Avataṁsaka Sūtra, 69, 141, 258, 260, 263

Baka Brahmā, 63, 124–25
Bassui Tokushō, 72, 161, 182, 190, 220, 272
bathing in holy places, does not cleanse sins, 271
Bhagavadgītā, 111, 115, 122, 126, 129, 131, 133, 203
bhakti, *see* devotion; faith
Bimbisāra, King, 42
Blissful Abode, *see* Sukhāvatī
bodhi, *see* enlightenment
Bodhicharyāvatāra, *see* Shāntideva
bodhichitta, 214–15, *see also* enlightenment
  experience of, 87
  meaning of, 86
Bodhidharma, 210
bodhisattva(s), 14, *see also* bodhichitta; Buddha(s); teacher(s), spiritual
  devotion to, 203
  embodiment of Dharma, 211
  purpose of, 148, 164
  vision of transcendent Buddha(s), 253
Brahmā
  Buddha superior to, 124
  distinction between Brahman and, 125
  erroneously believes that he is Creator-God, 122–25
  limits of knowledge of, 125
  not ultimate God, 126
Brahmā Sahampati, 35–37, 279–80
Brahmajāla Sutta, 122
Brahman, 136, *see also* Brahmakāya; Dharmakāya
  analogous to ultimate reality, 131–39
  attainment of, 135
  attributes of, 126
  beyond speech, 132
  is above evil, 132
  nature of, 132, 134, 142
  not affected by criticisms against Brahmā, 132
  pure consciousness of, 133
Brahmanimantanika Sutta, 124
Brahmapatta, *see* Brahman
Brahmayāna, *see* Noble Eightfold Path
brahmins, *see also* caste system
  futility of outer rituals of, 272
  not innately better than other castes, 275, 277
  taught according to their understanding, 265
  true, 190, 225, 270

Brihadāraṇyaka Upanishad, 120, 129, 142
Buddha(s), *see also* Dharmakāya; living spiritual teacher(s); Siddhārtha Gautama; Tathāgata; teacher(s), spiritual
  all emanations from Dharmakāya, 7, 202
  appearance of many, 143, 147, 170
  brought forth from the unconditioned, 71
  characteristics of, 142
  compassion of, *see* compassion
  Dharma-body of, 63
  embody Dharma and Dharmakāya, 211
  enlightenment of, 248, 246–48
  experience of sound and light by, 247
  found within, 150, 200
  historical, importance of, 68–71
  inner light of, 247
  manifest for the benefit of humanity, xv, 8, 41, 52, 69, 139, 147, 163, 200, 279
  meaning of name, 1
  need for physical form of, 36, 69
  past and future, xvi, 7, 38, 160
  pragmatism of, 6, 72, 127
  refuge in, 198
  reliance on personal experience of Dharma, 279
  teach from inner experience, 9
  teachings still alive today, xv
  ten unanswered questions of, 116
  three dimensions of, 61–68
  transcendent form of, 64, 65, 66, 72, 147, 148, 252–54
  transcendent sound of, 249–52
  transcendent, dwells in all, 113
  true nature of, 62, 140, 147, 198
  true worship of, 199
  wisdom of, *see* wisdom
Buddhacharita, 12, 20, 27, 29
Buddhahood, essence of, 70
Buddhism, 214, *see also* Four Noble Truths; Five Basic Precepts; Noble Eightfold Path; Three Jewels
  and recognition of primordial creative energy, 141
  centrality of meditation in, 7, 78, 219
  chief elements of, 6
  common elements of different schools of, 6
  complexities in reconstructing original teachings of, 3–5
  fundamentals of, 208
  inner sound and light in, 243, 245, 264
  path of, 13, 165, 243, 279
  perspective on God in, 121–28
  perspective on soul in, 108–21
  pragmatism of, xvii, 279
  priority of Dharma in, 182
  schools of, 2
  spread of, 3
  three main traditions of, 2

caste system
  development of, 274
  futility of, 99–100
  rejection of, 274, 276
  spiritual obstacle of, 277
Chandrakīrti, 250
Chhandaka, 25–29
Chhāndogya Upanishad, 115, 129, 132
Chinul, 80, 88, 92, 150
chitta, *see* mind
Chogyal Namkhai Norbu, *see* Norbu, Chogyal Namkhai
Chunda, 53

classes, four, *see* caste system
clinging
  root cause of suffering, 105
  to I-ness, 101, 105
compassion, 226, *see also* Avalokiteshvara
  interconnected with wisdom, 8
  is quality of Dharmakāya, 142
  of Primordial Buddha(s), 158, 167
  of spiritual teacher(s), 8, 151, 163, 167, 174, 181
  of the Buddha(s), xvi, 38, 41, 59, 139, 142, 148, 171, 202, 212, 248, 252
  power of, 49
conceit of 'I', *see* self, conceit of 'I'
concentration, 217, 258
  on sounds heard, 256
  right, 41, *see also* Noble Eightfold Path
  two features of, 240
  value of, 221
conduct
  after ordination, 150
  codes of, 212
  guided by the Five Basic Precepts, 218
  right, 216, *see also* Noble Eightfold Path
consciousness, *see also* ultimate reality
  analogous to ultimate reality, 142
  distinction between mundane and supramundane, 119
  infinite, 119
  oneness with reality, 143
  withdrawal of, 234
  worldly, extinguished in Nirvāṇa, 119
contemplation, *see* visualization
controlling the mind, 230, *see also* concentration; mind; Noble Eightfold Path
Conze, Edward, 7, 71, 97, 114, 141, 142, 200, 201, 202, 206, 207, 236, 237, 238, 246, 251
creative energy of the universe, 141
Creator-God, *see* God
cycle of birth and death, 74, *see also* death
  caused by erroneous sense of independent self, 104
  freedom from, 85, 87, 152, 154, 156, 160, 188, 281

Dalai Lama, XIV, 6, 228
death, *see also* cycle of birth and death
  always going towards, 95
  consciousness at, 234
  is great equalizer, 96
  motivation to practice, 96
  powerless against, 96
  visible sign of impermanence, 95
deathlessness, 248
  search for state of, 81
decay, visible sign of impermanence, 95
dependent origination
  beyond notion that cause always precedes effect, 104
  not easy to understand, 105
  teaching of, 104
desires
  bound by, 233
  freedom from, to attain Nirvāṇa, 85
  need to rise above, 233
  root in selfhood, 102
detachment, 232–33
Devadatta, 17
  attack on Siddhārtha Gautama, 47–49
  loss of powers, 273
devotion, 201, 206, *see also* love
  results of, 220

to spiritual teacher(s), 176, 184, 185, 187, 205
Dhamma, *see* Dharma
Dhammachakkappavattana Sutta, 265
Dhammapada, 230, 266
Dhammayāna, *see* Noble Eightfold Path
Dharma, 3–10, 214, *see also* Dharmakāya; transcendent reality
available to all, 170
beyond duality, 146, 149
Buddha urged to teach by Brahmā Sahampati, 35–37
Buddhist perspective of, 145–51
difficult to understand, 4, 35, 148–49, 250
emanation from Dharmakāya, 8
experience of, 168, 170, 254
is true nature of Buddha, 146
meanings of, 60, 146
needs living teacher to reveal, 148
path of, 51, 145, 190
practice of, 80, 90, 183, 209
proclaimed with one word, 251
refuge in, 171, 212
refuge in, after teacher's death, 51, 57
right effort on path of, 84
sound of, 253
true nature of, 147
unchanging nature of, 9, 12, 60, 148, 150, 165, 212
wheel of, 41, 248
Dharma-body, *see* Dharmakāya
Dharmakāya, 145, 252, *see also* Buddha; Tathāgata; triple body
analogous to Godhead, 139, 147
and true nature of Dharma, 146
descent of, 147
distinct from physical body of Buddha, 61
essence of Buddhahood, 70, 139, 147
inaccessible at level of physical, 69
is Buddha, 146
is pure consciousness, 67
nature of, 63
necessity of human form of, 201
realized through living spiritual teacher, 162
revealed only to true aspirants, 254
spiritual teachers emanate from, 8
two major qualities of, 142
worthy of love and faith, 198
Diamond Sūtra, 64, 71, 146
Dīpaṅkara, *see* Atīsha of Vikramashilā
disciple
advice to, 179
attitude of, 174–79
determination in meditation of, 186
duty of, 175, 179–88
emulation of spiritual teacher by, 186
necessity of practice by, 181
need for unconditional acceptance of teacher's instructions, 184, 183–88
three levels of service by, 187
disciple-teacher relationship, 166, 169, 171, 176, 177, 184, 185
discrimination, 208
cultivation of, 277
disease
afflicts all, 20
visible sign of impermanence, 95
Dōgen Zenji, 154, 183, 188
Dona, 62
Drogön Tsangpa Gyare, 184
duality
dissolved by Dharma, 146, 262
liberation from, 128
world of, 128

duḥkha, *see* suffering
dying while living, *see* meditation

Edward Conze, *see* Conze, Edward
effort
  need for, 84, 130, 180, 208
  right, 84, 216, *see also* Noble Eightfold Path
effort and grace
  link between, 86
  necessity of, 86
ego, *see also* self, conceit of 'I'
  distinct from Tathāgata-garbha, 113
  importance of discarding, 112
  inflated by reliance on own efforts, 86
  need to disentangle from, 107
Eightfold Path, *see* Noble Eightfold Path
Eihei Dōgen Zenji, *see* Dōgen Zenji
emotions
  calming of, 151, 156
  freedom from negative, 156, 159, 168
emptiness, 113, 138, 261, *see also* Suchness; ultimate reality
  consciousness of, 216
  of Nirvāṇa, 243
  sound of, 244
  wisdom of, 262
emptying of consciousness, 235
enlightenment, *see also* Nirvāṇa
  attainment as a householder, 24–27
  attainment of, 236
  goal of human life, xvi
  impeded by habitual tendencies, 243
  obstacles to, 265
  requires spiritual teacher(s), 151
  through detachment, 26
Epitome of the Great Symbol, 239
equality, Buddha's teaching of, 276
essence, 109, 167, 246, *see also* true nature
  germinal, 115
  hidden within, 114
  immortal, 117
  impersonal, not same as personal self, 114
  non-dual nature of, 109, 110
  of Buddhahood, 250
  three meanings of, 109
  true, 110, 146
Essence of Nectar, 163, 195
Evans-Wentz, W.Y., 8, 114, 167, 237
extremes, avoidance of, 266

faith, 193
  as basis for salvation, 206
  as basis of love and devotion, 198
  based upon understanding of teachings, 199
  first of five-fold requisites, 197
  in spiritual teacher(s), 197
  in Three Jewels, 214
  path of, open to all, 202
faith and devotion, 196–207
  indispensable need for, 176, 206
First Noble Truth, *see* suffering
Five Basic Precepts, 218–21
  adherence to, 218
  as basis of spiritual practice, 218, 219
  importance of, 221
five constituents of personality, *see* skandhas
Flower Ornament Scripture, see *Avataṁsaka Sūtra*
Four Noble Truths, 40
freedom, *see* liberation; Nirvāṇa

Gampopa Rinpoche, 8, 84, 91, 158, 170, 176
Gaṇḍa-Vyūha, 211, 240

Geshe Acharya Thubten Loden, *see* Thubten Loden, Geshe Acharya
Geshe Kharak Gomchung, *see* Gomchung, Geshe Kharak
God
belief in, does not replace need for effort, 131
Brahmā contained in, 126
Buddhist perspective on, 122–28
cannot be intellectually comprehended, 121
delusion of Brahmā as Creator-God, 123
impersonal, analogous to ultimate reality, 133–38
one notion of, rejected by Buddha, 122
personal, 139–43
personal, necessity of, 139
theistic view of, 201
within, 200
Gomchung, Geshe Kharak, 185
grace, 174–75, 180, 186, 202, 206, 207, *see also* effort and grace
necessity of, 86
grasping, 106, *see also* clinging
five groups of, 102, 106
gratitude, 197
Great Play Sūtra, 99, 233
greed, 259, 267
true nature of, 99
Guenther, Herbert, 177
guru, *see* teacher(s), spiritual
Guru Yoga, 185
intense devotion to guru in, 205

happiness, 90, 98, 223, 230
as a result of controlled mind, 230
as a result of non-violence, 224
impermanent nature of, 40, 97
source of, 156, 164, 168, 214
ultimate, realization of, 90, 98, 261
Herbert Guenther, *see* Guenther, Herbert
Heroic Progress Sūtra, 137
Hevajra Tantra, 80
householder
able to succeed in practice, 270
can attain enlightenment, 27
Hsüan-sha Shih-pei, *see* Shih-pei, Hsüan-sha
Huang-Po, 64
Hui-neng, *see Platform Sūtra*
human beings, innately pure, 80
human body, 81, *see also* human life
perishable nature of, 82
truth found within, 79
human life
difficulty in obtaining, 75, 74–77
impermanent and perishable, 77, 81–84, 94
not to be wasted, 87, 89, 91, 92
objective of, xv, 6
opportunity of, 84, 89, 90, 91, 149, 186, 208
rarity of, 74
rising above ups and downs of, 88
value of, 77
humility, 203, 205
approaching spiritual teacher with, 176
need to develop, 176
through focus on own shortcomings, 90

ignorance, 152
imperfect teachers, *see* teacher(s), spiritual
impermanence, 94–96, *see also* human life; phenomenal world
four visible signs of, 95
mark of phenomenal world, 93
of family relationships, 100
of five skandhas, 102

transcending, 88
impersonal consciousness
transcendent nature of, 115
indulgence, avoidance of, 266
I-ness, *see* ego; self, conceit of 'I'
inferior feelings, problems of, 92
initiation, *see* ordination
inner consciousness
attributes of, 112
potential of, 79
regions of, beyond mind, 78
inner light, 247, 254, 257, *see also* inner sound and light
inner sound, 38, 257, 263
attuning to, 258
description of, 249, 259, 261
differs in different realms, 260
hearing of, 254, 255
hearing of, takes practice, 259
is reality, 245
manifests from emptiness, 244
pervasive nature of, 244
source of everything, 245
inner sound and light, 251
appearance of, 246–48
benefit of, 259
experience of, 254–64
merging in, 261
peace and bliss of, 258, 263
intention, *see* action(s), intentional; bodhichitta
interdependent co-arising, *see* dependent origination
intoxicants, refraining from, 221
Īsha Upanishad, 131, 133

Jātaka, 25, 123
Jigme Gyalwai Nyugu, 154
Jina, 249
Buddha declares himself to be, 37
jīva, *see* ātman; soul
Jizō Bodhisattva, 161
Junjirō Takakusu, *see* Takakusu, Junjirō

Kalama Sutta, 193
Kalyāṇa-Mitra, 185–86
Kannon, *see* Avalokiteshvara
karma, 227, 247, *see also* cycle of birth and death; phenomenal world; saṁsāra
disease of, 159
law of, 130, 128–31
same in Buddhism and theistic Indian literature, 128
universal nature of, 129
karunā, 7, *see also* compassion
Kassapa, 117
Kena Upanishad, 132
Kern, H., 140
Kevaṭṭa Sutta, 124
Khemaka Sutta, 106
killing, 221, 223, 225, *see also* non-violence; vegetarian diet
consequences of, 224
five ways of accumulating negative karma, 222
responsibility for, 223
Kuei-feng Tsung-mi, 80

Lalitavistara, 12, 18, 25, 187, 199, 247
Lama Thubten Yeshe, *see* Yeshe, Lama Thubten
Laṅkāvatāra Sūtra, 78, 113, 143, 226
Larger Sukhāvatī-Vyūha, see *Pure Land Sūtra*
liberation, 87–88, 98, 214, 219, *see also* Nirvāṇa
achieved by taking refuge in the Buddha, 154
achieved through meditation, 235
achieved through vigilance, 84
attained only in human life, 74, 89

Liberation in the Palm of Your Hand, 75, 77, 83, 87, 91, 95, 96, 153, 157, 159, 163, 164, 166, 168, 172, 173, 176, 182, 184, 194, 195, 201, 228, 238, 239
light, *see* inner light
Lin-Chi, 242
livelihood
  forbidden means of, 224
  right, 216, *see also* Noble Eightfold Path
living spiritual teacher(s), 200, *see also* teachers(s), spiritual
  ability to communicate with disciple, 163
  necessity for physical form of, 160–64
  unbroken chain of, 165, 166
Longchenpa, 141, 151, 176, 179
Lord Krishṇa, see *Bhagavadgītā*
Lotus Sūtra, 38, 65, 66, 69, 140, 143, 160, 167, 169, 172, 203, 241, 242, 247, 248, 251, 253, 263
love, *see also* devotion
  for living teacher, 200
  message of, in dispute over Buddha's ashes, 58
  of Buddha(s), 167, 172, 196
  of spiritual teachers, 175
  result of faith, 197
loving-kindness, *see* compassion

Mādhyamaka, 113
Mahā Kāshyapa, 42, 58, 250
Mahāmati, 226
Mahāmāyā, Queen, 13, 15–17
Mahāprajāvatī, Queen, 17, 29, 45
Mahāratnakūṭa Sūtra, 262
Mahāsiddha, 149
Mahāvastu, 249
Mahāyāna, 2, 3, 7, 137–38, 200
  bodhichitta in, 214
  compassion root of, 228
  faith and devotion in, 199, 203, 207
  Suchness and Thusness in, 137–38
  triple body doctrine in, 61, 63
Mahāyāna doctrines, language of, 3
Maitrī Upanishad, 115, 120
majjhimā paṭipadā, *see* Middle Path
manaskāra, *see* attention
Māṇḍūkya Upanishad, 136
Mañjushrī, 254
  attuning to inner sound, 257
  personification of wisdom, 142
mantra, *see also* meditation
  benefits of repetition of, 241, 242
  not to be divulged, 238
  power of repetition of, 206
  provides protection, 237
  repeated while visualizing teacher's form, 238
  to be repeated under teacher's guidance, 237
  wrong use of, 238
Māra
  appearance to Siddhārtha before his death, 52
  attempt to prevent Siddhārtha's enlightenment, 33
Marpa, 236
master(s), *see* living spiritual teacher(s); teacher(s), spiritual
meat-eating, *see* vegetarian diet
meditation, 236, *see also* samādhi
  and realization of three characteristics of phenomenal world, 93
  benefit of repetition in, 241
  causes emptying of consciousness, 234
  centrality of, 7, 78
  determination in, 187
  dying while living, 234
  importance of, 256

liberation from birth and death through, 84
on form of spiritual teacher, 239
practice of, 221, 234–42, 257
practice of Vajrayāna, 237
purifies the mind, 80
result of, 34, 219, 253, 254, 255
right, 216, *see also* Noble Eightfold Path
technique of, 235

metaphysical questions
answers considered irrelevant to practice of Dharma, 72, 127
unanswered by Buddha, 116, 121, 126

Middle Path, 39, *see also* Noble Eightfold Path
avoidance of extremes in, 265

Middle Way, *see* Mādhyamaka; Middle Path

Milindapañhā, 134, 198

mind
and transformation through bodhichitta, 86
concentration of, 255
control of, 231, 229–32, 267
detachment of, 232
impediment to spiritual enlightenment, 229
method of purification of, 219
need to transcend, 78
not calmed by austerities, 267
originally pure but defiled by passions, 229
power of, 229
precedes all action, 230
purification of, 80
restless nature of, 230
suffering from, 231

mindfulness, 216–18
heart of Buddhist teachings, 216
practice of, 216
right, 216, *see also* Noble Eightfold Path
through company of spiritual teacher(s), 211, 240

morality, 41, *see also* shīla/sīla

motivation, right, *see* bodhichitta

Muṇḍaka Upanishad, 125

Musō Kokushi, 79, 88, 109, 114, 233

Nāgārjuna, 158, 202, 250

Nanda, 44

Nārada Sūtra, 237

Nāropa, 177, 235

nature, true, *see* true nature

Nhat Hanh, Thich, 104, 216

Nibbāna, *see* Nirvāṇa

Nirmāṇakāya, 68, 145, 252, *see also* triple body

Nirvāṇa, 118, *see also* enlightenment
attainment of, 33–38, 180
ceasing of five constituents of personality, 119
final release from suffering, 281
incomprehensible to the mind, 118
liberation from suffering, 128, 279
obtained by freedom from desires, 85
path to, 282
profound emptiness of, 243
state of, 135
transcends all, 134

noble conduct, 6, *see also* shīla/sīla

Noble Eightfold Path, 40, 136, 216
avoids empty ritual, 265
balanced spiritual practice of, 217
control of mind in, 232
eight practices of, 41, 215
three categories of practices in, 216

non-self, 94, *see also* self
basis of, 103
doctrine of, 100–107
mark of phenomenal world, 93

principle of, 100
non-violence, 223, 226
ethics of, 222–28
toward living creatures, 222
Norbu, Chogyal Namkhai, 244

obedience, 240
Ocean of Delight for the Wise, 277
old age, visible sign of impermanence, 95
One Mind, reality of, 64
ordination, and birth into Buddha's spiritual family, 150

Pabongka Rinpoche, see *Liberation in the Palm of Your Hand*
Padmasambhāvā, 189, 256
Pali, 1, 3
pañchashīla, *see* Five Basic Precepts
Pāthika Sutta, 124
Patrul Rinpoche, see *Words of My Perfect Teacher*
peace
attained from discarding ego, 111
Buddha always maintains, 178
Five Precepts bring, 220
found through the Middle Path, 266
not found in phenomenal world, 21
the highest happiness, 98
Perfection of Wisdom Sūtra in Eight Thousand Lines, 63, 69, 146
personality
impermanence of, 112
not the essential being, 120
phenomenal world
beginning of, incomprehensible, 127
impermanence of, 21, 28, 52, 81, 93
suffering of, 96
three characteristics of, 93
pilgrimages, *see* rituals, outer
Platform Sūtra, 80, 255
pleasures, worldly
drawbacks of, 89
impermanent nature of, 94
worthless snares of Māra, 95
pork, not eaten by Siddhārtha Gautama, 53, 225
powers, spiritual
not to be displayed, 273
practice, 26, *see also* Dharma; meditation; Noble Eightfold Path
importance of, 91, 172, 176
leads to liberation, 83
necessity of, 179, 182
need to follow instructions of spiritual teacher in, 157
prajñā/paññā, 7, 41, 216, *see also* wisdom
prakriti*s*, delusion of, 129
prejudice, obstacle to spirituality, 277
procrastination, dangers of, 90
Pure Abode, 20
Pure Land Sūtra, 67, 174, 246, 262

Rāhula
becomes disciple, 43
birth of, 22
reality, *see* ultimate reality
recluse(s), *see* ascetic(s)
refuge
foundation of all practice, 200
in Dharma, 171
in Dharma after teacher's death, 52
in Dharma leads to inner sound and light, 262
in saṅgha, 213
in spiritual teacher(s), 149, 152, 198, 203, 204, 209

in Three Jewels, 153
three forms of, 212
relationships, impermanence of, 83
renunciation, purpose of, 268
repetition, *see* mantra
resolve, right, 216, *see also* bodhichitta, Noble Eightfold Path
rituals, outer
fire, 271
futility of, 266, 270, 265–73
turn attention outward, 272
Ryokan, 77, 79

Sadāprarudita, 164
Saddharmapuṇḍarīka, see *Lotus Sūtra*
Sahampati Brahmā, *see* Brahmā Sahampati
sakkāyadiṭṭhi, false view of psycho-physical body, 101
samādhi, 6, 41, 216, *see also* meditation
Samādhirāja Sūtra, 182, 251
Samanta-Bhadra, 141
Sambhogakāya, 68, *see also* triple body
blissful body of Buddha(s), 66
meaning of, 62
saṁsāra, 214, *see also* cycle of birth and death; karma; phenomenal world
freedom from, 164
snare of, 151
Sangarava Sutta, 26
saṅgha, 209
cultivating company of, 213
growth of, 41–42
importance of, 212
support for spiritual practice, 213
Sanskrit, 1, 3
Saraha, 114, 137, 157, 272, 276
Sāramati, 113
self, *see also* non-self; prakritis; soul
clinging to I-ness, 101
conceit of 'I', 86, 106, 112, 129
absurdity of, 102
difficult to avoid, 105
must rid oneself of, 105
detrimental to spiritual pursuit, 105
fictitious nature of, 102–3, 107
notion of, leads to evils, 102
notion of, wrongly regarded as five skandhas, 102–3
only impermanent skandhas denied by Buddha, 110–11
physical and mental constituents of, 100
truth hidden within, 114
sense objects, *see* phenomenal world
separation, fixed law of, 28
service
through practice, body and speech, and material offerings, 187
value of, 204
Shākyamuni, 14
Shāntideva, 75, 76, 82, 83, 86, 87, 90, 148, 149, 186, 203, 204, 209, 211, 231, 237, 240
sharaṇa, *see* refuge
Shāriputra, 42, 168
Shih-pei, Hsüan-sha, 256
shīla/sīla, 6, 41, 216, *see also* noble conduct
Shorter Exhortation to Rāhula, 94
Shuddhadhivāsa, *see* Pure Abode
Shuddhodana, King, 13, 15–19, 22–24, 43
Shunryū Suzuki, *see* Suzuki, Shunryū
shūnya/shūnyatā, *see* emptiness; ultimate reality

Shūraṅgama Sūtra, 254
Shvetāshvatara Upanishad, 120, 132
sickness, *see* disease
Siddhārtha Gautama, 1, *see also* Buddha(s); Tathāgata
  and the bliss of Nirvāṇa, 35
  ascetic practices of, 31
  awareness of death and suffering by, 19–21
  biographical works about, 11–14
  death of, 52–59
  declares resolve to lead people to deathlessness, 37
  departure from Kapilavastu, 27–30
  did not eat pork at last meal, 225
  dispute over ashes of, 59
  donation of Jeta Grove to, 46–47
  early life of, 11–26
  early meditation of, 17, 30
  enlightenment of, 33–38
  first disciples of, 39–40
  growth of saṅgha of, 42
  initiates last disciple, 56
  last hours of, 53–56
  last life in Tushita heaven, 14
  last meal of, 53
  last words of, 57–58
  marriage of, 18–19
  meaning of name of, 16
  reasons for leaving home, 27
  reluctance to teach, 35
  renounces palace life, 24–26
  request of four boons by, 23
  resolve to attain enlightenment, 30, 33
  return to Kapilavastu, 43
  tells five ascetics of enlightenment, 39
six-fold higher powers, 34
skandhas
  five constituents, 102
  impermanence of, 102
  not permanent self, 110
skilful means, 65, 69, 265
soul, *see also* ātman
  and Nirvāṇa, 118–21
  beyond personality, 120
  bodiless, 115, 116
  Buddhist perspective on, 108–21
  Buddhist terms analogous to, 112
  different from impermanent self, 111
  existence of, affirmed by Kassapa, 117–18
  infinite nature of, 120
  relationship between body and, 116–18
  same as infinite consciousness, 118
  true essence, not impermanent self, 108
sound, *see also* inner sound
  is essence, 246
  secret, 244
  three kinds of, 244
Soyen Shaku, 245, 255, 264
speech
  right, 216, *see also* Noble Eightfold Path
  ultimate reality beyond, 136, 243
spiritual path, *see also* Dharma
  two conditions for following, 208
spiritual teacher, *see* teacher(s), spiritual
spirituality, difficult to know without a teacher, 155
Subha Sutta, 26
Subhadra, 56
submission, *see* surrender
subtle essence, *see* ultimate reality
Suchness or Thusness, *see* ultimate reality
suffering, 100–107, *see also* phenomenal world, suffering of
  as a result of attachments, 98

as First Noble Truth, 98, 100
avoided by rising above identification with impermanent self, 94, 103
Buddhist perspective on, 40
liberation from, 98, 242
mark of phenomenal world, 93
motivation to attain Nirvāṇa, 98
of old age, disease and death, afflicts all, 21
result of impermanence, 97, 102
sources of, 97, 99–100
universal nature of, 97
why Buddha emphasizes, 100
Sukhāvatī, 174
description of, 67
sound and light in, 246
Sukhāvatī-Vyūha, see *Pure Land Sūtra*
Supreme Divinity, *see* Dharmakāya
supreme reality, *see* ultimate reality
surrender, 112, 188, 198, 203, 207
Sūtra Arranged like a Tree, 159
Sūtra of Perfect Enlightenment, 221
Sutta Nipāta, 225, 274
Sutta Piṭaka, 2
Suzuki, D.T., 70, 139, 143, 147
Suzuki, Shunryū, 78

Taittirīya Upanishad, 133, 142
Takakusu, Junjirō, 62, 138, 202, 206, 256
Takuan Sōhō, 244
Tan-hsia Tzu-ch'un, 150
Tathāgata, 1, *see also* Buddha(s); Dharma-body
names for, denote embodiment of sound or light, 251
nature of, 140
rarity of, 66
Tathāgata-garbha, *see also* essence
distinct from ego, 113
dwells in all, 113
teacher(s), spiritual, *see also* Buddha(s); living spiritual teacher(s)
all teach same eternal truth, 7
always present in the world, 164, 167, 169, 170
benefit to the world, 167
careful assessment of, 192, 194
company of, 211, 213
compassion of, 8, 280, *see also* compassion
devotion to, 92, 153, 158, 163, 185, 186, 202
difficulty in distinguishing true from false, 188–96
do not attract disciples by miracles, 173
emanations from absolute, 142, 210
embodiment of all Buddhas, 167
faith and devotion to, 196, 202
false, 192
guidance of, 156
indispensability of, 153, 154–60
lead beyond mind, 152, 155
liberate through teachings, 173
like Buddha for disciple, 176, 179
motivation to teach, 145
necessity of physical form of, 68–71, 160–71, 201
need for, 149, 151, 154, 157, 160, 210
need for obedience to, 186
not limited to physical body, 170
pragmatic approach of, 10
protection of, 180
protection, after their death, 170, 253
protection, at disciple's death, 174, 204
purpose of, 160, 172
rarity of finding true, 191

refuge in, 148, 154, 199, 203, 210
release disciples from cycle of birth and death, 171
responsibilities of, 171–74
self-proclaimed not to be trusted, 190
submission to, 203
transmission of teachings by, 150, 280
true, 188, 189
value of admonition of, 184
value of meeting, 176
visualization on form of, 206, 239, 240
teachings
eternal nature of, 8
given according to students' understanding, *see* skilful mean
ten unanswered questions, *see* metaphysical questions
Thera, 3
Theravāda, 2
Theravāda scriptures, language of, 3
Thich Nhat Hanh, *see* Nhat Hanh, Thich
thought, right, 41, *see also* Noble Eightfold Path
Three Jewels
essentials for spiritual path, 209
faith in, 214
refuge in, 153, 209, 212
Tipiṭaka, 1
Thubten Loden, Geshe Acharya, 90
Thusness, *see* ultimate reality
Tokushō, Bassui, *see* Bassui Tokushō
transcendent reality, 146, *see also* Brahman; ultimate reality
Buddhist view of, 132
trikāya, *see* triple body
Tripiṭaka, 2
triple body
doctrine of, 61, 60–73
oneness of, 67
roots of doctrine of, 63
true essence, *see* essence
true master, *see* teacher(s), spiritual
true nature, 151, 215, 243, 282
appearance of, 236
found within, 80
innately pure, 236
is transcendent sound and light, 264
of teacher, difficult to recognize, 195
of the Buddha(s), 140, 146, 147, 198
truth, found within, 79, 81, 242, 262
Tsongkhapa, 100

Udraka Rāmaputra, 30, 37
ultimate reality, 113, *see also* Dharmakāya; essence; Tathāgata; transcendent reality
analogous to Brahman and impersonal God, 131–39
and transcendent consciousness in *Upanishads*, 136
as Suchness and Thusness, 137–38
beyond description, 137, 167
beyond duality, 128
beyond good and evil, 133
bliss of, 137
is personalized in the Buddha, 139
must manifest, 201
nature of, 132
need for direct experience of, 144
oneness of, 143, 281
personal and impersonal aspects of, 142
terms for, 136
transcends all, 134
Upaka, 248
Upanishads, 122, 125, 128, 131, 133
Uruvelā Kashyapa, 42

Vajrachchhedikā Prajñāpāramitā, see *Diamond Sūtra*
Vajrayāna, 2, 3, 79, 237
Vakkali Sutta, 61
vegetarian diet, 221, 222–28, *see also* killing; non-violence; violence
last meal of Siddhārtha Gautama not pork, 53, 225
quotes from Tibetan gurus on, 228
rationale for, 226
veneration, true, by living the teachings, 55, 175, 199
view, right, 41, 216, *see also* Noble Eightfold Path
vigilance, 218, 281
importance of, 84
Vimalakīrti Nirdesha Sūtra, 26, 229
Vinaya Piṭaka, 2
viññāṇa, *see also* consciousness
two kinds of, 118
violence, *see also* non-violence
avoidance of, 221
consequences of, 223
laying aside of, 225
towards animals, 228
vision, of transcendent Buddha(s), 253
visualization of one's spiritual teacher, 206, 211, 240, 238–42
like contemplating on the Buddha, 241
power of, 240
voice of the Buddha(s), transcendent, *see* Buddha(s), transcendent sound of
Void, *see* emptiness

wisdom, 41, 247, *see also* Noble Eightfold Path
achieved by controlling the mind, 231
adorned by conduct, 217
and faith, 202
attained through meditation, 217, 221, 247
compassionate, 8
development of, 185
difficult way of, 202
imparting of, 248
light of, 263
of the Buddha(s), 171, 252, 279
of emptiness, 262
personification of, 142
quality of Buddha(s), 196
quality of Dharmakāya, 142
through attainment of Nirvāṇa, 7
true, 263
Wisdom-Teachings of the Ādi-Buddha, 151
within, turning, *see* truth, found within
women, first ordination of, 44–46
Words of My Perfect Teacher, 8, 76, 89, 92, 153, 154, 156, 157, 159, 164, 165, 167, 169, 176, 181, 184, 185, 186, 187, 189, 192, 195, 196, 199, 205, 209, 210, 212, 214, 227
world, *see* phenomenal world
worldly perspective, limitations of, 10

Yājñavalkya, 120
Yashodharā, 18–19, 22, 29, 43, 45
Yeshe, Lama Thubten, 143, 244, 257

ADDRESSES FOR INFORMATION AND BOOKS

INDIAN SUB-CONTINENT

INDIA
The Secretary
Radha Soami Satsang Beas
Dera Baba Jaimal Singh
District Amritsar, Punjab 143204

NEPAL
Mr. Dal Bahadur Shreshta
Radha Soami Satsang Beas
P. O. Box 1646, Gongabu
Dhapasi, Kathmandu
☎+97-1-435-7765

PAKISTAN
Mr. Sadrang Seetal Das
Lahori Mohala
Larkana, Sindh

SRI LANKA
Mr. Chandroo Mirpuri
Radha Soami Satsang Beas
No. 45 Silva Lane
Rajagiriya, Colombo
☎+94-11-286-1491

SOUTHEAST ASIA

FOR FAR EAST
Mrs. Cami Moss
RSSB-HK
T.S.T., P.O. Box 90745
Kowloon, Hong Kong
☎+852-2369-0625

MALAYSIA
Mr. Bhupinder Singh
Radha Soami Satsang Beas
29 Jalan Cerapu Satu, Off Batu 3 ¼
Jalan Cheras, Kuala Lumpur 56100
☎ +603-9200-3073

THAILAND
Mr. Harmahinder Singh Sethi
Radha Soami Satsang Beas
58/32 Ratchadaphisek Road, Soi 16
Thapra, Bangkok Yai
Bangkok 10600
☎+66-2-868-2186 / 2187

INDONESIA
Mr. Ramesh Sadarangani
Jalan Pasir Putih IV/16, Block E 4
Ancol Timur, Jakarta
DKI Jakarta 14430

Yayasan Radha Soami Satsang
Jalan Transyogi KM. 5, Jatikarya
Pondok Gede
DKI Jakarta 17435
☎+62-21-845-1612

Yayasan Radha Soami Satsang
Jalan Bung Tomo
Desa Pemecutan Raya
Denpasar, Barat 80116
☎ +62-361-438-522

PHILIPPINES
Mr. Kay Sham
Science of the Soul Study Centre
9001 Don Jesus Boulevard
Alabang Hills, Cupang
Muntinlupa City, 1771
☎+63-2-772-0111 / 0555

SINGAPORE
Mrs. Asha Melwani
Radha Soami Satsang Beas
19 Amber Road
Singapore 439868
☎+65-6447-4956

ASIA PACIFIC

AUSTRALIA
Mr. Pradeep Raniga
Science of the Soul Study Centre
1530 Elizabeth Drive
Cecil Park, New South Wales 2178

NEW ZEALAND
Mr. Tony Waddicor
P. O. Box 5331, Auckland

Science of the Soul Study Centre
80 Olsen Avenue, Auckland
☎+64-9-624-2202

GUAM
Mrs. Hoori M. Sadhwani
115 Alupang Cove
241 Condo Lane, Tamuning 96911

HONG KONG
Mr. Manoj Sabnani
Radha Soami Satsang Beas Society HK Ltd
3rd Floor, Maxwell Centre
39-41 Hankow Road
Tsim Sha Tsui, Kowloon
☎+852-2369-0625

JAPAN
Mr. Jani G. Mohinani
Radha Soami Satsang Beas
1-2-18 Nakajima-Dori
Aotani, Chuo-Ku, Kobe 651-0052
☎+81-78-222-5353

KOREA
Mr. Haresh Buxani
Science of the Soul Study Group
613, Hopyeong-Dong
R603-18604 Sungbo Building
Nam Yangju, Gyeong Gi-Do
Nam Yangju Kyung-gi

TAIWAN, R.O.C.
Mr. Haresh Buxani
Science of the Soul Study Group
Aetna Tower Office, 15F., No. 27-9
Sec.2, Jhongjheng E.Rd.
Danshuei Township, Taipei 25170
☎+886-2-8809-5223

NORTH AMERICA

CANADA
Mr. John Pope
5285 Coombe Lane
Belcarra, British Columbia V3H 4N6

Mrs. Meena Khanna
149 Elton Park Road
Oakville, Ontario L6J 4C2

Science of the Soul Study Centre
2932 -176th Street
Surrey, B.C. V3S 9V4
☎+1-604-541-4792

Science of the Soul Study Centre
6566 Sixth Line, RR 1 Hornby
Ontario L0P 1E0
☎ +1-905-875-4579

MEXICO
Radha Soami Satsang Beas
Efrain Gonzalez Luna
2051 Col. Americana
Guadalajara, Jalisco 44090
☎+52-333-615-4942

Radha Soami Satsang Beas
Circuito Universidad S/N
Lomas San Nicolas
Puerto Vallarta 48290
☎+52-322-299-1954

UNITED STATES
Mr. Hank Muller
P.O. Box 1847
Tomball, TX 77377

Dr. Vincent P. Savarese
2550 Pequeno Circle
Palm Springs
CA 92264-9522

Dr. Frank E. Vogel
275 Cutts Road
Newport, NH 03773

Dr. Douglas Torr
P. O. Box 2360, Southern Pines
NC 28388-2360

Science of the Soul Study Centre
4115 Gillespie Street
Fayetteville, NC 28306-9053
☎+1-910-426-5306

Science of the Soul Study Centre
2415 Washington Street
Petaluma, CA 94954-9274
☎+1-707-762-5082

CARIBBEAN

FOR CARIBBEAN
Mr. Sean Finnigan
R.S.S.B. Foundation
P. O. Box 978, Phillipsburg
St. Maarten, N. A.

Mrs. Jaya Sabnani
1 Sunset Drive South
Fort George Heights
St. Michael BB111 02
Barbados

BARBADOS, W.I.
Mrs. Mukta Nebhani
Science of the Soul Study Centre
No. 10, 5th Avenue
Belleville BB11114
☎+1-246-427-4761

CURACAO, N.A.
Mrs. Hema Chandiramani
Science of the Soul Study Centre
Kaya Seru di Milon 6-9
Santa Catharina
☎+599-9-747-0226

ST. MAARTEN, N.A.
Mr. Prakash Daryanani
R.S.S.B. Foundation
P. O. Box 978, Phillipsburg
☎+599-547-0066

GRENADA, W.I.
Mr. Prakash Amarnani
P. O. Box 726, St. Georges

GUYANA
Mrs. Indu Lalwani
115, Garnette Street
Newtown Kitty, Georgetown

HAITI, W.I.
Mrs. Mousson Finnigan
P. O. Box 2314
Port-au-Prince

JAMAICA, W.I.
Mrs. Reshma Daswani
17 Colombus Height
First Phase, Ocho Rios

ST. THOMAS
Mrs. Hema Melwani
P. O. Box 600145
USVI-VI00801-6145

SURINAME
Mr. Chandru Samtani
15 Venus Straat, Paramaribo

TRINIDAD, W.I.
Mr. Chandru Chatlani
20 Admiral Court
Westmoorings-by-Sea
Westmoorings

FOR CENTRAL & SOUTH AMERICA

Mr. Hiro W. Balani
Paseo De Farola, 3, Piso 6
Edificio Marina, Malaga, Spain 29016

CENTRAL AMERICA

BELIZE
Mrs. Milan Hotchandani
4633 Seashore Drive
P. O. Box 830, Belize City

PANAMA
Mr. Ashok Tikamdas Dinani
P. O. Box 0301, 03524 Colon

SOUTH AMERICA

ARGENTINA
Ms. Fabiana Shilton
Leiva 4363 Capital Federal
C.P. 1427 Buenos Aires

BRAZIL
Mr. Guillerme Almeida
SQN 315, Bloco C
Apto. 306 Brasilia
DF 70-774-030

CHILE
Mr. Vijay Harjani
Pasaje Cuatro No. 3438
Sector Chipana, Iquique

Fundacion Radha Soami Satsang Beas
Av. Apoquindo 4770, Oficina 1504
Las Condes, Santiago

COLOMBIA
Mrs. Emma Orozco
Asociacion Cultural
Radha Soami Satsang Beas
Calle 48 No. 78A-30
Medellin 49744
☎+574-234-5130

ECUADOR
Dr. Fernando Flores Villalva
Radha Soami Satsang Beas
Calle Marquez de Varela
OE 3-68y Avda. America
P. O. Box 17-21-115, Quito
☎+5932-2-555-988

PERU
Mr. Carlos Fitts
P. O. Box 18-0658, Lima 18

Asociacion Cultural
Radha Soami Satsang Beas
Av. Pardo #231
12th Floor, Miraflores, Lima 18

VENEZUELA
Mrs. Helen Paquin
Radha Soami Satsang Beas
Av. Los Samanes con
Av. Los Naranjos Conj
Res. Florida 335
La Florida, Caracas 1012

EUROPE

AUSTRIA
Mr. Hansjorg Hammerer
Sezenweingasse 10, A-5020 Salzburg

BELGIUM
Mr. Piet J. E. Vosters
Driezenstraat 26, Turnhout 2300

BULGARIA
Mr. Deyan Stoyanov
Radha Soami Satsang Beas
P. O. Box 39, 8000 Bourgas

CYPRUS
Mr. Heraclis Achilleos
P. O. Box 29077, 1035 Nicosia

CZECH REPUBLIC
Mr. Vladimir Skalsky
Maratkova 916, 142 00 Praha 411

DENMARK
Mr. Tony Sharma
Sven Dalsgaardsvej 33
DK-7430 Ikast

FINLAND
Ms. Anneli Wingfield
P. O. Box 1422, 00101 Helsinki

FRANCE
Mr. Pierre de Proyart
7 Quai Voltaire, Paris 75007

GERMANY
Mr. Rudolf Walberg
P. O. Box 1544, D-65800 Bad Soden

GIBRALTAR
Mr. Sunder Mahtani
RSSB Charitable Trust, 15 Rosia Road
☎+350-200-412-67

GREECE
Mr. Themistoclis Gianopoulos
6 Platonos Str. 17672 Kallithea, Attiki

ITALY
Mrs. Wilma Salvatori Torri
Via Bacchiglione 3, 00199 Rome

THE NETHERLANDS (HOLLAND)
Mr. Henk Keuning
Kleizuwe2, Vreeland 3633AE

Radha Soami Satsang Beas
Middenweg 145 E
1394 AH Nederhorst den Berg
☎+31-294-255-255

NORWAY
Mr. Manoj Kaushal
Langretta 8, N-1279 Oslo

POLAND
Mr. Vinod Sharma
UL. Szyprow 2M12, 02-654 Warsaw

PORTUGAL
Mrs. Sharda Lodhia
Torres das Palmeiras, Lote 68, 11° C
2780-145 Oeiras

ROMANIA
Mrs. Carmen Cismas
C.P. 6-12, 810600 Braila

SLOVENIA
Mr. Marko Bedina
Brezje pri Trzicu 68, 4290 Trzic

SPAIN
Mr. J. W. Balani
Fundacion Cultural RSSB
Fca Loma del Valle S/N
Cruce de Penon de Zapata
Alhaurin De la Torre, Malaga 29130
☎+34-952-414-679

SWEDEN
Mr. Lennart Zachen
Norra Sonnarpsvägen 29
SE-286 72 Asljunga

SWITZERLAND
Mr. Sebastian Züst
Weissenrainstrasse 48
CH 8707 Uetikon am See

UNITED KINGDOM
Mr. Narinder Singh Johal
Radha Soami Satsang Beas
Haynes Park, Haynes
MK45 3BL Bedford
☎+44-1234-381-234

AFRICA

BENIN
Mr. Jaikumar T. Vaswani
01 Boite Postale 951
Recette Principale Cotonou 01

BOTSWANA
Dr. Krishan Lal Bhateja
P. O. Box 402539, Gaborone

CONGO
Mr. Prahlad Parbhu
143 Kasai Ave. Lubumbashi

GHANA
Mr. Murli Chatani
Radha Soami Satsang Beas
P. O. Box 3976, Accra
☎+233-242-057-309

IVORY COAST
Mr. Veerender Kumar Sapra
Avenue 7, Rue 19, Lot 196
Trechville, Abidjan 05

KENYA
Mr. Surinder Singh Ghir
Radha Soami Satsang Beas
P. O. Box 15134
Langata 00509, Nairobi
☎+254-20-890-329

LESOTHO
Mr. Sello Wilson Moseme
P. O. Box 750, Leribe 300

LIBYA (G.S.P.L.A.J.)
Mr. Abhimanyu Sahani
P. O. Box 38930, Bani Walid

MADAGASCAR
Mr. Francis Murat
Lote 126B, Ambohiminono
Antanetibe, Antananarivo 101

MAURITIUS
Dr. I. Fagoonee
Radha Soami Satsang Beas Trust
69 CNR Antelme /Stanley Avenues
Quatre Bornes
☎+230-454-3300

NAMIBIA
Mrs. Jennifer Carvill
P. O. Box 449, Swakopmund 9000

NIGERIA
Mr. Nanik N. Balani
G. P. O. Box 5054, Marina, Lagos

RÉUNION
Ms. Marie-Lynn Marcel
5 Chemin 'Gonneau, Bernica
St Gillesles Hauts 97435

SIERRA LEONE
Mr. Kishore S. Mahboobani
82/88 Kissy Dock Yard
P. O. Box 369, Freetown

SOUTH AFRICA
Mr. Gordon Clive Wilson
P. O. Box 47182, Greyville 4023

Radha Soami Satsang Beas
P. O. Box 5270, Cresta 2118
☎+27-11-792-7644

SWAZILAND
Mr. Mike Cox
Green Valley Farm, Malkerns

TANZANIA
Mr. Manmohan Singh
99 Lugalo Street
Dar-Es-Salaam 65065

UGANDA
Mr. Sylvester Kakooza
Radha Soami Satsang Beas
P. O. Box 31381, Kampala

ZAMBIA
Mr. Chrispin Lwali
P. O. Box 12094
Nchanga North Township, Chingola

ZIMBABWE
Mr. Gordon Clive Wilson
P. O. Box 47182
Greyville 4023, South Africa

MIDDLE EAST

BAHRAIN
Mr. Deepak Katyal
P. O. Box 76091-Juffair

ISRAEL
Mr. Michael Yaniv
Moshav Sde Nitzan 59
D.N. Hanegev 85470

KUWAIT
Mr. Vijay Kumar
Yousef AL Badar Street
Bldg 28, Block 10, Flat #8, Salmiya

U.A.E.
Mr. Daleep Jatwani
P. O. Box 37816, Dubai
☎+971-4-339-4773

Books on This Science

SOAMI JI MAHARAJ

Sar Bachan Prose (The Yoga of the Sound Current)
Sar Bachan Poetry (Selections)

BABA JAIMAL SINGH

Spiritual Letters

MAHARAJ SAWAN SINGH

The Dawn of Light
Discourses on Sant Mat
My Submission
Philosophy of the Masters, in 5 volumes
Spiritual Gems
Tales of the Mystic East

MAHARAJ JAGAT SINGH

The Science of the Soul
Discourses on Sant Mat, Volume II

MAHARAJ CHARAN SINGH

Die to Live
Divine Light
Light on Saint John
Light on Saint Matthew
Light on Sant Mat
The Master Answers
The Path
Quest for Light
Spiritual Discourses, in 2 volumes
Spiritual Heritage
Thus Saith the Master

BOOKS ABOUT THE MASTERS

Call of the Great Master—Daryai Lal Kapur
Heaven on Earth—Daryai Lal Kapur
Treasure Beyond Measure—Shanti Sethi
With a Great Master in India—Julian P. Johnson
With the Three Masters, in 3 volumes—Rai Sahib Munshi Ram

INTRODUCTION TO SPIRITUALITY

A Spiritual Primer—Hector Esponda Dubin
Honest Living—M. F. Singh
The Inner Voice—C. W. Sanders

Liberation of the Soul—J. Stanley White
Life is Fair: The Law of Cause and Effect—Brian Hines

BOOKS ON MYSTICISM

A Treasury of Mystic Terms, Part I: The Principles of Mysticism (6 volumes)—John Davidson
The Holy Name: Mysticism in Judaism—Miriam Caravella
Jap Ji – T. R. Shangari
Yoga and the Bible—Joseph Leeming

BOOKS ON SANT MAT IN GENERAL

In Search of the Way—Flora E. Wood
Living Meditation: A Journey beyond Body and Mind —Hector Esponda Dubin
Message Divine—Shanti Sethi
The Mystic Philosophy of Sant Mat—Peter Fripp
Mysticism: The Spiritual Path, in 2 volumes—Lekh Raj Puri
The Path of the Masters—Julian P. Johnson
Radha Soami Teachings—Lekh Raj Puri

MYSTICS OF THE EAST SERIES

Bulleh Shah—J. R. Puri and T.R. Shangari
Dadu: The Compassionate Mystic—K. N. Upadhyaya
Dariya Sahib: Saint of Bihar—K. N. Upadhyaya
Guru Nanak: His Mystic Teachings—J. R. Puri
Guru Ravidas: The Philosopher's Stone—K. N. Upadhyaya
Kabir: The Great Mystic—Isaac A. Ezekiel
Kabir: The Weaver of God's Name—V. K. Sethi
Mira: The Divine Lover—V. K. Sethi
Saint Namdev—J. R. Puri and V. K. Sethi
Saint Paltu: His life and teachings—Isaac A. Ezekiel
Sarmad: Martyr to Love Divine—Isaac A. Ezekiel
Sultan Bahu—J. R. Puri and K. S. Khak
Tukaram: The Ceaseless Song of Devotion—C. Rajwade
Tulsi Sahib: Saint of Hathras—J. R. Puri and V. K. Sethi
The Teachings of Goswami Tulsidas—K. N. Upadhyaya

BOOKS FOR CHILDREN

The Journey of the Soul—Victoria Jones
One Light Many Lamps—Victoria Jones

For Internet orders, please visit: www.rssb.org

For book orders within India, please write to:

Radha Soami Satsang Beas
BAV Distribution Centre, 5 Guru Ravi Dass Marg
Pusa Road, New Delhi 110005